This "O-P Book" is an authorized reprint of the original edition, produced by microfilm-Xerox by University Microfilms, Inc., Ann Arbor, Michigan, 1959.

THE STRUCTURE OF LABOR MARKETS

THE STRUCTURE OF LABOR MARKETS

Wages and Labor Mobility in Theory and Practice

by
LLOYD G. REYNOLDS
PROFESSOR OF ECONOMICS
YALE UNIVERSITY

Yale Labor and Management Center Series

HARPER & BROTHERS . NEW YORK

UNIVERSITY
LIBRARY
NOTTINGHAM

THE STRUCTURE OF LABOR MARKETS

Printed in the United States of America

FIRST EDITION

B-A

CONTENTS

PREFACE

THIS BOOK is two things in one. Part One reports a case study of labor mobility and wage determination carried out in a New England factory city during the years 1946–48. The distinctive feature of this study is the attempt to analyze wages and mobility together and to examine the relations between them. Some preliminary findings concerning mobility have already been published (*Job Horizons*, by Lloyd G. Reynolds and Joseph Shister, New York, Harper & Brothers, 1949). These findings are summarized in Chapters II and V of this book, though these chapters also contain a good deal of new material. On a few points subsequent analysis and reflection have led to some modification of the earlier conclusions, and on these points the statements made herein should be regarded as superseding those of the earlier book.

Part Two has a broader focus. It includes: (1) a reexamination of traditional labor-market theory in the light of the factual findings of Part One; (2) an attempt to sketch out a revised theory of local labor markets, consistent with the findings of this study and of other empirical work to date; (3) a discussion of the objectives of public policy concerning wages and mobility.

The title of the book derives from Part Two rather than Part One. The broad scope of the title is not meant to suggest that we now have anything like a complete theory of local labor markets. On the contrary, we are obviously at an early stage in the development of such a theory. My chief hope for this book is that it may give added impetus to both theoretical and empirical work.

Different portions of this book will probably appeal to somewhat different audiences. Students of wages will be most interested in Chapters VI–VII, while those whose primary interest is in mobility will want to read Chapters II–V. Readers whose interest is mainly theoretical may wish to pass over the factual material and go directly to Chapters VIII–IX. Employers and others with a practical interest in labor market operations will probably find Chapters II, IV, VI, VII and X most useful for their purposes.

PREFACE

THIS BOOK is two things in one. Part One reports a case study of labor mobility and wage determination carried out in a New England factory city during the years 1946–48. The distinctive feature of this study is the attempt to analyze wages and mobility *together* and to examine the relations between them. Some preliminary findings concerning mobility have already been published (*Job Horizons,* by Lloyd G. Reynolds and Joseph Shister. New York: Harper & Brothers, 1949). These findings are summarized in Chapters IV and V of this book, though these chapters also contain a good deal of new material. On a few points subsequent analysis and reflection have led to some modification of the earlier conclusions, and on these points the statements made herein should be regarded as superseding those of the earlier book.

Part Two has a broader focus. It includes (1) a reexamination of traditional labor market theory in the light of the factual findings of Part One; (2) an attempt to sketch out a revised theory of local labor markets, consistent with the findings of this study and of other empirical work to date; (3) a discussion of the objectives of public policy concerning wages and mobility.

The title of the book derives from Part Two rather than Part One. The broad scope of the title is not meant to suggest that we now have anything like a completed theory of local labor markets. On the contrary, we are obviously at an early stage in the development of such a theory. My chief hope for this book is that it may give added impetus to both theoretical and empirical work.

Different portions of this book will probably appeal to somewhat different audiences. Students of wages will be most interested in Chapters VI–VII, while those whose primary interest is in mobility will want to read Chapters II–V. Readers whose interest is mainly theoretical may wish to pass over the factual material and go directly to Chapters VIII–IX. Employers and others with a practical interest in labor market operations will probably find Chapters III, IV, VI, VII, and X most useful for their purposes.

Research workers who may wish to do similar work in other areas are referred to Appendix B, which describes the methods used in this study and discusses some things which we did not do but which might usefully be done in future studies. In a pioneer venture one never knows just what one should have done until one is finished. Looking back with the benefit of hindsight, one can see additional techniques which might have been tried and factual gaps which might have been filled with enough time and effort. I hope that future students may profit by our experience and that the gaps left in this work may be filled by later studies.

It is a pleasant duty to thank the many people who furthered the completion of this study in various ways. Financial support for the study was received from the Rockefeller Foundation. The study was sponsored by the Labor and Management Center of Yale University and owes much to the interest and encouragement of the Director of the Center, E. Wight Bakke.

In the planning stage of the work, I profited greatly by technical advice from Gladys Palmer, of the University of Pennsylvania, and Burton Fisher, then at Yale and now at the Survey Research Center, University of Michigan.

I am indebted to Dr. Joseph Shister, of the University of Buffalo, for carrying through much of the basic research of this study. Dr. Shister was associated with me in planning the general strategy of the enterprise, supervised the staff employed on the worker interviews, supervised the analysis and tabulation of these interviews, and himself conducted all the interviews with union officials and a good share of those with management officials. Over the three years of field work we had many fruitful discussions about the significance of what we were doing, and many of the ideas in this book had their origin in these discussions.

Mrs. Beverly Calsoyas, in addition to participating in the worker interviews, did a considerable amount of management interviewing and did much of the statistical work of the study. Mrs. Shirley Buttrick took over the statistical work at a later stage and was particularly helpful in the area wage survey and the preparation of the background data for Chapter I.

I am heavily indebted to the insight, persistence, and diligence of the people who knocked on workers' doors several evenings a week for more than a year in order to secure the basic data for Chapters II–V. Those who served on the interviewing staff include: Lee Adams, L. T. Calvert, George Churchill, John Daly, Karl de Schweinitz, Herchel Elliott, Alan

Ferguson, Marshall Fishwick, Charles Foy, Robert Hamilton, Jerome Korcyach, Robin Marshall, Warner Mills, Arnold Olena, Harold Quanbeck, Suzanne Petersen, Catherine Schlender, Leo Schnurer, Nevan Shaver, Nino Stracher, Stokes Tower, Dale Underwood, Otto Weber, Charles Winston, John Witkey, Homer Wood, and Florence Zacher. Those who had a hand in the clerical work on the study at one time or another were: Muriel Adams, Irene Booth, Ann Nevitt, Anne Orgain, Doris Shipman, and Irene Short.

Charles Myers and George Shultz, of the Massachusetts Institute of Technology, were kind enough to read and comment on Chapter VII, and also sent me the preliminary manuscript of a similar study which they have been conducting in another New England city. The general similarity between their findings and my own gave me courage to be more venturesome in Part II than I might otherwise have been. Several of my colleagues at Yale—Neil W. Chamberlain, C. E. Lindblom, and Warren S. Nutter—read drafts of Chapters VIII–X and made many useful suggestions.

My greatest debt of all is to the approximately one thousand workers and the several hundred management officials, union leaders, employment-service officials, and others who took time to answer the questions we put to them. I am sorry that the anonymity of the area prevents my making more explicit acknowledgment to several people who were particularly helpful, notably the manager of the local office of the State Employment Service, and the committee of local business leaders who worked closely with us on the management phase of the study. These men took many hours from their own business to meet with us, and without their help we would not have gotten anywhere on the management side. I hope that the courtesy and patience with which we were received by all these people is justified by the significance of our findings.

Lloyd G. Reynolds

New Haven, Connecticut
[illegible]

Ferguson, Marshall Fishwick, Charles Fox, Robert Hamilton, Jerome Kornreich, Robin Marshall, Warner Mills, Arnold Olena, Harold Orlansky, Suzanne Peterson, Catherine Sahlendar, Leo Schumer, Beverly Shaver, Nino Siracusa, Stokes Tolbert, Dale Underwood, Otto Weber, Charles Winston, John Withey, Hormer Wood, and Florence Zucker. Those who had a hand in the clerical work of the study at one time or another were: Muriel Adams, Irene Booth, Ann Nevitt, Ann Quinn, Doris Rapuano, and Irene Short.

Charles Myers and George Schultz, of the Massachusetts Institute of Technology, were kind enough to read and comment on Chapters I–VII, and also sent me the preliminary manuscript of a similar study which they have been conducting in another New England city. The general similarity between their findings and my own gave me courage to be more venturesome in Part II than I might otherwise have been. Several of my colleagues at Yale—Neil W. Chamberlain, C. E. Lindblom, and Warren G. Nutter—read drafts of Chapters VIII–X and made many useful suggestions.

My greatest debt of all is to the approximately one thousand workers and the several hundred management officials, union leaders, employment service officials, and others who took time to answer the questions we put to them. I am sorry that the anonymity of the area prevents my making more explicit acknowledgment to several people who were particularly helpful, notably the manager of the local office of the State Employment Service, and the committee of local business leaders who worked closely with us on the management phase of the study. These men took many hours from their own businesses to meet with us, and without their help we would not have gotten anywhere on the management side. I hope that the courtesy and patience with which we were received by all these people is justified by the significance of our findings.

LLOYD G. REYNOLDS

New Haven, Connecticut
July 1, 1950

THE STRUCTURE OF LABOR MARKETS

CHAPTER 1 The Problem of Labor Market Analysis

ECONOMIC theory focuses on the concept of the market. An economy is viewed as a system of interrelated markets, events in any one of which are ultimately conditioned by events in all the others. Product markets are linked by the substitutability of goods in consumers' budgets. Markets for productive services are linked by the possibility of alternative uses for the same service, and by substitutability of different services in producing the same output. The two types of market are related by the transformability of services into products. Economic statics sets forth the formal conditions for simultaneous equilibrium in all markets and, by the device of "comparative statics," attempts to trace the chain of events which will be set in motion by any change in the basic data—consumer preferences, supplies of productive services, and production techniques.

Labor appears in this schema as the leading type of productive service. A wage rate is the price for a particular species of labor. The market for each kind of labor is integrally related to the market for the product which it helps to produce; price-quantity changes in the product market are reflected in the labor market, and vice versa. The market for one kind of labor, moreover, is related to the market for every other kind by the willingness and ability of workers to change jobs in response to relative wage rates.

In this view, wage determination and movements of labor are intimately related. They are, in fact, simply different aspects of a single process by which members of the labor force are distributed to the points at which they can make the greatest productive contribution. Movements of labor are induced by wage differences, and the economic function of the wage structure is to ensure an optimum distribution of workers among occupations and industries. The wage structure is conditioned in turn by potential movement of labor. The only tenable (i.e., equilibrium) wage structure is one which provides no inducement for any worker to change his present employment.

This is the "economic" approach to the study of labor, an approach

which has aroused much controversy between "neoclassical theorists" and "institutionalists," between supporters and critics of "intervention" in the labor market by trade unions and government. This book is an attempt to clarify the issues in dispute and to make progress toward a resolution of the controversy.

Economists have always been somewhat diffident about integrating labor into the market schema. Marshall, Pigou, Taussig, and other leading theorists were troubled by the "peculiarities" of the labor market—the fact that the worker sells himself with his services, that his immediate financial need may place him at a disadvantage in negotiating with employers, that he is influenced by nonpecuniary motives, that he has limited knowledge of alternative opportunities, and that there are numerous objective barriers to free movement of labor. The imperfections which characterize almost any actual market seem particularly pronounced in the purchase and sale of labor. Most economists would agree that the notion of a "perfect labor market" is a highly abstract concept useful mainly for normative purposes. We can make a step forward, then, by avoiding any debate over this straw man and by relegating it to its proper role as a norm for welfare discussions. This narrows the range of controversy to genuine issues: what are the most significant sources of imperfection in labor markets? how important are these imperfections in checking the play of market forces? what can be done as a practical matter to improve labor market structure?

During the past twenty years it has become customary in theoretical writing to telescope every kind of limitation on labor mobility into a forward-sloping labor supply curve to the individual firm, occupation, or industry. This device is attractive because of its apparent simplicity and because it continues to yield a determinate wage structure and allocation of labor resources. Given workers' preferences among jobs, this allocation of labor may even be regarded as a sort of ideal—the best which can be done under imperfect market conditions. The sloped labor supply curve has also been welcomed by writers sympathetic to trade unionism; for it implies that the employer is a "monopsonist" who, in the absence of trade unionism, has power to vary his wage level. It follows by a familiar chain of argument that, if the employer wishes to maximize profit, he will hire fewer workers and pay a lower wage rate than he would do in a perfect labor market. A union entering on the scene may thus be able to raise wages to the competitive level while at the same time increasing employment in the firm.

Why should a union be content with merely offsetting the employer's monopsony power? Why should it not push wages above the competitive level in an effort to maximize the union's wage bill, or simply in a blind striving for "more, more, more"? Some theorizing on the assumption that union leaders behave like monopolistic sellers of a commodity, envisage a situation in which relative wage rates will be wrenched violently away from competitive levels as a result of collective bargaining. In industries where unions are especially powerful and aggressive, and where employers are in an unusually good position to translate wage increases into price increases, wage rates are likely to be set "too high"; and in the converse circumstances they will be set "too low." This will produce a distortion in the allocation of labor resources—too little employment in the high-wage industries, too much in the low-wage industries. It will also mean a good deal of personal frustration. Many people will wish to migrate from low-wage to high-wage jobs, but will be unable to do so because the very existence of unduly high wages restricts employment opportunities in those industries.

The merit of this argument will be evaluated in Chapter XI. The point to be emphasized here is that both parties to the argument have tended to assume that when one is talking about wages one is also talking about mobility, and vice versa. When one looks at actual behavior, however, one seems to see two quite distinct processes. Voluntary movement of labor—the only type of movement which is relevant here—seems to depend more largely on differences in availability of jobs than on differences in wage levels. Conversely, people engaged in setting wages often make little explicit reference to mobility as an influence on their decisions. The processes of wage determination and labor mobility seem to go on with only a peripheral relation to each other.

This cleavage is reflected also in the research literature. Studies of wages, if they go beyond statistical measurement of the wage structure, focus on the economic and political factors which influence wage administration. What criteria does management normally employ in setting the plant wage level and rates for specific jobs? What is the motivation of union leaders in wage bargaining, and how does collective bargaining alter the wage structure?

Studies of labor mobility, if they go beyond statistical measurement, focus on such things as the motivation of movement, the mechanism through which new jobs are found and possible improvements in this

Why should a union be content with merely offsetting the employer's monopsony power? Why should it not push wages above the competitive level in an effort to maximize the industry's wage bill, or simply in a blind striving for "more, more, more"? Some theorists, on the assumption that union leaders behave like monopolistic sellers of a commodity, envisage a situation in which relative wage rates will be wrenched violently away from competitive levels as a result of collective bargaining. In industries where unionism is especially powerful and aggressive, and where employers are in an unusually good position to translate wage increases into price increases, wage rates are likely to be set "too high," and in the converse circumstances they will be set "too low." This will mean a distortion in the allocation of labor resources—too little employment in the high-wage industries, too much in the low-wage industries. It will also mean a good deal of personal frustration. Many people will wish to migrate from low-wage to high-wage jobs, but will be unable to do so because the very existence of unduly high wage rates chokes off employment opportunities in those industries.

The merit of this argument will be evaluated in Chapter IX. The point to be emphasized here is that both parties to the argument have tended to assume that when one is talking about wages one is also talking about mobility, and vice versa. When one looks at actual behavior, however, one seems to see two quite distinct processes. Voluntary movement of labor—the only type of movement which is relevant here—seems to depend more largely on differences in availability of jobs than on differences in wage levels. Conversely, people engaged in setting wages often make little explicit reference to mobility as an influence on their decisions. The processes of wage determination and labor mobility seem to go on with only a peripheral relation to each other.

This cleavage is reflected also in the research literature. Studies of wages, if they go beyond statistical measurement of the wage structure, focus on the economic and political factors which influence wage administration. What criteria does management normally employ in setting the plant wage level and rates for specific jobs? What is the motivation of union leaders in wage bargaining, and how does collective bargaining alter the wage structure?

Studies of labor mobility, if they go beyond statistical measurement, focus on such things as the motivation of movement, the mechanism through which new jobs are found and possible improvements in this

mechanism, and the personal incidence of movement—why some workers rather than others are able to find new jobs, or to move up the occupational ladder. Much of the mobility literature has been stimulated by the phenomenon of unemployment—chronic unemployment in declining sections of the economy, heavy general unemployment arising from cyclical fluctuations, or dramatic instances of labor displacement by plant shutdowns or technological change. These studies have had such objectives as measuring the characteristics of the unemployed, trying to discover what characteristics make for rapid or slow reemployment, exploring the occupational and geographical readjustments necessary for reemployment to occur, and assessing the net gain or loss to the workers involved. Except for the conclusion that displaced workers typically lose in skill and earnings, the studies proceed with little direct reference to the wage structure.[1]

This discrepancy between the theoretical and research literature suggests two possibilities. The researchers may be operating at a superficial level and may have failed to discover that, at a more fundamental level (the cherished "long run" of economic theory), the wage structure is shaped by potential mobility and movements of labor occur in response to wage differentials. Alternatively, the researchers may know what they are doing and the relation between mobility and the wage structure may in fact be looser than theorists have assumed.

The central purpose of this book is to form a reasoned judgement on this matter. How close is the relation between labor mobility and wage determination? Do we need one theory or two? If the latter, what should our revised theories of wages and mobility look like, in general outline?

The argument proceeds in two stages. Chapters II–VII are a case study of a New England factory city, based on field work during the years 1946–48. The distinctive feature of this study is that it examines both labor mobility and wage determination in the same area at the same time, and tries to devise as many tests as possible of the closeness of relation between the two processes. The findings are conditioned, of course, by the characteristics of the area and by the economic climate during the period covered by the study. The main findings check rather closely with those of other comparable studies,[2] which suggests that

[1] The only published study I have seen which tries explicitly to appraise the relation between mobility and wage structure is Charles A. Myers and W. Rupert Maclaurin, *The Movement of Factory Labor* (New York, John Wiley and Sons, 1943).

[2] Particularly the study by Myers and Maclaurin cited above, a study of another New England city by Myers and Shultz which is to be published in the near future, and the studies of Gladys Palmer and her associates in the Philadelphia area.

they have more than purely local validity. More area studies using the same general techniques will be necessary, however, before one can speak with confidence on this point.

Chapters VIII–X are an essay in economic theory and public policy, stimulated by the findings of the case study, but not really dependent upon them. In these chapters I attempt to criticize existing conceptions of the labor market, to develop an alternative body of hypotheses, and to deal with some of the more pressing issues of labor market policy. These chapters necessarily draw on the results of our research on wages and labor mobility. The propositions advanced are not intended, however, as empirical generalizations, which would be quite premature in the present state of our knowledge. They are put forward simply as hypotheses not contradicted by the facts presently available, but obviously in need of further testing and refinement.

PRELUDE TO THE CASE HISTORY

The reader interested in generalizing about the economy will want to know to what extent the results presented in Chapters II–VII are peculiar to this area and this time period, and to what extent they may have wider significance. The remainder of this chapter, therefore, is devoted to a discussion of the circumstances under which our factual findings were obtained. The reader interested only in the findings themselves may omit this section and go directly to Chapter II.

The Area, the Industries, the Labor Force

The study was carried out in a medium-sized city, with a population in 1947 of 352,000.[1] The city is small enough so that leaders in industry, labor, and other walks of life meet frequently and are well known to each other; yet it is large enough so that labor does not move freely throughout the metropolitan area in search of employment.

It is a mature city, whose population in recent decades has been growing less rapidly than that of the United States as a whole. From 1920 to 1930, the population of the area grew by 12.7 per cent (United States, 16.1 per cent), and from 1930 to 1940 by only 4.4 per cent (United States, 7.2 per cent). From 1940 to 1947, however, the situation was reversed, the population of the area increasing by 14.2 per

[1] United States Bureau of the Census, *Current Population Reports*, Series P-21, No. 6. The population given is that of the metropolitan area. The population of the central city in 1947 is not known, but was probably about half that of the metropolitan area. In 1940, the most recent year for which a comparison is available, the population of the central city was 160,605 and of the metropolitan area 308,228.

they have more than purely local validity. More area studies using the same general techniques will be necessary, however, before one can speak with confidence on this point.

Chapters VIII–X are an essay in economic theory and public policy, stimulated by the findings of the case study, but not really dependent upon them. In these chapters I attempt to criticize existing conceptions of the labor market, to develop an alternative body of hypotheses, and to deal with some of the more pressing issues of labor market policy. These chapters necessarily draw on the results of past research on wages and labor mobility. The propositions advanced are not intended, however, as empirical generalizations, which would be quite premature in the present state of our knowledge. They are put forward simply as hypotheses, not contradicted by the facts presently available, but obviously in need of further testing and refinement.

PRELUDE TO THE CASE HISTORY

The reader interested in generalizing about the economy will want to know to what extent the results presented in Chapters II–VII are peculiar to this area and this time period, and to what extent they may have wider significance. The remainder of this chapter, therefore, is devoted to a discussion of the circumstances under which our factual findings were obtained. The reader interested only in the findings themselves may omit this section and go directly to Chapter II.

The Area, the Industries, the Labor Force

The study was carried out in a medium-sized city, with a population in 1947 of 352,036.[3] The city is small enough so that leaders in industry, labor, and other walks of life meet frequently and are well known to each other; yet it is large enough so that labor does not move freely throughout the metropolitan area in search of employment.

It is a mature city, whose population in recent decades has been growing less rapidly than that of the United States as a whole. From 1920 to 1930, the population of the area grew by 13.4 per cent (United States, 16.1 per cent), and from 1930 to 1940 by only 4.9 per cent (United States, 7.2 per cent). From 1940 to 1947, however, the situation was reversed, the population of the area increasing by 14.2 per

[3] United States Bureau of the Census, *Monthly Report on the Labor Force,* Series P-21, No. 4. The population given is that of the metropolitan area. The population of the central city in 1947 is not known, but was probably about half that of the metropolitan area. In 1940, the most recent year for which a comparison is available, the population of the central city was 160,605 and of the metropolitan area 308,228.

cent (United States, 8.9 per cent).[4] This bulge in the city's growth was due mainly to the fact that, as a metalworking center, it underwent an unusually large industrial expansion during the war.

It is a mature city also from an industrial standpoint. The remains of a factory constructed by Eli Whitney stand on the outskirts of the town. A watch and clock company organized in 1817 is still one of the major industries of the city. Of forty leading manufacturing companies, twenty were organized before 1900. Industry is more conscious of tradition and precedent than it might be in a younger area.

The metropolitan area extends some six miles from east to west and seven miles from north to south. To cross the area from east to west at a busy time of day takes about forty minutes by bus and twenty-five minutes by automobile. The corresponding times from north to south are fifty and thirty minutes. Distance and travel time are thus important barriers to labor mobility within the area, as will be explained more fully in Chapter III.

The economic life of the area is dominated to an unusual degree by manufacturing. In 1940, 39.0 per cent of those employed in the area were engaged in manufacturing, compared with 23.6 per cent for the United States as a whole.[5] This is reflected in the occupational composition of the labor force. In 1947, 45 per cent of the gainfully employed in the area were classified as skilled or semiskilled workers, compared with 35 per cent for the United States.[6] The area also has slightly more than the normal percentage of clerical, sales, and kindred workers—22 per cent in 1947, compared with 18 per cent for the United States. This is due to the presence of several corporation headquarters and a large university.

Metals and machinery provide almost half of the total manufacturing employment. The next largest industry is clothing manufacture, which provided 13.6 per cent of manufacturing employment in 1940.[7] All of the major census categories, however, are well represented in

[4] Data for the United States to 1940 are from the *16th Census of Population* (1940), Volume 1, p. 96. Data for the area to 1940 are from the Bureau of the Census, *The Growth of Metropolitan Districts in the United States, 1900–1940* (Government Printing Office, Washington, 1948), p. 39, table 3. Data for 1947 are from the Census publication cited previously (MRLF, Series P-21, No. 4).

[5] Bureau of the Census, *16th Census of Population* (1940), Volume 2, Part I, pp. 48–49 and 888.

[6] Bureau of the Census, *Monthly Report on the Labor Force*, Series P-51, No. 4. The census categories "craftsmen, foremen, and kindred workers" and "operatives and kindred workers" were added to obtain these totals.

[7] Bureau of the Census, *16th Census of Population* (1940), Volume 2, Part I, pp. 48 and 888.

the area. There are fifty-four food-processing companies, six tobacco manufacturers, six textile companies, ninety-six clothing producers, thirty-three plants producing furniture and finished lumber products, sixteen paper products companies, forty-seven printing establishments, nineteen producers of chemical products, and other companies, and nineteen in the "stone, clay, and glass" group.

The dominant metal-working group is not at all homogeneous, but includes a bewildering variety of products—marine gears, screws of every description, zippers, precision threading tools, automobile and aircraft parts, rifles, shotguns, pistols, ammunition, flashlights, steel wire, asbestos and rubber insulated wire and cable, hacksaw blades, machine screw products, clocks and watches, household appliances, mechanical toys, and so on almost endlessly. The number of individual metal products runs to many thousands.

Diversity of products is due partly to the large number of producing units and their small average size. The forty-five thousand manufacturing workers in the area in 1947 were employed in 587 establishments, yielding an average employment of less than one hundred workers per plant. Almost three-fifths of the plants (411 out of 587) had less than fifty employees. Only seven plants in the area had between five hundred and one thousand employees, and only nine had more than one thousand workers. Virtually all of the small companies, and most of the larger ones, are owned and controlled by residents of the area. Many of them have been handed down as family businesses for two or three generations.

Union organization is recent and relatively weak in the manufacturing industries of the area. Of thirty-nine leading companies from whom the Chamber of Commerce collects wage data, seventeen companies with a June, 1947, employment of 11,775 were operating under union contract, while twenty-two companies with an employment of 17,557 were nonunion. The degree of unionization is even lower than this comparison would suggest. There are more than twenty thousand workers in the smaller plants of the area and, while precise data are not available, a large majority of these are probably nonunion. Of the unionized workers in the major companies, about four-fifths are in CIO unions, the remainder in the AFL.

Most of the local unions in manufacturing have been established since 1940. Their growth was part of the vast expansion of unionism throughout the United States during the years of war and postwar prosperity. The development of unionism in this area, however, was

the area. There are fifty-four food processing companies, six tobacco manufacturers, six textile companies, ninety-six clothing producers, thirty-three plants producing furniture and finished lumber products, sixteen paper products companies, forty-seven printing establishments, nineteen producers of chemical products, ten rubber companies, and nineteen in the "stone, clay, and glass" group.

The dominant metalworking group is not at all homogeneous, but includes a bewildering variety of products—marine gears, hardware of every description, zippers, precision threading tools, automobile and aircraft parts, rifles, shotguns, pistols, ammunition, flashlights, steel wire, asbestos and rubber insulated wire and cable, hacksaw blades, machine screw products, clocks and watches, household appliances, mechanical toys, and so on almost endlessly. The number of individual metal products runs to many thousands.

Diversity of products is due partly to the large number of producing units and their small average size. The forty-five thousand manufacturing workers in the area in 1947 were employed in 537 establishments, yielding an average employment of less than one hundred workers per plant. Almost four-fifths of the plants (411 out of 537) had less than fifty employees. Only seven plants in the area had between five hundred and one thousand employees, and only nine had more than one thousand workers. Virtually all of the small companies, and most of the larger ones, are owned and controlled by residents of the area. Many of them have been handed down as family businesses for two or three generations.

Union organization is recent and relatively weak in the manufacturing industries of the area. Of thirty-nine leading companies from whom the Chamber of Commerce collects wage data, seventeen companies with a June, 1947, employment of 11,775 were operating under union contract, while twenty-two companies with an employment of 11,557 were nonunion. The degree of unionization is even lower than this comparison would suggest. There are more than twenty thousand workers in the smaller plants of the area and, while precise data are not available, a large majority of these are probably nonunion. Of the unionized workers in the major companies, about four-fifths are in CIO unions, the remainder in the AFL.

Most of the local unions in manufacturing have been established since 1940. Their growth was part of the rapid expansion of unionism throughout the United States during the years of war and postwar prosperity. The development of unionism in this area, however, was

less complete than in most other parts of the country. When the tide of postwar prosperity receded, it left perhaps two-thirds of the manufacturing workers still unorganized, and even some of the unions which had contractual relations with employers were relatively weak.[8]

The labor force of the area is characterized by an unusually high proportion of first- and second-generation immigrants from southern and eastern Europe. The 1940 Census indicated that 25.2 per cent of the male labor force of the area was born abroad, compared with 12.0 per cent for the United States as a whole.[9] There is unfortunately no cross classification of the labor force by nativity and occupational level. If there were, it would doubtless appear that a good majority of the manual labor force consists of first- and second-generation immigrants. The largest ethnic group in the city is the Italian. Of the total foreign-born population of the area in 1940, 34.7 per cent were born in Italy, 10.5 per cent in Poland, 10.4 per cent in Russia, and 9.0 per cent in Eire. Negroes constituted only 2.7 per cent of the city's labor force in 1940.

In most other respects the labor force of the area corresponds rather closely with that of the nation as a whole. The age distribution of the gainfully employed is almost identical with that for the United States. The labor force participation of various age and sex groups is also quite close to the average for the United States, except for a markedly higher labor force participation by women in the age group 14–24.[10] This may be due partly to the large amount of clerical and light manufacturing employment available in the area. It may also be that the cultural pattern of the immigrant groups in the city favors early leaving of school by women and continuation of work by the wife after marriage. The occupational distribution of the labor force necessarily

[8] Little need be said about the extent of union organization in nonmanufacturing industries. The focus of this study is on manufacturing and, moreover, there is nothing unusual about the pattern of unionism outside manufacturing. Most of the larger construction companies are organized, as are the newspapers and most of the commercial printers. Also operating under contract are the railroad company, the telephone company, the street railway, the truckers' association, and the university (for most of the nonfaculty employees). The remaining public utilities, wholesale and retail trade, the service and repair industries, and most other types of industry are predominantly nonunion.

[9] Bureau of the Census, *16th Census of Population* (1940), Volume 2, Part I, pp. 44, 47, 887.

[10] In April, 1947, 40 per cent of the girls aged 14–19 in the area were in the labor force, compared with 27.7 per cent for the United States; 60 per cent of the females aged 20–24 were in the labor force, compared with 44.3 per cent for the United States. (Bureau of the Census, *Current Population Reports,* Series P-51, No. 4; and Supplement to the *Monthly Report on the Labor Force,* Population, No. 59-S.)

corresponds with the distribution of available jobs in the area. This means a relatively high proportion of clerical workers, artisans, and factory operatives.

The relatively high ratio of home ownership is important from a mobility standpoint. In April, 1947, homes occupied by their owners represented 52 per cent of all occupied dwelling units in the area.[12] Home ownership makes people reluctant to move to other areas, and also has considerable effect on their choice of employment within the area.

Both union and management officials testify that the labor force of the area is "company minded" to an unusual degree. This frame of mind springs partly from the fact that much of the immigration to the area was sponsored by the major companies. Workers went directly from the boat to the factory, and often worked there for the remainder of their lives with little realization of the existence of other companies in the area. In many cases their sons and grandsons have followed him into the same plant. Companies in the area pride themselves on their high proportion of long-service workers, and both management and workers regard permanent attachment to one plant as the normal thing. This orientation of workers toward a particular company does not seem to have been basically disturbed by the rise of unionism. International union representatives in the area frequently complain about the "pro-company" attitude of union members and many local union officials, and assert that the locals in the area will not fight for as much as they could get by more aggressive tactics.

LIMITATION OF THE STUDY TO MANUAL LABOR

The study was restricted, for practical reasons of time and expense, to manual labor only. While manual workers formed 57 per cent[13] of the area labor force in 1940, some 23 per cent were engaged in clerical and sales activities, and 9 per cent were in professional and managerial occupations. We are unable to say anything about the markets for these other occupations, which doubtless differ in many ways from that for manual labor.

Focusing on the manual worker also prevents us from drawing

[12] Bureau of the Census, Current Population Reports, Housing Series, P-71, No. 18, Housing Characteristics of the [illegible] Metropolitan District, April, 1947.

[13] This includes in the manual group all workers in service industries, except domestic servants. It also includes foremen, who could not be separated out from the census category of craftsmen, foremen, and kindred workers. The line between manual and nonmanual occupations is necessarily somewhat arbitrary and difficult to define.

corresponds with the distribution of available jobs in the area. This means a relatively high proportion of clerical workers, artisans, and factory operatives.

The relatively high ratio of home ownership is important from a mobility standpoint. In April, 1947, homes occupied by their owners represented 52 per cent of all occupied dwelling units in the area.[11] Home ownership makes people reluctant to move to other areas, and also has considerable effect on their choice of employment within the area.

Both union and management officials testify that the labor force of the area is "company minded" to an unusual degree. This frame of mind springs partly from the fact that much of the immigration to the area was sponsored by the larger employers. Workers went directly from the boat to the factory, and often worked there for the remainder of their lives with little realization of the existence of other companies in the area. In many cases a man's sons and grandsons have followed him into the same plant. Companies in the area pride themselves on their high proportion of long-service workers, and both management and workers regard permanent attachment to one plant as the "normal" thing. This orientation of workers toward a particular company does not seem to have been basically disturbed by the rise of unionism. International union representatives in the area frequently complain about the "pro-company" attitude of union members and even of local union officials, and assert that the locals in the area will not fight for as much as they could get by more aggressive tactics.

Limitation of the Study to Manual Labor

The study was restricted, for practical reasons of time and expense, to manual labor only. While manual workers formed 57 per cent[12] of the area labor force in 1947, some 22 per cent were engaged in clerical and sales activities, and 19 per cent were in professional and managerial occupations. We are unable to say anything about the markets for these other occupations, which doubtless differ in many ways from that for manual labor.

Focusing on the manual worker also prevents us from drawing

[11] Bureau of the Census, *Current Population Reports,* Housing Series, P-7, No. 4: Housing Characteristics of the________Metropolitan District, April, 1947.

[12] This includes in the manual group all workers in service industries, except domestic servants. It also includes foremen, who could not be separated out from the census category of "craftsmen, foremen, and kindred workers." The line between manual and nonmanual occupations is actually very unclear and difficult to define.

definite conclusions about the amount and types of movement between manual and nonmanual occupations. There is clearly a good deal of interchange between white-collar and manual work. The manual workers whom we interviewed included some who had done white-collar work at an earlier time and the experience of these people is analyzed in Chaper V. We are not able, however, to examine the other side of the coin: people who are now in white-collar work, and therefore excluded from our samples, but who have done manual work at an earlier time. It would be necessary to take work histories from a cross section of the entire gainfully employed population in order to obtain a clear picture of the interchange between manual and white-collar occupations.

The Time Period

The fact that a sample census of population and employment was conducted in the area in April, 1947, enables us to describe the main economic developments since the Census of April, 1940. The course of events was broadly similar to that in other manufacturing areas of the country. A war of unprecedented magnitude, financed in part by inflationary methods, produced an abnormally high level of money demand for goods and services, which in turn led to capacity production and employment plus a wage-price inflation.

The population of the metropolitan area increased by about 14 per cent between the two censuses. Natural increase was reinforced by migration into the area to man the expanding war industries. About 10 per cent of the 1947 population had moved into the area since April, 1940. The labor force rose slightly more than the population of the area, due to an increase in labor force participation; 83 per cent of the males and 34 per cent of the females aged 14 and over were in the labor force in 1947, compared with 80 and 33 per cent in 1940.

The most striking change was the much fuller utilization of the labor force in 1947. At the time of the 1940 Census, 13 per cent of the labor force was totally unemployed and many of the employed had only part-time work. In April, 1947, only 3 per cent of the labor force was unemployed. Part-time work had also been virtually eliminated and many plants were working overtime. The work week in the thirty-nine manufacturing companies reporting to the Chamber of Commerce averaged 41.5 hours in April, 1947.

There were also important changes in the composition of employment over the period. Manufacturing, while below its wartime peak, still had

definite conclusions about the amount and types of movement between manual and nonmanual occupations. There is clearly a great deal of interchange between white-collar and manual work. The manual workers whom we interviewed included some who had done white-collar work at an earlier time and the experience of these people is analyzed in Chapter V. We are not able, however, to examine the other side of the coin, people who are now in white-collar work and therefore excluded from our samples, but who have done manual work at an earlier time. It would be necessary to take work histories from a cross section of the entire gainfully employed population in order to obtain a clear picture of the interchange between manual and white-collar occupations.

THE TIME PERIOD

The fact that a sample census of population and employment was conducted in the area in April, 1947, enables us to describe the main economic developments since the Census of April, 1940. The course of events was broadly similar to that in other manufacturing areas of the country. A war of unprecedented magnitude, financed in part by inflationary methods, produced an abnormally high level of money demand for goods and services, which in turn led to capacity production and full employment plus a wage-price inflation.

The population of the metropolitan area increased by about 14 per cent between the two censuses. Natural increase was reinforced by migration into the area to man the expanding war industries. About 10 per cent of the 1947 population had moved into the area since April, 1940. The labor force rose slightly more than the population of the area, due to an increase in labor force participation; 83 per cent of the males and 34 per cent of the females aged 14 and over were in the labor force in 1947, compared with 80 and 28 per cent in 1940.

The most striking change was the much fuller utilization of the labor force in 1947. At the time of the 1940 Census, 13 per cent of the labor force was totally unemployed and many of the employed had only part-time work. In April, 1947, only 3 per cent of the labor force was unemployed. Part-time work had also been virtually eliminated and many plants were working overtime. The work week in the forty-nine manufacturing companies reporting to the Chamber of Commerce averaged 41.5 hours in April, 1947.

There were also important changes in the composition of employment over the period. Manufacturing, while below its wartime peak, still had

about [illegible] per cent of area employment in 1947, compared with [illegible] per cent in 1940. Service industries, on the other hand, declined from 26 per cent of total employment in 1940 to 22 per cent in 1947. There was a particularly sharp drop in domestic service, which fell from 5.5 per cent of the labor force in 1940 to 1.8 per cent in 1947. These figures suggest a reduction of disguised unemployment over the period, i.e., a movement of people from occupations in which their productivity and earnings were relatively low to others in which productivity and earnings were higher.

The years 1946–48, during which the main field work of the study was conducted, were marked by an extremely low unemployment rate. Employers in the aggregate needed more labor than they were able to get, and unfilled vacancies were plentiful. The situation was one of "more than full" employment. The excess of labor demand over supply gradually declined during the period, however, and had disappeared by the end of 1948. In consequence of excess demand for labor, workers had unusual opportunities to change jobs if they wished to do so. Many of them took advantage of the opportunity, and the voluntary quit rate remained high, though it fell below the wartime level. Both wage and retail prices rose continuously, with prices somewhat in the lead. It will be worthwhile to present briefly the statistical evidence on each of these points.

There is no current measure of aggregate employment or unemployment in the area. The best indicators of unemployment are probably the number of registrations for work at the local office of the State Employment Service, and the number of people in receipt of unemployment compensation payments. While neither of these accurately measures the level of unemployment, they are likely to move in the same direction as the level of unemployment.[18] The data in Chart 1 and Table A-1[19] suggest that, except for seasonal variations, the level of unemployment

[18] The number of unemployment compensation recipients is presumably less than the number of unemployed, since at any one time some of the unemployed will be serving their waiting period, others will have exhausted their benefit rights, while others may never have acquired benefit rights because they worked in uncovered industries or because their employment in covered industries was too irregular. It should be remembered, on the other hand, that the unemployment compensation recipients include some partially unemployed people, which tends to offset [illegible]. The size of the active file at the State Employment Service is closely related to the size of the claimant load, since receipt of unemployment compensation is the main positive pressure on workers to register for work with the service. A fuller explanation of the significance of these two series will be found in connection with our discussion of Employment Service operations in Chapter III.

[19] Tables A-1, etc., refer to tables in Appendix A.

about 43 per cent of area employment in 1947, compared with 39 per cent in 1940. Service industries, on the other hand, declined from 23 per cent of total employment in 1940 to 19 per cent in 1947. There was a particularly sharp drop in domestic service, which fell from 3.6 per cent of the labor force in 1940 to 1.0 per cent in 1947. These figures suggest a reduction of disguised unemployment over the period, i.e., a movement of people from occupations in which their productivity and earnings were relatively low to others in which productivity and earnings were higher.

The years 1946–48, during which the basic field work of the study was conducted, were marked by an extremely low unemployment rate. Employers in the aggregate needed more labor than they were able to get, and unfilled vacancies were plentiful. The situation was one of "more than full" employment. The excess of labor demand over supply gradually declined during the period, however, and had disappeared by the end of 1948. In consequence of excess demand for labor, workers had unusual opportunities to change jobs if they wished to do so. Many of them took advantage of the opportunity and the voluntary quit rate remained high, though well below the wartime level. Both wages and retail prices rose continuously, with prices somewhat in the lead. It will be worthwhile to present briefly the statistical evidence on each of these points.

There is no current measure of aggregate employment or unemployment in the area. The best indicators of unemployment are probably the number of registrants for work at the local office of the State Employment Service, and the number of people in receipt of unemployment compensation payments. While neither of these actually measures the level of unemployment, they are likely to move in the same *direction* as the level of unemployment.[13] The data in Chart 1 and Table A-1[14] suggest that, except for seasonal variations, the level of unemployment

[13] The number of unemployment compensation recipients is presumably less than the number of unemployed, since at any time some of the unemployed will be serving their waiting period, others will have exhausted their benefit rights, while others may never have acquired benefit rights because they worked in uncovered industries or because their employment in covered industries was too irregular. It should be remembered, on the other hand, that the unemployment compensation recipients include some partially unemployed people, which tends to bring the total claim load above the number of full-time unemployed. The size of the active file at the State Employment Service is closely related to the size of the claim load, since receipt of unemployment compensation is the main positive pressure on workers to register for work with the Service. A fuller appraisal of the significance of the active file will be made in connection with our discussion of Employment Service operations in Chapter III.

[14] Tables A-1, etc., refer to tables in Appendix A.

was stable and very low from mid-1946 until the end of 1948. The active file at the State Employment Service fluctuated around four thousand, or about 2.5 per cent of the area labor force. Even allowing

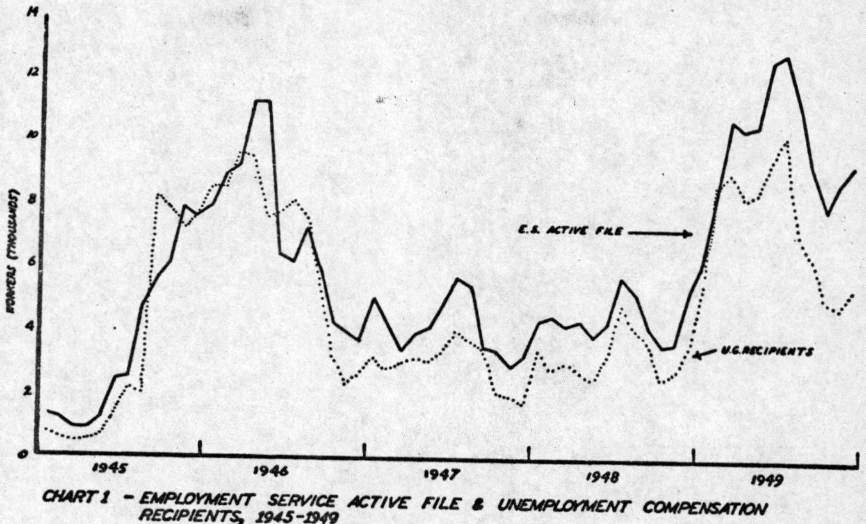

CHART 1 – EMPLOYMENT SERVICE ACTIVE FILE & UNEMPLOYMENT COMPENSATION RECIPIENTS, 1945–1949

for the fact that some of the unemployed do not register at the Service, unemployment cannot have been much above 3 per cent of the labor force during this period.

The statement that employers needed more workers than they could get cannot be documented thoroughly, but several pieces of evidence point in this direction. First, manufacturers' hiring rates were considerably in excess of separation rates over the period. The accession rate ran between 5 and 6 per cent per month during 1947 and 1948, while total separations averaged only about 4 per cent per month. The result, as appears from Chart 2, and Table A-2, was a gradual increase in the level of manufacturing employment. The only thing which prevented employment from rising more rapidly seems to have been unavailability of labor. Most of the larger manufacturers, when we interviewed them in 1947 and again in 1948, said that they had unfilled vacancies and were anxious to expand their employment if they could find people to hire.

Second, most plants in the area continued to operate some overtime. Hours actually worked in the companies reporting to the Chamber of Commerce averaged about forty-two per week over the years 1946–48,

representing an average scheduled work week of forty-four or forty-five hours. Employers would doubtless have preferred to cut back to forty hours and avoid overtime payments but since the labor necessary to do this was not available, they continued to pay whatever overtime was needed to meet production requirements.

A third indication of labor scarcity is the number of unfilled orders for workers at the State Employment Service. Over the period 1945–48, the Employment Service typically had on its hands at any time more than a thousand unfilled orders.[4] These orders, moreover, were distributed over the whole range of skilled, semiskilled, and laboring work, so that one could really speak of a general shortage of labor. It is interesting to note, however, that the trend of unfilled orders was downward throughout the period. The number of unfilled orders at the end of each month averaged 1,176 in 1946, 1,135 in 1947, and 905 in 1948. This seems to indicate that there was a gradual "softening up" of the labor market, a gradual decline in the excess demand for labor, over the period.

A situation of excess demand for labor is clearly favorable to volun-

[4] A more significant measure of labor scarcity might be the average length of time during which orders remained unfilled, but data on this point are not available. The reader may wonder how the Employment Service could consistently, month after month, have more than a thousand unfilled orders for work and at the same time more than four thousand unplaced applicants for employment. This apparent paradox will be discussed when we come to consider the operation of the Employment Service in Chapter VI.

representing an average scheduled work week of forty-four to forty-five hours. Employers would doubtless have preferred to cut back to forty hours and avoid overtime payments but, since the labor necessary to do this was not available, they continued to run whatever overtime was needed to meet production requirements.

A third indication of labor scarcity is the number of unfilled orders for workers at the State Employment Service. Over the period 1946–48, the Employment Service typically had on its hands at any time more than a thousand unfilled orders.[15] These orders, moreover, were dis-

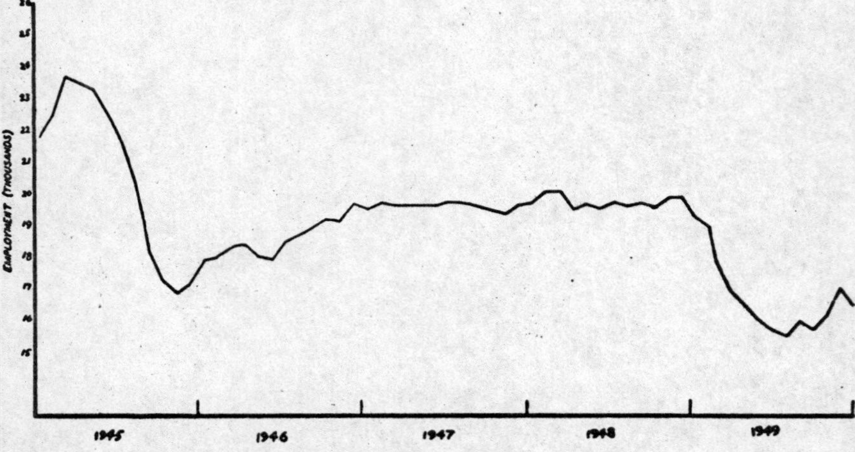

CHART 2 - EMPLOYMENT IN 39 MANUFACTURING COMPANIES, 1945-1949

tributed over the whole range of skilled, semiskilled, and laboring work, so that one could really speak of a general shortage of labor. It is interesting to note, however, that the trend of unfilled orders was downward throughout the period. The number of unfilled orders at the end of each month averaged 1774 in 1946, 1135 in 1947, and 905 in 1948. This seems to indicate that there was a gradual "softening up" of the labor market, a gradual decline in the excess demand for labor, over the period.

A situation of excess demand for labor is clearly favorable to volun-

[15] A more significant measure of labor scarcity might be the average length of time during which orders remained unfilled, but data on this point are not available. The reader may wonder how the Employment Service could consistently, month after month, have more than a thousand unfilled orders for work and at the same time more than four thousand unplaced applicants for employment. This apparent paradox will be discussed when we come to consider the operation of the Employment Service in Chapter III.

tary mobility. Workers have an unusually good chance to quit undesirable jobs and look for better ones. While there are no data on quit rates for all industries in the area, we do have data for the thirty-nine manufacturing companies reporting to the Chamber of Commerce. It will be noted from Chart 3 and Table A-3 that the voluntary quit

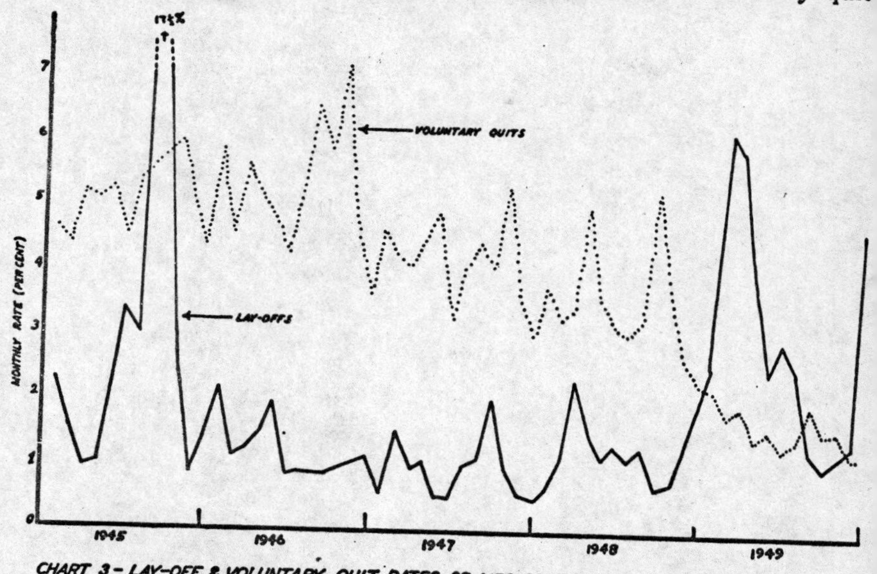

CHART 3 - LAY-OFF & VOLUNTARY QUIT RATES, 39 MFG. COMPANIES, 1945-1949

rate in these companies during 1946–48, while below the wartime peak, continued far above the prewar level. Voluntary quits, which had been running between 1 and 2 per cent per month in 1940, ran between 4 and 6 per cent in the postwar period. The trend of quit rates, however, was downward from 1946 on. The quit rate averaged 5.3 per cent per month in 1946, 4.1 per cent in 1947, and 3.5 per cent in 1948. This may indicate that by 1948 most people had found their postwar niche and had less desire to change jobs. In addition, as the excess demand for labor declined, there were fewer opportunities for advantageous moves.

A final feature of the period was a marked wage-price inflation. The course of average hourly and weekly earnings in the thirty-nine manufacturing companies, and of the retail price level in the area, is shown in Chart 4 and Table A-4.[16]

[16] The earnings data were compiled by the local Chamber of Commerce from monthly reports submitted to them by each company; the hourly earnings figure is a gross figure, including overtime. The retail price data were obtained from the National Industrial Conference Board.

tary mobility. Workers have an unusually good chance to quit unsatisfactory jobs and look for better ones. While there are no data on quit rates for all industries in the area, we do have data for the thirty-nine manufacturing companies reporting to the Chamber of Commerce. It will be noted from Chart 3 and Table A-3 that the voluntary quit

rate in these companies during 1946–48, while below the wartime peak, continued far above the prewar level. Voluntary quits, which had been running between 1 and 2 per cent per month in 1940, ran between 4 and 6 per cent in the postwar period. The trend of quit rates, however, was downward from 1946 on. The quit rate averaged 5.5 per cent per month in 1946, [illegible] per cent in 194[illegible], and 3.5 per cent in 1948. This may indicate that by 1948 most people had found their postwar niche and had less desire to change jobs. In addition, as the excess demand for labor declined, there were fewer opportunities for advantageous moves.

A final feature of the period was a marked wage-price inflation. The course of average hourly and weekly earnings in the thirty-nine manufacturing companies, and of the retail price level in the area,[illegible] is shown in Chart 4 and Table A-[illegible].

[illegible] The earnings data were furnished by the local Chamber of Commerce from monthly reports submitted to them by each company. The hourly earnings figure is a gross figure, including overtime. The retail price data were obtained from the National Industrial Conference Board.

While the economic conditions of 1946-47 were definitely unusual, they were at least approximately constant over the period. We were

not placed in the awkward situation of having obtained part of our material during prosperity and the remainder during depression.

Sources of Data

Proper appraisal of the results of this study requires that the reader be aware, not only of the milieu within which it was conducted, but of the techniques used in gathering the basic data. Since a full discussion of methods would have extended this chapter to undue length, this discussion has been placed in Appendix B. In addition to an explanation of sampling and interviewing methods, Appendix B contains the main interview schedules and questionnaires used in the study.

Briefly, data were drawn from three main sources:

1. Worker interviews. We interviewed three separate groups of workers, which are identified in the following chapters as Samples 1, 2, and 3. The workers in Sample 1, some 450 in number, are a cross section of the manual working population of the city as of October, 1945 (the date of the most recent city Directory available when we began work). This group, which included few war veterans, turned out to be relatively old, skilled, and immobile. In order to learn more about mobility we decided to draw a second sample made up entirely of people whose job listing in the 1947 Directory differed from their listing in the 1946 Directory. Sample 2 was limited further to men currently employed in manufacturing industries. This group, numbering some 350 workers is relatively young, with a large proportion of war

While the economic conditions of 1946–48 were distinctly unusual, they were at least approximately constant over the period. We were

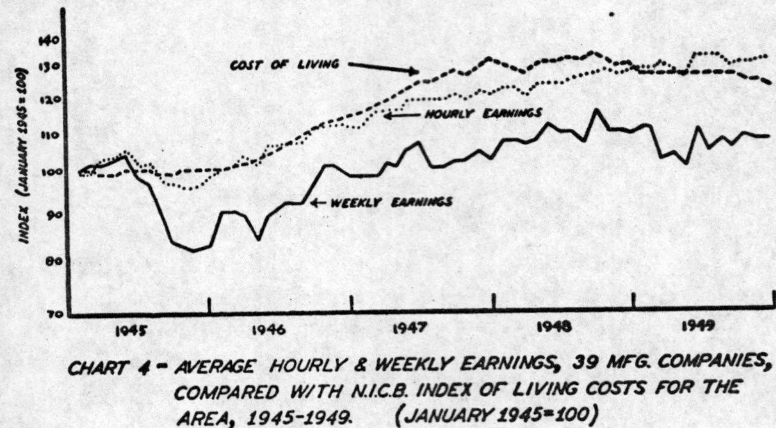

CHART 4 – AVERAGE HOURLY & WEEKLY EARNINGS, 39 MFG. COMPANIES, COMPARED WITH N.I.C.B. INDEX OF LIVING COSTS FOR THE AREA, 1945-1949. (JANUARY 1945=100)

not placed in the awkward situation of having obtained part of our material during prosperity and the remainder during depression.

Sources of Data

Proper appraisal of the results of this study requires that the reader be aware, not only of the milieu within which it was conducted, but of the techniques used in gathering the basic data. Since a full discussion of methods would have extended this chapter to undue length, this discussion has been placed in Appendix B. In addition to an explanation of sampling and interviewing methods, Appendix B contains the main interview schedules and questionnaires used in the study.

Briefly, data were drawn from three main sources:

1. Worker interviews. We interviewed three separate groups of workers, which are identified in the following chapters as Samples 1, 2, and 3. The workers in Sample 1, some 450 in number, are a cross section of the manual working population of the city as of October, 1945 (the date of the most recent city Directory available when we began work). This group, which included few war veterans, turned out to be relatively old, skilled, and immobile. In order to learn more about mobility, we decided to draw a second sample made up entirely of people whose job listing in the 1947 Directory differed from their listing in the 1946 Directory. Sample 2 was limited further to men currently employed in manufacturing industries. This group, numbering about 350 workers, is relatively young, with a large proportion of war

veterans, and a considerably higher mobility rate than Sample 1. The third sample is a small group of 50 unemployed workers, who were questioned intensively on their methods of job hunting and their minimum standards of an acceptable job.

2. Management interviews. We made several visits to each of some fifty manufacturing companies in the area. The list included virtually all plants with more than two hundred employees, and a sampling of plants below this level. In these visits we tried to make a thorough exploration of the company's procedures and policies in recruiting, selecting, assigning, promoting, and separating workers from the company; the kind of wage system used and methods of internal wage administration; the criteria used in making general wage changes, including the details of contract negotiations in unionized plants; and the adjustments made by the company to offset the cost increases resulting from wage increases. We also requested statistical data on employment, turnover, general wage changes, key job rates, average weekly earnings, and average hourly earnings over the period 1940–48. The coverage of the statistical survey was smaller than that of the interviews, due partly to inadequate personnel records in some of the smaller companies, but usable returns were obtained from twenty-six companies.

3. Other sources of statistical and interview information. Statistical information on wages and mobility in the area was assembled from a wide variety of sources, including the manufacturers' division of the Chamber of Commerce, the state headquarters of the National Metal Trades Association, the local office of the State Employment Service, the central files at state headquarters of the unemployment compensation system, the State Department of Labor, and the records of the local school system. In addition, we spent a good deal of time in discussion with union officials, Employment Service officials, school officials, and others in the area who become involved in labor market operations.

These remarks are intended merely to suggest the general scope of the study. Each of these types of activity is described in greater detail in Appendix B, and readers interested in method might well read this Appendix before proceeding.

PART I

WAGES AND MOBILITY: A CASE STUDY

CHAPTER II

Pattern of Labor Mobility

THE area case study falls into two main parts: information on the amount and determinants of labor mobility in the area (Chapters II–V) and information on wage determination and the evolution of the area wage structure (Chapters VI–VII). The purpose of this chapter is to introduce the discussion of mobility by presenting some statistical measurements drawn primarily from the lifetime employment histories of workers in the area. It is necessary to have a detailed picture of the phenomena of mobility before entering on an explanation of these phenomena. The function of this chapter is to suggest questions, while the function of Chapters III–V is to provide answers. In Chapters III and IV we shall examine the factors which influence the movement of workers between employers in the area, while Chapter V will deal with movement from one occupational level to another.

Labor mobility is of several sorts: movement into and out of the labor force, between employment and unemployment, between employers, industries, occupational levels, and geographical areas. A single job change may involve several types of movement simultaneously; the worker may take a job at a different occupational level, with a company in a different industry, located in a different part of the country. An interesting question about mobility is how far one of these types of movement is likely to involve others as well.

The focus of this study is on movement between employers, industries, and occupational levels. The nature of the study made it impossible to obtain much information on the other three types of movement.[1] All of the workers interviewed were in the labor force at the

[1] A full analysis of all types of mobility and their interrelations would require selecting a sample, not merely of persons currently in the labor force, but of the entire adult population of the United States. Persons [illegible] of the sample would then have to be followed over a long period of time, with provision also for replacement of the sample by adding new entrants to the labor force. The Social Security Board has experimented in this direction, but the data available from employers' quarterly payroll reports are [illegible] for this purpose [illegible]. Some [illegible] might be collected [illegible] history [illegible] year or at some other regular interval from the families already being interviewed by the Census Bureau for the Monthly Report on the Labor Force. The cost of this operation would be small relative to the significance of the information obtained.

HAPTER II Patterns of Labor Mobility

THE area case study falls into two main parts: infor-ıation on the amount and determinants of labor mobility in the area Chapters II–V), and information on wage determination and the ehavior of the area wage structure (Chapters VI–VII). The purpose f this chapter is to introduce the discussion of mobility by presenting ome statistical measurements, drawn primarily from the lifetime em-loyment histories of workers in the area. It is necessary to have a letailed picture of the phenomena of mobility before entering on an xplanation of these phenomena. The function of this chapter is to uggest questions, while the function of Chapters III–V is to provide .nswers. In Chapters III and IV we shall examine the factors which nfluence the movement of workers between employers in the area, vhile Chapter V will deal with movement from one occupational level o another.

Labor mobility is of several sorts: movement into and out of the abor force, between employment and unemployment, between em-loyers, industries, occupational levels, and geographical areas. A ingle job change may involve several types of movement simultane-usly: the worker may take a job at a different occupational level, vith a company in a different industry, located in a different part of he country. An interesting question about mobility is how far one of hese types of movement is likely to involve others as well.

The focus of this study is on movement between employers, indus-ries, and occupational levels. The nature of the study made it im-ossible to obtain much information on the other three types of move-nent.[1] All of the workers interviewed were in the labor forces at the

[1] A full analysis of all types of mobility and their interrelations would require electing a sample, not merely of persons currently in the labor force, but of the entire dult population of the United States. The employment status of this sample would hen have to be followed over a long period of time, with provision also for replenish-nent of the sample by adding new entrants to the labor force. The Social Security Board has experimented in this direction, but the data available from employers' uarterly payroll reports are quite incomplete for this purpose. A more hopeful pro-edure might be to collect a work history, once a year or at some other regular interval, rom the families already being interviewed by the Census Bureau for its Monthly Report on the Labor Force. The cost of this operation would be small relative to the ignificance of the information obtained.

time of interview, and the proportion unemployed was negligible. A analysis of geographical movement would have had to extend over tim and include outflow from the area as well as inflow. Our study, a snap shot at a point of time including only workers currently in the are could do no more than discover the past range of geographical move ment of those workers. This matter is of some interest, however, an we shall say as much about it as the evidence warrants.

We are concerned primarily with *voluntary* movement from one jo to another. If there is anything purposive or constructive about labo mobility, it must operate through voluntary rather than involuntar movement. It is voluntary movement which has been supposed to hol wage differentials within reasonable limits and to enable workers t maximize their satisfaction from work. Moreover, we know much les about the characteristics of voluntary movement than we do abou layoffs and discharges, the incidence of which was studied intensivel during the depression of the thirties.

At many points the data will oblige us to work with average mobilit rates which lump together voluntary and involuntary moves over worker's lifetime. This does not, however, impair the usefulness of th data as much as one might think. It would do so if voluntary movemen were correlated with one set of worker characteristics and if involuntar movement were correlated with precisely opposite characteristics. Thi is not the case. It is a familiar fact that layoffs bear heaviest on th young, the short-service workers, and the unskilled. The results o the present study indicate that these groups also show the highest rat of voluntary movement. Thus, when the two types of movements ar lumped together, one gets a reinforcement of results rather than cancelling-out of opposites.

INTERPLANT MOVEMENT: CHARACTERISTICS OF THE VOLUNTARY CHANGERS

Special interest attaches to voluntary changes of employment, sinc they involve positive action by the worker and thus present problem of worker motivation. Since the study was made during a period o peak employment in which voluntary turnover was unusually large we were able to obtain a good deal of information about it. Fourteen per cent of the workers in Sample 1 had changed jobs voluntarily sinc the end of the World War II, 10 per cent had changed jobs involun tarily, and 76 per cent had not changed. This enabled us to compar

the characteristics of those who had moved of their own accord and those who had not moved.

A problem should be noted here which will recur throughout the chapter. A worker's propensity to move may be influenced by numerous factors—notably age, sex, occupational level, length of service, industrial attachment, family status, and union membership. These variables, however, are interrelated with each other. A worker of 40 is likely to have greater length of service, more dependents, a higher occupational level, and a longer period of union membership than a worker of 20. A tabulation of turnover rates against age usually shows that the older workers have a markedly lower propensity to move. But is this due to age per se, or is it due to the influence of other variables which happen to be correlated with age? The same question arises concerning any other tabulation of mobility rates against a single variable. This problem was met in part by preparing three-way tabulations, in which the influence of a particular variable was examined while holding each of the other major variables constant in turn.[4] Thus the relation of mobility to age was examined first with length of service constant, then with occupational level constant, and so on; similar subtabulations were prepared for each of the other variables. A variable was held to have a significant influence on mobility only if a clear relationship continued to exist in these subtabulations, so that the relationship could not be explained by the presence of other variables correlated with the first. These subtabulations are much too numerous to be presented here, though some of the more significant of them are included in Appendix A.

The clearest differentiating feature of the voluntary job changers is length of service. Table 1 indicates that the propensity to move declines sharply with increasing length of service, falls sharply after three years, and is negligible after ten years of work in the same plant. This relationship persists through all the subtabulations involving length of service, and there can be little doubt of its strength.

The other relationships revealed by the analysis are considerably weaker. There is some relation, though not a very strong one, between voluntary movement and occupational level. 18 per cent of the skilled workers in Sample I had changed jobs voluntarily since the end of the war, compared with 25 per cent of the unskilled. There is an apparent

[4] It would have been preferable, of course, to hold all the other variables constant simultaneously, but this would have required a population much larger than the 450 workers in Sample I. Even with only three variables, the number of cases in many cells of the tables was frequently too small to permit significant conclusions.

the characteristics of those who had moved of their own accord and those who had not moved.

A problem should be noted here which will recur throughout the chapter. A worker's propensity to move may be influenced by numerous factors—notably age, sex, occupational level, length of service, industrial attachment, family status, and union membership. These variables, however, are intercorrelated with each other. A worker of 40 is likely to have greater length of service, more dependents, a higher occupational level, and a longer period of union membership than a worker of 20. A tabulation of turnover rates against age usually shows that the older workers have a markedly lower propensity to move. But is this due to age per se, or is it due to the influence of other variables which happen to be correlated with age? The same question arises concerning any other tabulation of mobility rates against a single variable. This problem was met in part by preparing three-way tabulations, in which the influence of a particular variable was examined while holding each of the other major variables constant in turn.[2] Thus the relation of mobility to age was examined first with length of service constant, then with occupational level constant, and so on; similar subtabulations were prepared for each of the other variables. A variable was held to have a significant influence on mobility only if a clear relationship continued to exist in these subtabulations, so that the relationship could not be explained by the presence of other variables correlated with the first. These subtabulations are much too numerous to be presented here, though some of the more significant of them are included in Appendix A.

The clearest differentiating feature of the voluntary job changers is length of service. Table 1 indicates that the propensity to move declines sharply with increasing length of service; it is slight after three years and negligible after ten years of work in the same plant. This relationship persists through all the subtabulations involving length of service, and there can be little doubt of its strength.

The other relationships revealed by the analysis are considerably weaker. There is some relation, though not a very strong one, between voluntary movement and occupational level; 15 per cent of the skilled workers in Sample 1 had changed jobs voluntarily since the end of the War, compared with 19 per cent of the unskilled. There is an apparent

[2] It would have been preferable, of course, to hold all the other variables constant *simultaneously*, but this would have required a population much larger than the 450 workers in Sample 1. Even with only three variables, the number of cases in certain sections of the tables was frequently too small to permit significant conclusions.

relation between mobility and age; the average age of the voluntar changers was 37, compared with 45 for the nonchangers. This relatio is due almost entirely, however, to the strong correlation of age wit length of service. When length of service is held constant, the influenc of age alone becomes very slight.

There seems also to be some relation between the propensity to mov and union membership. At first glance, this relation appears striking Only 6 per cent of those who had been union members more than fou

TABLE 1

VOLUNTARY MOVEMENT AND LENGTH OF SERVICE*
(Sample 1)

Length of Service (Years)	Voluntary Changers (%)	Nonchangers (%)
Less than 1	44	2
1–3	27	9
3–5	9	20
5–10	14	24
10–20	5	22
20 and over	1	23
Total	100	100

* "Voluntary changers" means workers who had changed jobs voluntarily between August 1, 1945, and th date of interview (a period of about eighteen months). "Nonchangers" means workers who had not changed job during this period. Those who changed jobs involuntarily are not included in the tabulation.

Length of service means service with *last previous employer* in the case of jobchangers, service *with presen employer* in the case of nonchangers.

years had changed jobs voluntarily, compared with 16 per cent of those who had been union members four years or less, and 22 per cent of those not union members. This turns out, however, to be due largely to a correlation between length of union membership and length of service. When length of service is held constant the relation with union membership is much weakened, though not eliminated.

The dominant influence of length of service suggests the hypothesis that voluntary mobility is essentially a form of job shopping by workers. For reasons which will be developed in Chapters III–IV, workers have great difficulty in judging the attractiveness of a job by talking it over in the company's employment office. The only way to judge it accurately is to work on it a while. After a few weeks or months of work, one can tell whether the job is worth keeping. This explains why quits are most frequent during the first few months of service and diminish rapidly after that point. The data suggest also that the difficulty of

appraise jobs from the outside is much the same for all occupational levels, industry groups, and age groups so that one finds little systematic variation in the quit rates of these groups.

While the quit rates of different categories of workers do not seem to differ greatly, the general level of voluntary quits fluctuates widely with changes in the demand for labor. This is in accord with the hypothesis just suggested. The low quit rates during depression do not mean that workers are more satisfied with their jobs. But the fact a worker who finds he has made a bad bargain will cling to the job during depression because of the slight probability of finding another. He will nurse his discontent until the demand for labor rises sufficiently so that he dares risk a change. During prosperity, workers whose job shopping has turned out badly seek, then, to leave immediately in search of better opportunities.

If this view is correct, there are no "natural" differentials in quit rates between different categories of labor. Differences in the actual quit rates of workers in different occupations, areas, and industries at any time are due, not to intrinsic characteristics of the jobs or the workers, but to the behavior of labor demand. If, for example, the demand for unskilled labor in an area is rising much more rapidly than that for skilled workers, the quit rate of laborers may be much above that of craftsmen. If the demand situation is reversed, however, one may find that the relative quit rates are also reversed. The limited data presented here cannot fully confirm this hypothesis, but it is sufficiently plausible to deserve further study.

INTERPLANT MOVEMENT: LIFETIME MOBILITY RATES

Each worker in Sample 1 was asked for a chronological listing of all jobs held since starting to work. While these work histories have certain defects, which are described in Appendix 2, they enable us to calculate an approximate mobility rate for each worker throughout his working life.[4] It seemed most understandable to calculate mobility in terms of

[4] Workers were not asked their reason for leaving each job because it was thought that the answers for earlier years would be quite unreliable and because addition of this question would have extended the interview unduly. This makes it impossible to distinguish voluntary from involuntary mobility in the work histories. The data thus indicate merely rate of movement, not reason for movement. The workers in Sample 2 were asked only for jobs held since January 1, 1940—mainly primarily to reduce the length of the questionnaire. Since this was a relatively young group, the schedules did include the whole of the job history in most cases. Since the starting date is not the same in all cases, however, the calculation of mobility rates for Sample 2 are not strictly comparable with those for Sample 1 and are not presented here. In general, however, the results conform quite closely to those for Sample 1.

appraising jobs from the outside is much the same for all occupational levels, industry groups, and age groups so that one finds little systematic variation in the quit rates of these groups.

While the quit rates of different categories of workers do not seem to differ greatly, the general level of voluntary quits fluctuates widely with changes in the demand for labor. This is in accord with the hypothesis just suggested. The low quit rates during depression do not mean that workers are more satisfied with their jobs than before. A worker who finds he has made a bad bargain will cling to the job during depression because of the slight probability of finding another. He will nurse his discontent until the demand for labor rises sufficiently so that he dares risk a change. During prosperity, workers whose job shopping has turned out poorly feel freer to leave immediately in search of better opportunities.

If this view is correct, there are no "natural" differentials in quit rates between different categories of labor. Differences in the actual quit rates of workers in different occupations, areas, and industries at any time are due, not to intrinsic characteristics of the jobs or the workers, but to the behavior of labor demand.[9] If, for example, the demand for unskilled labor in an area is rising much more rapidly than that for skilled workers, the quit rate of laborers may be much above that of craftsmen. If the demand situation is reversed, however, one may find that the relative quit rates are also reversed. The limited data presented herein cannot fully confirm this hypothesis, but it is sufficiently plausible to deserve further study.

INTERPLANT MOVEMENT: LIFETIME MOBILITY RATES

Each worker in Sample 1 was asked for a chronological listing of all jobs held since starting to work. While these work histories have certain defects, which are described in Appendix B, they enable us to calculate an approximate mobility rate for each worker throughout his working life.[8] It seemed most understandable to calculate mobility in terms of

[8] Workers were not asked their reason for leaving each job because it was thought that the answers for earlier years would be quite unreliable, and because addition of this question would have extended the interview unduly. This makes is impossible to distinguish voluntary from involuntary mobility in the work histories. The data thus indicate merely *rate* of movement, not reasons for movement. The workers in Sample 2 were asked only for jobs held since January 1, 1940—again primarily to reduce the length of the questionnaire. Since this was a relatively young group, the schedules do contain the worker's entire job history in most cases. Since this is not true in all cases, however, the tabulations of mobility rates for Sample 2 are not strictly comparable with those for Sample 1 and are not presented here. In general, however, the results conform quite closely to those for Sample 1.

average length of job, i.e., by dividing the number of jobs held into the number of years of employment. In what follows, then, it must be remembered that a *high* number of years per job indicates a *low* rate of mobility, and vice versa.

Table 2 indicates that there is a great variation in the mobility rates of different workers. The average rate for all workers in Sample 1 was 7.0 years per job. The most mobile 16 per cent, however, had averaged less than two years per job, while at the opposite extreme were 19 per cent who had averaged ten years or more per job.

TABLE 2
DISTRIBUTION OF WORKERS BY LIFETIME MOBILITY RATE
(Sample 1)

Mobility Rate (Years per job)	Distribution of Workers (%)
0–0.9	4
1–1.9	12
2–2.9	13
3–4.9	23
5–9.9	29
10–19.9	14
20 and over	5
Total	100

When the characteristics of the less mobile and more mobile workers are analyzed, the strongest relation which appears is between mobility rate and age. Table 3 indicates a progressive retardation of movement with increasing age. The youngster out of school usually moves about a good deal for several years, trying out various jobs and eventually settling into a more or less permanent line of work. After this "settling-down period" his rate of movement decreases. If he is able to stay five or ten years in a single job, his propensity to move becomes very low indeed.

There appears to be some relation between mobility rate and occupational level, the unskilled having the highest rate of movement and skilled workers the lowest. In Sample 1, the skilled workers had averaged 7.6 years per job, the semiskilled 7.0, and the unskilled 6.6. Corresponding figures for Sample 2 were 4.0, 3.6, and 2.5 years. No other significant relations were revealed by statistical analysis.

An interesting question is whether a high mobility rate means simply

more movement *of the same kind,* or whether it also extends the worker's *range* of movement. Is a highly mobile worker likely to have worked in a wider range of industries, occupational levels, and localities than a worker with lower mobility? Or does he simply move around more rapidly within the same orbit?

The work histories from Sample 1 provide tentative answers to these questions. As regards *employer,* a higher mobility rate definitely means a wider range of movement. Workers who change jobs frequently do not simply shuttle back and forth between the same two or three

TABLE 3
RELATION OF MOBILITY RATE TO AGE
(Sample 1)

Age	Mobility Rate (Years per job)
Under 25	2.0
25–34	4.2
35–44	6.2
45–54	7.9
55–64	10.1
65 and over	13.0

companies, but move on from one new company to another. The same thing is true, though less strikingly, of *interindustry* shifting. Workers with a high mobility rate are more likely to have worked in a wide variety of industries than are low-mobility workers. Thus of workers who had averaged less than one year per job, 35 per cent made five or more interindustry shifts; of workers who had averaged ten years or more per job, only 2 per cent had made this many shifts (Table A-5). Moreover, about three-quarters of the job changes by workers in the sample involved a change of industry as well. The ties binding the worker to a particular industry seem to be rather loose,[4] and this impression will be confirmed by data to be presented later in this chapter.

The situation is different as regards changes of *occupational level.*

[4] What one counts as "an interindustry shift" will depend, of course, on one's classification of industries. A fine industry classification will yield many more "shifts" than a coarse one. The classification used here was quite coarse. Manufacturing was divided only into gun plants, other metalworking, clothing, rubber, paper, printing, and other manufacturing; other major industry groups were not subdivided at all. It is all the more striking, therefore, that we should have found so much shifting even between these very broad categories.

Shifts from one occupational level to another are less frequent than interindustry shifts.[5] Moreover, the workers with high mobility rates show little more occupational shifting than do those with low mobility (Table A-6). The worker does not seem to alter his chances of rising or falling in the occupational scale by a more rapid rate of movement.

There is least shifting of all as regards *locality* of work and residence. Fifty-seven per cent of the workers in Sample 1 had never worked outside of this community, and another 18 per cent had worked in only one other locality. Nor is a high mobility rate associated with

TABLE 4
PERCENTAGE DISTRIBUTION OF WORKERS BY FREQUENCY OF INDUSTRIAL, OCCUPATIONAL, AND GEOGRAPHICAL SHIFTING
(Sample 1)

Number of Shifts	Type of Shift		
	Industrial (%)	Occupational (%)	Geographical (%)
0	19	17	57
1	19	34	18
2	17	19	11
3	15	14	6
4	11	8	4
5 or more	19	8	4
Total	100	100	100

wide geographical movement (Table A-7). Workers who have been very mobile geographically must, of course, have changed jobs frequently; but the converse is not true. Workers who change jobs frequently seem about as likely to remain in the same area as those who change infrequently.

The data on the relative frequency of different types of movement among the workers in the Sample are summarized in Table 4. Interindustry movement is clearly the commonest type of job shift. In a large majority of cases, a change of employer involves a change of industrial attachment as well. Changes of occupational level are less common. There is, to be sure, some tendency for industry shifts to involve occupational shifts as well. It will be noted from Table 5 and

[5] This result, however, may be due partly to the fact that the occupational categories used here were even fewer and broader than the industry categories. The "semiskilled" category, for example, embraces a great variety of jobs. If it had been possible to use a finer occupational classification, there would have been more apparent "shifts" of occupation. We shall have more to say in Chapter V about the inadequacy of the occupational categories in general use at the present time.

as more detailed classifications in Tables A-8 and A-9 show. Workers with a larger number of industry shifts have also, on the average, a larger number of occupational shifts. The number of occupational shifts, however, is consistently well below the number of industry shifts. Geographical shifting is less common than any other type, and the highly mobile worker seems to enjoy little more range of geographical movement than the worker with a much lower mobility rate.

Before leaving the subject of mobility rates we should note one other conclusion, derived from a different body of data. It is a familiar

TABLE 5
Frequency of Occupational and Industrial Shifting

Number of Interindustry Changes	Average Number of Changes in Occupational Level	
	Sample 1	Sample 2
[illegible]	[illegible]	[illegible]
1	[illegible]	[illegible]
[illegible]	[illegible]	[illegible]
[illegible]	[illegible]	[illegible]
[illegible]	[illegible]	[illegible]
5 or more	[illegible]	[illegible]

fact that, of the workers who change jobs in a particular year, some change several times during the year, so that a minority of the job changers account for a large part of the total movement. It follows that turnover rates showing *number of job changes* give a misleading impression of the *proportion of employed workers* who have changed jobs during the year. The turnover rate will always exceed the proportion of job-changers by a considerable margin, but there has been little investigation of the probable size of this discrepancy.

We were able to form an impression on this point by using data drawn from the state unemployment compensation files. For each of the years 1941, 1945, and 1946 we drew a 10 per cent sample of covered workers in the area who had changed jobs during the year. The main objective was to determine the direction of movement in each year; the results on this point will be discussed in the next section, as will the methods used in drawing the sample. As an incidental result, however, we were able to compute the number of moves by each job-changer in a particular year. The data on this point are shown in Table 6. While most of the job changers moved only once or twice during the year, the minority of very mobile people accounted for a

the more detailed distributions in Tables A-8 and A-9 that workers with a larger number of industry shifts have also, on the average, a larger number of occupational shifts. The number of occupational shifts, however, is consistently well below the number of industry shifts. Geographical shifting is less common than any other type, and the highly mobile worker seems to enjoy little more range of geographical movement than the worker with a much lower mobility rate.

Before leaving the subject of mobility rates we should note one other conclusion, derived from a different body of data. It is a familiar

TABLE 5
RELATION OF OCCUPATIONAL TO INDUSTRIAL SHIFTING

Number of Interindustry Changes	Average Number of Changes in Occupational Level	
	Sample 1	Sample 2
0	0.62	0.59
1	1.04	1.23
2	1.60	1.27
3	2.08	1.67
4	2.68	2.25
5 or more	3.42	2.58

fact that, of the workers who change jobs in a particular year, some change several times during the year, so that a minority of the job-changers account for a large part of the total movement. It follows that turnover rates showing *number of job changes* give a misleading impression of the *proportion of employed workers* who have changed jobs during the year. The turnover rate will always exceed the proportion of job-changers by a considerable margin, but there has been little investigation of the probable size of this discrepancy.

We were able to form an impression on this point by using data drawn from the state unemployment compensation files. For each of the years 1941, 1943, and 1946, we drew a 10 per cent sample of covered workers in the area who had changed jobs during the year. The main objective was to determine the *direction* of movement in each year; the results on this point will be discussed in the next section, as will the methods used in obtaining the sample. As an incidental result, however, we were able to count the *number* of moves by each job-changer in a particular year. The data on this point are shown in Table 6. While most of the job-changers moved only once or twice during the year, the minority of very mobile people accounted for a

disproportionate share of the total movement. In 1941, for example, one-third of the group had moved three times or more, and these people accounted for 60 per cent of the total moves during the year.

The average number of moves per worker was 2.3 in 1941, 1.9 in 1943, and 1.9 in 1946. This suggests that, at the turnover levels prevailing in these years, one could approximate the proportion of the labor force who had changed jobs by dividing the gross turnover rate by 2, i.e., if cumulative monthly separation rates for the year totaled 50 per cent of the labor force, one could conclude that about 25 per cent of all workers had changed jobs. This suggestion should be treated with caution, however, for a different ratio might obtain at turnover rates much higher or much lower than those of 1941–46. In general, one would expect that the higher the gross turnover rate, the greater the average number of moves per man. Thus at an annual turnover rate of 100 per cent, the number of moves per man might be 3.0, while at a rate of 20 per cent it might be only 1.5. This would mean that the percentage of workers changing jobs is not only *lower* than the gross turnover rate at a given time, but also that it *fluctuates* less over the course of time.

TABLE 6
FREQUENCY OF MOVEMENT BY WORKERS WHO CHANGED JOBS WITHIN COVERED EMPLOYMENT
1941, 1943, AND 1946

Number of Job Changes During Year	Distribution of Workers (%)			Distribution of "Man-Moves" (%)		
	1941	1943	1946	1941	1943	1946
1	35	47	49	15	23	26
2	29	29	31	25	28	33
3	18	13	11	23	20	17
4	10	5	4	17	10	8
5	4	3	2	9	8	5
More than 5	4	3	3	11	11	11
Total	100	100	100	100	100	100

DIRECTION AND SCOPE OF MOVEMENT: INTERINDUSTRY SHIFTS

It has already been noted that interindustry shifting is common. Forty-five per cent of the workers in Sample 1 had made three or more interindustry shifts during their working lives. Moreover, these shifts

are not a mere shuttling back and forth between two industries. In most cases the worker goes on to a new industry instead of returning to one in which he has already worked.* Interindustry shifting is somewhat more common among unskilled workers than among skilled men, as is indicated by Table 2. This appears to be a genuine relationship not attributable to the influence of age or any other third variable. It probably stems from the fact that certain trade skills can be used in only one industry. Men in these trades have an incentive to avoid interindustry movement which the unskilled worker does not have.

TABLE [illegible]

Frequency of Interindustry Shifts by Occupational Level

Occupational Level	Average Number of Interindustry Shifts	
	Sample 1	Sample 2
Skilled	[illegible]	[illegible]
Semiskilled	[illegible]	[illegible]
Unskilled	[illegible]	[illegible]

We wish now to examine the *direction* of these interindustry shifts. The central question is whether interindustry movement is random or whether it exhibits a regular pattern. Are certain industries close "neighbors" of other industries, so that workers leaving a particular industry are more likely to go to a "neighbor" industry than to others? Or do workers leaving a particular industry distribute themselves among other industries according to chance?

Two types of information are available on this subject. The first is the lifetime employment histories of the workers in Sample 1, tabulated to show the *kinds* of industry as well as the number of industries in which each person has worked. The information obtained from these histories is summarized in Tables 3 and [illegible].

Table 3 bears on the extent to which each industry is a self-contained

* Workers in Sample 1 who had made two shifts had worked, on the average, in [illegible] industries; those with three shifts had worked in [illegible] industries; those with four shifts in [illegible] industries; and those with five or more shifts in [illegible] industries. If a worker shuttled back and forth between two industries, the number of industries in which he had worked could never be greater than two; if on the other hand he always went on to a new industry, the number of industries in which he had worked would always be one greater than the number of shifts. The results are intermediate, but closer to the latter pole; i.e., while there is some tendency to return to industries in which one has worked previously, this tendency is not predominant. Even where the worker does return, the main attraction, as we shall see in Chapter III, is usually a particular employer rather than the industry as such.

are not a mere shuttling back and forth between two industries. In most cases the worker goes on to a new industry instead of returning to one in which he has already worked.[6] Interindustry shifting is somewhat more common among unskilled workers than among skilled men, as is indicated by Table 7. This appears to be a genuine relationship not attributable to the influence of age or any other third variable. It probably stems from the fact that certain trade skills can be used in only one industry. Men in these trades have an incentive to avoid interindustry movement which the unskilled worker does not have.

TABLE 7
FREQUENCY OF INTERINDUSTRY SHIFTS BY OCCUPATIONAL LEVEL

Occupational Level	Average Number of Interindustry Shifts	
	Sample 1	Sample 2
Skilled	2.1	1.1
Semiskilled	2.4	1.4
Unskilled	2.7	2.1

We wish now to examine the *direction* of these interindustry shifts. The central question is whether interindustry movement is random or whether it exhibits a regular pattern. Are certain industries close "neighbors" of other industries, so that workers leaving a particular industry are more likely to go to a "neighbor" industry than to others? Or do workers leaving a particular industry distribute themselves among other industries according to chance?

Two types of information are available on this subject. The first is the lifetime employment histories of the workers in Sample 1, tabulated to show the *kinds* of industry as well as the number of industries in which each person has worked. The information obtained from these histories is summarized in Tables 8 and 9.

Table 8 bears on the extent to which an industry is a self-contained

[6] Workers in Sample 1 who had made two shifts had worked, on the average, in 2.6 industries; those with three shifts had worked in 3.0 industries; those with four shifts in 3.9 industries; and those with five or more shifts in 5.1 industries. If a worker shuttled back and forth between two industries, the number of industries in which he had worked could never be greater than two; if on the other hand he *always* went on to a new industry, the number of industries in which he had worked would always be one greater than the number of shifts. Our results are intermediate, but closer to the latter pole; i.e., while there is some tendency to return to an industry in which one has worked previously, this tendency is not predominant. Even where the worker does return, the main attraction, as we shall see in Chapters III–IV, is usually a *previous employer* rather than the industry per se.

entity, with workers moving about only within the industry. It will be noted that in only four of the twelve industry groups have as many as a quarter of the workers spent their entire working life in their present industry. The nearest thing to a self-contained industry is clothing, in which half of the employees have never worked in any other industry. At the opposite extreme, the metalworking industries appear to be extremely "open" industries, the majority of their employees having worked in at least two or three other industries. Even

TABLE 8
NUMBER OF OTHER INDUSTRIES WORKED IN, BY CURRENT INDUSTRIAL ATTACHMENT
(Sample 1)

Current Industrial Attachment	Number of Other Industries in Which Employed (%)				
	Total	0	1	2	3 or more
Gun Plants	100	9	32	23	36
Other Metalworking	100	15	23	3	59
Clothing	100	50	39	6	5
Rubber	100	45	22	22	11
Paper	100	18	41	18	23
Printing	100	35	24	18	23
Other Manufacturing	100	18	22	30	30
Construction	100	21	7	36	36
Transportation and Utilities	100	16	23	31	30
Wholesale and Retail Trade	100	14	14	18	54
Service	100	18	22	18	42
Miscellaneous	100	16	18	22	34

construction, which one tends to think of as a quite specialized line of work, has had less than one-quarter of its workers engaged continuously in the industry. Table 8 as a whole confirms our earlier conclusion that labor flows back and forth quite freely across industry lines.

It is still possible, however, that workers might move more frequently between certain industries than others. How much is there to this hypothesis of "neighboring" industries? Table 9 tells us in *which* industries, other than the one to which they are presently attached, the workers in Sample 1 have been employed. The existence of neighboring industries would be indicated by a figure in a particular box of the table which is significantly larger than the figure at the foot of the column in which the box is located.[7] Looking at the foot of the first

[7] The construction of this table requires explanation. The unit of calculation is a "man-industry," i.e., one man having worked in one industry other than the one to

column, for example, one finds that for the sample as a whole gun plants account for 13 per cent of all "outside" employment. If interindustry movement were completely random, then, one would expect to find the figure 13 in each box of this column, i.e., workers presently attached

TABLE 9
OTHER INDUSTRIES WORKED IN, BY CURRENT INDUSTRIAL ATTACHMENT
(Sample 1)

Current Industrial Attachment	Other Industries in Which Employed (%)											
	Gun Plants	Other Metalworking	Clothing	Rubber	Paper	Printing	Other Manufacturing	Construction	Transp., Comm., Utilities	Wholesale and Retail Trade	Service	Total
Gun Plants	—	21	—	5	1	2	10	5	17	19	20	100
Other metalworking	12	—	4	6	2	1	11	10	17	22	15	100
Clothing	—	21	—	7	—	—	—	—	21	29	22	100
Rubber	9	18	—	—	9	—	9	18	9	—	28	100
Paper	9	13	17	—	—	9	22	8	—	13	9	100
Printing	22	22	—	9	4	—	9	4	13	4	13	100
Other Manufacturing	14	12	3	3	—	2	14	7	9	19	17	100
Construction	20	13	2	2	4	—	7	—	18	27	7	100
Transp., Comm., Utilities	17	20	1	7	2	1	7	10	—	19	16	100
Wholesale and Retail Trade	26	17	5	4	—	—	6	11	13	—	18	100
Service	20	20	2	7	—	—	10	9	15	17	—	100
Total	13	13	3	6	1	1	10	8	13	18	14	100

to any industry should have had, on a chance basis, 13 per cent of their outside employment in gun plants. If it now appeared that workers in a particular industry—say, clothing—had had 50 per cent of their outside jobs in gun plants, one would conclude that there is an unusually close relation between employment in these two industries. In the

which he is presently attached. A man who has worked in three other industries is represented three times in the table, whereas a man who has always worked in his present industry does not appear at all. The absolute figures in the original tabulation were reduced to comparable form by percentaging horizontally. These percentage distributions, however, relate to "man-industries," not to individuals. A particular row indicates that, of all "outside" jobs held by workers now engaged in industry A, a certain percentage were in industry B, industry C, and so on. It should be noted also that, in order to reduce the coding and tabulation work, no more than three entries were made for any individual, although some workers had actually worked in four or more "outside" industries. The number of jobs excluded in this way was too small, however, to have a significant effect on the results.

example chosen, the evidence is the reverse. None of the clothing workers in the sample has ever been employed in a gun plant, nor have any of the workers now in gun plants ever been employed in a clothing factory.

Careful inspection of Table 9 does not reveal a close relation between any pair of industries. The few relations which appear strong at first glance turn out on examination to be due to special circumstances. Thus a relatively large proportion of trade and service workers who have been employed in gun plants and other metalworking is doubtless due to the fact that the study was made just after World War II, during which large numbers of trade and service workers were drawn temporarily into war industries. Again, the large number of workers in certain industries who have also worked in wholesale and retail trade is probably due to the fact that many youngsters spent a short time in a retail store on first leaving school; these jobs are of little significance in the total work history of the individual.

In general, then, the hypothesis of "neighboring" industries is not borne out by the evidence. On the contrary, the pattern of interindustry employment is close to what one would expect on a random basis. The implication is that workers looking for a new job are more concerned with the occupational level of the job, characteristics of the employer, geographical location, and other factors than with the industry in which the job is located.

A different sort of conclusion can be drawn by comparing the percentages in the "total" row at the bottom of Table 9 with the distribution of total area employment in these industries. Thus although the clothing industry provided about 10 per cent of area employment in these industries in 1947, only 3 per cent of the "outside" jobs held were in clothing. This confirms our previous finding that clothing is more nearly a "closed" industry than are most others. At the opposite extreme, construction accounted for only about 4 per cent of 1947 employment, and the transportation—communication—utilities group for another 4 per cent. Yet 13 per cent of the "outside" jobs were in construction, and 18 per cent were in transportation, communications, and utilities. These industries are thus very "open" in the sense that a disproportionately large number of workers pass through them on their way to other industries.

Our second body of data on interindustry movement is more sharply focussed, since it relates to the direction of movement in specific years—1941, 1943, and 1946. When a worker covered by the state

unemployment compensation system is hired or separated from employment, this fact is reported to state headquarters, and an accession or separation slip is clipped to the worker's card in the central file. Thus, if a man changes jobs several times during the year, by the end of the year a corresponding number of slips will be attached to his card, each showing the name of the employer, from which one can determine the industry in which the job was held. A separate file is kept for each year. Thus by going to the 1947 file one can find a record of all moves made by workers in covered employment during that year, and similarly for any other year one wishes to examine.

We selected for study the last prewar year (1940), the year of peak wartime employment (1943), and the first full year of postwar demobilization (1946). For each year, we took a 10 per cent sample of all covered workers in the area who had changed jobs once or more during the year. The samples were substantial, averaging some two thousand workers and four thousand "moves" in each year. For each move, we recorded the firm and industry from which the worker was separated and the firm and industry to which he went. It was then possible to compute the extent and direction of interindustry movement in each year. The results are summarized in Tables 10, A-15 and A-16.[3]

Table 10 shows the proportion of accessions to firms in each industry which come from other firms in the industry, compared with the proportion which one would have expected on a random basis, i.e., on the basis of relative employment in the industry. A table was also prepared showing the proportion of workers separated from firms in each industry who moved to other firms in the same industry, but the results were so similar that it seemed unnecessary to present them.

[3] Certain limitations of the basic data should be noted at this point. (1) The data for the area are maintained by Social Security number. Since continuous blocks of Social Security numbers have been assigned to particular areas, one can identify workers by the area in which they originally received a Social Security number, i.e., in which they first entered covered employment. In compiling our figures, considering numbers assigned to this community, it was possible to include workers currently employed in other areas. It was not possible, however, to include in the sample workers whose numbers were assigned in other areas and who have since moved to this community. What we have, in other words, is a sample of workers who first entered covered employment in this locality and are still working there. The sample thus understates geographical mobility. (2) The data cover only movement within covered employment. While an effort is made to get large employers to report their accessions to state headquarters, this reporting is far from complete. This limitation is not very serious, however, since the great bulk of urban industrial workers are in covered industries and movement among these industries is our main concern. (3) It was impossible to locate some of the very small employers in any industrial directory of the city or state. Where the industry in which a firm belonged could not be determined, it was necessary to exclude the move from our summary tables.

unemployment compensation system is hired or separated from employment, this fact is reported to state headquarters, and an accession or separation slip is clipped to the worker's card in the central file. If he changes jobs several times during the year, by the end of the year a corresponding number of slips will be clipped to his card, each bearing the name of the employer, from which one can determine the industry in which the job was held. A separate file is kept for each year. Thus by going to the 1941 file one can find a record of all moves made by workers in covered employment during that year, and similarly for any other year one wishes to examine.

We selected for study the last prewar year (1941), the year of peak wartime employment (1943), and the first full year of postwar demobilization (1946). For each year, we took a 10 per cent sample of all covered workers in the area who had changed jobs once or more during the year. The samples were substantial, averaging some two thousand workers and four thousand "moves" in each year. For each move we recorded the firm and industry from which the worker was separated and the firm and industry to which he went. It was then possible to compute the extent and direction of interindustry movement in each year. The results are summarized in Tables 10, A-10, and A-11.[8]

Table 10 shows the proportion of accession to firms in each industry which come from other firms in the industry, compared with the proportion which one would have expected on a random basis, i.e., on the basis of relative employment in the industry. A table was also prepared showing the proportion of workers separated from firms in each industry who moved to other firms in the same industry, but the results were so similar that it seemed unnecessary to present them

[8] Certain limitations of the basic data should be noted at this point. (1) The card files are maintained by Social Security number. Since continuous blocks of Social Security numbers have been assigned to particular areas, the workers are really filed by the area in which they originally received a Social Security number, i.e., in which they first entered covered employment. In sampling the drawers containing numbers assigned to this community, it was possible to exclude workers currently employed in other areas. It was not possible, however, to include in the sample workers whose numbers were assigned in other areas and who have since moved to this community. What we have, in other words, is a sample of workers who first entered covered employment in this locality and are still working there, i.e., a sample with low geographical mobility. (2) The data cover only movement within covered employment. While an effort is made to get large employers in uncovered industries to report their accessions to state headquarters, this reporting is far from satisfactory. This limitation is not very serious, however, since the great bulk of urban manual workers are in covered industries and movement among these industries is our main concern. (3) It was impossible to locate some of the very small employers in any industrial directory of the city or state. Where the industry to which a firm belonged could not be determined, it was necessary to exclude the move from our summary tables.

here. Several conclusions emerge from an examination of Table 10. In the years 1941 and 1943, the industries studied showed a moderate degree of internal recruitment, approaching 50 per cent in most cases and appreciably larger than would be encountered on a random basis.[9] Construction and clothing manufacture showed a particularly high degree of internal recruitment.

The degree of internal recruitment was lower in 1946 than in the earlier years. This was due partly to the fact that a large proportion

TABLE 10
INTERNAL AND EXTERNAL RECRUITMENT OF LABOR, SELECTED INDUSTRIES, 1941, 1943, AND 1946

	Percentage of Accessions From Within the Industry			Employment in Industry as Percentage of Area Employment (1940)
	1941	1943	1946	
Metalworking	32	43	26	20
Apparel	57	31	38	5
Construction	54	36	32	5
Transp., Comm., and Utilities	6	18	9	8
Wholesale and Retail Trade	34	27	24	18
Service Industries	46	30	18	10

of the accessions during 1946 consisted of returning war veterans. Most of this was actually internal recruitment in the sense that the veterans were returning to their previous jobs, but it was not counted as such in our tabulations. Moreover, during 1946 large numbers of workers who had been engaged in war work for several years returned to their old occupations or sought new ones. Because of this churning around of the labor market during 1946, one would expect a high degree of interindustry movement and an unusually low proportion of intraindustry movement. The data for 1941 are doubtless more indicative of what one should expect in normal high employment conditions.

[9] On a random basis, the percentage of the accessions to firms in an industry who came from other firms in the same industry would be very nearly the same as the percentage which employment in that industry forms of total employment, i.e., the columns under each year in Table 10 would closely parallel the right-hand column. (The percentages would not be *precisely* the same because, in calculating the probability of accessions to a particular firm, the employment of that firm would have to be subtracted from that of the industry to which it belongs.) Actually, however, the figures are substantially above those in the right-hand column, indicating a considerable degree of industry attachment.

1940-1941 and 1946

	Percentage of Accessions From Within the Industry			Employment in Industry as Percentage of Area Employment (1946)
	1940	1941	1946	
Manufacturing	12		23	70
Apparel		31	13	6
Construction	62	66	47	3
Transp., Comm. and Utilities	4	11	7	6
Wholesale and Retail Trade	25	32	31	18
Service Industries	40	30	8	10

The direction of interindustry shifting during 1941, 1942, and 1946 is summarized in Tables A-10 and A-11, which were placed in the appendix because they are rather voluminous. Table A-10 shows the workers who left each industry in a particular year, classified according to the industries to which they went. [A companion table was prepared showing the workers entering each industry, classified according to the industries from which they came, but this is not included here because it simply pictures the pattern depicted in Table A-10 from the opposite side.]

Table A-15 presents a different measure of the "closeness" of particular pairs of industries. This is the number of workers moving between the two industries during a year in both directions, taken as a percentage of aggregate employment in the two industries. This kind of calculation is necessary because two large industries would naturally have a larger absolute interchange of workers than two small industries; the absolute movement must be reduced to a ratio of employment before accurate comparisons can be drawn.

Tables A-10 and A-11 will repay careful study. They are dominated, of course, by the fact that during 1941–42 great numbers of workers were drawn into metalworking and other war industries, while during 1945 and 1946 workers were demobilized from these industries into others. Table A-10 suggests that the war industries drew very evenly from other types of industries. One might have expected, for example, that the expanding metalworking industries would have drawn much more heavily on other branches of manufacturing than on industry in general. The evidence is, however, that metalworking drew quite as heavily on trade, service, utilities, and other lines of industry—relative, of course, to the number of people employed in those industries, in both 1941 and 1942. Almost every industry shows between 40 and 50 per cent of its departing workers going into metal manufacturing. Such barriers to interindustry movement as may have existed before the war apparently crumbled before the intense demand for labor and the special rewards offered to workers in war industry.

The main conclusion which emerges from careful study of Table A-15 is that movement is more intense between certain pairs of industries than others. The trade and service industries, for example, show a marked interchange of labor with each other and also considerable interchange with manufacturing. The various branches of manufacturing show somewhat more interchange with each other than with nonmanufacturing industries. Clothing manufacture, however, as has

The *direction* of interindustry shifting during 1941, 1943, and 1946 is summarized in Tables A-10 and A-11, which were placed in the Appendix because they are rather voluminous. Table A-10 shows the workers *leaving* each industry in a particular year, classified according to the industries to which they went. (A companion table was prepared showing the workers *entering* each industry, classified according to the industries from which they came, but this is not included here because it simply pictures the process described in Table A-10 from the opposite side.)

Table A-11 presents a different measure of the "closeness" of particular pairs of industries. This is the number of workers moving between the two industries during a year, in both directions, taken as a percentage of aggregate employment in the two industries. This kind of calculation is necessary because two large industries would naturally have a larger absolute interchange of workers than two small industries; the absolute movement must be reduced to a ratio of employment before accurate comparisons can be drawn.

Tables A-10 and A-11 will repay careful study. They are dominated, of course, by the fact that during 1941–44 great numbers of workers were drawn into metalworking and other war industries, while during 1945 and 1946 workers were demobilized from these industries into others. Table A-10 suggests that the war industries drew very evenly from other types of industries. One might have expected, for example, that the expanding metalworking industries would have drawn much more heavily on other branches of manufacturing than on industry in general. The evidence is, however, that metalworking drew fully as heavily on trade, service, utilities, and other lines of industry—relative, of course, to the number of people engaged in those industries. In both 1941 and 1943, almost every industry shows between 40 and 50 per cent of its departing workers going into metal manufacturing. Such barriers to interindustry movement as may have existed before the war apparently crumbled before the intense demand for labor and the special rewards offered to workers in war industry.

The main conclusion which emerges from careful study of Table A-11 is that movement is more intense between certain pairs of industries than others. The trade and service industries, for example, show a marked interchange of labor with each other, and also considerable interchange with manufacturing. The various branches of manufacturing show somewhat more interchange with each other than with non-manufacturing industries. Clothing manufacture, however, as has

been noted repeatedly, occupies a relatively isolated position. Its receipts of labor from other industries are consistently below what one would expect on a random basis, indicating barriers to ready entrance. Construction seems to have somewhat more interchange with transportation and utilities than with other industries.

This finding that movement is more intense between certain pairs of industries than others may seem to contradict our earlier finding that there are no definite patterns of interindustry movement in the work histories from Sample 1. The explanation, I think, is that we are dealing with two quite different things—in the one case with a single move at a particular time, in the other case with a series of moves over the worker's entire career. Putting the two types of material together, three conclusions appear justified: first, when a worker leaves a firm the probability that he will go to another firm in the same industry is considerably greater than one would expect on a random basis. This is particularly true of certain industries, notably clothing. Second, if he moves outside the industry, he is somewhat more likely to go to certain industries than to others. Third, even though these things are true of *single moves,* when one aggregates the entire past careers of workers in a particular industry their movements will have been so numerous and varied that neighborhood relationships between industries become blurred and indistinguishable. If a worker moves often enough, he will eventually run the gamut of industries; yet each one of these moves may have been influenced considerably by the industry of his last employment.

One other useful bit of information can be derived from our unemployment compensation material. When a worker leaving a company in the area took a new job in another locality, this fact was noted and later tabulated. It is thus possible to tell what percentage of the workers leaving each industry in a particular year moved to jobs outside the area. These data, presented in Table 11, tell something about the relative geographical mobility of workers in different industries.[10]

It is apparent from Table 11 that construction workers show a relatively high propensity to take jobs in other areas, and clothing workers an unusually low propensity, with other industries occupying an inter-

[10] The information is not precise, because of the limitations of the sample and because we do not know whether the job in the new area was in the same *industry* as before. We do not know, therefore, whether the geographical movement is attributable to characteristics of the *industry* or of the *worker*. It should be recalled also that these changes in the location of the worker's job did not necessarily involve a change of residence. There are several large industrial centers within easy commuting distance of this community.

majority position. In most industries the extent of outward movement declined from 1941 to 1946, possibly because of housing shortages and the postwar decline in demand for labor which reduced the chances of locating jobs in other areas. A companion table (not reproduced here) showing the percentage of recruitments in each industry which came

TABLE 11

PROPORTION OF SEPARATED WORKERS MOVING TO JOBS IN OTHER AREAS, BY EXIT INDUSTRY

Ex. Industry	Percentage Moving to Jobs in Other Areas		
	1941	1945	1946
Metalworking	13	10	5
Apparel	1	4	4
Other Manufacturing	13	[illegible]	3
Construction	17	17	10
Trans., Comm., and Utilities	4	2	8
Retail and Wholesale Trade	9	4	7
Service	10	3	[illegible]

from outside the area yielded similar results, except that recruitment of outside workers into the area dropped off rather sharply in 1946 as compared with 1941 and 1945. There was a pronounced demobilization of the area's war industries in 1945, and by 1946 the area was in the position of exporting more workers to other areas than it imported from them.

DIRECTION AND SCOPE OF MOVEMENT— GEOGRAPHICAL SHIFTS

The lifetime work histories from Sample 1 yielded additional information about geographical mobility of labor. This information is one-sided in the sense that we were able to interview workers from other areas now working in this one, but could not interview people from this area now working elsewhere. It is of some interest, however, to explore the past movements of those presently in the area.

Fifty-nine per cent of the people in Sample 1 had never held a job in the United States outside of this area, and an additional 17 per cent had never worked outside of the state. In this respect the community differs markedly from newer industrial areas in the midwest and Pacific coast regions, whose labor force has been built up largely through immigration from other areas. Twelve per cent of Sample 1

mediate position. In most industries the extent of outward movement declined from 1941 to 1946, possibly because of housing shortages and the postwar decline in demand for labor which reduced the chances of locating jobs in other areas. A companion table (not reproduced here) showing the percentage of the *accessions* to each industry which came

TABLE 11
PROPORTION OF SEPARATED WORKERS MOVING TO JOBS IN OTHER AREAS, BY EXIT INDUSTRY

Exit Industry	Percentage Moving to Jobs in Other Areas		
	1941	1943	1946
Metalworking	13	10	8
Apparel	7	4	4
Other Manufacturing	13	6	5
Construction	17	17	19
Trans., Comm., and Utilities	0	8	5
Retail and Wholesale Trade	9	5	7
Service	10	5	6

from outside the area yielded similar results, except that recruitment of outside workers into the area dropped even more sharply in 1946 as compared with 1941 and 1943. There was large-scale demobilization of the area's war industries in 1945, and by 1946 the area was in the position of exporting more workers to other areas than it imported from them.

DIRECTION AND SCOPE OF MOVEMENT: GEOGRAPHICAL SHIFTS

The lifetime work histories from Sample 1 yielded additional information about geographical mobility of labor. This information is one-sided in the sense that we were able to interview workers from other areas now working in this one, but could not interview people from this area now working elsewhere. It is of some interest, however, to explore the past movements of those presently in the area.

Fifty-nine per cent of the people in Sample 1 had never held a job in the United States outside of this area, and an additional 17 per cent had never worked outside of the state. In this respect, the community differs markedly from newer industrial areas in the midwest and Pacific coast regions, whose labor force has been built up largely through immigration from other areas. Twelve per cent of Sample 1

had worked in other New England States,[11] and only 12 per cent had worked outside of New England. Even those who had worked in other areas had not changed their place of work very frequently. Only 14 per cent of those in Sample 1 had changed localities more than twice during their working life, and only 4 per cent had changed five or more times. It should be remembered that these figures relate to change of workplace, not residence; changes of residence would be somewhat less frequent, since some jobs are held on a commuting basis and can be changed without moving one's home.

The older workers in Sample 1 had made more changes of workplace than the younger workers, though by no means in full proportion to their greater age. Sixty-four per cent of those under 25 had never worked outside the area, while only 51 per cent of those aged 55–64 had never worked outside. The most striking difference, however, is between the mobility record of men and women workers. Eighty-seven per cent of the women in Sample 1 had never worked outside the area, compared with only 54 per cent of the men workers. This is a genuine difference, attributable only in small measure to differences in age and other characteristics of the two groups.

The frequency and scope of geographical movement in Sample 1 bears no relation to current occupational level, current industrial attachment, or any variable other than sex and age. This does not necessarily mean that occupation and industry are unrelated to geographical movement. It would, indeed, be surprising if this were the case. It is more likely that, since the members of Sample 1 have moved about a good deal occupationally and industrially over their working lives, their *current* occupational and industrial attachment is not a good indicator of their career as a whole. The problem is similar to that with respect to lifetime movement among industries.

CONCLUDING OBSERVATIONS

The conclusions of this chapter may be restated briefly under four heads: factors affecting a worker's mobility rate; the relative frequency of different types of movement—industrial, occupational, and geographical; the characteristics of interindustry movement; and the significant lines of cleavage within the labor market.

[11] For this purpose, New York City was treated as part of New England, since it is readily accessible from the area studied.

FACTORS INFLUENCING MOBILITY RATES

Our findings on this point serve mainly to buttress the conclusions of earlier mobility studies. They are four in number:

1. Most labor turnover occurs within a small segment of the labor force. Only a minority of the labor force changes jobs in a given year; and it is a minority of this minority—those who move two or more times during the year—which accounts for most of the movement. Thus the usual statistics of accessions and separations of workers give an exaggerated impression of the number of *individuals* changing jobs, particularly during periods of very high turnover such as 1941–46.

2. Unskilled workers change jobs more frequently than the semiskilled, and these in turn move more frequently than skilled workers. This conclusion emerges whether one is dealing with turnover in a single year, or lifetime mobility rates, or data on frequency of interindustry shifts. There is reason to suspect that the relation between mobility rate and occupational level is actually even stronger than our statistics suggest. The relationship is blurred in our tabulations by at least two factors. First, the skilled group includes a good many highly mobile people, such as building construction workers and stationary engineers, as well as the railroad operating crafts. A similar heterogeneity appears among semiskilled and unskilled workers. Industry influences, in other words, are intermingled with occupational influences proper. Second, most of the craftsmen and skilled workers have not been skilled all their lives, and their over-all mobility record may be influenced by high mobility in unskilled or semiskilled work at an earlier stage of their career. If one calculated only their mobility rate while engaged in skilled occupations, this would probably be appreciably below their over-all rate.

3. The propensity to change employers diminishes rapidly with increasing length of service. It is not entirely correct, however, to say that it is length of service which "causes" a worker to remain with an employer. It is at least equally correct to regard the accumulation of years of service as the result of a prior decision by the employee that the company is a good place to work. This decision is usually made early in his work record. If the decision is adverse to the company, he will leave immediately if jobs are good, or after some lapse of time if other opportunities are scarce. For this reason voluntary turnover typically occurs after only a short period of service. The more easily an

Factors Influencing Mobility Rates

Our findings on this point serve mainly to buttress the conclusions of earlier mobility studies. They are four in number:

1. Most labor turnover occurs within a small segment of the labor force. Only a minority of the labor force changes jobs in a given year; and it is a minority of this minority—those who move two or more times during the year—which accounts for most of the movement. Thus the usual statistics on accessions and separations of workers give an exaggerated impression of the number of *individuals* changing jobs, particularly during periods of very high turnover such as 1941–46.

2. Unskilled workers change jobs more frequently than the semiskilled, and these in turn move more frequently than skilled workers. This conclusion emerges whether one is dealing with turnover in a single year, or lifetime mobility rates, or data on frequency of inter-industry shifts. There is reason to suspect that the relation between mobility rate and occupational level is actually even stronger than our statistics suggest. The relationship is blurred in our tabulations by at least two factors: first, the skilled group is heterogeneous, including such mobile people as building construction workers and such immobile groups as the railroad operating trades. A similar heterogeneity appears among semiskilled and unskilled workers. Industry influences, in other words, are intermingled with occupational influences proper. Second, most of the current skilled workers have not been skilled all their lives, and their over-all mobility record may be influenced by high mobility in unskilled or semiskilled work at an earlier stage of their career. If one calculated only their mobility rate *while engaged in skilled occupations*, this would probably be appreciably below their over-all rate.

3. The propensity to change employers diminishes rapidly with increasing length of service. It is not entirely correct, however, to say that it is length of service which "causes" a worker to remain with an employer. It is at least equally correct to regard the acquisition of years of service as the *result* of a prior decision by the employee that the company is a good place to work. This decision is usually made early in his work record. If the decision is adverse to the company, he will leave immediately if times are good, or after some lapse of time if other opportunities are scarce. For this reason voluntary turnover typically occurs after only a short period of service. The rare cases in

which a long-service worker quits his job arise usually from the sudden development of some personal frustration—a new and uncongenial supervisor, a failure of promotion, or some other untoward incident.

4. The propensity to change employers decreases also with increasing age (which is correlated, of course, with increasing length of service). In most cases this indicates that the worker, after a certain amount of "shopping around" in early life, has arrived at a satisfactory occupational adjustment and has settled down to piling up seniority, pension rights, and other forms of security for his later years. In other cases the propensity to move declines because, while the worker may not be satisfied with his present job, he realizes that at his age he has a poor chance of finding a good job elsewhere; he therefore stays where he is and adjusts to the situation as best he can.

It should be repeated that these factors, and others which we shall examine later in the book, help to account for the *propensity* of a worker to change jobs, and for differences in this propensity from one worker to the next. The extent of *actual movement* is quite a different matter, depending mainly on the rate of expansion in the aggregate demand for labor. Movement may increase five- or tenfold from deep depression to peak prosperity, as the appearance of job vacancies releases the propensity to move which lies latent in bad times. The extent of actual movement is influenced also by at least two other factors: the *direction* of the expansion in labor demand—geographically, industrially, and so on—relative to the location of labor supplies; and the *facilities* for movement—channels of information, placement agencies, and so on. The importance of these factors will appear as we proceed.

Relative Frequency of Different Types of Movement

Interplant movement is most frequent because (except for intraplant promotions) it is a prerequisite for any other sort of movement. Next most common is interindustry movement. It will be recalled that slightly more than three-quarters of the job changes by workers in Sample 1 involved changes of industry as well. Shifts from one occupational level to another are less frequent than shifts from one industry to another. The force of this conclusion is reduced, of course, by the wide span of the occupational categories used. The "semiskilled" group is especially unsatisfactory, including jobs which at the time of the study paid anywhere from \$0.70 an hour to \$1.50 or more an hour. A worker can thus progress or retrogress greatly in terms of earnings

and pleasantness of work without changing his occupational category. If one could devise a way of detecting significant shifts within broader occupational bands, these might turn out to be fully as frequent as interindustry shifts; and if one worked in terms of changes of job title these would probably be more frequent than any other, because of the ever-growing number of specialized job titles in modern industry. Changes of locality are least frequent of all. The reasons are almost self-evident, but something more will be said on this matter in Chapter IV.

CHARACTERISTICS OF INTERINDUSTRY MOVEMENT

The evidence suggests that the walls around particular industries are quite porous. Few workers remain in the same industry throughout their working lives, and some show an amazing variety of movement. Even within the span of a single year something like half the workers hired by firms in the area came from other types of industry. It must be remembered, too, that the industry categories used in this study are very broad. Metalworking, for example, comprises a large number of quite distinct industries. If a detailed classification of industries had been used, the amount of interindustry movement would have been even greater.

Industry influences are not negligible. A worker leaving a company is somewhat more likely to go to another company in the same industry; in a few cases, such as clothing manufacture, the probability of this occurring is quite high. If he leaves the industry he is more likely to go to certain "neighboring" industries than to others. This tendency, however, is not very strong and seems capable of being overridden by war emergencies or other drastic shifts in the demand for labor. To the extent that it does exist, it is probably due to the fact that certain occupations overlap two or more industries and that a worker must go to one of those industries if he wants to stay within the same occupational group.

THE SCOPE OF "THE LABOR MARKET"

The findings of this chapter support the impression that the most important boundaries between labor markets run along geographical lines. It is approximately correct to identify "a labor market" with a locality small enough so that people can readily travel from homes in any part of the area to jobs in any other part. May there not, however, be significant lines of cleavage within the locality as well? One must

and pleasantness of work without changing his occupational category. If one could devise a way of detecting significant shifts *within* broader occupational bands, these might turn out to be fully as frequent as interindustry shifts; and if one worked in terms of changes of *job title*, these would probably be more frequent than any other, because of the ever-growing number of specialized job titles in modern industry. Changes of locality are least frequent of all. The reasons are almost self-evident, but something more will be said on this matter in Chapter IV.

Characteristics of Interindustry Movement

The evidence suggests that the walls around particular industries are quite porous. Few workers remain in the same industry throughout their working lives, and some show an amazing variety of movement. Even within the span of a single year something like half the workers hired by firms in the area came from other types of industry. It must be remembered, too, that the industry categories used in this study are very broad. Metalworking, for example, comprises a large number of quite distinct industries. If a detailed classification of industries had been used, the amount of interindustry movement would have been even greater.

Industry influences are not negligible. A worker leaving a company is somewhat more likely to go to another company in the same industry; in a few cases, such as clothing manufacture, the probability of his doing so is quite high. If he leaves the industry, he is more likely to go to certain "neighboring" industries than to others. This tendency, however, is not very strong and seems capable of being overridden by war emergencies or other drastic shifts in the demand for labor. To the extent that it does exist, it is probably due to the fact that certain occupations overlap two or more industries and that a worker must go to one of those industries if he wants to stay within the same occupational orbit.

The Scope of "The Labor Market"

The findings of this chapter support the impression that the most important boundaries between labor markets run along geographical lines. It is approximately correct to identify "a labor market" with a locality small enough so that people can readily travel from homes in any part of the area to jobs in any other part. May there not, however, be significant lines of cleavage within the locality, so that one must

think in terms of a honeycomb of submarkets rather than a single market for the area as a whole?

The answer seems to be that, as far as manual labor is concerned, the most significant boundary lines within an area are those which surround individual employing units. Other boundaries are of some importance: geographical neighborhoods are significant—people would rather work close to home than far from home; industrial attachment is important in certain industries; skilled trades present certain barriers to occupational movement. It remains true, however, that the firm is the hiring unit and that each company employment office is really a distinct market for labor. The employed worker is attached basically to a *company,* rather than to an industry or an occupation. If he leaves one company, his path of movement within the area is conditioned mainly by the hiring techniques and requirements of other *companies.* He will usually not encounter any other decisive boundary until he hits the outer limit of the area, beyond which he is restrained by reluctance to change his place of residence.

The labor market is best conceived, then, as an outer circle defined by geography (really, by transportation time and cost rather than distance per se), within which are many smaller circles or nuclei consisting of individual employing units. Other types of boundary within the area are hazier and easier to cross, at least during the early years of a man's working life. The most important single problem in labor market analysis, then, is to explore the factors which attach the worker to a particular firm and condition his movement between firms. Chapters III and IV are devoted to this matter. A second problem, examined in Chapter V, is how far workers are able to progress occupationally by movement within firms and between firms, and what are the significant limitations on such progress.

CHAPTER III Determinants of Interplant Movement: The Structure of the Market

WORKERS' decisions about jobs are made in a context which may be divided into two parts: the objective limitations imposed by the structure of the market, and particularly by employers' hiring techniques and requirements; and the preferences, attitudes, and habit patterns of the workers themselves. This separation is only an analytical one, for workers' attitudes and habit patterns are largely a reflection of employer hiring practices and other features of the external environment. The purpose of this chapter is to describe the objective structure of the market as it presents itself to the worker in search of employment. The way in which workers respond to this environment will be considered in the next chapter.

It will be useful to keep in mind throughout the discussion the economic concept of a perfect market, perhaps best exemplified by a securities market or an organized commodity exchange. In such a market the goods being exchanged are strictly defined, all persons interested in buying or selling these goods are either present or represented in a single place, the willingness of any participant to buy or sell a specified quantity at a specified price is readily communicated to all other participants, the number of buyers and sellers is too great to permit of collusion, and the total quantities demanded and supplied are kept in continuous balance by frequent changes in market price. Most actual markets, of course, differ in greater or lesser degree from this prototype; and it has always been recognized that these deviations are particularly serious in labor markets. The problem of Chapters III and IV is to determine as precisely as possible the nature and extent of these deviations.

The structural features of the labor market in this community may be arranged for discussion under three heads: (1) The nature of labor demand and labor recruitment in the area. This is mainly a matter of employers' hiring preferences and practices. One must take account, however, of union contract rules which limit employers' behavior; and also of factors, such as the nature of modern production processes and

the geographical layout of the city, which are external to both employers and unions. (2) The extent to which the State Employment Service provides a central clearing house for labor, and the main factors limiting its effectiveness in this respect. (3) The way in which labor market structure is influenced by fluctuations in the level of employment. This subject cuts across the first two, but it will be convenient to segregate discussion of it at one point.

CHARACTERISTICS OF LABOR DEMAND AND LABOR RECRUITMENT

This section will consider the main ways in which labor demand and the hiring process fail to meet the specifications of an ideal market. The points to be discussed are: (1) the limitation of active trading to certain types of skill, and the lack of a general market for other types of skill; (2) the lack of a mechanism for disseminating wage information rapidly and accurately throughout the area; (3) the even more marked absence of information on significant job characteristics other than wages; (4) the lack of a mechanism for notifying all interested workers simultaneously of job vacancies; (5) limitations on active competition for labor among employers; (6) the effects of geographical dispersion of plants; (7) the heterogeneity of the commodity "labor," and the differences in employers' conceptions of what they are buying; (8) the influence of union rules and practices. The list could be lengthened, but the most significant points can be brought under these headings.

The Extent of the "Market"

The concept of an active market for labor rests on an implicit assumption that job vacancies are typically filled by recruiting workers from outside the plant. It is conceivable, however, that vacancies on all but the poorest jobs might be filled by promotion from within the present labor force. In this event there would be an area-wide market only for untrained workers, and no general market at all for specialized skills.

The actual promotion policies of employers in the area are discussed in Chapter V, since they bear most directly on the process of occupational mobility. Briefly, vacancies on skilled maintenance and service jobs are typically filled from the outside, and this is true also of vacancies on completely unskilled jobs. Vacancies on semiskilled production jobs, on the other hand, are usually filled from within the plant. Thus

workers at the two extremes—the skilled mechanic and the day laborer—find something like a general market for their services. Semiskilled workers, however, who constitute the great bulk of the factory labor force, have difficulty in penetrating a new plant because of the usual rule that present employees get first chance at vacancies. If they do get in, they are likely to get undesirable jobs [illegible]. The development of a market for semiproduction workers is further impeded by the great heterogeneity of production processes in modern industry. Many jobs are found only in one industry, and even when the same job title is found in numerous plants in the area, job content often differs widely among plants.

The growing practice of in-plant promotion might be taken into account through the concept of an "internal market," in which workers already in a plant compete for desirable vacancies. It is not really accurate, however, to regard all in a plant as actually in competition with each other for jobs. Eligibility for vacancies is normally limited to a particular department of the plant, and sometimes to a particular operation within the department. Nor is the selection of workers for promotion "competitive" in the usual sense; seniority is frequently the dominant consideration and there is no opportunity for workers to underbid each other with respect to wages and terms of employment. Insofar as internal recruitment prevails, then, it is probably better to abandon market concepts and to think in terms of status and hierarchy.

THE AVAILABILITY OF WAGE INFORMATION

In an organized commodity exchange, sellers can learn almost instantaneously both the prices being offered by buyers (or bids) and the prices at which past transactions have been concluded. If there were a similar mechanism in labor markets, workers would be able to discover the rates at which people in other plants are already working as well as the rates offered on vacant jobs. It is obvious that nothing of this sort exists at the present time. Interviews with workers in our samples revealed that most of them had only a vague and frequently inaccurate idea of earnings in other plants. The principal exceptions were workers who had recently moved from another plant in the area and remember something about earnings there, and union members who tended to assume—not always correctly—that the union scale prevailed in all unionized establishments in their industry.

There are several reasons for this lack of adequate wage information. One reason is a lack of curiosity among workers about rates

workers at the two extremes—the skilled mechanic and the day laborer —find something like a general market for their services. Production workers, however, who constitute the great bulk of the factory labor force, have difficulty in penetrating a new plant because of the usual rule that present employees get first chance at vacancies. If they do get in, they are likely to get undesirable jobs which present employees do not want. The development of a market for production workers is further impeded by the great heterogeneity of production processes in modern industry. Many jobs are found only in one industry; and even where the same job title exists in numerous plants in the area, job content often differs widely among plants.

The growing practice of in-plant promotion might be taken into account through the concept of an "inside market," in which workers already in a plant compete for desirable vacancies. It is not really accurate, however, to regard all in a plant as actually in competition with each other for jobs. Eligibility for vacancies is normally limited to a particular department of the plant, and sometimes to a particular operation within the department. Nor is the selection of workers for promotion "competitive" in the usual sense; seniority is frequently the dominant consideration and there is no opportunity for rivals to underbid each other with respect to wages and terms of employment. Insofar as internal recruitment prevails, then, it is probaby better to abandon market concepts and to think in terms of status and hierarchy.

The Availability of Wage Information

In an organized commodity exchange, sellers can learn almost instantaneously both the prices being offered by buyers for *future* sales and the prices at which *past* transactions have been concluded. If there were a similar mechanism in labor markets, workers would be able to discover the rates at which people in other plants are already working as well as the rates offered on vacant jobs. It is obvious that nothing of this sort exists at the present time. Interviews with workers in our samples revealed that most of them had only a vague and frequently inaccurate idea of earnings in other plants. The principal exceptions were workers who had recently moved from another plant in the area and remember something about earnings there, and union members who tended to assume—not always correctly—that identical rates prevailed in all unionized establishments in their industry.

There are several reasons for this lack of adequate wage information. One reason is a lack of curiosity among workers satisfactorily

employed in one plant about earnings in other plants—a point which will be developed further in the next chapter. Another reason is that no one in the area is responsible for collecting wage information and disseminating the results to *workers;* the only regular wage surveys in the area are made by employers' organizations for their own use. Another factor in the situation is the reticence of employers about revealing wage information to outsiders.[1] While this reticence is less than it was a decade ago, it is still quite marked. Wage rates and earnings are not publicized, even in advertisements designed to recruit labor. Nonwage inducements are used as the principal talking points in recruitment, doubtless because of a feeling that direct wage competition would call forth reactions from other employers.

A less obvious but fundamental difficulty is the inherent complexity of modern wage structures. Suppose that one wanted to post all "wage rates" on a billboard in the town square for the information of interested workers, and suppose that employers were willing to open their records for this purpose. What precisely would one put on the billboard? Average plantwide earnings would not be very useful. Workers are interested in earnings on a particular job. Apart from the practical difficulty of compiling data on thousands of individual jobs, there are serious questions as to what figure one should put opposite each job.

Should one, for example, put the starting rate at which a new worker would normally be hired? Many companies in the area hire all unskilled and semiskilled employees either at the plant minimum or at a "starting rate" 5 or 10 cents an hour below the plant minimum. The worker is then brought up gradually to the minimum rate for the job to which he is assigned, over a probationary period which varies from a few weeks to three months or more in some companies. To many workers, however, it is the starting rate rather than the eventual job rate which is significant. If the starting rate is low, the worker may become discouraged and drop out before the probationary period is over. In order to prevent this and to attract labor during the "tight" market of 1941–48, some companies in the area abandoned the start-

[1] Some employers in the area are willing to give wage rates in confidence to other companies hiring the same types of labor. The wage surveys published by the National Metal Trades Association and other groups use code numbers, however, and the identity of individual plants is not revealed even to other employers. Even the public employment service, as will be noted below, has difficulty in getting accurate rate information on job orders filed with it. It should be added that there are understandable reasons for a certain amount of employer reticence about wage rates and earnings. The data are complex and susceptible of misinterpretation in untrained hands. It should be said also that employers in the area were entirely cooperative in providing wage information for the present study.

employed in one plant about earnings in other plants—a point which will be developed further in the next chapter. Another reason is that no one in the area is responsible for collecting wage information and disseminating the results to workers. The only regular wage surveys in the area are made by employers' organizations for their own use. Another factor in the situation is the reticence of employers about revealing wage information to outsiders.[5] While this reticence is less than it was a decade ago, it is still quite marked. Wage rates and earnings are not publicized, even in advertisements designed to recruit labor. Nonwage inducements are used as the principal selling points in recruitment, doubtless because of a feeling that direct wage competition would call forth retaliation from other employers.

A less obvious but fundamental difficulty is the inherent complexity of modern wage structures. Suppose that one wanted to post all "wage rates" on a billboard in the town square for the information of interested workers, and suppose that employers were willing to open their records for this purpose. What precisely would one put on the billboard? Average plant-wide earnings would not be very useful. Workers are interested in earnings on a particular job. Apart from the practical difficulty of compiling data on thousands of individual jobs, there are serious questions as to what figure one should put opposite each job. Should one, for example, put the starting rate at which a new worker would normally be hired? Many companies in the area hire all unskilled and semiskilled employees either at the plant minimum or at a starting rate 5 or 10 cents an hour below the plant minimum. The worker is then brought up gradually to the minimum rate for the job to which he is assigned, over a probationary period which varies from a few weeks to three months or more in some companies. To many workers, however, it is the starting rate rather than the eventual job rate which is significant. If the starting rate is low, the worker may become discouraged and drop out before the probationary period is over. In order to prevent this and to attract labor during the "tight" market of 1946–48, some companies in the area abandoned the start-

[5] Some employers in the area are willing to give wage rates in confidence to other companies hiring the same types of labor. The wage surveys published by the National Metal Trades Association and other groups use code numbers, however, and the identity of individual plants is not revealed even to other employers. Even the public employment service, as will be noted below, has difficulty in getting accurate rate information on job orders filed with it. It should be added that there are understandable reasons for [illegible] of employers [illegible] rate data are complex and susceptible of misinterpretation. It should be said also that employers in the area were entirely cooperative in providing wage information for the present study.

ing rate device and began to hire new employees at the minimum of the rate range for their job. Moreover, workers on incentive jobs with short learning times are often allowed to earn a bar incentive rate within a week or two of being hired. For such workers the hiring rate, if high enough to yield expected incentive earnings, which they expect to their best rate, is not very important. Skilled maintenance workers are normally hired at the minimum of the range for their job, unless they are able to get a better rate out of the foreman and the employment manager because of special experience or individual bargaining power. If, then, by "hiring rate for the job" one means the rate at which a new worker will normally be hired, this rate is not uniformly comparable among companies and may be quite flexible even within a single company.

Instead of the starting rate, one might post the amount which a worker could expect to earn on the job after some months of experience. In the case of jobs paid on an output basis, should one put the base rate or expected incentive earnings? Actual earnings on the job will depend partly on the worker himself. Can he be assumed to make an adequate estimate of his own capacity? Should one put average weekly rather than hourly earnings, since the former figure is more significant to many workers? If so, what assurance has the worker that the figure may not be drastically altered by subsequent variations in the plant work week? Reflection on these questions suggests the serious difficulties in the "billboard" concept, and also helps one to understand why the typical worker is not an encyclopedia of wage information.

THE EVALUATION OF NONWAGE FACTORS

An even more serious difficulty is that the worker, in order to make an informed choice among alternative jobs, would need to know many things besides the probable earnings on each job. He would need to know such things as physical working conditions on the job, the extent of variety and interest in the work, opportunities for promotion to better jobs, probable stability of employment in the company, the congeniality of the foreman and fellow workers in the department, and company policies concerning vacations, pensions, and other benefits. Some of these things might possibly be determined objectively and posted on a central bulletin board. Some of them, however, are unknown to the company itself—for example, the probable growth rate of the company and the consequent possibilities of rapid promotion. Other things, such as whether the work is "too heavy" or "too fast," or whether one will get along well with the foreman, depend partly on

ing rate device and began to hire new employees at the minimum of the rate range for their job. Moreover, workers on incentive jobs with a short learning time are often allowed to go on an incentive basis within a week or two of being hired. If their output is high enough to yield expected incentive earnings, what happens to their base rate is not very important. Skilled maintenance workers are normally hired at the minimum of the range for their job, unless they are able to get a better rate out of the foreman and the employment manager because of "special experience," i.e, individual bargaining power. If, then, by "the rate for the job" one means the rate at which a new worker will normally be hired, this rate is not entirely comparable among companies and may be quite flexible even within a single company.

Instead of the starting rate, one might post the amount which a worker could expect to earn on the job after some months of experience. In the case of jobs paid on an output basis, should one put the base rate or expected incentive earnings? Actual earnings on the job will depend partly on the worker himself. Can he be assumed to make an accurate estimate of his own capacity? Should one perhaps post weekly rather than hourly earnings, since the former figure is more significant to many workers? If so, what assurance has the worker that the figure may not be drastically altered by subsequent variations in the plant work week? Reflection on these questions suggests serious difficulties in the "billboard" concept, and also helps one to understand why the typical worker is not an encyclopedia of wage information.

The Availability of Nonwage Information

An even more serious difficulty is that the worker, in order to make an informed choice among alternative jobs, would need to know many things besides the probable earnings on each job. He would need to know such things as physical working conditions on the job, the extent of variety and interest in the work, opportunities for promotion to better jobs, probable stability of employment in the company, the congeniality of the foreman and fellow workers in the department, and company policies concerning vacations, pensions, and other benefits. Some of these things might possibly be determined objectively and posted on a central bulletin board. Some of them however, are unknown to the company itself—for example, the probable growth rate of the company and the consequent possibilities of rapid promotion. Other things, such as whether the work is "too heavy" or "too fast" or whether one will get on well with the foreman, depend partly on

characteristics of the individual worker and can be learned only through experience.

For these reasons the worker cannot make an accurate comparison of two or more jobs on the basis of what he hears about them from the employment manager. He can determine the suitability of a job only by working at it for a while and then quitting if it does not prove satisfactory. This leads to a high rate of turnover among new employees during the probationary period. There was widespread agreement among the companies interviewed that a large proportion of voluntary quits occur during the first few months of employment, and that if a worker can be held for the first year there is much less chance of his leaving thereafter. One company said that three-quarters of its new employees quit during the probationary period, and others gave proportions ranging between one-quarter and three-quarters. The proportion of early quits seems to be particularly high in plants where the work is heavy, hot, smelly, or otherwise unpleasant. As one manager said, "They just won't believe that the jobs are as heavy as we tell them. They insist on trying them out anyway. When they find out that everything we said was true, most of them quit." Others quit because of inability to develop enough speed to "make piecework," or because their performance is not good enough to win merit increases, or because of some other unsatisfactory feature of the job.

This suggests the observation that in any analysis of labor turnover it is important to distinguish between quitting by new employees and by long-service employees. An unusually high quit rate among new employees may indicate only unpleasant physical conditions, faulty selection of workers, or an inadequate structure of probationary wage rates. A high quit rate among longer-service workers is likely to indicate more serious maladjustments within the organization. An analysis which lumps together *all* voluntary quits and correlates them with wage levels or other characteristics of the company may have little significance.

Channels of Recruitment

Regardless of how much workers know about conditions in other plants, movement is possible only when a vacancy exists. A perfect market mechanism would ensure that news of a vacancy was spread simultaneously to all workers who might be interested in it, so that all would have an equal chance to apply. In actuality, word of vacancies spreads gradually and in such a way that some workers have a much

greater chance of being hired than others. The best chance is enjoyed by those who have numerous friends, relatives, and other "contacts" in the area. The next best chance falls to those who are willing to make the rounds of company employment offices and the public employment service at frequent intervals. Those who simply fill out application forms and then sit home waiting to be called have little chance of being hired.

When a job becomes vacant and cannot be filled by internal promotion, initial responsibility for action falls on the foreman. He may simply fill out a requisition and send it to the employment office, but he is likely also to comb his mind for people who have worked for him before or live in his neighborhood, or to ask other workers in the department to recommend friends of theirs. When word gets around the shop that there is a vacancy, workers in the department may "sponsor" friends on their own initiative. Actual hiring must, of course, be routed through the employment office. A worker's chances are greatly improved, however, if he has been tipped off to appear at the employment office on a certain morning, if he knows of a specific vacancy for which to apply, and if he has his credentials organized with this vacancy in mind. A casual word from the foreman to the employment manager can be influential and, if necessary, the foreman can use his veto power over hiring to secure the man he wants. Thus, while the screening of applicants for employment is done nominally by the employment manager, the actual initiative in getting a particular man into a particular job often comes from the foreman or from someone else in the work group. The result is a strong tendency for the more desirable jobs to be filled from among friends and relatives of present employees before outsiders have a chance to hear about them.

This tendency has the general approval of higher management in the area. There is a widespread feeling that if the present employees of the plant are more likely to stay with the company than those desirable qualities; that the mixing of groups of friends makes for congeniality in the work force; and that workers from the neighborhood of the plant are more likely to stay with the company than those farther away. One-fifth of the companies interviewed, on the other hand,

In a few of the larger plants of the area, the employment manager has sole power to select and assign workers to jobs, the foreman having only the authority to demand the removal of poor performers during the probationary period. The usual procedure, however, is for the employment manager to send all applicants whom he considers qualified for an interview with the foreman, who must also approve the selection before the man is hired.

greater chance of being hired than others. The best chance is enjoyed by those who have numerous friends, relatives, and other "contacts" in the area. The next best chance falls to those who are willing to make the rounds of company employment offices and the public employment service at frequent intervals. Those who simply fill out application forms and then sit home waiting to be called have little chance of being hired.

When a job becomes vacant and cannot be filled by internal promotion, initial responsibility for action falls on the foreman. He may simply fill out a requisition and send it to the employment office, but he is likely also to comb his mind for people who have worked for him before or live in his neighborhood, or to ask other workers in the department to recommend friends of theirs. When word goes around the shop that there is a vacancy, workers in the department may "tip off" friends on their own initiative. Actual hiring must, of course, be routed through the employment office. A worker's chances are greatly improved, however, if he has been tipped off to appear at the employment office on a certain morning, if he knows of a specific vacancy for which to apply, and if he has his credentials organized with this vacancy in mind. A casual word from the foreman to the employment manager can be influential and, if necessary, the foreman can use his veto power over hiring[2] to secure the man he wants. Thus, while the screening of applicants for employment is done nominally by the employment manager, the actual initiative in getting a particular man into a particular job often comes from the foreman or someone else in the work group. The result is a strong tendency for the more desirable jobs to be filled from among friends and relatives of present employees before outsiders have a chance to hear about them.

This tendency has the general approval of higher management in the area. There is a widespread feeling that if the present employees of the plant are more likely to stay with the company than those desirable qualities; that hiring of groups of friends makes for congeniality in the work force; and that workers from the neighborhood of the plant are more likely to stay with the company than those farther away. Certain of the companies interviewed, on the other hand,

[2] In a few of the larger plants of the area, the employment manager has sole power to select and assign workers to jobs, the foreman having only the authority to dismiss the man for poor performance during the probationary period. The usual procedure, however, is for the employment manager to send on applicants whom he considers qualified for an interview with the foreman, who must also approve the selection before the man is hired.

felt that hiring too many friends and relatives leads to favoritism, formation of cliques, and poorer production. Some of the companies expressing a *preference* for a diversified work force, however, felt unable to do much about it. Certain nationality groups and kinship groups had become so firmly established in the plant that it was no use trying to add an outsider as he would be "frozen out" in short order.[8]

If a vacancy is not filled through personal recommendation, the onus of recruitment falls on the employment manager. Employment managers in the area rely mainly on the day-to-day flow of applicants at the plant. This is particularly true of the larger companies which, because their names are known throughout the area, have a considerable stream of applicants at all times. Little use is made of application files; some companies keep no application file at all, while others take applications only when a specific vacancy exists or is expected. A serious difficulty with application files is that they become obsolete very quickly. The better workers in the file have usually found other jobs before a vacancy develops for them in the company, and those remaining in the file are the least desirable people. Moreover, applicants are flowing through the office every day, and it is more convenient to catch them on the wing as they are needed. The man who gets hired, therefore, is the one who appears in the employment office with the right qualifications on the morning when a vacancy actually exists. If he is asked to fill out an application form and sent away, the odds against his ever being hired are heavy.

This is a point of some importance. A market in which employers filed all applicants, rated the applications in priority order, and filled all vacancies by going down the priority list, would operate quite differently from a market in which the first man on the spot gets the job. This is not to say that an application file system is actually feasible. It would require, for one thing, that workers who find jobs should immediately notify all plants at which they have filed applications, so that their applications could be withdrawn and the files kept current. The paradox of the present situation is that, since workers do not take the filing of an application seriously and do not bother to tell the company when they have found other employment, employers cannot afford to take the files seriously either and the whole system becomes unworkable.

If the company is unable to secure qualified workers by direct appli-

[8] For a fuller discussion of the advantages and disadvantages of hiring people recommended by present employees, see William Noland and E. Wight Bakke, *Workers Wanted* (New York, Harper & Brothers, 1949) pp. 109–111.

cation, resort is frequently had to the public employment service. The operations of the employment service will be explored in the next section. It will appear that at the employment service office, as at company employment offices, the worker who is physically present has a superior chance of employment.

EMPLOYER OPPOSITION TO "LABOR PIRATING"

Another interesting feature of the market is that it is mainly unemployed workers who are exposed to vacancies which develop. Employed workers are largely outside the range of consideration. The main reason for this is lack of interest by workers in job openings outside their own establishment, the basis for which will be explained in the next chapter. Another important factor, however, is the reluctance of employers to consider people already working in other plants.

Aggressive "pirating" of workers employed in another plant is definitely against the code of employers in the area. If the personnel manager of company A learns that someone from company B has approached an A worker and tried to hire him, he will immediately telephone the personnel manager of company B and ask him to let the worker alone. This protest is usually sufficient, for each personnel manager knows that, if he steals a worker today, someone else will steal from him tomorrow, and all have an interest in playing by the rules. As one personnel manager said, "You might get away with it once, but it wouldn't be much fun to see the other fellow glaring at you at the next meeting of the Personnel Managers' Association. So you probably wouldn't do it again." If the personnel manager in company B should be uncooperative, a call from a higher official of company A to his opposite number in company B will usually dispose of the problem.

What if the worker himself takes the initiative and applies at company A while still employed by company B? Employer practice in this situation varies considerably. Some companies in the area will not consider such an application at all. Most companies, however, take account of the circumstances of each case. If the worker has a good personal reason for wishing to change employers—a change of residence in the area, desire for day work rather than night work, or health problems—the application will usually be considered. In such cases the personnel manager of company A will probably call company B and ask whether they are willing to release the worker in question. Most personnel managers are reasonable about releasing workers who

cation, resort is frequently had to the public employment service. The operations of the employment service will be explored in the next section. It will appear that at the employment service office, as at company employment offices, the worker who is physically present has a superior chance of employment.

Employer Opposition to "Labor Pirating"

Another interesting feature of the market is that it is mainly *unemployed* workers who are exposed to vacancies which develop. Employed workers are largely outside the range of consideration. The main reason for this is lack of interest by workers in job openings outside their own establishment, the basis for which will be explained in the next chapter. Another important factor, however, is the reluctance of employers to consider people already working in other plants.

Aggressive "pirating" of workers employed in another plant is definitely against the code of employers in the area. If the personnel manager of company A learns that someone from company B has approached an A worker and tried to hire him, he will immediately telephone the personnel manager of company B and ask him to let the worker alone. This request is usually sufficient; for each personnel manager knows that, if he steals a worker today, someone else will steal from him tomorrow, and all have an interest in playing by the rules. As one personnel manager said, "You might get away with it once. But it wouldn't be much fun to see the other fellow glaring at you at the next meeting of the Personnel Managers' Association. So you probably wouldn't do it again." If the personnel manager in company B should be uncooperative, a call from a higher official of company A to his opposite number in company B will usually dispose of the problem.

What if the worker himself takes the initiative and applies at company B while still employed by company A? Employer practice in this situation varies considerably. Some companies in the area will not consider such an applicant at all. Most companies, however, take account of the circumstances of each case. If the worker has a good personal reason for wishing to change employers—a change of residence in the area, desire for day work rather than night work, or a health problem—the application will usually be considered. In such cases the personnel manager of company B will probably call company A and ask whether they are willing to release the worker in question. Most personnel managers are reasonable about releasing workers who

have a genuine desire to move, since if they refuse the worker may quit anyway. If the worker is at all uncertain, however, the practice of advance clearance between companies gives his present employer a chance to persuade him to stay.

An employed worker who wants to change jobs, then, must usually win the acquiescence of his present employer and must bring a good recommendation with him. If he quits against the wish of his present employer, he may not get a good recommendation and other employers may have doubts about his dependability. This constitutes a considerable obstacle to voluntary movement among plants. The situation is quite different from that of a commodity exchange in which sellers are free to shift to alternative buyers without notice and with no questions asked.

Distance as an Obstacle to Movement

Even in a medium-sized city, distance from home to work is an important consideration. Travel time and expense makes workers reluctant to live on one side of the area and work on another. If a man is out of a job, he tends to apply first at plants near his home. Employers also prefer workers who live near the plant, because they are more likely to stay with the company than are people who come from some distance away and may eventually leave for a job in their home neighborhood. Distance from home to work is also a factor in the definition of "suitable" employment for unemployment compensation purposes; a man is not expected to take a job much farther away from his home than his previous job.

The fact that people like to live near their work would not constitute a barrier to interplant mobility if residential preferences were slight. In this event a worker would shop for work throughout the city and, having located a job, move to a new residence near the plant. This is not, however, the predominant pattern of behavior. Residential preferences are strong, particularly in the case of home owners, and place of work tends to be adapted to place of residence rather than vice versa. During the years 1946–48, even tenants were bound to their place of residence by the housing shortage, which made it difficult to find a new rental dwelling at reasonable cost. As this situation is gradually corrected by new construction, mobility of tenants will doubtless increase.

Transportation lines radiate from the center of the city, and manufacturing plants stretch out in different directions along these lines.

In order to check the significance of this point, we listed the home addresses of employees in selected plants throughout the city, and then spotted these addresses on a block map of the city. This revealed a strong tendency for employees to live within walking distance either of the plant itself or of a bus line leading directly to the plant. The frequency of employees usually dropped sharply beyond the point of transfer to another bus line.

It was noted in Chapter II that workers in the area show little tendency to remain within a particular industry. One reason is that, with the exception of clothing, there is no tendency for plants in the same industry to be located in the same area. As between types, workers may usually choose then, between continuing in the same industry and remaining in the same neighborhood. Except for small groups of highly specialized and highly paid workers, neighborhood attachment seems to outweigh industry attachment. It should be noted that workers living near the center of the city, from which all bus lines radiate, are in the best position to consider jobs in all parts of the area. Similarly, plants located in the central area are in the best position to draw workers from the entire city. Outlying plants and workers located near the ends of transportation routes, which find their labor markets most severely limited by geography.

Heterogeneity of Labor Services and Employers

In an organized commodity or securities exchange the articles being traded are defined unambiguously. Both buyers and sellers know precisely what is meant by a bushel of No. 1 Northern hard wheat, and can feel safe in concluding transactions without even seeing the wheat in question. Labor services, on the other hand, are extremely heterogeneous. There are thousands of separate jobs in modern industry, and workers differ greatly in their experience and capacity to perform these jobs. Moreover, in selecting among applicants for work, employers take into account a wide range of personal characteristics such as education, age, race, sex, character, personality traits, nationality, family status, and place of residence.[6] Some of these factors are related to productive efficiency, but others are not. In addition to efficient workers, employers want people who will be pleasant to have around, and who will do credit to the company in the community. These de-

[6] For a detailed discussion of the relative importance attached to these factors by employers in two localities, see William Noland and E. Wight Bakke, op. cit., especially Chapters 2 and 10.

In order to check the significance of this point, we listed the home addresses of employees in selected plants throughout the area, and then spotted these addresses on a block map of the city. This revealed a strong tendency for employees to live within walking distance either of the plant itself or of a bus line leading directly to the plant. The frequency of employees usually dropped sharply beyond the point of transfer to another bus line.

It was noted in Chapter II that workers in the area show little tendency to remain within a particular industry. One reason is that, with the exception of clothing, there is no tendency for plants in the same industry to be located in the same area. An unemployed worker must usually choose, then, between remaining in the same industry and remaining in the same neighborhood. Except for small groups of highly specialized and highly paid workers, neighborhood attachment seems to outweigh industry attachment. It should be noted that workers living near the center of the city, from which all bus lines radiate, are in the best position to consider jobs in all parts of the area. Similarly, plants located in the central area are in the best position to draw workers from the entire city. It is plants and workers located near the ends of transportation routes which find their labor market most severely limited by geography.

Heterogeneity of Labor Supplies and Demands

In an organized commodity or securities exchange, the articles being traded are defined unambiguously. Both buyers and sellers know precisely what is meant by a bushel of No. 1 Northern hard wheat, and can feel safe in concluding transactions without ever seeing the wheat in question. Labor services, on the other hand, are extremely heterogeneous. There are thousands of separate jobs in modern industry, and workers differ greatly in their experience and capacity to perform these jobs. Moreover, in selecting among applicants for work employers take into account a wide range of personal characteristics such as education, age, race, sex, character, personality traits, nationality, family status, and place of residence.[4] Some of these factors are related to productive efficiency, but others are not. In addition to high-output workers, employers want people who will be pleasant to have around, and who will do credit to the company in the community. These de-

[4] For a detailed discussion of the relative importance attached to these factors by employers in two localities, see William Noland and E. Wight Bakke, *op. cit.*, especially Chapters 2 and 10.

tailed hiring preferences differ considerably from one company to the next, and are largely unknown to the man looking for work. It is thus very difficult for a worker to have any idea of where he will "fit" best or where he will have the best chance of being hired.

The hiring transaction amounts to an exchange of an unspecified amount of productive power plus personal agreeableness and cooperation, on the one hand, for a package of compensations including important nonwage as well as wage elements. Neither the worker nor the employer can be at all sure of what he is getting at the time the transaction is made. The employer cannot make a precise estimate of the worker's productive efficiency, particularly since few companies in the area use preemployment tests of any kind. His estimate of the worker's personal characteristics is bound to be even more incomplete. The worker cannot know much about the job except its general nature and approximate earnings. Gross misjudgments by either worker or employer can be corrected by quitting or discharge during the first few months of work. There is, however, a considerable range of tolerance on both sides. The worker will keep the job if it is not too far below his original expectations, and the employer will keep the worker if his performance is not too much below normal.

Collective Bargaining and Market Structure

The most important types of union contract provision affecting mobility appear to be:

1. The general requirement that present employees be notified of vacant jobs and given an opportunity to bid on them before outsiders are recruited. This reduces the number of jobs which come into the "outside market" and limits workers' chances of interplant movement, while at the same time it stimulates and redirects upward occupational movement within the plant.

2. Provisions which ensure that the worker's position in the company is automatically bettered by increasing length of service. In this category come provisions for automatic wage increases within established rate ranges; pension and other rights whose value increases with the passage of time, and which are lost by voluntary quitting; provision for the use of seniority as a factor in promotion; and provisions for layoffs on a seniority basis, which ensures greatest job security to the workers with longest service. These provisions mean that a worker is almost certain to lose by a change of employers, even if he gets the same type of job and the new employer has as high a wage structure as the old.

3. Provisions for recall of laid-off workers in order of seniority before new workers are hired. This strengthens the tendency, which would exist in any event, for laid-off workers to wait around for weeks or months in the hope of recall to their old jobs before beginning an active search for new employment.

4. Rules protecting workers against discharge after the end of the probationary period, except for violation of specified company rules. This prevents employers from using periods of heavy unemployment to weed out the less efficient people in the plant and replace them with better workers.

Collective bargaining thus tends to reduce both the incentives to and the opportunities for interplant movement. It was noted in Chapter 3 that, even under nonunion conditions, the most significant labor market boundaries in a locality are those around individual employing units. The growth of collective bargaining reinforces this conclusion and makes the walls around individual establishments even higher than before. The worker trades reduced opportunities of interplant movement for greater security of job tenure and greater opportunities for upward movement within the plant.

Collective bargaining also clearly affects the personal incidence of movement. By its effect on the policies of hiring and layoff, unionism helps to determine which individuals will get readiest access to particular occupations or industries. Moreover, where labor demand is insufficient to provide those already in an industry with full-time employment, collective bargaining influences the allocation of such work as is available.

THE PUBLIC EMPLOYMENT SERVICE: A GREAT EXCHANGE FOR LABOR?

The accepted prescription for labor market imperfections is to strengthen the local offices of the State Employment Services so that labor supplies and demands in an area can be brought together at a single point. More precisely, the objective is to bring together vacant jobs and unemployed workers. It is not seriously contemplated that employed workers will run down to the employment service every week to see whether a better job is available in the area. Indeed, if this ever began to happen on any scale, there would doubtless be pressure for speedy abolition of the Employment Service!

An adequate matching of unemployed workers and vacant jobs would, however, be sufficient to bring about the marginal adjustments contemplated in economic theory. The idea would presumably be a

3. Provisions for recall of laid-off workers in order of seniority before new workers are hired. This strengthens the tendency, which would exist in any event, for laid-off workers to wait around for weeks or months in the hope of recall to their old jobs before beginning an active search for new employment.

4. Rules protecting workers against discharge after the end of the probationary period, except for violation of specified company rules. This prevents employers from using periods of heavy unemployment to "weed out" the less efficient people in the plant and replace them with better workers.

Collective bargaining thus tends to reduce both the incentives to and the opportunities for interplant movement. It was noted in Chapter II that, even under nonunion conditions, the most significant labor market boundaries in a locality are those around individual employing units. The growth of collective bargaining fortifies this conclusion and makes the walls around individual establishments even higher than before. The worker trades reduced opportunities of interplant movement for greater security of job tenure and better opportunities for upward movement within the plant.

Collective bargaining also clearly affects the personal *incidence* of movement. By its effect on the politics of hiring alone, unionism helps to determine which individuals will get readiest access to particular occupations or industries. Moreover, where labor demand is insufficient to provide those already in an industry with full-time employment, collective bargaining influences the allocation of such work as is available.

THE PUBLIC EMPLOYMENT SERVICE: A GRAIN EXCHANGE FOR LABOR?

The accepted prescription for labor market imperfections is to strengthen the local offices of the State Employment Services so that labor supplies and demands in an area can be brought together at a single point. More precisely, the objective is to bring together vacant jobs and *unemployed* workers. It is not seriously contemplated that employed workers will run down to the Employment Service every week to see whether a better job is available in the area. Indeed, if this ever began to happen on any scale, there would doubtless be pressure for speedy abolition of the Employment Service!

An adequate matching of unemployed workers and vacant jobs would, however, be sufficient to bring about the marginal adjustments contemplated in economic theory. The ideal would presumably be a

thoroughgoing labor exchange, in which any worker could get a simultaneous view of all vacancies which might interest him, and any employer could have simultaneous choice among all workers qualified for his positions. The purpose of this section is to examine how far and in what respects the Employment Service office in this community currently falls short of the ideal. This will lay a foundation for our discussion in Chapter X of the practical steps which might be taken to create a closer approach to a comprehensive labor exchange.

The Employment Service office in this area is a superior one—well managed, well staffed, and enjoying good repute in the community. Yet at the time of our study it was filling only about 20 per cent of the vacancies arising in manufacturing industry.[5] Why was this? The answer involves a variety of considerations: the established hiring procedures of employers in the area and their limited use of the Service, worker attitudes toward the Service, the inherent complexity of the placement job and the technical impossibility of matching all applicants against all vacancies, and the involvement of the Employment Service in unemployment compensation operations. The difficulties which the Service faces in each of these respects must be explored in order to discover how far they may be remediable and by what methods.

Employer Use of the Service

Some of the obstacles to full use of the Service by employers have already been noted. Most employers prefer to hire workers who are brought in by present employees or who apply to the company of their own accord. Direct application at the plant is taken as an indication that the man really wants to work and possesses initiative, and also that he has some reason for preferring this plant over others. If the man wants specifically to work at their company, employment managers reason, he must be a better employment risk than someone who comes out merely because the Employment Service sent him. Moreover, employers want to make their own selection from among the workers available and are reluctant to accept preselection of applicants by the Employment Service or anyone else. This is related to the fact that the employer is building a work team, not merely a

[5] The basis of this estimate is explained in this section. The term "vacancy" here is limited to vacancies filled by recruitment from outside the company, since the Employment Service has no occasion to concern itself with internal transfers and promotions.

production mechanism in which workers can be treated as interchangeable parts. He wants people who can become congenial members of the group, who have certain attributes of personality and character, who are "our type of worker." He will not trust anyone outside his own organization to pick such people for him.

These difficulties might be met if the Employment Service limited itself to funneling candidates into the plant employment office, leaving selection among them entirely up to the company. The Employment Service cannot function in this way, however, for it must keep in good standing with workers as well as employers. If it were to send dozens of workers to one vacancy, workers' confidence in and use of the Service would diminish. The practice of referring only a few selected workers, which implies a prejudgment by the Service of who are the "best" workers available, is thus unavoidable; but this means that the Service exercises more discretion than some employers would prefer.

Another obstacle to full acceptance of the Service by employers is the fact that Employment Service registrants do not constitute a random sample of unemployed workers in the area, but rather a sample which is biased downward in terms of employability. There are two reasons for this adverse selection. First, workers drawing unemployment compensation or public assistance, which includes most of the long-term unemployed, are obliged to register at the Service. Workers changing jobs voluntarily, who include some of the better employment risks, do not have to register. Second, workers with good qualifications and good contacts often prefer to seek work directly, which means that the Service tends to inherit those whose personal contacts are poor. This worker behavior, of course, is a direct reflection of employers' hiring practices. Many of the best workers avoid the Service because many employers do not use the Service to fill their best jobs; neither group can afford to use the Service unless the other does. How to break through this circle is the most difficult single problem of Employment Service organization.

It should be noted that when an employer places an order for a particular kind of worker, this does not ensure that the Service will actually get a chance to fill the job. The company still has the right to hire "at the gate" if it can. In periods of slack employment and plentiful labor supplies, the ink is sometimes scarcely dry on an order before the employer calls back to say that the job is already filled.

Still more disturbing, he may neglect to call back and a worker referred by the Service may arrive at the plant only to find that someone else has already been hired.

Despite all these difficulties, employer use of the Service is substantial and seems to be increasing over the long run. Both the proportion of vacancies listed with the Service and the percentage filled through it are considerably above the prewar level, partly because employers had extensive and generally favorable experience in using the Service during the war years. The use made of the Service naturally varies with the general level of demand for labor; employers are more likely to call on it when labor is scarce and direct recruitment difficult than when labor is abundant. Employer use of the Service varies also with the type of labor in question; it is used much more heavily for unskilled and low-skilled jobs than for skilled work on which individual qualifications are particularly important.

There is some reason to think that use of the Service varies also with the employer's ability to do his own recruiting. Companies which have special difficulties in recruiting because of an isolated geographical location, or because they are too small to have a specialized employment manager, or because their names are not well enough known to attract applicants, appear to use the Service more than do employers more favorably situated. This fact, plus the fact that in all companies the best jobs tend to be picked off by present employees and their friends, means that the Employment Service gets an adverse selection of job vacancies in manual labor just as it gets an adverse selection of registrants for work. It is thus faced with the unappetizing task of matching "hard to place" workers with "hard to fill" jobs, and producing results satisfactory to all concerned.

The wide variation in the wage rates and working conditions offered by different plants in the area presents an additional complication in Employment Service work. Orders come in for unskilled workers at rates varying from, say, sixty cents to ninety cents an hour. If the Employment Service presents all these jobs simultaneously to workers, and allows them to take their choice, the poorest jobs will presumably remain unfilled. If employers are to be given equal service, in the sense of filling all orders with equal rapidity, this will require hiding some of the better jobs while an effort is made to sell workers on the poorer jobs. What should the Service do?

The official policy, for obvious reasons, is one of equal service to all employers. The individual referral interviewer, however, who

actually decides which jobs shall be shown to a particular worker. He has a practical interest in filling as many vacancies as possible. He knows that it is easier to sell a worker on a ninety-cent job than a sixty-cent job, and that the chances of a satisfactory placement will be greater. There is a natural tendency for interviewers to "deal from the top of the deck," to fill better jobs before poorer ones. Employers offering good wages and conditions thus tend to get quicker service. Employers whose jobs are least attractive, and who therefore need most help in recruiting, get least assistance from the Employment Service. This is doubtless as it should be; in a perfectly competitive labor market good jobs would certainly be filled before poor ones. The market, however, is an impersonal instrument, which it is difficult to blame for one's misfortunes. In the Employment Service one has instead an administrative mechanism which is all too readily blamed for "inefficiency" or "favoritism" when it fails to refer workers rapidly to good jobs.

WORKERS' USE OF THE SERVICE

While there is more pressure on workers than on employers to use the Employment Service, its use is still essentially voluntary. A laid-off worker in an industry covered by the unemployment compensation system must register with the Service in order to be eligible for benefit payments. He must also report to the Employment Service at least once every thirty days in order to continue eligible for benefits. The fact of registration at the Service, however, does not prevent the worker from seeking work on his own, and many registrants do not rely at all heavily on the Service. They report to the office at the prescribed intervals, but meanwhile carry on an independent search for work. Workers who are not eligible for or in receipt of payments, and workers in industries not covered by the compensation system need not register at the Service unless they choose to do so.

In practice, however, workers do rely rather heavily on the Service in their search for employment. The people in Sample A—relatively young workers in manufacturing industry who had changed jobs recently—were asked whether they had ever used the Service and what their experience had been with it. Only 30 per cent said that they had never used the Service at any time; 44 per cent said that they had found the Service helpful in finding work, while 26 per cent had used it but had not found it helpful. There was a marked difference in this respect between workers at different skill levels.

actually decides which jobs shall be shown to a particular worker, has a practical interest in filling as many vacancies as possible. He knows that it is easier to sell a worker on a ninety-cent job than a sixty-cent job, and that the chances of a satisfactory placement will be greater. There is a natural tendency for interviewers to "deal from the top of the deck," to fill better jobs before poorer ones. Employers offering good wages and conditions thus tend to get quickest service. Employers whose jobs are least attractive, and who therefore need most help in recruiting, get least assistance from the Employment Service. This is doubtless as it should be; in a perfectly competitive labor market, good jobs would certainly be filled before poor ones. The market, however, is an impersonal instrument which it is difficult to blame for one's misfortunes. In the Employment Service one has instead an administrative mechanism which is all too readily blamed for "inefficiency" or "favoritism" when it fails to refer workers rapidly to poor jobs.

Workers' Use of the Service

While there is more pressure on workers than on employers to use the Employment Service, its use is still essentially voluntary. A laid-off worker in an industry covered by the unemployment compensation system must register with the Service in order to be eligible for benefit payments. He must also report at the Employment Service at least once every thirty days in order to continue eligible for benefits. The fact of registration at the Service, however, does not prevent the worker from seeking work on his own, and many registrants do not rely at all heavily on the Service. They report to the office at the prescribed intervals, but meanwhile carry on an independent search for work. Workers who are not eligible for compensation payments, and workers in industries not covered by the compensation system, need not register at the Service unless they choose to do so.

In practice, however, workers do rely rather heavily on the Service in their search for employment. The people in Sample 2—relatively young workers in manufacturing industry who had changed jobs recently—were asked whether they had ever used the Service and what their experience had been with it. Only 30 per cent said that they had never used the Service at any time, 44 per cent said that they had found the Service helpful in finding work, while 26 per cent had used it but had not found it helpful. There was a marked difference in this respect between workers at different skill levels.

Thus 63 per cent of the unskilled workers had found the Service helpful at one time or another, compared with only 29 per cent of the skilled men.

Most of those who had never used the Service said simply that they had never needed it. Skilled men, in particular, frequently have enough contacts so that they can readily locate vacancies when they need to. As one toolmaker said: "I never bother with the State Employment Service. I know most of the shops in town and have friends who let me know when they are hiring." Other workers believe, with considerable reason, that they get a better selection of jobs by shopping around on their own than by relying on an Employment Service interviewer to make a selection for them. Still others fail to distinguish the placement operations of the local office from the unemployment compensation operations. They tend to regard the whole office as a charitable enterprise, and believe that to apply there for work indicates lack of initiative and self-reliance.

Among those who had used the Service but found it unsatisfactory, the most common complaint concerned the quality of the jobs listed at the Service. There is a widespread (and largely justified) opinion that employers tend to list at the Service jobs which are at the bottom of the occupational ladder in the plant or are otherwise unattractive, while the more attractive jobs are filled by direct recruiting. Workers conclude, therefore, that one has to detour the Service in order to get a really good job. This limitation on the effectiveness of the Service reflects employers' hiring procedures, and any expansion in the scope of its activities must probably be initiated mainly from the employer side. If more of the good jobs were listed at the Service, more of the better workers would rely on it for work.

The Placement Mechanism

The kind of market provided by the Employment Service office depends on the specific procedures used in referring workers to jobs. One tends to think of the office as a place at which all registered workers are "exposed" to all the listed jobs, so that both workers and employers get a maximum range of choice among alternatives. In actuality, however, the Service does not and cannot function in this way. It effects at best a limited matching of men and jobs, which is better than what would happen without it but is still far from the ideal of a competitive market.

Consider the process which is set in motion by receipt of a job order from a manufacturer in the area. Data concerning the job are

taken down over the telephone by one of the reception interviewers who make up the intake/orders unit of the office. Details of the job are often somewhat fragmentary despite the best efforts of the interviewers. Most employers, for example, are quite conservative in quoting wage rates to the Employment Service. If a rate range is involved, they will cite only the minimum of the range. If the job cannot be classified at several different rates, depending on individual qualifications, only the lowest rate will be quoted. Some companies quote only the plant starting rate, and say that what the worker will get over that depends on what he turns out to be suited for. This is especially likely where an order is placed for several workers at once. The employer's reasoning is as follows: "Suppose we give you a rate for a higher labor grade. Then you send a man who doesn't fit into that labor grade. We try to sell him a lower job. But he won't take the job because it's below the rate he has been quoted." The strategy is to get as many workers referred as possible, and then fit them in to the job structure wherever they seem to fit. The practice of quoting only the minimum opportunity in the plant, however, makes it more difficult for the Employment Service to induce workers to accept referral. It also interferes with the accuracy of price information which characterizes a good market.

Information about job duties and physical conditions of work is also likely to be incomplete, unless the interviewer is able to round out the picture from previous visits to the plant or discussions with the employment manager. Other important matters—probable stability of employment, quality of supervision, congeniality of the work group—can scarcely be predicted at all. The job order, in short, is not a full bill of particulars; it leaves many things for the worker to find out for himself, just as he would do if he applied directly at the company.

A file containing all unfilled orders for a particular type of work sits on the corner of the interviewer's desk where it is available for ready reference. Workers coming into the office, whose registration cards[4] indicate a background in this type of work, are directed to this interviewer. The interviewer's first problem is to determine which of

[4] Incoming workers are registered by a separate registration section before being passed on to a cycle of interviewers. The worker's file card, covering his work history and key items of personal information, is checked for accuracy and completeness by a member of the registration staff. It is then coded, using the code numbers of the Dictionary of Occupational Titles, so as to show both the worker's primary skill and any supplementary skills he may possess. This makes it possible, by running through the registration file, to determine quickly which workers are qualified for a specific vacancy.

taken down over the telephone by one of the referral interviewers who make up the manufacturing unit of the office. Details of the job are often somewhat fragmentary despite the best efforts of the interviewer. Most employers, for example, are quite conservative in quoting wage rates to the Employment Service. If a rate range is involved, they will cite only the minimum of the range. If the job might be classified at several different rates, depending on individual qualifications, only the lowest rate will be quoted. Some companies quote only the plant starting rate, and say that what the worker will get over that depends on what he turns out to be suited for. This is especially likely where an order is placed for several workers at once. The employer's reasoning is as follows: "Suppose we give you a rate for a higher labor grade; then you send a man who doesn't fit into that labor grade. We try to sell him a lower job, but he won't take the job because it is below the rate he has been quoted." The strategy is to get as many workers referred as possible, and then tuck them in to the job structure wherever they seem to fit. The practice of quoting only the minimum opportunity in the plant, however, makes it more difficult for the Employment Service to induce workers to accept referral. It also interferes with the accuracy of price information which characterizes a good market.

Information about job duties and physical conditions of work is also likely to be incomplete, unless the interviewer is able to round out the picture from previous visits to the plant or discussions with the employment manager. Other important matters—probable stability of employment, quality of supervision, congeniality of the work group—can scarcely be predicted at all. The job order, in short, is not a full bill of particulars; it leaves many things for the worker to find out for himself, just as he would do if he applied directly at the company.

A file containing all unfilled orders for a particular type of work sits on the corner of the interviewer's desk where it is available for ready reference. Workers coming into the office whose registration cards[6] indicate a background in this type of work are directed to this interviewer. The interviewer's first problem is to determine which of

[6] Incoming workers are registered in a separate registration section before being passed on to a referral interviewer. The worker fills out a card, covering his recent work history and key items of personal information, which is checked for accuracy and completeness by a member of the registration staff. It is then coded, using the code numbers of the Dictionary of Occupational Titles, so as to show both the worker's primary skill and any supplementary skills he may possess. This makes it possible, by running through the registration file, to determine rapidly which workers are qualified for a specific vacancy.

the unfilled orders most nearly matches the applicant's past work record. If there are several jobs for which the worker might be suitable, there is a problem of which one to mention to him first. As was noted earlier, interviewers tend to pick the best jobs in the file first on the ground that it will be easier to get workers interested in these jobs.

The worker is not told the name of the employer unless he indicates a definite interest in the job. If the worker does not express interest in the first job mentioned, the interviewer will pull out a second, perhaps even a third or fourth. In the end, however, the worker will often come back to the first job mentioned by the interviewer, which turns out after all to be most attractive to him. Two aspects of this process need to be emphasized: first, unless the worker has enough initiative and persistence to request that he be shown several jobs, he will learn only about the one job which, *in the opinion of the interviewer* (not the worker himself), is most suitable for a person of his qualifications. Second, even when the worker is shown more than one job, he will not be *referred* to more than one employer at the same time, since multiple referral creates resentment among employers. The worker must decide to accept referral to a particular plant and then, if the employer does not hire him or he does not like the job, come back to the Service for another referral. The only exceptions are in cases of plants located near each other and at a considerable distance from the office, in which case the worker will sometimes be given two referral cards at once to save carfare.

In addition to the workers physically present in the office on a particular day, the interviewer has at his disposal for filling an employer order the "active file," which contains the registration cards of all workers who have reported to the office during the preceding thirty days. If there does not seem to be any well-qualified candidate among the "floor traffic," the interviewer goes through the active file to see whether it may contain someone who meets the employer's specifications. As among people with approximately equal qualifications, however, there is a tendency to select people "from the floor" rather than from the file. A spot-check for the first four months of 1950 indicated that, of all the selection interviews conducted, four-fifths were with workers who had come into the office of their own accord and only one-fifth were with workers who had been called in after a canvass of the active file.

An important consideration here is that recruitment "from the

fecor is much faster, and in placement work speed is of prime importance. It may take two or three days to send a postcard to someone in the file, get him into the office, and refer him to the job; by this time the employer may already have filled the job. The active file also gets out of date rapidly, particularly during a period of high employment. Many of those called in from the file for referral never report because they have already found work, left town, or changed their minds about the kind of work they want. In the spring of 1950 the proportion of workers called in who actually reported to the office was running at only about 40 per cent.

The referral interviewer's job is a skilled and difficult one requiring years of experience and unusual qualities of tact and judgment. He must be able to clothe the bare bones of an employer's job order with flesh and blood, preferably on the basis of actual plant visits. He must be able to "size up" the worker, to distinguish real capacity from mere pretension. He must judge whether a certain set of job conditions will satisfy a particular worker well enough so that he will not merely take the job but stay with it. The employer must also be satisfied; the interviewer must be careful to send out only people whom he is fairly sure will meet employer specifications, else the long-run standing of the service will suffer. Here is no mechanical balancing of supply and demand, but rather an intricate task of matching highly specialized personal qualifications and job requirements in such a way that both parties to the transaction are content. When one considers the vagueness of the information at the interviewer's disposal, the conflicting interests of the workers and employers involved, and the necessity for rapid decision and action, it is really remarkable how well the job is done.

It is not done perfectly, for only about half the workers referred to employers are actually hired. In some cases the interviewer has misjudged the employer's requirements, and the worker referred is unacceptable. In other cases, particularly where referral has been delayed, the employer has already hired someone else. The worker sometimes decides, after visiting the plant and talking with the employment manager, that he does not want the job. In many cases, as we shall see in a moment, workers go through the motions of accepting referral to a job in order to remain eligible for unemployment compensation, but without any intention of actually taking the job. Some workers simply drop out of sight after being given a referral card and never show up at the plant. The local labor section of the office

floor" is much faster, and in placement work speed is of prime importance. It may take two or three days to send a postcard to someone in the file, get him into the office, and refer him to the job; by this time the employer may already have filled the job. The active file also gets out of date rapidly, particularly during a period of high employment. Many of those called in from the file for referral never report because they have already found work, left town, or changed their minds about the kind of work they want. In the spring of 1950 the proportion of workers called in who actually reported to the office was running at only about 40 per cent.

The referral interviewer's job is a skilled and difficult one, requiring years of experience and unusual qualities of tact and judgment. He must be able to clothe the bare bones of the employer's job order with flesh and blood, preferably on the basis of actual plant visits. He must be able to "size up" the worker, to distinguish real capacity from mere pretensions. He must judge whether a certain set of job conditions will satisfy a particular worker well enough so that he will not merely take the job but stay with it. The employer must also be satisfied; the interviewer must be careful to send out only people whom he is fairly sure will meet employer specifications, else the long-run standing of the Service will suffer. Here is no mechanical balancing of supply and demand, but rather an intricate task of matching highly specialized personal qualifications and job requirements in such a way that both parties to the transaction are content. When one considers the vagueness of the information at the interviewer's disposal, the conflicting interests of the workers and employers involved, and the necessity for rapid decision and action, it is really remarkable how well the job is done.

It is not done perfectly, for only about half the workers referred to employers are actually hired. In some cases the interviewer has misjudged the employer's requirements and the worker referred is unacceptable. In other cases, particularly where referral has been delayed, the employer has already hired someone else. The worker sometimes decides, after visiting the plant and talking with the employment manager, that he does not want the job. In many cases, as we shall see in a moment, workers go through the motions of accepting referral to a job in order to remain eligible for unemployment compensation, but without any intention of actually taking the job. Some workers simply drop out of sight after being given a referral card and never show up at the plant. The casual labor section of the office

can recount many incidents of men who stopped off to celebrate their "new job" at so many taverns en route that they never arrived to report for work.

An interesting facet of Employment Service operations is the typical coexistence in the local office of unfilled orders and unplaced registrants. Throughout 1947, which was a year of peak prosperity and high employment, the local office in the area had on the average about 1,500 unfilled orders from employers. At the same time it had some 3,500 unplaced registrants in the active file. In an effort to determine the reasons for this situation, the manager of the office made several checks of the composition of the active file. These studies revealed that a substantial proportion of those in the file were unavailable. When post cards were sent out to a sample of one thousand workers, asking them to report in for referral, only 60 per cent responded. The remainder had presumably found jobs already or were not actively seeking work. Of those who responded, more than half failed to meet employers' hiring specifications at the time. Some were overage, others had physical defects, some were available only for part-time work. Others were what the Employment Service terms its "chronic customers"—people with low intelligence or personality difficulties, who had already been referred to numerous plants in the area but had not been able to hold a job in any of them.[7]

There was also considerable discrepancy between the sex- and skill-distribution of the job orders and the available workers. Certain types of skilled worker in great demand—for example, power sewing machine operators, compositors, and upholsterers—were not to be found in the active file. At the semiskilled level, there was an active demand from metalworking plants for female machine operators. Virtually no women in this category were registered at the Service, partly because large numbers of women retired from the labor market soon after the end of the war. An obvious possibility was to substitute low-

[7] These marginal workers, who in good years constitute a high proportion of Employment Service registrants, present a peculiarly difficult problem. They return repeatedly to the interviewers and plead for employment. The interviewer sympathizes with their need for income, but knows from experience that a referral will probably prove unavailing and will simply alienate the employer. He is forced to become adept, therefore, in putting the worker off and explaining why there are no jobs available at the moment. The only hope for these people lies in the orders which the Service receives for poorly paid and unattractive jobs in small enterprises—jobs which cannot be sold to the more capable workers. These employers are perforce resigned to getting poor workers in return for their low wages, and are accustomed also to a high rate of turnover. An interviewer will therefore ship out some of his chronic customers to these jobs, even though he has good reason to suspect that they will be back on his shoulder in a few weeks' time.

an economy—many accounts of men who stopped off to celebrate their "new job" at so many taverns en route that they never arrived to report for work.

An interesting facet of Employment Service operations is the typical coexistence in the local office of unfilled orders and unplaced applicants. Throughout 1947, which was a year of peak prosperity and high employment, the local office in the area had on the average about 1,500 unfilled orders from employers. At the same time it had some 4,500 unplaced applicants in the active file. In an effort to determine the reasons for this situation, the manager of the office made several checks of the composition of the active file. These studies revealed that a substantial proportion of those in the file were unavailable. When post cards were sent out to a sample of one thousand workers, asking them to report in for referral, only 60 per cent responded. The remainder had presumably found jobs already or were not actively seeking work. Of those who responded, more than half failed to meet employers' hiring specifications at the time. Some were overage, others had physical defects, some were available only for part-time work. Others were what the Employment Service terms its "chronic customers"—people with low intelligence or personality difficulties, who had already been referred to numerous plants in the area but had not been able to hold a job in any of them.[1]

There was also considerable discrepancy between the sex and skill distribution of the job orders and the available workers. Certain types of skilled worker in great demand—for example, power sewing machine operators, compositors, and upholsterers—were not to be found in the active file. At the semiskilled level, there was an active demand from metalworking plants for female machine operators. Virtually no women in this category were registered with the Service, partly because large numbers of women retired from the labor market soon after the end of the war. An obvious possibility was to substitute low-

[1] These marginal workers, who in good years constitute a high proportion of Employment Service registrants, present a peculiarly difficult problem. They return repeatedly to the interviewer and plead for employment. The interviewer, sympathizing with their need for income, but knowing from experience that a referral will probably prove unavailing, [illegible] simply [illegible] the interviewer [illegible] to become adept, therefore, in [illegible] the worker off and explaining why there are no jobs available at the moment. The only hope for these people lies in [illegible] the Service receives [illegible] paid and unattractive jobs in small enterprises—jobs which cannot be sold to the more capable workers. These employers [illegible] poor workers in return for their low wage and [illegible] also [illegible] rate of turnover. An interviewer will [illegible] customers to these jobs, even though he has good reason to [illegible] within a few weeks' time.

skilled male workers, of whom the Service had a surplus at the time. The jobs in question, however, had been set up for many years as "women's work," at wage rates too low to attract male workers. Employers were unwilling to raise these rates merely to meet what they hoped would be a temporary shortage of labor. Nor were they willing to lower hiring standards and take in marginal workers to fill the vacant jobs. The long-run objectives of maintaining a "sound" wage structure and a "desirable" type of worker were given precedence over the short-run objective of filling all vacancies and attaining maximum production.

The situation underlines once more the great heterogeneity of labor supplies and demands, and the inadequacy of simple comparisons between total workers available and total workers required. It also suggests serious ambiguities in the concept of "full employment." There seems little doubt that full employment should be regarded, not as a point, but as a zone which is perhaps three or four million workers "broad." The level of employment actually achieved within this zone probably depends mainly on the rate of inflation in the economy. The greater the prospect of immediate money profits, the more willing will employers be to lower hiring standards, readjust wage structures, and do whatever else is necessary to achieve maximum employment.

The Employment Service and Unemployment Compensation

In order to remain eligible for compensation payments, an unemployed worker must stand willing to accept "suitable" employment if it is offered to him. The test of willingness is applied by the Employment Service, which alone knows what opportunities are available in the area. A worker filing an initial claim for compensation must register for employment, and must report back to the Employment Service at least once every thirty days. In this area, as in most others, employment service and unemployment compensation officials are housed in a single large office. They can thus keep in close touch with each others' operations, and workers can move back and forth between the two groups without inconvenience.

If there are no vacancies in a man's line of work, no problem arises. If the referral interviewer has a job which he regards as suitable, and if the worker refuses to accept referral to the job, this fact is certified to the unemployment compensation staff. If the unemployment compensation people agree that the job was suitable, the worker's

benefits may be stopped. The worker is then entitled to appeal to the Unemployment Commission, which handles all disputed cases arising in the state. Either the worker or the unemployment compensation administrator may appeal to the courts from a Commission decision, but such appeals are quite rare.

The meaning of "suitable" employment, then, is shaped by administrative rulings of the Unemployment Compensation Department, by decisions of the Unemployment Commission, and by occasional court decisions. As matters now stand in the area, the interpretation of suitable work is quite favorable to the worker, and there is little pressure on workers to deviate from the conditions of their last previous job. The job offered must pay as much as the worker earned before; if it is an incentive job, the apparent earnings opportunities must be as good as on the last job. If the man has been working on the first shift, he cannot be required to take a job on the second or third shift. It he has been running a certain kind of machine, he cannot be required to shift to another sort of machine, even though little retraining might be required. The new job must be about as close to his place of residence as the last job, and must be comparable as regards physical effort and working conditions.

There is some tendency for the interpretation of suitable work to become less restrictive as the period of unemployment lengthens. After a man has been unemployed for two or three months, the unemployment compensation people may put some pressure on him to shift to a different type of work and may ask the Employment Service to refer him out to the most appropriate job it can find, even though the job is not as good as his last one. The worker has another line of defense, however, to which he can fall back. He is in trouble only if he *refuses to accept referral* to a job and, unless he is very naive, there is no reason why he could do this. If he does not want the job, he can take the referral card, go out to the plant, conduct himself in such a way that the company will not offer him the job, then come back to the Service and say, "Well, it's too bad, but they wouldn't hire me after all." An experienced employment manager can tell in a few minutes from the worker's general attitude whether he wants the job or not and, if he does not, there is clearly no point in hiring him.

This is not meant to imply that most of the unemployed prefer to draw unemployment compensation for as long as possible before taking jobs. On the contrary, most of them would prefer to work—

but at "reasonable" terms. The main effect of unemployment compensation is to strengthen the worker's hand in holding out for the kind of work and the level of wages he wants. As we shall see in Chapter IV, the main factor influencing the wages and conditions an unemployed worker will take is the length of time he has been unemployed. Today, as in earlier times, it is exhaustion of personal resources which really compels a search for work. Since the installation of unemployment compensation, however, exhaustion of resources occurs only after a much longer period of unemployment. The availability of compensation payments lengthens the period during which the worker can hold off the market. It also enables workers to resist poorly paid jobs and sets a kind of minimum wage, although at a rather low level. It gives the worker a kind of bargaining power which is different from, and supplementary to, the bargaining power achieved through union organization.

The conditions under which workers should be assisted and encouraged to hold off the market will be discussed in Chapter X. The main point to be noted here is that the Employment Service derives additional problems from its connection with the unemployment compensation system. It is obliged to register large numbers of workers who have no intention of using its placement service, and whose cards simply sit idle in the file. In order to apply the "willingness to work" test, it must often make referrals which the workers involved do not want and which fail to eventuate in placement. It is sometimes put under pressure by unemployment compensation officials to refer a worker with several months' unemployment to jobs which do not match closely with the worker's qualifications. This creates additional work for employers in interviewing and rejecting unsuitable candidates, and weakens employer cooperation with the Service. Employers would doubtless use the Service with more confidence if it were entirely divorced from compensation operations. While a complete divorce is not practicable, it will be pointed out in Chapter X that the relation between the two operations could be reexamined and improved in some respects.

THE WORK LOAD OF THE SERVICE

The most significant measure of the Service's performance would be the percentage which Employment Service placements form of all new hires in the area. There is unfortunately no way of estimating this percentage for most types of industry in the area, since to do this

but at "reasonable" terms. The main effect of unemployment compensation is to strengthen the worker's hand in holding out for the kind of work and the level of wages he wants. As we shall see in Chapter IV, the main factor influencing the wages and conditions an unemployed worker will take is the length of time he has been unemployed. Today, as in earlier times, it is exhaustion of personal resources which really compels a search for work. Since the installation of unemployment compensation, however, exhaustion of resources occurs only after a much longer period of unemployment. The availability of compensation payments lengthens the period during which the worker can hold off the market. It thus fortifies worker resistance to poorly paid jobs and sets a kind of minimum wage, although at a rather low level. It gives the worker a kind of bargaining power which is different from, and supplementary to, the bargaining power achieved through union organization.

The conditions under which workers should be assisted and encouraged to hold off the market will be discussed in Chapter X. The main point to be noted here is that the Employment Service derives additional problems from its connection with the unemployment compensation system. It is obliged to register large numbers of workers who have no intention of using its placement services and whose cards simply sit idle in the file. In order to apply the "willingness to work" test, it must often make referrals which the workers involved do not want and which fail to eventuate in placements. It is sometimes put under pressure by unemployment compensation officials to refer a worker with several months' unemployment to jobs which do not match closely with the worker's qualifications. This creates additional work for employers in interviewing and rejecting unsuitable candidates, and weakens employer cooperation with the Service. Employers would doubtless use the Service with more confidence if it were entirely divorced from compensation operations. While a complete divorce is not practicable, it will be pointed out in Chapter X that the relation between the two operations could be reexamined and improved in some respects.

The Work Load of the Service

The most significant measure of the Service's performance would be the percentage which Employment Service placements form of all new hires in the area. There is unfortunately no way of determining this percentage for most types of industry in the area, since no data

are available on the volume of hiring. It is possible to make a rough estimate of total hirings in manufacturing by applying the average accession rate of the thirty-nine companies reporting to the Chamber of Commerce to the total manufacturing employment of the area. Employment Service placements in manufacturing can then be reduced to a percentage of estimated hires.

This calculation suggests that, during the years 1946–48, the Service filled about 20 per cent of all manufacturing vacancies in the area. The proportion of manufacturing vacancies which the Service got a chance to fill, i.e., which were listed with it by employers, cannot be determined at all precisely but was probably in the neighborhood of 30 per cent.[8] For all types of industry in the area, the proportion of vacancies listed with and filled by the Employment Service is probably somewhat lower, since the Service is particularly active in the manufacturing field.

It cannot be expected, of course, that the Service will ever fill *all* job vacancies, nor would it be socially efficient for it to do so. Where a worker has definite reason to prefer a particular plant, or where an employer has a definite preference for a particular worker, it may be more efficient for them to deal directly rather than via the Employment Service. It must be remembered also that many accessions represent recall of laid-off workers who have never severed their connection with the company. The Service could, however, reduce the amount of wandering by workers from one plant gate to another. Where the employer has no preference for a particular worker, the Service could canvass more workers on his behalf than he would get by waiting for them to drop into his employment office, and canvass them more quickly. In order for the Service to attain its maximum usefulness in these respects, it should probably fill at least half of the job vacancies in the area. There is thus much room for the Service to expand its activities with benefit to all concerned. The practical steps which might be taken in this direction will be considered in Chapter X.

Chart 5 presents monthly data on placements made, unfilled orders at the end of the month, and registrants in the active file for the years 1945–48. The number of registrants reflects the volume of unemployment in the area. It is interesting to note that the marked increase in unemployment during early 1949 brought little decline

[8] The ratio of placements made to orders received by the local office runs between two-thirds and three-quarters in most months. Since the data on orders received are not broken down by type of industry, however, it is not possible to say how closely this ratio applies to manufacturing alone.

in the number of placements. This confirms the familiar observation that there is a considerable volume of hiring even in bad years, and that fluctuations in employment result mainly from variations in layoff rates rather than in accession rates. The number of unfilled orders shows a downward trend over the period, indicating a gradual softening of the labor market.

[illegible]

A breakdown of these data by occupational level throws some interesting light both on the operation of the Service and on the state of the labor market itself during these years. Table 12 shows the distribution of unfilled orders, active file, and placements for 1940, the latest full year available. It is apparent that the Service's work is concentrated very heavily in unskilled labor and service occupations, more than three quarters of total placements having been in these categories. The figures are somewhat misleading, of course, because many of the placements in casual labor and domestic service are of very short duration. A distribution of steady jobs obtained through the Service would look rather different. The other interesting fact revealed by a comparison of the first two columns of the Table is the relatively high level of demand for clerical, sales, and service

See on this point H. W. Singer, "The Process of Unemployment in the Depressed Areas," Review of Economic Studies, June, 19[illegible], pp. [illegible]; and "Regional Labor Markets and the Process of Unemployment," ibid., October, 1939, pp. [illegible].

in the number of placements. This confirms the familiar observation that there is a considerable volume of hiring even in bad years, and that fluctuations in employment result mainly from variations in layoff rates rather than in accession rates.[9] The number of unfilled orders shows a downward trend over the period, indicating a gradual softening of the labor market.

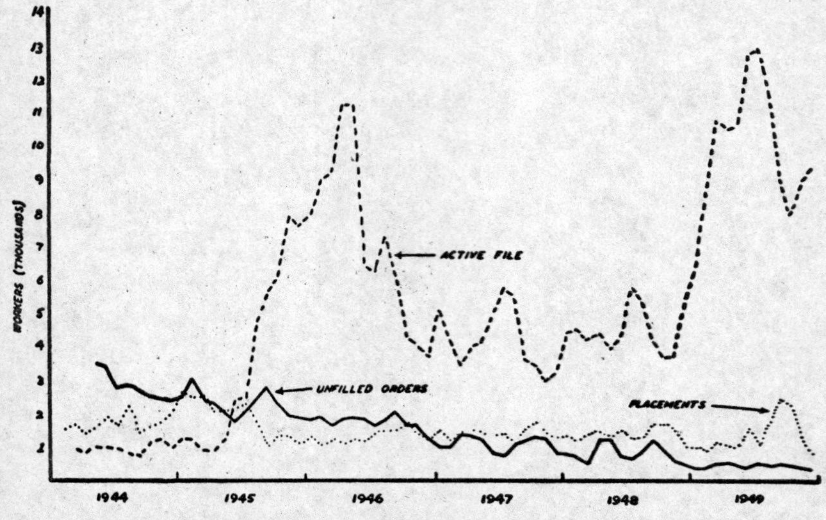

CHART 5 - ACTIVE FILE, PLACEMENTS, & UNFILLED ORDERS AT THE LOCAL OFFICE OF THE S.E.S., 1944-1949

A breakdown of these data by occupational level throws some interesting light both on the operation of the Service and on the state of the labor market itself during these years. Table 12 shows a distribution of unfilled orders, active file, and placements for 1948, the latest full year available. It is apparent that the Service's work is concentrated very heavily in unskilled labor and service occupations, more than three-quarters of total placements having been in these categories. This figure is somewhat misleading, of course, because many of the placements in casual labor and domestic service are of very short duration. A distribution of steady jobs obtained through the Service would look rather different. The other interesting fact, revealed by a comparison of the first two columns of the table, is the relatively high level of demand for clerical, sales, and service

[9] See on this point H. W. Singer, "The Process of Unemployment in the Depressed Areas," *Review of Economic Studies,* June, 1939, pp. 177–188; *idem.,* "Regional Labor Markets and the Process of Unemployment," *ibid.,* October, 1939, pp. 42–58.

workers in 1948 in relation to the available supply. The market for these occupations continued tight for some time after the market for manufacturing workers had softened up. Unskilled workers, at the other extreme, were clearly in excess supply by 1948.

TABLE 12
UNFILLED ORDERS, ACTIVE FILE, AND PLACEMENTS, BY OCCUPATIONAL LEVEL, 1948*

Occupational Level	Unfilled Orders at End of Month (%)	Registrants in Active File (%)	Placements Made (%)
Professional and Managerial	2.2	4.6	0.7
Clerical and Sales	17.6	12.8	9.3
Service	32.4	11.0	29.0
Skilled	10.1	10.1	4.3
Semiskilled	17.6	18.1	8.8
Unskilled	20.1	43.4	47.9
Total	100.0	100.0	100.0

* The basic data relate to operations for each month, and have been averaged to obtain a picture of the year as a whole.

Another aspect of the same situation is shown in Table 13, which shows the number of unfilled orders at the end of each month as a percentage of the registrants in the active file, by occupations, for the years 1946–48. A high ratio of unfilled openings reflects a relative

TABLE 13
UNFILLED ORDERS AT END OF MONTH AS A PERCENTAGE OF REGISTRANTS IN THE ACTIVE FILE, BY OCCUPATIONAL LEVEL, 1946–48*

Occupational Level	Year		
	1946	1947	1948
Professional and Managerial	3.9	11.8	9.1
Clerical and Sales	17.6	38.2	25.2
Service	70.1	66.8	54.4
Skilled	17.7	27.4	18.3
Semiskilled	30.9	27.2	17.9
Unskilled	19.7	14.2	8.5

* As in Table 12, the annual data presented here are averages of monthly data.

scarcity, a low ratio a relative surplus, of the type of skill in question. This table confirms the previous finding that clerical, sales, and service workers were in relatively scarce supply in 1948, while

unskilled labor was in excess supply. It should also be noted that, for all occupations, the ratio of unfilled orders declined from 1947 to 1948, indicating a general loosening of the market.

Why was there a continued shortage of white-collar workers and domestic servants in 1948 at a time when most manual skills were in excess supply? The situation seems to have resulted from a combination of three factors. (1) During World War II, new entrants to the labor market were funneled mainly into war industries, and large numbers of people previously engaged in white-collar and domestic service work were also siphoned off from those occupations into manual labor. (2) After the war, therefore, the white-collar and service occupations had to recapture an unusually large number of people in order to regain their prewar share of the labor force. (3) This recapture was impeded by the fact that wage levels in clerical, sales, and domestic service work compared unfavorably with those in manufacturing, so that unemployed manufacturing workers had little inducement to transfer and tended rather to wait and hope for eventual reabsorption into manufacturing.

The Feasibility of a "Clear" Exchange for Labor

A realistic view of Employment Service operations suggests that creation of a thoroughgoing labor exchange, after the pattern of organized commodity exchanges, is not a feasible objective for public policy. This conclusion is sufficiently important that it will be worthwhile, even at the risk of tedium, to restate some of the main reasons for it. First, many jobs do not come into the general market at all because of rules concerning promotion from within, recall of laid-off workers, and so on. Second, personal friendships and contacts will probably always influence the hiring process to some extent. Third, complete information about vacancies can never be obtained and posted. Employers are reluctant to provide certain types of information, other things they are unable to give, and the full details of numerous jobs would be too bulky for the worker to peruse in any event. Fourth, workers are not capable of matching their capacities against job requirements and finding their own way to the "right" vacancies. Fifth, the labor services being purchased and sold are extremely heterogeneous and difficult to appraise in advance. Finally, it is not administratively or politically feasible to refer all qualified workers to a particular vacancy, or all vacancies to a particular worker.

unskilled labor was in excess supply. It should also be noted that, for all occupations, the ratio of unfilled orders declined from 1947 to 1948, indicating a general loosening of the market.

Why was there a continued shortage of white-collar workers and domestic servants in 1948 at a time when most manual skills were in excess supply? The situation seems to have resulted from a combination of three factors: (1) During World War II, new entrants to the labor market were funneled mainly into war industries, and large numbers of people previously engaged in white-collar and domestic service work were also siphoned off from those occupations into manual labor. (2) After the war, therefore, the white-collar and service occupations had to recapture an unusually large number of people in order to regain their prewar share of the labor force. (3) This recapture was impeded by the fact that wage levels in clerical, sales, and domestic service work compared unfavorably with those in manufacturing, so that unemployed manufacturing workers had no inducement to transfer and tended rather to wait and hope for eventual reabsorption into manufacturing.

The Feasibility of a "Grain Exchange" for Labor

A realistic view of Employment Service operations suggests that creation of a thoroughgoing labor exchange, after the pattern of organized commodity exchanges, is not a feasible objective for public policy. This conclusion is sufficiently important that it will be worthwhile, even at the risk of tedium, to restate some of the major reasons for it. First, many jobs do not come into the general market at all because of rules concerning promotion from within, recall of laid-off workers, and so on. Second, personal friendships and contacts will probably always influence the hiring process to some extent. Third, complete information about vacancies can never be obtained and posted. Employers are reluctant to provide certain types of information, other things they are unable to give, and the full details of numerous jobs would be too bulky for the worker to peruse in any event. Fourth, workers are not capable of matching their capacities against job requirements and finding their own way to the "right" vacancies. Fifth, the labor services being purchased and sold are extremely heterogeneous and difficult to appraise in advance. Sixth, it is not administratively or politically feasible to expose *all* qualified workers to a particular vacancy, or *all* vacancies to a particular worker.

One must aim instead at a more limited objective—a public Employment Service which, while it cannot function automatically and will always be limited by human judgment and fallibility, will yet produce better results than could be achieved without it. The Employment Service can assemble *better* information on *more* jobs than would otherwise exist. It can send out a *suitable* man to the employer, though doubtless not the *best* man who might be located by an omniscient observer. The Employment Service can hope to function as a central hiring point bearing somewhat the same relation to each company in the area that a company employment office now does to each department of the plant. It can yield about as good results as one would get by crowds of workers actually traveling from one company employment office to the next, and with a saving of time and effort to all concerned.

The present operation of the Employment Service is admittedly some distance from this ideal, and there are serious difficulties in the way of attaining it. The gravest difficulties stem from conflicts of interest among the Service's clients, which it must somehow mediate in order to survive. Different employers are in competition for labor, so that the public employment office is forced to serve many masters simultaneously. Each employer naturally expects the Service to skin the cream from the available labor supply for his own benefit. Yet all employers cannot get the "best" workers—someone must hire those who are left over. Similarly, the workers registered with the Service are in competition for jobs; yet only part of them can be sent to the "best" jobs. There is a further conflict between the two groups as a whole; the referral policies which would best serve the interests of employers will not be most desirable from the workers' standpoint. Should the Service, in filling orders, accept employers' hiring specifications concerning race, nationality, religion, and other personal characteristics of workers? How many jobs shall be shown to each worker, how many workers shall be referred to a particular job, how much shall the interviewer be allowed to tell the worker about the characteristics of the job and the company? On each point, the procedure most serviceable to employers will not be ideal from the workers' standpoint, and vice versa. There is no possibility, then, of the Employment Service being ideally satisfactory to *all* who have an interest in its operation. Its procedures must always represent a working compromise among conflicting interests and pressures. Our

One must aim instead at a more limited objective—a public Employment Service which, while it cannot function automatically and will always be limited by human judgment and fallibility, will yet produce better results than could be achieved without it. The Employment Service can assemble order information on more jobs than would otherwise exist. It can send out a suitable man to the employer, though doubtless not the best man who might be located by an omniscient observer. The Employment Service can hope to function as a central hiring point bearing somewhat the same relation to each company in the area that a company employment office now does to each department of the plant. It can yield about as good results as one would get by crowds of workers aimlessly traveling from one company employment office to the next, and with a saving of time and effort to all concerned.

The present operation of the employment service is admittedly some distance from this ideal, and there are serious difficulties in the way of attaining it. The gravest difficulties stem from conflicts of interest among the Service's clients, which it must somehow mediate in order to survive. Different employers are in competition for labor, so that the public employment office is forced to serve many masters simultaneously. Each employer naturally expects the Service to skim the cream from the available labor supply for his own benefit. Yet all employers cannot get the "best workers"—someone must hire those who are left over. Similarly, the workers registered with the Service are in competition for the jobs, yet only part of them can be sent to the "best" jobs. There is a further conflict between the two groups as a whole; the general policies which would best serve the interests of employers will not be most desirable from the workers' standpoint. Should the service, in filling orders, accept employers' hiring specifications concerning race, nationality, religion, and other personal characteristics of workers? How many jobs shall be shown to each worker, how many workers shall be referred to a particular job, how much shall the interviewer be allowed to tell the worker about the characteristics of the job and the company? On each point, the procedure most satisfactory to employers will not be ideal from the workers' standpoint, and vice versa. There is no possibility, then, of the Employment Service being ideally satisfactory to all who have an interest in its operation. Its procedures must always represent a working compromise among conflicting interests and pressures. One

practical suggestions for Employment Service procedure on these points and others, are deferred until Chapter X.

EMPLOYMENT FLUCTUATIONS AND LABOR MOBILITY

We should not conclude this chapter without noting that the level and rate of change of employment, while it does not basically alter either the motivation of workers or the objective structure of the market, does have a great effect on actual movements of labor. The moderate recession of 1948–49, which occurred near the end of our study, provided some indication of what happens during a period of declining employment. The main effects observed were as follows:

First, employer hiring requirements tend to rise—the definition of an "acceptable" worker is tightened up. This was noticeable particularly as regards maximum age limits for hiring, increased insistence on specialized job experience, and increased reluctance to hire "floaters" with a high mobility record.

Second, opportunities to change employers and to learn new skills diminish. Accessions to manufacturing employment, which averaged 5.4 per cent per month during 1947 and 1948, fell to 2.0 per cent per month in 1949. During a recession, many of the people who retire or quit are not replaced or are replaced by recalling laid-off workers. Thus the wall between the establishment's "internal" labor force and the outside labor market, rather porous in periods of peak employment, becomes much thicker in bad years. Within each enterprise, demotions tend to exceed promotions. When it is necessary to fill a job from the outside, employers insist on training and experience on the specific job in question—a requirement which is feasible because of the large number of experienced workers among the unemployed. Thus young people have little opportunity to acquire occupational skills, and other workers have little opportunity to change occupations.

Third, workers cling tightly to their present jobs. Even those who are dissatisfied and plan to change jobs eventually realize that a depression is no time to make a change. Voluntary turnover falls to a very low level. In this area, the rate of voluntary separations from the thirty-nine manufacturing companies reporting to the Chamber of Commerce fell from an average of 3.5 per cent per month in 1948 to 1.8 per cent in 1949.

Fourth, employers generally, and nonunion employers in particular, tend to tighten up on worker performance in a variety of ways: by insisting on better time-keeping and avoidance of absenteeism, by

practical suggestions for Employment Service procedure on these points and others are deferred until Chapter X.

EMPLOYMENT FLUCTUATIONS AND LABOR MOBILITY

We should not conclude this chapter without noting that the level and rate of change of employment, while it does not basically alter either the motivation of workers or the objective structure of the market, does have a great effect on actual movements of labor. The moderate recession of 1948–49, which occurred near the end of our study, provided some indication of what happens during a period of declining employment. The main effects observed were as follows: first, employer hiring requirements tend to rise—the definition of an "acceptable" worker is tightened up. This was noticeable particularly as regards maximum age limits for hiring, increased insistence on specialized job experience, and increased reluctance to hire "floaters" with a high mobility record.

Second, opportunities to change employers and to learn new skills diminish. Accessions to manufacturing employment, which averaged 5.4 per cent per month during 1947 and 1948, fell to 3.0 per cent per month in 1949. During a recession, many of those who retire or quit are not replaced or are replaced by recalling laid-off workers. Thus the walls between establishments, rather porous in periods of peak employment, become much thicker in bad years. Within each enterprise, demotions tend to exceed promotions. When it is necessary to fill a job from the outside, employers insist on training and experience on the specific job in question—a requirement which is feasible because of the large number of experienced workers among the unemployed. Thus young people have little opportunity to acquire occupational skills, and older workers have little opportunity to change occupations.

Third, workers cling tightly to their present jobs. Even those who are dissatisfied and plan to change jobs eventually realize that depression is no time to make a change. Voluntary turnover falls to a very low level. In this area, the rate of voluntary separations from the thirty-nine manufacturing companies reporting to the Chamber of Commerce fell from an average of 3.5 per cent per month in 1948 to 1.6 per cent in 1949.

Fourth, employers generally and nonunion employers in particular, tend to tighten up on worker performance in a variety of ways: by insisting on better time-keeping and avoidance of absenteeism; by

insisting on better quality of output and reduction of waste; by tightening up time standards on incentive jobs which had been allowed to become loose during prosperity; and by weeding out the least efficient members of the labor force. The motive is a need to offset falling profit margins. Since it is usually unfeasible to reduce wages, employers try to get more in return for the same wage. They are able to do this because workers have few alternative opportunities for employment.

Fifth, the Employment Service develops a large excess of registrants over applicants, and use of the Service tends to decline. Employers have little difficulty in obtaining all the labor they need "at the gate." Workers, realizing that the probability of getting jobs through the Service are low, are discouraged from using it.

If the depression is severe, these tendencies will not be reversed as soon as employment begins to rise. Not until full-time unemployment in the area has fallen below, say, 10 per cent of the labor force will one notice a change in the operation of the market.[10] As the area approaches nearer and nearer to full employment, one will observe tendencies the opposite of those just described. Employer hiring specifications will be adjusted downward. Opportunities for movement within enterprises and between enterprises will increase. Voluntary turnover will rise. Pressure for high worker performance will tend to relax. Employment Service orders and placements will rise and registrations will fall.

These facts suggest several general observations. First, labor markets contain great possibilities of adjustment to over-all economic fluctuations *by methods other than changes in wage rates*. Changes in hiring specifications, in the quality of employed labor, and in pressure for worker performance permit a marked divergence between the behavior of wage rates and unit labor costs. Were this not so, downward rigidity of wages would doubtless be more serious than it actually is. In practice, the rigidity of wage rates cannot be taken as an indication of inflexibility in the *total* adjustment of the market to changing economic circumstances.

[10] This figure of 10 per cent is illustrative only, and may be too low or too high. Moreover, the shift from a "loose" to a "tight" labor market occurs gradually over (roughly) the second half of a cyclical upswing, and it is not certain that one could find any clear breaking-point in the process. Rather, the labor market tendencies characteristic of high employment gradually develop behind the facade of unemployment, and finally come to preponderate over the opposing tendencies. One reason for the gradualness of the change is that, even within a single area, one finds quite different unemployment ratios and unemployment trends for different occupational groups. Conditions have already become tight in certain sectors of the market while they continue loose in others.

Second, one cannot set up tenable assumptions about labor mobility in abstraction from the behavior of aggregate employment. Labor markets in which full employment had existed long enough for everyone to assume its continued existence would operate quite differently from labor markets in a highly cyclical economy.

Third, the possibility of rationalizing the labor market through public employment offices and other devices is largely contingent on maintenance of a high level of aggregate employment. General underemployment is much the most serious obstacle to optimum distribution of workers among jobs and maximum opportunity for individual advancement. Maintenance of a high general level of economic activity has priority over improved labor market organization per se—not because the former is "more important" in some quantitative sense, but because it is a structural prerequisite to the latter.

CHAPTER IV Determinants of Interplant Movement: Worker Attitudes and Behavior

THE second group of factors influencing interplant movement includes workers' job preferences, their knowledge and beliefs about the labor market, and their customary ways of seeking work. These attitudes and practices are derived mainly from the worker's own job experience. They thus mirror the objective characteristics of the market described in the previous chapter. Part of what we have to say concerning them has already been said in a preliminary report.[1] Since that report was issued, however, the data obtained from our two samples of employed workers have been subjected to further statistical analysis. In addition, interviews with a group of unemployed workers (referred to hereafter as Sample 3) have yielded information on the work-seeking behavior of the unemployed.

The questionnaires used, the characteristics of the three worker samples, the technique of interviewing, and other matters of method are discussed in Appendix B. The technique was that of a "fixed question-free response" interview. The data obtained by this technique, and particularly responses involving beliefs and attitudes rather than actions, are not quantitative in the same sense as wage or employment data. The method is highly suggestive of hypotheses about worker behavior; but whether these hypotheses can ever be subjected to rigorous quantitative tests is uncertain. In any event, the reader interested in problems of method and reliability is referred to Appendix B.

As the study progressed, we were increasingly impressed with the homogeneity of the findings on many points. Where we tried to get at a problem through a series of different questions, the replies to these questions agreed closely with each other. Instances of this will appear as we proceed. Again, when the replies to a particular question

[1] See Lloyd G. Reynolds and Joseph Shister, *Job Horizons* (New York, Harper & Brothers, 1949), especially Chs. 2, 3, and 6. This chapter will say both more and less than was said in the earlier volume. More, because we now have additional data and additional analysis of the earlier data. Less, because it is not necessary to repeat here the numerous quotations from interviews which were used for illustrative purposes in the earlier report.

were broken down by age, skill, income level, union membership, and other variables, the results were usually strikingly similar for all groups in the population. There seems, therefore, to be a basic pattern of attitudes and reactions toward jobs which is characteristic of manual workers as a whole. While deviations from this pattern occur, they are less significant than the pattern itself.

This chapter is divided into three main sections. First, we shall describe the general attitudes, beliefs, and objectives which shape the worker's conduct in the labor market. Second, we shall examine in some detail the criteria which workers use in deciding whether a job is worth taking or worth keeping, or whether one job is better than another. Third, we shall consider how and why workers change jobs, how they find out about new jobs, and how they choose among them. This pattern of behavior, while it could scarcely have been anticipated on *a priori* grounds, turns out to be quite reasonable in view of the structure of the market and the nature of workers' attitudes and objectives.

GENERAL ATTITUDES, BELIEFS AND OBJECTIVES

The material to be presented in this section will be grouped under five headings: the attachment of most workers to a particular locality; the additional attachment to a particular employer; the workers' limited knowledge of job vacancies, wages, and conditions of employment in other companies; the belief that good jobs are scarce and that the better jobs are obtained only through "pull" or "contacts"; and the strong urge toward security and avoidance of risk.

ATTACHMENT TO A LOCALITY

Our findings on this point may well be unrepresentative, since New Englanders may show a stronger attachment to one area than people in the Midwest or Far West. The workers interviewed in this area certainly showed a strong attachment to their community and their homes. It will be recalled from Chapter II that 69 per cent of those in Sample II (the only group for which a lifetime work history was obtained) had never worked outside of the area, while three-quarters had never worked outside the state.[2]

[2] There was, of course, a slight bias toward immobility in this sample, because about a year elapsed between the compilation of the City Directory from which the sample was drawn and the date of our interviews. During this period, two per cent of those drawn in the sample had moved out of the city and were not interviewed. Inclusion of these people would have changed the results somewhat.

were broken down by age, skill, income level, union membership, and other variables, the results were usually strikingly similar for subgroups in the population. There seems, therefore, to be a basic pattern of attitudes and reactions toward jobs which is characteristic of manual workers *as a whole*. While deviations from this pattern occur, they are less significant than the pattern itself.

This chapter is divided into three main sections. First, we shall describe the general attitudes, beliefs, and objectives which shape the worker's conduct in the labor market. Second, we shall examine in some detail the criteria which workers use in deciding whether a job is worth taking or worth keeping, or whether one job is better than another. Third, we shall consider how and why workers change jobs, how they find out about new jobs, and how they choose among them. This pattern of behavior, while it could scarcely have been anticipated on *a priori* grounds, turns out to be quite reasonable in view of the structure of the market and the nature of worker attitudes and objectives.

GENERAL ATTITUDES, BELIEFS, AND OBJECTIVES

The material to be presented in this section will be arranged under five headings: the attachment of most workers to a particular *locality;* the additional attachment to a particular *employer;* the worker's limited knowledge of job vacancies, wages, and conditions of employment in other companies; the belief that good jobs are scarce and that the better jobs are obtained only through "pull" or "contacts"; and the strong urge toward security and avoidance of risks.

Attachment to a Locality

Our findings on this point may well be unrepresentative, since New Englanders may show a stronger attachment to one area than people in the Midwest or far West. The workers interviewed in this area certainly showed a strong attachment to their community and their homes. It will be recalled from Chapter II that 60 per cent of those in Sample 1 (the only group for which a lifetime work history was obtained) had never worked outside of the area, while three-quarters had never worked outside the state.[2]

[2] There was, of course, a slight bias toward immobility in this sample, because about a year elapsed between the compilation of the City Directory from which the sample was drawn and the date of our interviews. During this period, two per cent of those included in the sample had moved out of the city and were not interviewed. Inclusion of these people would have changed the results somewhat.

The workers in Sample 1 were asked how much they knew about the availability of jobs and about terms of employment in other localities. Almost two-thirds replied that they knew nothing whatever about other areas. The remainder had picked up a certain amount of information through working in other areas, through their trade union, through friends and acquaintances, or from odd items in newspapers. This knowledge was meager, however, except in the case of people who had recently moved from another area and a few skilled workers belonging to craft unions.

Members of Sample 1 were next asked how large a wage increase would be necessary to induce them to move to another area. Only 12 per cent said that they would move for a moderate increase in their weekly earnings, i.e., an increase of 25 per cent or less. These responses no doubt implied that the new job would be as good as the present job in matters other than wages, and also that it could be obtained *before* making the move. While workers were not asked specifically on this point, one may conjecture that scarcely any of them would have abandoned a job in this area to pursue "a bird in the bush" somewhere else, regardless of relative wage rates. This question, indeed, struck most of the respondents as unreal; few of them had any serious interest in or intention of moving outside the area. Thirty per cent said that they would move for a large (25 to 100 per cent) increase in weekly earnings. Forty-five per cent said that they would not move under any circumstances; and the remaining 13 per cent said that they would move only if they could be assured of housing in the new area. Younger workers showed a greater willingness to move than did older workers, and tenants were more willing to move than were home owners. Sixty per cent of those who owned their homes indicated that they would not move under any circumstances, compared with 35 per cent of the tenants.

In order to check the effect of employment status on propensity to move, the unemployed workers in Sample 3 were asked whether they would be willing to move to another area to secure work. The replies indicated a markedly greater willingness to move than in the case of the employed workers in Sample 1. One-third of those in Sample 3 said that they would go to another area if necessary to get a job. Within the unemployed there was a marked difference between single people and members of family groups. Only one-fifth of those who were members of families expressed willingness to move, compared

The workers in Sample 1 were asked how much they knew about the availability of jobs and about terms of employment in other localities. Almost two-thirds replied that they knew nothing whatever about other areas. The remainder had picked up a certain amount of information through working in other areas, through the trade union, through friends and acquaintances, or from odd items in newspapers. This knowledge was meagre, however, except in the case of people who had recently moved from another area and a few skilled workers belonging to craft unions.

Members of Sample 1 were next asked how large a wage increase would be necessary to induce them to move to another area. Only 12 per cent said that they would move for a moderate increase in their weekly earnings, i.e., an increase of 25 per cent or less. These responses no doubt implied that the new job would be as good as the present job in matters other than wages, and also that it could be obtained before making the move. Where workers were not asked specifically on this point, one may conjecture that scarcely any of them would have abandoned a job in Nashua to pursue "a bird in the bush" somewhere else, regardless of relative wage rates. This question, indeed, struck most of the respondents as unreal; few of them had any serious interest in or intention of moving outside the area. Thirty per cent said that they would move for a large (75 to 100 per cent) increase in weekly earnings. Forty-five per cent said that they would not move under any circumstances; and the remaining 13 per cent said that they would move only if they could be assured of housing in the new area. Younger workers showed a greater willingness to move than did older workers, and tenants were more willing to move than were home owners. Sixty per cent of those who owned their homes indicated that they would not move under any circumstances, compared with 15 per cent of the tenants.

In order to check the effect of employment status on propensity to move, the unemployed workers in Sample 3 were asked whether they would be willing to move to another area to get other work. The replies indicated a markedly greater willingness to move than in the case of the employed workers in Sample 1. One-third of those in Sample 3 said that they would go to another area if necessary to get a job. Within the unemployed there was a marked difference between single people and members of family groups. Only one-fifth of those who were members of families expressed willingness to move, compared

with two-thirds of those who were single, widowed, or divorced. This finding is in accord with the familiar fact that geographical movement is greatest among the young and unattached.[8] It should be noted that, while one-third of the sample expressed willingness to move, only one-fifth had actually visited nearby areas in search of work and in many cases the search had been rather perfunctory. This suggests that, even where unemployment exists, the job must often seek the man rather than vice versa.

Unemployed workers seem, then, to have a higher propensity to move than employed workers. In many cases, however, willingness to move does not lead to a systematic search for work in other areas. It leads rather to inquiries of friends and relatives in other areas and greater receptiveness to "tips." Often, a specific job vacancy is necessary to convert propensity to move into actual movement. The incidence of geographical movement, moreover, is likely to be uneven. Movement is greatest among the young and unattached. As between occupational levels, movement is likely to be greatest at the skilled craft occupations. From the employers' standpoint it is cheaper to meet a local shortage of a skilled trade by importing labor than by training it; for semiskilled jobs the reverse is true. From the workers' side, skilled men in craft unions have unusually good facilities for finding out about vacancies in other areas.

Attachment to a Particular Employer

Most workers do not shift readily from one employer to another. While this factor has been recognized, however, it has not been stressed as heavily as it should be. Our interviews indicate that employer attachment is strong, and that most employed workers have little interest in what is going on elsewhere in the market.

Attachment to a particular employer is commonly stronger than attachment to a particular occupation or industry. It is true that many workers, including most skilled workers, prefer to continue working in the same occupation. These preferences, however, are usually not

[8] Many workers in the sample, especially among the middle-age group, responded somewhat as follows: "Sure, I'd be willing to move to another city if I knew there was a job there. But things are bad here, so they're probably bad in A______, B______, and C______ too. What's the use? I might as well stay here and see what happens." Skilled craftsmen, on the other hand, tended to regard the union as a source of information. A steamfitter laughed at this and simply telephones the business agents in A______, B______, and C______, thereby determining almost at once what jobs are available and under what conditions.

with two-thirds of those who were single, widowed, or divorced. This finding is in accord with the familiar fact that geographical movement is greatest among the young and unattached. It should be noted that, while one-third of the sample expressed willingness to move, only one-fifth had actually visited nearby areas in search of work and in many cases the search had been rather perfunctory. This suggests that, even when unemployment exists, the job must often seek the man rather than vice versa.

Unemployed workers seem, then, to have a higher *propensity to move* than employed workers. In many cases, however, willingness to move does not lead to a systematic search for work in other areas.[3] It leads rather to inquiries of friends and relatives in other areas, and greater receptiveness to "tips" and rumors. A specific job vacancy is necessary to convert propensity to move into actual movement. The incidence of geographical movement, moreover, is likely to be uneven. Movement is greatest among the young and unattached. As between occupational levels, movement is likely to be greatest in the skilled craft occupations. From the employers' standpoint, it is cheaper to meet a local shortage of a skilled trade by importing labor than by training it; for semiskilled jobs, the reverse is true. From the workers' side, skilled men in craft unions have unusually good facilities for finding out about vacancies in other areas.

Attachment to an Employer

Most workers do not shift readily from one employer to another. While this factor has been recognized, however, it has not been stressed as heavily as it should be. Our interviews indicate that employer attachment is strong, and that most employed workers have little interest in what is going on elsewhere in the market.

Attachment to a particular employer is normally stronger than attachment to a particular occupation or industry. It is true that many workers, including most skilled workers, prefer to continue working in the same occupation. These preferences, however, are usually not

[3] Many of those in Sample 3, especially among the semiskilled group, reasoned about as follows: "Sure, I'd be willing to move to another city if I knew there was a job there. But things are bad here, so they're probably bad in A________, B________, and C________ too. What's the use? I might as well stay here and see what happens." Skilled craftsmen, on the other hand, tended to use the union as a source of information. A steamfitter laid off in this area simply telephones the business agents in A________, B________, and C________, thereby determining almost at once what jobs are available and under what conditions.

rigid; the great majority of workers, if they cannot find work in the preferred occupation, are willing to consider the next best thing.[4] A change of occupation is not regarded as so great a disaster as severance from a company after some years of employment. Industry preferences seem to be even less marked, except where a certain occupation is found only in a particular industry—garment cutting, clock adjusting, gun testing, and so on. In these cases what appears to be an industry preference is really an occupational preference. It is doubtful, indeed, whether there is any such thing as a separate industry preference, i.e., anything which cannot be resolved either into preference for a particular occupation or a particular employer.

The strength of attachment to a particular employer was tested in several ways, all of which yielded the same general result. Workers in Samples 1 and 2 were asked whether they planned to continue working for their present employer. Eighty-eight per cent of those in Sample 1, and 78 per cent of those in Sample 2, said that they expected to continue where they were; the remainder were dissatisfied and wanted to change employers. Analysis of the characteristics of the satisfied and dissatisfied workers revealed only two clear relationships—with years of service, and with amount of education. Desire to move is concentrated among the short-service workers and decreases rapidly with increasing length of service;[5] this conclusion is perhaps tautological, since the fact that a worker has stayed with a company for many years must indicate a reasonably good adjustment to the job. Desire to change employers seems also to be positively correlated with years of schooling. Workers with a high school education or better showed a noticeably greater desire to change jobs, probably reflecting in some cases a desire to escape from manual work alto-

[4] The unemployed workers in Sample 3, for example, were asked what kind of work they would like to get. About half the group, including virtually all the skilled men, said that they would like to continue with the kind of work they had been doing. When asked about second choices, however, most of these people showed marked flexibility of outlook. If they couldn't get what they wanted, they would take the next best thing; for skilled mechanics, this usually meant stepping down to a machine-operating job on production. Only about 10 per cent of the sample said they were so determined to continue in their usual line of work that they would refuse to consider anything else. Even in these cases, prolonged unemployment would probably produce some shift in attitude.

[5] In Sample 1, 30 per cent of those with less than one year of service expressed a desire to change employers; but only 22 per cent of those with one to three years of service, 12 per cent of those with three to five years of service, 9 per cent of those with five to ten years of service, and 8 per cent of those with ten to twenty years of service wanted to change. The results for Sample 2 were similar. Three-way tabulations by length of service and age indicated that the former is the more significant variable.

gether. There was no significant relation with earnings level, occupational level, or any other variable. Workers earning $30.00 a week were just as anxious to keep their present jobs as workers earning $80.00 a week.

A second piece of evidence relates to the behavior of World War II veterans, who formed a considerable proportion of Sample 2. All veterans in this Sample were asked whether they had returned to their prewar jobs after discharge from service. Our initial hypothesis was that the veterans, whose horizons had been enlarged by travel, contact with men from other areas and occupations, and in many cases additional trade training, would show a greater propensity to change employers than did workers in general. This hypothesis, however, was not supported by the results. Eighty-eight per cent of the veterans in the sample had returned to the company for which they were working when they entered the service. Seventy-six per cent had not even looked around for another job; 12 per cent had looked around but had finally decided to go back to their previous employer. About half of those who went back to their old employer mentioned accumulated seniority as the main reason for their decision. Others were influenced by the fact that their previous employer was legally obligated to reemploy them, whereas they were not sure that they could obtain employment elsewhere.

A third piece of evidence comes from the unemployed workers in Sample 3. These workers, it will be recalled, were interviewed at an early stage in the 1948–49 recession. Most of them had been laid off in the recent past. Two-thirds had been unemployed three months or less; three-quarters were receiving unemployment compensation or veterans' unemployment allowances; and almost all of the remainder belonged to family units which had income from other wage earners. Each worker was asked whether he would like to go back to work for his previous employer. In a few cases the question was inapplicable because the employer had gone out of business. In the cases where it was applicable, however, 87 per cent of the workers said they would like to go back to their previous jobs, and 50 per cent believed that they would actually be able to do so.

Of those with more than twelve years of education, 34 per cent in Sample 1 and 29 per cent in Sample 2 wanted to leave their present job. Of those with four years or less of education, on the other hand, only 15 per cent in Sample 1 and none in Sample 2 wanted to leave.

Those who wanted to go back but did not believe they would be able to fall into two main categories: (1) Workers with very low seniority. As one man said, "I'm

gether.[6] There was no significant relation with earnings level, occupational level, or any other variable. Workers earning $30.00 a week were just as anxious to keep their present jobs as workers earning $80.00 a week.

A second piece of evidence relates to the behavior of World War II veterans, who formed a considerable proportion of Sample 2. All veterans in this Sample were asked whether they had returned to their prewar jobs after discharge from service. Our initial hypothesis was that the veterans, whose horizons had been enlarged by travel, contact with men from other areas and occupations, and in many cases additional trade training, would show a greater propensity to change employers than do workers in general. This hypothesis, however, was not supported by the results. Eighty-eight per cent of the veterans in the sample had returned to the company for which they were working when they entered the service. Seventy-six per cent had not even looked around for another job; 12 per cent had looked around but had finally decided to go back to their previous employer. About half of those who went back to their old employers mentioned accumulated seniority as the main reason for their decision. Others were influenced by the fact that their previous employer was legally obligated to reemploy them, whereas they were not sure that they could obtain employment elsewhere.

A third piece of evidence comes from the unemployed workers in Sample 3. These workers, it will be recalled, were interviewed at an early stage in the 1948–49 recession. Most of them had been laid off in the recent past. Two-thirds had been unemployed three months or less; three-quarters were receiving unemployment compensation or veterans unemployment allowances; and almost all of the remainder belonged to family units which had current income from other wage earners. Each worker was asked whether he would like to go back to work for his previous employer. In a few cases the question was inapplicable because the employer had gone out of business. In the cases where it was applicable, however, 87 per cent of the workers said they would like to go back to their previous jobs, and 50 per cent believed that they would actually be able to do so.[7]

[6] Of those with more than twelve years of education, 36 per cent in Sample 1 and 48 per cent in Sample 2 wanted to leave their present job. Of those with four years or less of education, on the other hand, only 13 per cent in Sample 1 and none in Sample 2 wanted to leave.

[7] Those who wanted to go back but did not believe they would be able to fall into two main categories: (1) Workers with very low seniority. As one man said, "Well,

These replies suggest that unemployment does not necessarily break the worker's attachment to a particular employer and push him into the general labor market. If the layoff is expected to last for only a few weeks or months, most workers will tend to "sit it out," supporting themselves from unemployment compensation, odd jobs, and savings. If pressure is put on them to take another job, they will "talk their way out of the job" in the way described in Chapter III. This behavior is quite rational from the worker's standpoint; for to take another job might make him unavailable for instantaneous recall to his old job, which is the one he really wants. Even if the employer announces an indefinite layoff, many of the work force will hold off from other jobs in the hope of eventual recall. It is remarkably hard to convince a worker who wants his old job back that the job has really disappeared and that he must look elsewhere.

Turning from the *indicators* of employer attachment to the *reasons* for it, we may note first that most people prefer an established routine for its own sake. The worker gets accustomed to going to and from work in the same way at the same hours, going through the same motions in the plant, seeing the same people day after day. If the existing routine is generally satisfactory, why change?

A second major consideration is security. Particularly in companies where layoffs are governed by union contract, workers are well aware that their chance of continued employment in bad years depends directly on their years of service with the company. Even in good years such as 1946–48, many workers are bearish about the economic outlook. Again and again in our interviews, workers would say, "I'm doing my best to get set before the big bust comes." Their main method of "getting set" was to roll up as many years of seniority as possible with the same company.

There are other risks involved in a change of employers, arising from the fact that a new job cannot be "sized up" accurately until you have worked on it for a while. If you give up your present job and the new job does not turn out as expected, you have made a serious and irretrievable error. Risk-bearing is unpleasant to most people, and particularly so when one's whole manner of life is intimately involved, as it is in a change of employment. Workers tend, therefore,

---

they've laid off up to eight years now, and I've only got eighteen months. I don't think they'll get back down to me for a long while." (2) People whose work record had been unsatisfactory and who didn't think the company would want them back. Some of these people had probably been discharged rather than laid off, though not a single member of the sample was willing to admit discharge as his reason for leaving!

to apply a heavy risk-discount to alternative jobs. The fact that a worker satisfied with his present job takes little interest in informing himself about other jobs in the area may be interpreted as meaning that the discounted value of these (hypothetical) possibilities is so low that it is not worthwhile to bother looking for them.

Even apart from the risk element, a change of employers is likely to worsen one's position rather than improve it. Because of the prevailing custom of hiring in at the bottom and promoting from within, a man who has got part way up the ladder in one plant is likely to slip back some distance when he shifts to a new plant. This is less true, of course, of skilled craftsmen than it is of production workers. A change of employers also means loss of pension and other rights which accrue with length of service.

It should be noted, finally, that not all workers have an effective choice among employers. Workers beyond the age of 45 or 50 realize that they would have serious difficulty in getting another job and are anxious to keep their present job on this account. This is true also of workers whose skills can be used by only one plant in the area—tire builders in the tire plant, wire drawers in the steel-wire plant, clock adjusters in the clock company, and so on. For these people, a change of employers would inevitably mean retrogression in skill and earning power.

These factors in combination produce virtually a separate labor market in each plant. Even in the good years 1946-48, something like 80 per cent of the manual workers in the area were not really available to other employers. Their horizon was bounded by the enterprise.

Information on Job Openings, Wages, and Working Conditions

The workers in sample 1 were asked a series of questions (A 4 to A 41) designed to draw out information about wages and conditions in other plants. Because of the length of the interview as a whole, it was not possible to go as thoroughly into this matter as would be desirable. The results are suggestive, however, and are in general accord with previous writings by informed observers.

The workers were first asked where they would go to look for work,

The only limitation of the questions asked was their generality. If one wanted to probe the quality of a worker's knowledge of the labor market (which would take perhaps half to three-quarters of an hour to do), it might be best to start by asking him to mention each company in the area which he has heard of. One could then go down the list and, with respect to each company mentioned, try to appraise the worker's information and determine his sources of information. Our interviews were not nearly this intensive, and the results should be regarded as suggestive only.

to apply a heavy risk-discount to alternative jobs. The fact that a worker satisfied with his present job takes little interest in informing himself about other jobs in the area may be interpreted as meaning that the discounted value of these (hypothetical) possibilities is so low that it is not worthwhile to bother looking for them.

Even apart from the risk element, a change of employers is likely to worsen one's position rather than improve it. Because of the prevailing custom of hiring at the bottom and promoting from within, a man who has got part way up the ladder in one plant is likely to slip back some distance when he shifts to a new plant. This is less true, of course, of skilled craftsmen than it is of production workers. A change of employers also means loss of pension and other rights which accrue with length of service.

It should be noted, finally, that not all workers have an effective choice among employers. Workers beyond the age of 45 or 50 realize that they would have serious difficulty in getting another job and are anxious to keep their present job on this account. This is true also of workers whose skills can be used by only one plant in the area—tire builders in the tire plant, wire drawers in the steel wire plant, clock adjusters in the clock company, and so on. For these people, a change of employers would inevitably mean retrogression in skill and earning power.

These factors in combination produce virtually a separate labor market in each plant. Even in the good years 1946–48, something like 80 per cent of the manual workers in the area were not really available to other employers. Their horizon was bounded by the enterprise.

Knowledge of Job Openings, Wages, and Working Conditions

The workers in Sample 1 were asked a series of questions (A-4c to A-4f) designed to draw out information about wages and conditions in other plants. Because of the length of the interview as a whole, it was not possible to go as thoroughly into this matter as would be desirable.[8] The results are suggestive, however, and are in general accord with previous writings by informed observers.

The workers were first asked where they would go to look for work

[8] The chief limitation of the questions asked was their generality. If one wanted to probe thoroughly into a worker's knowledge of the labor market, which would take perhaps half to three-quarters of an hour to do, it might be best to start by asking him to mention each company in the area which he has heard of. One could then go down the list and, with respect to each company mentioned, try to exhaust the worker's information and determine his sources of information. Our interviews were not nearly this intensive, and the results should be regarded as suggestive only.

if out of a job. Three-quarters did not mention a specific plant; the remaining quarter mentioned one or more plants as desirable places to work. About half of those who had a preference mentioned plants in which they had worked previously. The remainder usually mentioned plants in their home neighborhood, or plants in the same industry as their present employer, or plants which are so large that most people in the area know their names. The workers were next asked whether there were any plants in the area in which they would not like to work. Again, 60 per cent of the group did not give a specific answer; the remaining 40 per cent mentioned one or more plants as undesirable. Only about a third of those expressing dislike for a particular plant had actually worked in the plant, the remainder going on the basis of hearsay evidence. There was some tendency to condemn large plants in general, mainly because of their greater impersonality and tighter discipline. As one man remarked, "I wouldn't want to work in any large plants in town. Why, they're jailhouses. They treat you like a machine instead of a human being. When you punch in on the time clock you punch your freedom away."

The members of the sample were next asked specifically *what* they knew about the plants they had mentioned. The answers to this question were quite meager. It usually turned out that the worker had only a vague impression that "they treat you right at the A——— company," or "a friend told me that B——— is really a good shop." Very few knew whether jobs were actually available at the plant in question, or how much they could expect to earn per week there, or what the nonwage conditions of employment were like. The principal exceptions were workers who had recently moved from another plant or who had a relative in another plant, in which case they had some information about at least *one job* in the plant; and skilled workers in trade unions, who were rather well informed about union scales and availability of work in the area. The final question asked concerned the worker's sources of information about jobs in other plants. A majority (56 per cent) replied that they get their information mainly from friends and relatives. The next most frequent sources were unions (19 per cent), newspaper advertisements (8 per cent), shopping around from plant to plant (8 per cent), and visiting the State Employment Service (4 per cent).

These results confirm the prevalent impression that workers are poorly informed about job opportunities. Moreover, it is doubtful how far the situation can be altered by collecting and disseminating addi-

tional job information. The basic difficulty is that satisfactorily employed workers are almost entirely uninterested in employment conditions in other companies. This lack of interest is an even more serious obstacle than the difficulty of compiling accurate job information which was noted in Chapter III.

"Good" Jobs Are Scarce; "Contacts" Are Important

It is clear from the previous section that the typical worker has no sensation of being in a "labor market." He has no idea of the full range of jobs, wage rates, and working conditions prevailing in the area, nor does he have any realization of the hundreds or thousands of job vacancies available on a particular day. At most, he knows about a few jobs which have come to his attention in the haphazard way just described.

The worker sorts the jobs which he knows about into two broad categories—"good" and "bad," or "jobs worth taking" and "jobs not worth taking." The general criteria used in deciding whether a job is good or bad, which will be described in the next section, appear to be reasonably constant for all workers. The specific minimum standards for a good job, i.e., the degree to which it must possess the desired qualities, differ considerably from one worker to the next, depending mainly on his past experience. Any worker can tell whether a particular job is a good job by his own minimum standards. He does not, however, conceive of all jobs in the area as arrayed in a hierarchy of "good," "better," and "best." He evaluates jobs one at a time, on the basis of his minimum standards, instead of trying to compare each job with the full array of possible alternatives. If he comes across a "good" job, he takes it without worrying over whether a "better" job may be available somewhere else.

Behind this lies a deep-seated conviction that good jobs are scarce, that if you find one you are lucky and should grab it without delay. The intensity of this feeling among our respondents was rather surprising, since 1947 was a year of high employment and abundant job opportunities. A little reflection, however, suggests that even *when* jobs are abundant in the aggregate they are likely to be scarce for a particular individual. The great majority of vacancies existing in an area are irrelevant to a particular worker since, in the absence of an effective market mechanism, he has no way of learning about them. Moreover, most of the jobs which a worker does learn about may not be possibilities for him, because he is ruled out by the elaborate series

tional job information. The basic difficulty is that satisfactorily employed workers are almost entirely uninterested in employment conditions in other companies. This lack of interest is an even more serious obstacle than the difficulty of compiling accurate job information which was noted in Chapter III.

"Good" Jobs Are Scarce; "Contacts" Are Important

It is clear from the previous section that the typical worker has no sensation of being in "a labor market." He has no idea of the full range of jobs, wage rates, and working conditions prevailing in the area; nor does he have any realization of the hundreds or thousands of job vacancies available on a particular day. At most, he knows about a few jobs which have come to his attention in the haphazard way just described.

The worker sorts the jobs which he knows about into two broad categories—"good" and "bad," or "jobs worth taking" and "jobs not worth taking." The *general criteria* used in deciding whether a job is good or bad, which will be described in the next section, appear to be reasonably constant for all workers. The specific *minimum standards* for a good job, i.e., the degree to which it must possess the desired qualities, differ considerably from one worker to the next, depending mainly on his past experience. Any worker can tell whether a particular job is a good job by his own minimum standards. He does not, however, conceive of all jobs in the area as arrayed in a hierarchy of "good," "better," and "best." He evaluates jobs one at a time, on the basis of his minimum standards, instead of trying to compare each job with the full array of possible alternatives. If he comes across a "good" job, he takes it without worrying over whether a "better" job may be available somewhere else.

Behind this lies a deep-seated conviction that good jobs are scarce, that if you find one you are lucky and should grab it without delay. The intensity of this feeling among our respondents was rather surprising, since 1947 was a year of high employment and numerous job opportunities. A little reflection, however, suggests that even when jobs are abundant in the aggregate they are likely to be scarce for a particular individual. The great majority of vacancies existing in an area are irrelevant to a particular worker since, in the absence of an effective market mechanism, he has no way of learning about them. Moreover, most of the jobs which a worker does learn about may not be possibilities *for him*, because he is ruled out by the elaborate series

of employer hiring specifications described in the last chapter. Other jobs which he has a chance of getting may be below his own minimum standards of acceptability. Finally, workers feel that they are in competition for vacancies with many other workers, that there is a chronic excess of applicants over jobs, that they are in a "buyer's market" for labor. This belief is particularly strong among low-skilled workers, who feel that their limited qualifications give them no competitive advantage over a multitude of others. The result is a feeling that "If you're offered a job, you don't look twice. You just take it and feel lucky about it."

Even at a time of peak employment and active hiring, therefore, the number of jobs which a worker *actually hears about*, which are *good enough to take*, and for which he is *reasonably well qualified*, may be small. If he passes up one such job, it may be some time before he hears of another.

Another widely held belief is that the best jobs are obtained through "pull" and "contacts." Knowing the right people is more important than applying "cold" at various plants or sitting in the public employment service. Apart from contacts, workers believe that finding a good job is largely a matter of luck. They are skeptical of the notion that jobs go to those who are best qualified or who search most diligently for them. The world of employment appears to them as more nearly a lottery than a market.

The Importance of Security

The value which most workers attach to security of employment can scarcely be overemphasized. Almost every worker has either experienced unemployment himself or had relatives and close friends unemployed. Even with unemployment compensation systems, unemployment of more than a few weeks' duration usually means a drop in the family's standard of living. The loss of skill and self-respect, the nagging uncertainty about the future, and the other ill effects of unemployment have been too frequently described to need repetition. Protection against unemployment, therefore, is a major element in workers' calculations about jobs. They are unwilling to gamble with their family's livelihood and their own peace of mind.

This desire for protection against loss of income appeared at numerous points in the present study. It appeared in the general eagerness to pile up as many years of seniority as possible on the same job; in the eagerness of returning veterans and laid-off workers to go back to

jobs on which they have accumulated seniority rather than start over again on a new job; and in the reluctance of many workers to accept promotions even within the same enterprise if the change would mean loss of seniority on their old job.

The questionnaire used for Sample I contained a question aimed directly at the workers' concern with job security: "Suppose you had a choice on your present job of getting a wage increase or getting a guarantee of steady work throughout the year. Which would you take?" Several possible amounts of wage increase were then mentioned by the interviewer in an attempt to determine the worker's point of indifference. Fifty per cent of the workers replied that they would take the guarantee of steady employment under any circumstances. An additional 23 per cent said that they would take the employment guarantee unless the wage increase was very large, i.e., 75 to 100 per cent above their present wage. The remaining 27 per cent said that they would prefer the wage increase. About one-third of this group, however, said that they did not believe an employment guarantee was feasible, and another third were planning to leave the labor force soon because of marriage, retirement, or other reasons. Thus, of those who expected to remain in the labor force, and who could visualize an effective choice between steady work and higher wages, the great majority preferred steady employment. This appears to mean that if a prospective job is uncertain as to steadiness and duration this defect cannot be offset by a moderate differential in wage rates.

WORKERS' DECISIONS ABOUT JOBS: THE CRITERIA OF CHOICE

It was noted in the previous section that workers tend to evaluate jobs on an absolute rather than a comparative basis. They do not think in terms of an array of hypothetical alternatives. Their attention is focused on a single job—the job they now hold or a job of which they are thinking of accepting. Their problem is to determine whether that job is worth keeping or worth taking.

What criteria are used in making this sort of decision? This question is of practical interest to employers faced with the problem of recruiting and retaining labor. It is also of great theoretical interest. Labor supply curves, for example, show the relation between wage level and quantity of labor offered on the assumption that nonwage terms of employment are given and constant. The logical feasibility of this sort of abstraction is not open to question. Its practical use-

a job on which they have accumulated seniority rather than start over again on a new job; and in the reluctance of many workers to accept promotions even within the same enterprise if the change would mean loss of seniority on their old job.

The questionnaire used for Sample 1 contained a question aimed directly at the worker's concern with job security: "Suppose you had a choice on your present job of getting a wage increase or getting a guarantee of steady work throughout the year; which would you take?" Several possible amounts of wage increase were then mentioned by the interviewer in an attempt to determine the worker's "point of indifference." Fifty per cent of the workers replied that they would take the guarantee of steady employment under any circumstances. An additional 23 per cent said that they would take the employment guarantee unless the wage increase was very large, i.e., 25 to 100 per cent above their present wage. The remaining 27 per cent said that they would prefer the wage increase. About one-third of this group, however, said that they did not believe an employment guarantee was feasible; and another third were planning to leave the labor force soon because of marriage, retirement, or other reasons. Thus of those who expected to remain in the labor force, and who could visualize an effective choice between steady work and higher wages, the great majority preferred steady employment. This appears to mean that if a prospective job is uncertain as to steadiness and duration this defect cannot be offset by a moderate differential in wage rates.

WORKERS' DECISIONS ABOUT JOBS: THE CRITERIA OF CHOICE

It was noted in the previous section that workers seem to evaluate jobs on an absolute rather than a comparative basis. They do not think in terms of an array of hypothetical alternatives. Their attention is focussed on a single job—the job they now have, or a job offer which they are thinking of accepting. Their problem is to determine whether this job is worth keeping or worth taking.

What criteria are used in making this sort of decision? This question is of practical interest to employers faced with the problem of recruiting and retaining labor. It is also of great theoretical interest. Labor supply curves, for example, show the relation between wage level and quantity of labor offered on the assumption that nonwage terms of employment are given and constant. The logical feasibility of this sort of abstraction is not open to question. Its practical use-

fulness, however, is obviously greater if wages are the dominant consideration in workers' job decisions than if they are only one of five or six more or less equal factors.

Three separate questions are involved here. First, what are the important variables? What characteristics of jobs enter most prominently into workers' job decisions? It is easy to list fifteen or twenty factors which might be important. Which of these are actually of major importance, and which have only a minor effect? Second, considering only the major elements, can one posit continuous indifference curves relating these elements to each other? Can one assume, in other words, that a worsening of job conditions in one respect can always be offset by an improvement in some other element?

Third, if one can assume continuous indifference curves, what do they look like? Does it take a large wage increase, or only a small one, to offset a worsening of the foreman's temper? This is the only precise sense in which one can speak of the "importance" of a particular job characteristic for worker's decisions. A statement that physical conditions of employment have a weight of 25 per cent in worker's decisions would not make much sense. Importance can be defined only in terms of marginal rates of substitution. Physical conditions of work are important relative to wage rates if a small worsening of physical conditions must be offset by a considerable rise in wage rates in order for the worker to feel as well off as before.

It follows that statements about the importance of different job elements are necessarily relative to the actual characteristics of jobs at a particular place and time. If wages are very high and working conditions very bad, the "importance" of working conditions (i.e., the marginal rate of substitution of wages for conditions) will obviously be greater than it would be if conditions were very good and wages very low. One should not expect, therefore, that studies of different groups of workers at different times and places, even if fully comparable as regards *method,* will yield similar results.

The most reliable approach to these questions is probably to catch workers in the act of evaluating a job—their present job or a prospective offer—and to explore the basis for their evaluation as fully as possible. This was, in any event, the approach used in the present study. The results are adequate to answer the first question of what job characteristics stood out prominently in workers' thinking at this time and place. They do not provide definite answers to the two remaining questions, but suggest some hypotheses which may be useful for further work.

Before presenting this material, we should pause to note that there is already an extensive literature on workers' criteria of a satisfactory job.[7] The most puzzling feature of this literature is the wide variation in the conclusions reached by different writers. Factors which stand out as very important in some studies are of secondary or minor importance in others.

These apparent conflicts in the evidence stem mainly from differences in the groups studied, the concept of what was being studied, terminology, and techniques of measurement. Some of the studies cover workers on a particular job, others all workers in a particular plant or company, others all workers in a locality. Some of the studies relate to prosperous years, some to depressed years. There are wide differences in the ethnic background, age and sex distribution, occupational level, and industrial attachment of the workers. Such differing situations are bound to yield different results.

A more fundamental difficulty is that there have been wide differences in the concept of what was being measured. Some studies start from the vague concept of "morale" and attempt first to assess the morale of each person in the group. They then try to explain differences in morale in terms of characteristics of the job situation or of the worker himself. Other studies start from some item of observed behavior—high or low productivity on the job, absenteeism, voluntary quitting of a job, and so on—and attempt to explain differences in the behavior of different workers. These various approaches naturally yield different results. In general, studies which start from observed behavior are to be preferred. Unless the concept of "morale" is related to behavior, it is doubtful whether it has any clear meaning or any use that warrants research.

Some of the difficulties are terminological. The elements in a job situation are classified differently in different studies. Some do not distinguish six elements, others twenty. Different names are used for

[7] See, in particular, Wilfred Brown and Winifred Raphael, *Managers, Men and Morale* (London, MacDonald and Evans, 1948); J. David Houser, *What People Want from Business* (New York, McGraw-Hill Book Co., 1938); [illegible] (New York, [illegible], 1938); [illegible] (Stanford, Stanford University Press, 1946); Robert Hoppock, *Job Satisfaction* (New York, Harper & Brothers, 1935); [illegible] (New York, Harper & Brothers, 1946); [illegible] "Findings on Productivity, Supervision, and Morale," in [illegible] (Institute for Social Research, University of Michigan, 1949); Clifford E. Jurgensen, "Selected Factors Which Influence Job Preferences," *Journal of Applied Psychology*, Vol. 31 (1947); [illegible] (Survey Research Center, University of Michigan, 1950); National Industrial Conference Board, *Factors Affecting Employee Morale*, Studies in Personnel Policy No. 85, 1947.

Before presenting this material, we should pause to note that there is already an extensive literature on workers' criteria of a satisfactory job.[9] The most puzzling feature of this literature is the wide variation in the conclusions reached by different writers. Factors which stand out as very important in some studies are given only minimal importance in others.

These apparent conflicts in the evidence stem mainly from differences in the groups studied, the concept of what was being studied, terminology, and techniques of measurement. Some of the studies cover workers on a particular job, others all workers in a particular plant or company, others all workers in a locality. Some of the studies relate to prosperous years, some to depressed years. There are wide differences in the ethnic background, age and sex distribution, occupational level, and industrial attachment of the workers. Such differing situations are bound to yield different results.

A more fundamental difficulty is that there have been wide differences in the concept of what was being measured. Some studies start from the vague concept of "morale," and attempt first to assess the morale of each person in the group. They then try to explain differences in morale in terms of characteristics of the job situation or of the worker himself. Other studies start from some item of observed behavior—high or low productivity on the job, absenteeism, voluntary quitting of a job, and so on—and attempt to explain differences in the behavior of different workers. These various approaches naturally yield different results. In general, studies which start from observed behavior are to be preferred. Unless the concept of "morale" is related to behavior, it is doubtful whether it has any clear meaning or any usefulness in research.

Some of the difficulties are terminological. The elements in a job situation are classified differently in different studies. Some authors distinguish six elements, others twenty. Different names are used for

[9] See, in particular: Wilfred Brown and Winifred Raphael, *Managers, Men and Morale* (London, MacDonald and Evans, 1948); J. David Hauser, *What People Want From Business* (New York, McGraw-Hill Book Co., 1938); Patricia Hall and H. W. Locke, *Incentives and Contentment* (New York, Pitman, 1938); Alexander R. Heron, *Why Men Work* (Palo Alto, Stanford University Press, 1948); Robert Hoppock, *Job Satisfaction* (New York, Harper & Brothers, 1935); Schuyler D. Hoslett (ed.), *Human Factors in Management* (New York, Harper & Brothers, 1946); Nathan Jacoby, "Research Findings on Productivity, Supervision, and Morale," in *Research on Human Relations in Administration* (Institute for Social Research, University of Michigan, 1949); Clifford Jurgensen, "Selected Factors Which Influence Job Preferences," *Journal of Applied Psychology*, Vol. 31 (1947), pp. 553–564; Daniel Katz, *Morale and Motivation in Industry* (Survey Research Center, University of Michigan, 1949); National Industrial Conference Board, "Factors Affecting Employee Morale" (Studies in Personnel Policy, No. 85, 1947).

the same thing, and there is an almost perverse delight in coining a private language.

Finally, differing techniques are used to discover the relative importance of different job elements.[10] The commonest technique used in management "morale surveys" is the printed questionnaire containing a check list of predetermined job elements which the worker is asked to rate in order of their importance to him. The deficiencies of this technique are such that any results obtained by it are highly questionable.[11] The results of the semiguided interviews used in the present study are less readily quantified, but are fuller, more reliable, and generally more informative.

The differing results of past studies, then, are not really capable of being reconciled; certainly no effort in this direction can be made here. Our object is simply to present an additional body of data, with a careful explanation of how it was obtained and the precautions which should be observed in interpreting it.

The interview schedules used for Samples 1 and 2 contained a variety of questions, connected either with some past action or with some future aspiration or plan, which gave the worker a chance to elaborate on the job characteristics most significant to him. Thus, the workers in Sample 1 were asked why they left their last job (if they had quit a job voluntarily within the previous year); whether they planned to stay with their present job or leave it; and which other plants in the area they would or would not consider working in. The members of Sample 2 (a considerably younger and more mobile group) were asked to rate their last three jobs as "good" or "bad" and explain why; to give reasons for leaving their last job (if they left voluntarily); whether they planned to stay with their present job or leave it; and whether they would be interested in transfer to any other job

[10] An excellent analysis of some of the principal techniques in current use is found in Arthur Kornhauser, "Psychological Studies of Employee Morale," in Schuyler D. Hoslett (ed.), *Human Factors in Management* (New York, Harper & Brothers, 1946).

[11] Some of the difficulties with this approach are: (1) The use of a fixed check list channels all responses into predetermined categories. (2) The words used in describing these categories—"security," "advancement," "wages," etc.—may mean something quite different to the respondents than they mean to the persons making the survey, and may mean different things to different respondents. (3) Since the response is not connected in any way with observable behavior, there is no way of telling whether the respondent means what he says or how strongly he feels about the different items checked. A high percentage of the replies received are probably perfunctory. (4) The responses are biased by the fact that the project is sponsored by management, that only part of the labor force usually takes the trouble to fill out the questionnaire, and that those who do respond are bound to be an unrepresentative sample of the group as a whole.

the same things and there being almost perverse delight in confusing another's language.

in the same plant. The object was to obtain a considerable number of independent observations on the components of job satisfaction, which could then be cross-checked for consistency.

With respect to each question, the worker was encouraged to express himself as fully as possible, the interviewer confining himself to simple follow-up questions of a neutral character. The interview reports were then coded by a skilled analyst in terms of categories not known to either the interviewers or the respondents. The categories to be used, indeed, were selected after the interviewing had been completed, and the selection was made partly by reading enough interviews to get the general drift of the results. The code sheets and the tabulations based on them include only those elements which stood out most prominently in the worker's response to a particular question. The limit of three was set partly to reduce the tabulating work, partly because few workers dwelt at any length on more than three features of the job situation. The tabulations, then, show the frequency with which a particular element showed up in worker responses, and are not distributions of individual workers.[5]

The relative frequency with which different job elements were mentioned in the answers to various questions is indicated in Tables 14 and A-13. The frequencies themselves are shown in Table A-13, while Table 14 shows simply the ranking of the different job characteristics. An entry of "1" in a particular column of Table 14 means that this job element was mentioned more frequently than any other in response to a particular question; an entry of "2" indicates that that element was mentioned next most frequently; and so on. The exact percentage frequencies in Table A-13 should not be taken too seriously in view of the lack of quantitative precision in this type of analysis. The rank order shown in Table 14 can be taken, however, as a rough measure of relative significance.

Some of the terms used in the table require a word of explanation. "Wages" includes two different elements. In some cases the worker expressed satisfaction or dissatisfaction with the adequacy of his

[5] An alternative method would be to classify the single most important element in a worker's response, and to classify workers on this basis. This type of tabulation was made for the questions asked of Sample 1, but the results differed very little from those of the more inclusive tabulations. The latter were therefore preferred for presentation. In interpreting the tables it should be remembered that some of the questions were answered by only part of the respondents. Thus only a minority of those in Sample 1 had concrete preferences concerning other jobs (cf. the size of Columns 11 and 12 of Table 14), and only a small minority of those in Sample 2 had left their jobs voluntarily (Column 2 of Table 14). The remaining columns, however, are based on substantially 100 per cent response.

in the same plant. The object was to obtain a considerable number of independent observations on the components of job satisfaction, which could then be cross-checked for consistency.

With respect to each question, the worker was encouraged to express himself as fully as possible, the interviewer limiting himself to simple follow-up questions of a neutral character. The interview reports were then coded by a skilled analyst in terms of categories not known to either the interviewers or the respondents. The categories to be used, indeed, were selected *after* the interviewing had been completed; and the selection was made partly by reading enough interviews to get the general drift of the results. The code sheets, and the tabulations based on them, include the *three* elements which stood out most prominently in the worker's response to a particular question. The limit of three was set partly to reduce the tabulating work, partly because few workers dwelt at any length on more than three features of the job situation. The tabulations, then, show the *frequency* with which a particular element showed up in worker responses, and are not distributions of individual workers.[12]

The relative frequency with which different job elements were mentioned in the answers to various questions is indicated in Tables 14 and A-13. The frequencies themselves are shown in Table A-13, while Table 14 shows simply the ranking of the different job characteristics. An entry of "1" in a particular column of Table 14 means that that job element was mentioned more frequently than any other in response to a particular question; an entry of "2" indicates that that element was mentioned next most frequently; and so on. The exact percentage frequencies in Table A-13 should not be taken too seriously in view of the lack of quantitative precision in this type of analysis. The rank order shown in Table 14 can be taken, however, as a rough measure of relative significance.

Some of the terms used in the table require a word of explanation. "Wages" includes two different elements: in some cases the worker expressed satisfaction or dissatisfaction with the adequacy of his

[12] An alternative method would be to identify the *single* most important element in a worker's response, and to classify workers on this basis. This type of tabulation was made for the questions asked of Sample 1, but the results differed very little from those of the more inclusive tabulations. The latter were therefore selected for presentation here. In interpreting the tables, it should be remembered that some of the questions were answered by only part of the respondents. Thus, only a minority of those in Sample 1 had concrete preferences concerning other plants in the area (Columns 12 and 13 of Table 14), and only a small minority of those in Sample 1 had left their last jobs voluntarily (Column 2 of Table 14). The remaining columns, however, are based on substantially 100 per cent responses.

wages to cover living costs; in other cases, he seemed to be mainly concerned with whether he was being paid fairly as compared with workers in other jobs or in other plants. The cost-of-living element was mentioned about twice as frequently as the comparative wage rate element, possibly because the study was made during a period of rapid increase in living costs. "Physical characteristics of the job" includes three things: the nature of the job itself—clean or dirty, light or heavy, safe or dangerous; physical plant conditions—cleanliness, lighting, ventilation, etc.; and the type of machinery—modern or obsolete, and in good or bad condition. The first element—the intrinsic nature of the work—was much the most frequently mentioned. By "independence and control" is meant primarily two things—freedom from too close supervision, and a chance to voice one's opinion on how the job should be done. Broadly speaking, then, this factor amounts to adequacy of the worker's relation with his supervisor. "Relations with fellow workers" refers to such things as the type of person with whom the worker is associated on the job, the presence or absence of a cooperative spirit in the group, and the extent to which others in the group look to the worker for leadership. The other terms used require no special explanation.

The detailed content of each of these categories, and the reasons for their importance to workers, were discussed and illustrated at some length in a preliminary report of the study.[13] There is no need to repeat this material here. It is desirable, however, to point up the general conclusions and to qualify them more carefully than was done in the earlier volume.

There is marked consistency in the ranking of various factors throughout the table. Thus, "wages" appears in either first or second place in each instance, while "physical characteristics of the job" stands almost invariably in second or third place. At the lower end of the ranking, "steadiness of work" stands at the bottom in ten of the thirteen columns. This indicates at least a certain *consistency* in the workers' responses to different questions. It may also indicate—though this cannot be asserted so definitely—a basic *reliability* in the responses, i.e., a correspondence between the worker's statements to the interviewer and his actual feelings and behavior.

There are, however, some interesting variations among the responses to different questions. Independence and control, for example, while ranking only third in over-all standing, rises to first place when the

[13] See Lloyd G. Reynolds and Joseph Shister, *op. cit.*, Chapter 2.

TABLE 14

FACTORS IN JOB SATISFACTION*

Factor	Average Rank	Left Last Job Because		Dissatisfied with Present Job Because		Satisfied with Present Job Because		Last 3 Jobs Rated "Good" or "Bad" Because (S2)		Int. in Transfer to Other Job in Plant Because (S2)		Would or Would Not Work in Other Specified Plants Because (S1)		What Makes a Job a "Good Job"? S2
		S1	S2	S1	S2	S1	S2	Good	Bad	Int.[a]	Not Int.[b]	Would Work	Would Not Work	
	(1)	(2)	(3)	(4)	(5)	(6)	(7)	(8)	(9)	(10)	(11)	(12)	(13)	(14)
Wages	1	1	1	2	2	2	1	1	2	1	2	2	1	1
Physical characteristics of the Job	2	2	2	3	3	4	3	2	1	3	3	3	2	2
Independence and Control	3	3	3	1	1	1	2	4	3	6	4	5	4	3
Job Interest	4	4	4	5	5	7	4	3	5	2	1	1	6	4
Fairness of Treatment	5	5	5	4	4	6	5	6	4	5	5	6	3	5
Relations with Fellow Workers	6	6	6	6	6	3	7	5	7	4	6	4	5	6
Steadiness of Work	7	7	7	7	7	5	6	7	6	7	7	7	7	7

* Rankings based on frequency distributions shown in Table A-13.
[a] Interested [b] Not interested.
The symbols S1 and S2 refer to Samples 1 and 2 respectively.
The over-all ranking of a factor (Column 1) was obtained by taking an arithmetic mean of its rank in the other thirteen columns of the table.

worker is appraising his present job (Columns 4–7). The lower standing of this factor in other columns may mean that the worker forgets fairly readily how good or bad his supervisors were on *previous* jobs, and that he has no way of judging how good they will be on *prospective* jobs. Again, job interest, while standing fourth on average, rises to the top when the worker is considering a transfer to another job (Columns 10–12). Among workers who said they would not consider a transfer to any other job in the plant, the most common reason was the interesting nature of their present job (Column 11). Those who wanted to transfer to another job gave wages as the commonest reason, but job interest ranked second (Column 10). Those who expressed a preference for work in some other plant in the area also gave the interesting nature of the work as the most common reason (Column 12).

The first five categories, as will be noted from Table A-13, account for about 80 per cent of the total responses to all questions involving job satisfaction. The over-all distribution (Column 1 of Table A-13) was as follows: Wages, 24 per cent; physical characteristics of the job, 20 per cent; independence and control, 14 per cent; job interest, 12 per cent; and fairness of treatment, 9 per cent. There is a marked drop in frequency from these five to the two remaining categories. Relations with fellow workers received only about 5 per cent of the total responses, which suggests that this element may have been somewhat overemphasized in recent writings on human relations in industry. Steadiness of work received very few mentions indeed. This is doubtless because full employment had prevailed throughout the area for six or seven years, so that unsteady work was not an immediate problem for many workers. It should be pointed out, to prevent misconceptions, that *steadiness* of work is somewhat different from *security of employment*. Security means having a regular job; steadiness means having an opportunity to put in a full week's work on that job. Workers are very much concerned indeed with security. The desire for security, however, is something which causes the worker to cling to whatever job he may have; it is not a factor which he used in selecting among alternative jobs.

The workers interviewed made little mention of some of the things which have bulked large in the literature of personnel management, such as pensions, insurance plans, other types of "fringe payment," rest rooms and cafeterias, recreational programs, and other company welfare activities. This illustrates the dangers of the check list approach used in so many management studies of "employee morale."

worker is approaching his present job (Columns 4–6). The lower standing of this factor in other columns may mean that the worker forgets fairly readily how good or bad his supervisors were on previous jobs, and that he has no way of judging how good they will be on prospective jobs. Again, job interest, while standing fourth on average, rises to the top when the worker is considering a transfer to another job (Columns 10–12). Among workers who said they would not consider a transfer to any other job in the plant, the most common reason was the interesting nature of their present job (Column 11). Those who wanted to transfer to another job gave wages as the commonest reason, but job interest ranked as both (Column 10). Those who expressed a preference for work in some other plant in the area also gave the interesting nature of the work as the most common reason (Column 12).

The first five categories, as will be noted from Table A-13, account for about 90 per cent of the total responses to all questions involving job satisfaction. The overall distribution (Column 1 of Table A-13) was as follows: Wages, 24 per cent; physical characteristics of the job, 20 per cent; independence and control, 14 per cent; job interest, 12 per cent; and fairness of treatment, 9 per cent. There is a marked drop in frequency from these five to the two remaining categories. Relations with fellow workers received only about 6 per cent of the responses, which suggests that this element may have been somewhat overemphasized in recent writings on human relations in industry. Steadiness of work received very few mentions indeed. This is doubtless because full employment had prevailed throughout the area for six or seven years, so that unsteady work was not an immediate problem for many workers. It should be pointed out, to prevent misconceptions, that steadiness of work is somewhat different from security of employment. Security means having tenure on a job; steadiness means having an opportunity to work a full week's work on that job. Workers are very much concerned indeed with security. The desire for security, however, is something which causes the worker to cling to whatever job he may have; it is not a factor which he used in selecting among alternative jobs.

The workers interviewed made little mention of some of the things which have bulked large in the literature of personnel management, such as pensions, insurance plans, other types of "fringe payments," rest rooms and cafeterias, recreational programs, and other company welfare activities. This illustrates the dangers of the check list approach used in so many management studies of "employee morale."

The items included on the check list are bound to be selected in the light of existing preconceptions about worker motivation. The check list is a composite of management's hopes, fears, and guesses. Faced with such a list, the worker may go through all the motions of ranking the items in order. The results may nevertheless be spurious, because most of the items included may be of little significance to workers one way or the other. When workers are given an opportunity to volunteer their own ideas without any prompting, they may give little weight to many of the things which management has previously considered important.

There is bound to be a bias toward including on the check list items which management thinks it may be able to do something about. Much of the impetus for "morale surveys" has come from the hope that if management could only find out "what's on the worker's mind" it could then take remedial action to remove sources of dissatisfaction and ensure a contented labor force. This hope turns out to be in considerable measure illusory. Management cannot do very much—at least, in the short run—about the fact that certain jobs are heavy, dirty, dangerous, or otherwise unpleasant, or about the uninteresting or unsatisfying character of the job, or about the fact that many workers are unable to maintain what they regard as an adequate scale of living, which is the most prominent source of worker dissatisfaction with wage levels. It can do something about inequitable wage differentials within the plant; it can foster equity in job assignments, promotions, and other aspects of "fair treatment"; and it can do something to improve the quality of supervisors and of worker-supervisor relations, though one should not exaggerate the influence of higher management in this respect. On the whole, however, the determinants of job satisfaction which lie outside the immediate control of management appear to be at least as important as those within its control. If this is correct, it is wrong to conceive of management's problem as solely one of removing sources of job dissatisfaction. The more important part of the problem may be to offset or adapt to sources of dissatisfaction which, in the nature of the case, cannot be removed.

It is unnecessary to reemphasize the qualifications attaching to these general conclusions. The problems involved in obtaining reliable responses in a semiguided interview, and the efforts which were made to overcome these problems, are described in Appendix B. Apart from inaccuracies in the responses themselves and errors of judgment in

The items included on the check list are bound to be selected in the light of existing preconceptions about worker motivation. The check list is a composite of management's hopes, fears, and hunches. Faced with such a list, the worker may go through all the motions of ranking the items in order. The results may nevertheless be spurious, because most of the items included may be of little significance to workers one way or the other. When workers are given an opportunity to volunteer their own ideas without any prompting, they may give little weight to many of the things which management has previously considered important.

There is bound to be a bias toward including on the check list items which management thinks it may be able to do something about. Much of the impetus for "morale surveys" has come from the hope that if management could only find out "what's on the worker's mind" it could then take remedial action to remove sources of dissatisfaction and ensure a contented labor force. This hope turns out to be in considerable measure illusory. Management cannot do very much—at least, in the short run—about the fact that certain jobs are heavy, hot, dirty, dangerous, or otherwise unpleasant; or about the interesting or uninteresting character of the job; or about the fact that many workers are unable to maintain what they regard as an adequate scale of living, which is the most prominent source of worker dissatisfaction with wage levels. It can do something about inequitable wage differentials within the plant; it can foster equity in job assignments, promotions, and other aspects of "fair treatment"; and it can do something to improve the quality of supervisors and of worker-supervisor relations, though one should not exaggerate the influence of higher management in this respect. On the whole, however, the determinants of job satisfaction which lie outside the immediate control of management appear to be at least as important as those within its control. If this is correct, it is wrong to conceive of management's problem as solely one of *removing* sources of job dissatisfaction. The more important part of the problem may be to offset or adapt to sources of dissatisfaction which, in the nature of the case, cannot be removed.

It is necessary now to reemphasize the qualifications attaching to these general conclusions. The problems involved in obtaining reliable responses in a semiguided interview, and the efforts which were made to overcome these problems, are described in Appendix B. Apart from inaccuracies in the responses themselves and errors of judgment in

the coding process, the significance of the results is obviously limited by the time and place at which the study was made. The attitudes are those of a cross section of *employed manual workers* from a wide variety of *industries* and *occupations*, in a particular *locality*, at a time of very *high employment*, following after some seven years of high employment and rising wage levels. The answers obtained were conditioned also by the specific questions asked; different questions should not be expected to yield comparable results.

Two limitations of the technique used deserve special mention. First, there was no careful attempt to measure the *intensity* of the worker's feelings about each of the job characteristics which he mentioned. It was assumed for coding purposes that the amount which the worker had to say on each subject was a rough indicator of its importance to him, so that the three points on which he talked longest were normally the ones selected for tabulation. This is admittedly a crude procedure. It would be desirable, in a study oriented mainly at job attitudes,[14] to try to measure the intensity of these attitudes. This would yield, as it were, a three-dimensional picture of the components of job satisfaction, instead of the two-dimensional view given here.

Second, there was no systematic exploration of how far the worker's job attitudes were conditioned, not by characteristics of the job itself, but by the worker's own personality characteristics, intelligence level, family life, and other factors operating apart from the job. A worker's satisfaction on the job depends partly on his total personality adjustment to his environment; the job cannot be neatly separated from the remainder of his life. While we were not able to do any work in this direction, it would seem to be a promising field for psychological and sociological study.

When one considers what is already known about the intricacies of personal motivation, it may well be that statistical analysis of job satisfaction is both unwise and impracticable. Kornhauser, after a careful examination of employee attitude surveys, concludes that "valid practical conclusions in this field must be closely akin to clinical judgments regarding total individual personalities or to the balanced administrative decisions of social policy-makers. While

[14] It should be remembered that the primary orientation of our worker interviews was toward *mobility*—the work history of the individual, the circumstances of his recent job changes, and his methods of job-hunting. The questions on attitudes toward present and past jobs were a minor part of the questionnaire, and only a fraction of the total interview was allotted to them. A thorough exploration of job attitudes per se would require a lengthy interview in itself, perhaps even several interviews with each individual.

scientific procedures constitute useful leads and fragments of evidence which are valuable aids in reaching toward conclusions, this material must always be combined with various other types of information and insight if the conclusions are to become sound practical judgments."[16]

With all these limitations, the evidence does warrant a conclusion that the main criteria which workers use in evaluating a job are money income, the physical nature of the work, the degree of independence on the job and the agreeableness of supervision, the interesting or uninteresting character of the work, and the fairness with which the worker feels he has been treated by management. Moreover, a careful reading of the interviews suggests that one can reasonably assume a relation of substitution between money income and other elements in the job situation. Higher wage rates can serve as an offset to poor working conditions, irregular employment, disagreeable supervision, and so on. The relationship is perhaps not a continuous one, for the indications are that workers are not very sensitive to small variations in income. It seems justifiable, however, to apply indifference analysis to workers' job preferences.

The most reasonable hypothesis about the shape of the indifference functions is that, as matters stood in this area in 1948, the marginal rate of substitution of income for the other key variables was quite high. It would have required sizable increases in wage rates to compensate for a worsening of jobs in other respects. In this sense each of the other four variables was "important" relative to wage rates. This conclusion has implications for the estimation of labor supply functions based on wage rates alone, a problem to which we shall return in Chapter VIII.

Criteria of a Satisfactory Wage

The relation between wage differentials and job choices has played a central role in theoretical writings on the labor market. The theoretical and policy conclusions of Chapters XII–XIV will turn to a considerable extent on the nature and strength of this relation. For this reason a special effort was made to determine how workers decide whether a particular wage rate is good enough to warrant taking (or staying on) the job. Is this an absolute judgment, based solely on the income required to meet established living standards? Is it a comparative judgment, based on how the wage rate for this job compares with rates for other jobs? If the latter, what is the scope of the com-

[16] D. Ecum [illegible], pp. 218-219.

scientific procedures contribute useful hints and fragments of evidence which are valuable aids in reaching toward conclusions, this material must always be combined with various other types of information and insight if the conclusions are to become sound practical judgments."[15]

With all these limitations, the evidence does warrant a conclusion that the main criteria which workers use in evaluating a job are money income, the physical nature of the work, the degree of independence on the job and the agreeableness of supervision, the interesting or uninteresting character of the work, and the fairness with which the worker feels he has been treated by management. Moreover, a careful reading of the interviews suggests that one can reasonably assume a relation of substitution between money income and other elements in the job situation. Higher wage rates can serve as an offset to poor working conditions, irregular employment, disagreeable supervision, and so on. The relationship is perhaps not a continuous one, for the indications are that workers are not very sensitive to small variations in income. It seems justifiable, however, to apply indifference analysis to workers' job preferences.

The most reasonable hypothesis about the shape of the indifference functions is that, as matters stood in this area in 1947, the marginal rate of substitution of income for the other key variables was quite high. It would have required sizeable increases in wage rates to compensate for a worsening of jobs in other respects. In this sense, each of the other four variables was "important" relative to wage rates. This conclusion has implications for the usefulness of labor supply functions based on wage rates alone, a problem to which we shall return in Chapter VIII.

Criteria of a Satisfactory Wage

The relation between wage differentials and job choices has played a central role in theoretical writings on the labor market. The theoretical and policy conclusions of Chapters VIII–X will turn to a considerable extent on the nature and strength of this relation. For this reason a special effort was made to determine how workers decide whether a particular wage rate is good enough to warrant taking (or staying on) the job. Is this an absolute judgment, based solely on the income required to meet established living standards? Is it a comparative judgment, based on how the wage rate for this job compares with rates for other jobs? If the latter, what is the scope of the com-

[15] S. D. Hoslett, *op. cit.*, pp. 318–319.

parison? What other jobs does the worker look at in appraising the adequacy of his own wage?

Each person in Samples 1 and 2 was asked whether he regarded his present wage as fair or unfair, and why he held this opinion. A sizeable majority—70 per cent in Sample 1 and 75 per cent in Sample 2—said that they regarded their wage as fair; the remainder stated that it was unfair.

The fact that a worker regards his wage as fair does not necessarily mean that it is adequate for the standard of living to which he aspires, that he has "all the money he needs." On this matter, the workers in Sample 1 were asked: "How much (per week) do you think a family your size *should* have to live comfortably and without worry?" The answers were then compared with the actual weekly income of the family, including receipts from supplementary wage earners and other sources. The results confirm the tested economic truth that people's needs have a way of keeping ahead of their current incomes. Only 44 per cent of the Sample stated that their present income was adequate. The percentage satisfied with their income varied directly with size of income, rising from 26 per cent in the $30.—$40. per week bracket to 79 per cent of those making $80. or more per week. Among those who expressed a need for additional income the median increase desired was 27 per cent. The percentage increase needed varied inversely with income level, i.e., the higher the present income the lower the percentage increase required (Table A-14). In absolute terms, the size of increase desired remained rather steady at about $12.–$13. per week.

The proportion of workers regarding their wages as "fair" increases as one goes from lower to higher income levels (Table A-15). There seems also to be an appreciable difference between the attitudes of men and women workers. Thus, in Sample 1 79 per cent of the women stated that their wage was fair compared with only 66 per cent of the men, despite the fact that the average earnings of the women were much *lower* than those of the men (about $36. per week compared with $54. per week). The explanation is doubtless the lesser responsibility of women workers for the support of others. The great majority are either supplementary wage earners in a household with other employed members, or single women whose income requirements are considerably below those of family heads. There was no marked statistical relationship between the worker's satisfaction with his wage and skill level,

age, union membership, number of dependents,[16] or any other variable. The absence of any relationship with number of dependents is somewhat surprising. It may mean that a family's living standard adjusts itself over the course of time to the number of children, so that those with many children do not feel any worse off than those with few children. At any rate, if they do feel worse off, they apparently do not blame this on the employer by denouncing their wage as unfair.

The reasons which workers gave[17] for regarding their wage as fair or unfair are shown in Table 15.

TABLE 15
WORKERS' STANDARDS OF FAIR WAGES

Factor	Reasons for Regarding Wage as Unfair (%)		Reasons for Regarding Wage as Fair (%)	
	Sample 1	Sample 2	Sample 1	Sample 2
Cost of Maintaining an Adequate Standard of Living	35	30	15	30
Rates for Similar Work in Other Plants	10	27	27	27
Nature of the Work	35	21	23	21
Rates for Other Jobs in the Same Plant	6	6	8	6
Union Scale	2	2	5	2
Length of Service	1	2	4	2
Company's Ability to Pay	6	1	2	0
Others, and no Reason Given	5	11	16	12
Total	100	100	100	100

It will be noted that the cost-of-living element stands out prominently in the replies. It should be remembered in this connection that virtually all the interviewing was done during 1947. The weekly earnings of most workers at this time were below their peak wartime earnings because of a general reduction in the work week and the elimination of many remunerative wartime jobs. At the same time, price controls had been eliminated in the fall of 1946 and consumer

16 This relationship was tested by a three-way tabulation involving earnings, number of dependents, and "fairness" of wage. With income held constant, there was no clear relation between number of dependents and percentage of respondents regarding their wage as "fair."

17 The *two* most important elements in the worker's reply were coded and included in the tabulation. This table, therefore, like the tables relating to job satisfaction discussed earlier, gives a frequency distribution of *responses* rather than of *individuals.*

goods prices were rising rapidly. Most workers had thus experienced a drop in real weekly earnings, and this drop doubtless affected the replies to our interviews. A study conducted after a period of falling price levels and rising real incomes might reveal less concern with the cost-of-living factor.

Another frequent element in the responses was an attempt to appraise the fairness of the wage in terms of its relation to the *kind of work* done. In cases entered under the heading "nature of the work," the worker seemed to be expressing an absolute judgment that a certain kind of work is worth just about so much. In actuality, these judgments must rest on an implicit comparison with previous jobs held by the worker or with other jobs which he sees around him in the plant; but the basis of comparison was not made explicit. In explaining why a certain kind of work deserves a certain rate of pay, the job elements most heavily stressed by workers were: (1) the degree of physical effort required, tempo of work, or quantity of work accomplished during the day; (2) safety hazards and other working conditions; (3) degree of responsibility. The emphasis was on various sources of "disutility" in the job. The job evaluation systems used by management in setting relative wage rates, on the other hand, usually give heavy weight to such attributes as skill, education, experience, and training requirements. There seems to be considerable difference between management and worker criteria for "proper" ranking of jobs.

Where workers made an explicit comparison of their wage rates with those of other workers, the most common comparison was with workers in other firms or industries. These comparisons were quite imprecise. Workers' impression that another plant paid more or less than their own for comparable work were usually based on hearsay (and in some cases inaccurate) information. Comparisons tended to run in terms of weekly take-home rather than hourly earnings, with little attention to possible differences in the work week. Moreover, the type of work chosen for comparison was often not strictly comparable with the worker's own occupations. Railroad engineers compared their earnings with those of bricklakers, tool- and diemakers with plumbers, trolley operators with piece workers in manufacturing. In many of these cases one suspects that the worker was really dissatisfied with his wage because of living costs or for some other reason, and that the comparison with other occupations was simply a peg on which to hang his discontent.

Explicit comparisons with other jobs in the same plant were less frequent than interplant comparisons, averaging only about 6 per cent of all the replies received. This is apt to be misleading, however, for many of the cases classified under "nature of the work" probably involved implicit intraplant comparisons. If this is correct, intraplant comparisons may be more significant than one would judge from Table 15.

There was little mention of the company's ability to pay or similar abstract concepts, nor was much mention made of union scales for the work in question. The worker's judgment of the adequacy of his wage seems to rest on a limited and concrete basis, deriving mainly from the kind of work he does and the living needs of his family.

WORKERS' DECISIONS ABOUT JOBS: THE PROCESS OF CHOICE

Having considered the background of general attitudes and beliefs with which workers approach the labor market and the criteria which they use in deciding whether a particular job is satisfactory or unsatisfactory, we may proceed to examine how jobs are actually chosen. We shall consider in turn the question of what workers are in the market for jobs at a particular time, the ways in which they learn about job vacancies, and the extent to which they "shop around" and make careful comparison before accepting a particular job.

Who Is In The Market?

Discussions of labor supply usually imply that all workers in an area are "in the market" in the sense of being potentially available to any employer in the area who offers sufficiently good terms. The differences among them which give the supply curve of labor to the firm its upward slope are regarded as mainly differences in their evaluation of different sets of job conditions, differences in knowledge of job opportunities, and perhaps differences in willingness to undertake the risks of a change in employment.

In addition to these differences, however, one must recognize the importance of differences in employment status. As a minimum, one should distinguish (a) employed workers who are satisfied with their present jobs; (b) employed workers who are dissatisfied with their jobs; (c) unemployed workers on temporary layoff or part-time work; (d) unemployed workers who have quit their jobs, who have been permanently laid off or discharged, or who are entering employment

Explicit comparisons with other jobs *in the same* plant were less frequent than interplant comparisons, averaging only about 6 per cent of all the replies received. This is apt to be misleading, however, for many of the cases classified under "nature of the work" probably involved implicit intraplant comparisons. If this is correct, intraplant comparisons may be more significant than one would judge from Table 15.

There was little mention of the company's ability to pay or similar abstract concepts; nor was much mention made of union scales for the work in question. The worker's judgment of the adequacy of his wage seems to rest on a limited and concrete basis, deriving mainly from the kind of work he does and the living needs of his family.

WORKERS' DECISIONS ABOUT JOBS: THE PROCESS OF CHOICE

Having considered the background of general attitudes and beliefs with which workers approach the labor market, and the criteria which they use in deciding whether a particular job is satisfactory or unsatisfactory, we may proceed to examine how jobs are actually chosen. We shall consider in turn the question of what workers are in the market for jobs at a particular time, the ways in which they learn about job vacancies, and the extent to which they "shop the market" and make careful comparison before accepting a particular job.

Who Is In The Market?

Discussions of labor supply usually imply that all workers in an area are "in the market" in the sense of being potentially available to any employer in the area who offers sufficiently good terms. The differences among them, which give the supply curve of labor to the firm its upward slope, are regarded as mainly differences in their evaluation of different sets of job conditions, differences in knowledge of job opportunities, and perhaps differences in willingness to undertake the risks of a change in employment.

In addition to these differences, however, one must recognize the importance of differences in *employment status*. As a minimum, one should distinguish (a) employed workers who are satisfied with their present jobs; (b) employed workers who are dissatisfied with their jobs; (c) unemployed workers on temporary layoff or part-time work; (d) unemployed workers who have quit their jobs, who have been permanently laid off or discharged, or who are entering employment

for the first time. The effective labor supply at a particular time consists mainly of people in group d. To a more limited extent, it includes people in groups b and c. It does not include those in group a, who at most times are the large majority of the gainfully employed.

It may be argued that even those in group a are available *at a price;* if they are not willing to change employers, this means only that the price has not been pushed high enough. Such an argument, while formally correct, has little relevance to reality. In order to induce a satisfied worker to shift to another plant it would usually be necessary to offer him a substantial increase in earnings (that is, an increase of the order of 25 to 50 per cent), in order to offset accumulated seniority and other vested rights in his present job. Moreover, the job would have to seek the man rather than vice versa; for one of the clearest findings of our study is that satisfactorily employed workers have little interest in or knowledge of vacancies in other enterprises. The employer needing labor would have to take the initiative in locating a suitable worker, give him definite assurance of employment, and induce him to leave his present (satisfactory) job by the promise of substantial advantages. Now this is just the kind of behavior one does *not* find among employers in the area. It would constitute "labor piracy" of the grossest sort, would be condemned immediately by other employers, and would probably turn out to be bad business for the employer attempting it.

The relative unimportance of satisfied workers as a source of labor supply is indicated by the data from Sample 1. It will be recalled that only 14 per cent of the sample had changed jobs voluntarily between August, 1945, and the date of interview (early 1947). Only 15 per cent of the voluntary changers, (i.e., approximately 2 per cent of the entire sample) said that they had left a satisfactory job in order to take a better one. Deliberate movement from good to better jobs thus appears to be rare, even during periods of high employment.

Twelve per cent of the workers in Sample 1, and 22 per cent of those in Sample 2, said that they were dissatisfied with their present jobs and did not expect to stay with them indefinitely. It would appear that we have here a large shiftable group capable of bringing about the marginal adjustments contemplated in economic theory. It should be remembered, however, that we have no measure of the intensity of feeling behind these statements. We do not know what proportion of the group were dissatisfied *enough* to make them take an active interest in other opportunities. It is significant, however, that of those who

said they were dissatisfied with their present jobs only 18 per cent in Sample 1 and 23 per cent in Sample 2 said that they had taken any steps to locate a new job. The great majority were apparently content to wait around until something better showed up. As one man commented: "No sir, I don't like this job, and I'd leave it, if something breaks for me." The prevalence of this attitude leads one to suspect that much of the alleged dissatisfaction was not very deep-seated.

This suspicion is confirmed by examining the subsequent behavior of these individuals. A check of the most recent City Directory[16] reveals that, of those who said in 1947 that they were dissatisfied with their present jobs and were looking around for something else, 35 per cent had moved to a different company by the latter date. Of those who said they were dissatisfied but were not looking around for a new job, only 20 per cent had changed employers. Of those who said they were satisfied with their jobs, 20 per cent had moved by the fall of 1949.[17]

The evidence suggests that serious dissatisfaction, i.e., dissatisfaction to the point of quitting the job and taking the risks of new employment, was less prevalent than one might have concluded from statements made in the interviews. It suggests also that even genuine dissatisfaction does not typically lead to an active search for new employment. Some four-fifths of the (reportedly) dissatisfied workers in our samples were not looking actively for new jobs. This is due partly to the fact that employers do not carry on active recruiting among employed workers. It is also difficult for a worker who still has a job to absent himself from work in order to canvass opportunities in other plants. The best he can do is to pass the word out among friends and acquaintances that he is interested in a change and hope that he may get some leads in this way.

Unless a vacancy happens to turn up, the worker eventually has to decide whether to swallow his dissatisfaction or to quit and take

[16] The 1949 Directory, listings for which were taken in August 1948.

[17] These figures are not so informative as one would wish, since it is not possible to tell from the Directory listings alone whether the change of employers was voluntary or involuntary. A reasonable hypothesis would be that most of the moves by dissatisfied workers were voluntary, while most of those by satisfied workers were involuntary. Without information on this point, however, one can go no further than to note that these interviews do not provide a very firm basis for predicting the future behavior of the workers involved. One can say only that those who claimed to be satisfied were least likely to move, those who were dissatisfied but not looking around were more likely to move, and those who were dissatisfied and also looking around were most likely to change employers in the near future.

said they were dissatisfied with their present jobs only 18 per cent in Sample 1 and 23 per cent in Sample 2 said that they had taken any steps to locate a new job. The great majority were apparently content to wait around until something better showed up. As one man commented, "No sir, I don't like this job, and I'll leave it *as soon as something breaks for me.*" The prevalence of this attitude leads one to suspect that much of the alleged dissatisfaction was not very deep-seated.

This suspicion is confirmed by examining the subsequent behavior of these individuals. A check of the most recent City Directory[18] reveals that, of those who said in 1947 that they were dissatisfied with their present jobs and were looking around for something else, only 57 per cent had moved to a different company by the fall of 1948. Of those who said they were dissatisfied but were not looking around for a new job, only 40 per cent had changed employers. Of those who said they were satisfied with their jobs, 26 per cent had moved by the fall of 1948.[19]

The evidence suggests that serious dissatisfaction, i.e., dissatisfaction to the point of quitting the job and taking the risks of new employment, was less prevalent than one might have judged from the statements made in our interviews. It suggests also that even genuine dissatisfaction does not typically lead to an active search for new employment. Some four-fifths of the (reportedly) dissatisfied workers in our samples were not looking actively for new jobs. This is due partly to the fact that employers do not carry on active recruiting among employed workers. It is also difficult for a worker who still has a job to absent himself from work in order to canvass opportunities in other plants. The best he can do is to pass the word out among friends and acquaintances that he is interested in a change, and hope that he may get some leads in this way.

Unless a vacancy happens to turn up, the worker eventually has to decide whether to swallow his dissatisfaction or to quit and take

[18] The 1949 Directory, listings for which were taken in August, 1948

[19] These figures are not as informative as one would wish, for it is not possible to tell from the Directory listings alone whether the change of employers was voluntary or involuntary. A reasonable hypothesis would be that most of the moves by dissatisfied workers were voluntary, while most of those by satisfied workers were involuntary. Even without information on this point, however, one can conclude that the replies to our interviews did not provide a very firm basis for predicting the future behavior of the workers involved. One can say only that those who claimed to be satisfied were least likely to move, those who were dissatisfied but not looking around were more likely to move, and those who were dissatisfied and also looking around were most likely to change employers in the near future.

his chances of finding another job. The choice is doubtless affected both by the temperament of the individual and by the general level of employment at the time. Low employment will weight the scales in favor of sticking with his present job, while high employment and numerous vacancies will incline the worker to "take a chance." In any event, the typical sequence of events is from an unsatisfactory job to unemployment to a new job, rather than directly from one job to another. Of those in Sample 1 who had left their previous job voluntarily, 60 per cent said that they had quit before they had a new job in sight, while 40 per cent had the new job lined up before they quit. The corresponding figures for Sample 2 were 67 per cent and 33 per cent.

Turning to the unemployed, it must be noted that in periods of active business a large proportion of all unemployment results from layoffs which both the employer and the workers expect will be only temporary. In some industries such layoffs are regular and customary. Thus workers laid off from a garment factory during the slack season do not become available to other employers, but simply wait to be recalled to their regular job. Even workers on indefinite layoff tend to wait and hope for recall by their previous employer. A majority of the unemployed in Sample 3, who were interviewed during a period of moderate business recession, were on indefinite layoff and had been given no assurance of reemployment. Almost every member of this group, however, said that he wanted to return to his former employer, and two-thirds said that they actually expected to be recalled.

The worker's expectation of recall seems to depend mainly on his seniority standing and on the severity of the layoff. Typical comments among the group who expected recall were: "My chances are good. The layoff only went up to seven years, and I've got six and a half"; and, "Sure, I'm all right—I've got ten years' service out there." Those who thought their chances were poor tended to stress low seniority: "I don't think I'll get back. They laid off 160 out of 200 toolmakers, and I've only been there a year"; and, "Things don't look good; I've only got four years seniority and there are fifty men ahead of me."

People with substantial seniority will usually wait around for some months without making an active search for work elsewhere. They are frequently encouraged to do this by foremen and others in the plant. Out of kindness and out of a practical desire to have good workers available when they are needed, the foreman will say "Sure, Jim, things will probably pick up after a while and I'll let you know first

thing—get what you lack." This strengthens the worker's regular orientation toward his old job. The unemployment compensation system also enables people to hold off the market for a while. The system, for reasons noted in Chapter III, does not put severe pressure on people to take new jobs. Even if the worker should be referred to a job by the Employment Service, he can usually talk his way out of it if he wants to.[20]

One may ask why laid-off workers do not seek temporary work during the period in which they are awaiting recall. There are at least three reasons for not doing this. First, it would require deception of prospective employers; few employers would hire a man if they knew that he might stay with them for only a few weeks or months. Second, it might reduce the worker's chances of recall to his previous job; he fears that if he does not show up fairly frequently at the old plant, or that if the employer hears that he is "taken care of" in another job, he may not be called back when the time comes. Third, with a system of unemployment compensation, there may be little financial advantage in taking a new job. It may be better to piece out the compensation payments with odd jobs which, though they should legally be reported, are rarely reported in practice and cannot be checked on effectively.

The result is that a recession of six to twelve months does not produce much immediate increase in effective labor supply. A prolonged depression, of course, would gradually force more and more people into the market as their resources became exhausted, their benefit rights under unemployment compensation expired, and their hope of recall to their previous job declined.

The core of the effective labor supply at any time, then, may consist of unemployed workers without a regular job attachment. This means primarily people who are entering the market for the first time, who have been discharged, who have quit their previous jobs because of dissatisfaction, or who have been unemployed long enough for their benefit rights to be exhausted. To this must be added some laid-off workers who have little hope of recall to their previous jobs, and also some dissatisfied workers who are looking around for new jobs while still employed. The size of this fluid pool is difficult to estimate. Judg-

[20] This does not necessarily mean unwillingness to work. The worker's desire to maintain an established connection with a previous employer may be quite rational from the worker's standpoint and may be valuable also from the employer's standpoint. The conditions under which it is and is not desirable to encourage unemployed workers to hold off the market will be examined in Chapter III.

thing—we want you back." This strengthens the worker's natural orientation toward his old job. The unemployment compensation system also enables people to hold off the market for a while. The system, for reasons noted in Chapter III, does not put severe pressure on people to take new jobs. Even if the worker should be referred to a job by the Employment Service, he can usually "talk his way out of it" if he wants to.[20]

One may ask why laid-off workers do not seek temporary work during the period in which they are awaiting recall. There are at least three reasons for not doing this. First, it would require deception of prospective employers; few employers would hire a man if they knew that he might stay with them for only a few weeks or months. Second, it might reduce the worker's chances of recall to his previous job; he fears that if he does not show up fairly frequently at the old plant, or that if the employer hears that he is "taken care of" in another job, he may not be called back when the time comes. Third, with a system of unemployment compensation, there may be little financial advantage in taking a new job. It may be better to piece out the compensation payments with odd jobs which, while they should legally be reported, are rarely reported in practice and cannot be checked on effectively.

The result is that a recession of six to twelve months does not produce much immediate increase in effective labor supply. Prolonged depression, of course, would gradually force more and more people into the market as their resources became exhausted, their benefit rights under unemployment compensation expired, and their hope of recall to their previous job declined.

The core of the effective labor supply at any time, therefore, consists of unemployed workers without a regular job attachment. This means primarily people who are entering the market for the first time, who have been discharged, who have quit their previous jobs because of dissatisfaction, or who have been unemployed long enough for their benefit rights to be exhausted. To this must be added some laid-off workers who have little hope of recall to their previous jobs; and also some dissatisfied workers who are looking around for new jobs while still employed. The size of this fluid pool is difficult to estimate. During

[20] This does not necessarily mean "unwillingness to work." It may simply indicate a desire to maintain an established connection with a previous employer. This is quite rational from the worker's standpoint, and may be desirable also from the employer's standpoint. The conditions under which it is and is not desirable to encourage unemployed workers to hold off the market will be examined in Chapter X.

1946–48, however, it probably did not exceed 10 per cent of the manual workers in this area.

Methods of Learning About Jobs

We must next inquire how workers who are in the market learn about job openings. The members of Samples 1 and 2 were asked how they had located their present jobs. The replies are classified in Table 16. The members of Sample 1 were also asked a general question on this point: "Supposing you were out of a job, how would you go about finding another?" The replies to this question showed marked consistency[21] with the actual behavior reported in Table 16.

TABLE 16

Method of Learning about Present Job

Method	Sample 1 (%)	Sample 2 (%)
Acquaintances or Relatives: Working in Plant	24	24
Acquaintances or Relatives: Not Working in Plant	4	3
Direct Application at Plant	20	42
Returning to Plant Where He had Previously Worked	13	8
State Employment Service	13	13
Advertisement	13	5
Union	5	1
Other	8	4
Total	100	100

It is apparent that there are some differences between the behavior of manufacturing workers (Sample 2), and manual workers in general (Sample 1). The manufacturing workers make more use of direct application, and less use of advertisements and of the union. For both groups, however, the two commonest ways of learning about new jobs are through "tips" from friends and relatives and through direct application at a plant.

It is interesting to inquire what sort of selection among available vacancies is involved in the use of these various channels of information. The tips received from friends and relatives normally concern jobs in the plants where these people are employed. To the extent that a worker relies on this channel, therefore, his view of labor demand in the area depends on his network of personal relationships and on where

[21] The replies were distributed as follows: acquaintances or relatives, 34 per cent; direct application, 18 per cent; return to plant where he had previously worked, 15 per cent; State Employment Service, 11 per cent; advertisements, 11 per cent; union, 7 per cent; and others, 4 per cent.

1940–50, however, it probably did not exceed 10 per cent of the manual workers in this area.

METHODS OF LEARNING ABOUT JOBS

We must next inquire how workers who are in the market learn about job openings. The members of Samples I and II were asked how they had located their present jobs. The replies are classified in Table 16. The members of Sample I were also asked a general question on this point: "Supposing you were out of a job, how would you go about finding another?" The replies to this question showed marked consistency with the actual behavior reported in Table 16.[6]

TABLE 16
METHOD OF LEARNING ABOUT PRESENT JOB

Method	Sample I (1949)	Sample II (1951)
Acquaintances or Relatives Working in Plant	24	21
Acquaintances or Relatives not Working in Plant	4	5
Direct Application at Plant	30	47
Returning to Plant Where He had Previously Worked	18	4
State Employment Service	[illegible]	13
Advertisement	[illegible]	3
Union	[illegible]	1
Other	8	
Total	100	100

It is apparent that there are some differences between the behavior of manufacturing workers (Sample II) and manual workers in general (Sample I). The manufacturing workers make more use of direct application, and less use of advertisements and of the union. For both groups, however, the two commonest ways of learning about new jobs are through "tips" from friends and relatives and through direct application at a plant.

It is interesting to inquire what sort of selection among available vacancies is involved in the use of these various channels of information. The tips received from friends and relatives normally concern jobs in the plants where these people are employed. To the extent that a worker relies on this channel, therefore, his view of labor demand in the area depends on an intricate network of personal relationships and on a great

[6] The replies were distributed: friends, acquaintances or relatives, 25 per cent; direct application, 35 per cent; [illegible] 17 per cent; [illegible]

his friends happen to be working. This network should be regarded as including also former employers, since it appears from Table 40 that workers frequently go back to a plant where they had been satisfactorily employed at some earlier time. Direct application at plant employment offices involves selective factors of a different sort. There is a definite tendency for workers to apply at plants close to their homes before trying those farther away. There is a tendency also to gravitate to the largest plants in the area, partly because most people know these plants, partly because of a feeling that there will be more vacancies in a larger establishment. There is also a tendency, more marked in some industries than in others, to apply at plants in the same industry as one's last job.

Direct application does not necessarily involve systematic choice. In many cases the selection appears to be almost completely haphazard. The worker happens to be going across town or walking along a certain street, sees a "help wanted" sign, and applies for work on the spur of the moment. Even where there is premeditation, it is not of the sort which one might expect from economic reasoning. The worker does not try to array the plants in the area either in terms of wage level or of total job attractiveness and then go down the list from top to bottom. The data which would be needed to do this are not available to him, for the reasons described in Chapter III.

Use of the State Employment Service, and of "help wanted" advertisements in newspapers, would make for a more systematic selection of places at which to apply for work. It is apparent from Table 40, however, that these channels play only a restricted role in the labor market. The channels on which workers predominantly rely make for fragmentary knowledge and an (economically) haphazard selection of places at which to apply. It should be emphasized once more that this pattern of behavior is not due mainly to a lack of rationality or self-interest among manual workers. It stems rather from objective circumstances beyond the control of the individual worker, notably employer hiring practices. So long as employers prefer to do their own screening of applicants, and so long as they believe in the efficacy of recruiting new workers via their present employees, workers can scarcely do anything but accommodate themselves to these practices.

Comparison and Deliberation in Job Choices

Even though workers learn about jobs in a haphazard way, it is conceivable that they might offset this by waiting until they had discovered several vacancies and then selecting the one which looked

his friends happen to be working. This network should be regarded as including also former employers, since it appears from Table 16 that workers frequently go back to a plant where they had been satisfactorily employed at some earlier time. Direct application at plant employment offices involves selective factors of a different sort. There is a definite tendency for workers to apply at plants close to their homes before trying those farther away. There is a tendency to go first to the largest plants in the area, partly because most people know their names, partly because of a feeling that there will be more vacancies in a larger establishment. There is also a tendency, more marked in some industries than in others, to apply at plants in the same industry as one's last job.

Direct application does not necessarily involve systematic choice. In many cases the selection appears to be almost completely haphazard. The worker happens to be riding around town or walking along a certain street, sees a "help wanted" sign, and applies for work on the spur of the moment. Even where there is premeditation, it is not of the sort which one might expect from economic reasoning. The worker does not try to array the plants in the area, either in terms of wage level or of total job attractiveness, and then go down the list from top to bottom. The data which would be needed to do this are not available to him, for the reasons described in Chapter III.

Use of the State Employment Service, and of "help wanted" advertisements in newspapers, would make for a more systematic selection of places at which to apply for work. It is apparent from Table 16, however, that these channels play only a restricted role in the labor market. The channels on which workers predominantly rely make for fragmentary knowledge and an (economically) haphazard selection of places at which to apply. It should be emphasized once more that this pattern of behavior is not due mainly to a lack of rationality or self-interest among manual workers. It stems rather from objective circumstances beyond the control of the individual worker, notably employer hiring practices. So long as employers prefer to do their own screening of applicants, and so long as they believe in the efficacy of recruiting new workers via their present employees, workers can scarcely do anything but accommodate themselves to these practices.

Comparison and Deliberation in Job Choices

Even though workers learn about jobs in a haphazard way, it is conceivable that they might offset this by waiting until they had discovered several vacancies, and then selecting the one which looked

most promising. In order to explore this matter, all workers in our samples who had changed jobs recently were asked whether they had had any offers apart from the one they took and, if so, why they chose their present job. Sixty-three per cent of the job-changers in Sample 1, and 68 per cent of those in Sample 2, said that they took the first job they found. The remainder said that they had had one or more offers in addition to the one they took.

These data do not mean quite what may appear on the surface. It might be thought that we have here two different types of workers: planful, rational individuals who realize the necessity of careful shopping and job selection; and impetuous or short-sighted people who wander into any job available at the moment. The results do not actually imply any such distinction. The workers who said that they took the first job they found clearly did not mean that they were willing to take *anything* which came along. The situation was rather that the first job they found struck them as reasonably satisfactory. The workers who said they had had more than one offer rarely meant that they had passed by a *suitable* job in the hope of finding a better one. Rather, the first job or jobs offered to them did not meet their minimum standards, and so they kept on looking until they found one which did. In both groups, therefore, the dominant pattern was the same, to take the first *suitable* job offered. Job shopping, in the sense of holding off on a suitable job while one tries to locate other suitable jobs and select among them, seems to be very rare indeed.[22]

The reasons for the virtual absence of job shopping are not at all obscure. A major reason is that personnel managers are unwilling to hold a job open while the worker canvasses other possibilities. When they offer a man a job, they expect it to be accepted or refused at once. If the worker says "Well, I'll think about it," this is treated as a refusal and the personnel man continues his search. Only if labor is very scarce, and if the worker has specialized skills or other unusual qualifications, will the employer be willing to wait on his convenience.

The other important factor is that the worker himself does not want to carry on a protracted search for work. He is usually in fairly immediate need of funds, and the sooner he takes a job the better. He is convinced, for reasons already pointed out, that good jobs are scarce and that it is tempting fortune to reject a suitable vacancy.

[22] Only a handful of such cases were found among all the workers in both samples. These were workers of unusual ambition and drive who, because of specialized trade skills and the high level of labor demand, were in a strong bargaining position and able to make prospective employers wait while they made up their mind.

He has little conception of the full array of job opportunities available in the area, nor do his infrequent changes of employer enable him to develop much experience in job-hunting. When one adds to this the intrinsic difficulty of "window shopping" for jobs, and the fact that many of the most important features of a job cannot be appraised until one has worked on it, the absence of job shopping is entirely understandable.

If an unemployed worker typically takes the first suitable job he finds, it is important to determine what criteria he uses in deciding whether a job is suitable. Some evidence on this point is provided by the statements of the workers who had had more than one job offer as to why they took their present job rather than something else. Ninety per cent of the Sample 1 workers in this category, and 85 per cent of those in Sample 2, said that their decision was based on one or both of the following factors: Probable weekly take-home pay (a very rough estimate in many cases), and the general nature of the work. The heavy reliance on these two factors does not mean, of course, that they are the only things which workers consider important. It means rather that they are the only things which can be ascertained with any certainty before one has actually worked on the job, and they therefore constitute the only feasible bases for selection.

Interviews with the unemployed workers who constituted Sample 3 brought out additional information on the minimum supply-price of the unemployed. This is a matter of great importance, for, since employers recruit almost entirely from the unemployed, it is the minimum wage demanded by this group which sets a bottom to the wage structure of the area.

Each of the workers in Sample 3 was asked what was the lowest wage for which he would be willing to work. The answers to this question were in most cases frank and well considered. The determinant factors appeared to be: (1) The worker's earnings on his last previous job. In general, the higher the worker's previous earnings, the higher was his conception of an acceptable wage. For the group as a whole, the minimum acceptable wage averaged [illegible] per cent of earnings on the last previous job. (2) The period of unemployment. When the ratio of the minimum acceptable wage to the last previous wage was tabulated against length of unemployment, a strong inverse relation appeared. For people unemployed less than three months, the median expected wage was [illegible] per cent of the last previous wage. For people unemployed three to six months, this figure dropped to 90 per cent, and those un-

He has little conception of the full array of job opportunities available in the area, nor do his infrequent changes of employer enable him to develop much experience in job hunting. When one adds to this the intrinsic difficulty of "window shopping for jobs," the fact that many of the most important features of a job cannot be appraised until one has worked on it, the absence of job shopping is entirely understandable.

If an unemployed worker typically takes the first suitable job he finds, it is important to determine what criteria he uses in deciding whether a job is suitable. Some evidence on this point is provided by the statements of the workers who had had more than one job offer as to why they took their present job rather than something else. Ninety per cent of the Sample 1 workers in this category, and 85 per cent of those in Sample 2, said that their decision was based on one or both of the following factors: Probable weekly take-home pay (a very rough estimate in many cases), and the general nature of the work. The heavy reliance on these two factors does not mean, of course, that they are the only things which workers consider important. It means rather that they are the only things which can be ascertained with any certainty before one has actually worked on the job, and they therefore constitute the only feasible bases for selection.

Interviews with the unemployed workers who constituted Sample 3 brought out additional information on the minimum supply-price of the unemployed. This is a matter of great importance for, since employers recruit almost entirely from the unemployed, it is the minimum wage demanded by this group which sets a bottom to the wage structure of the area.

Each of the workers in Sample 3 was asked what was the lowest wage for which he would be willing to work. The answers to this question were in most cases frank and well considered. The dominant factors appeared to be: (1) The worker's earnings on his last previous job. In general, the higher the worker's previous earnings, the higher was his conception of an acceptable wage. For the group as a whole, the minimum acceptable wage averaged 85 per cent of earnings on the last previous job. (2) The period of unemployment. When the ratio of the minimum acceptable wage to the last previous wage was tabulated against length of unemployment, a strong inverse relation appeared. For people unemployed less than three months, the median expected wage was 90 per cent of the last previous wage. For people unemployed three to six months, this figure dropped to 60 per cent; and those un-

employed six months or longer were willing, on the average, to work for only 50 per cent of their last previous wage. (3) For workers drawing unemployment compensation (about three-quarters of the group in question), the level of benefit payments seems clearly to influence the minimum supply-price. The people interviewed had made quite precise calculations on this point. Suppose one is offered a job paying $40. a week. From this one must deduct income tax, social security contributions, possibly union dues, carfare, lunches, possibly extra work clothing, and other expenses. The net is perhaps $35. per week. A worker with three dependents and an adequate level of past earnings can draw $36. per week in unemployment compensation, and this can be eked out from part-time work and other sources. The conclusion is that it does not pay to take the job. At the time of this study, the effect of unemployment compensation was to establish a minimum supply-price of something like $1.00 per hour for the short-term unemployed covered by the system. About one-third of those interviewed stated that they had turned down job offers because the prospective earnings compared unfavorably with compensation payments as well as with their own previous earnings.

Discussion with these workers revealed several other interesting things about their wage expectations. Their responses tended to run in terms of weekly income rather than hourly rates. Many said immediately, "Well, I guess we could get by on about $——— a week." A number said explicitly that in order to earn the desired weekly amount they would be willing to work forty-eight hours or more per week.

The minimum wage demanded was also clearly related to the type of work in question. Workers frequently said that they would take one rate on light work, but would expect more for heavy work; or that they would take a certain rate on a day-rated job, but should average more on piece work; or that they would start at a lower rate on a job with a future, and take their chances of working up. Skilled men sometimes gave one minimum for work at their trade and a lower rate for other types of work. One man for example, said that his trade should pay $1.50 per hour. Rather than debase the trade by working for less, he would take semiskilled work at $1.10 to $1.20 per hour.

The wage expectations of the unemployed worker are thus determined in a rather complex way, being influenced by the type of work, previous earnings, length of unemployment, and (as a minimum) the level of unemployment compensation or relief payments. The implica-

tions of these findings for labor supply concepts will be developed in Chapter VIII.

The typical pattern of behavior in choosing jobs may be summarized briefly as follows: the worker seeks word of vacancies from friends and relatives, and by dropping into the employment offices of a few companies. He also registers at the State Employment Service, but does not usually rely mainly on the Service to find him a job. As soon as he finds a job which meets his minimum standards as regards income and type of work, he takes it. This is a tentative decision; the worker takes the job "on probation," just as the employer employs the worker on probation for a certain period. After he has worked at the job for a few months, he is able to tell whether it meets his original expectations concerning income and type of work, and also how it measures up as regards supervision, fellow employees, chance for advancement, and other factors which could not be gauged in advance. If it measures up to his standards of a satisfactory job on all counts, he gradually makes a firmer mental commitment to stay with it. If it does not measure up, he begins to cast around for other possibilities in the way described earlier, and perhaps eventually quits the job and starts looking again.

It is this process which accounts for a large proportion of the voluntary quits among short-service employees. Some of the voluntary turnover is due to personal instability of individual workers, some is due to faulty selection and assignment to work by employers, and some to other managerial inadequacies which could be corrected with sufficient effort. A large part of it, however, is unavoidable in a situation where individual capacities and tastes have to be matched with job characteristics by a process of experiment. It follows that absence of voluntary turnover is a sign of economic ill-health rather than the reverse. It indicates that the general demand for labor is so low that workers who have made a mistake in choice must nevertheless stay with the job because they dare not quit. At the other extreme, voluntary turnover can clearly be greater than is necessary or desirable. Somewhere between these extremes there is an optimum rate of turnover which permits workers adequate scope to correct their undesirable situations. This optimum rate is primarily a function of the worker's ability to make an accurate appraisal of jobs before taking them, and of the employer's ability to make an accurate estimate of the worker's probable performance on the job.

tions of these findings for labor supply concepts will be developed in Chapter VIII.

The typical pattern of behavior in choosing jobs may be summarized briefly as follows: the worker seeks word of vacancies from friends and relatives, and by dropping into the employment offices of a few companies. He also registers at the State Employment Service, but does not usually rely mainly on the Service to find him a job. As soon as he finds a job which meets his minimum standards as regards income and type of work, he takes it. This is a tentative decision; the worker takes the job "on probation," just as the employer considers the worker on probation for a certain period. After he has worked at the job for a few months, he is able to tell whether it meets his original expectations concerning income and type of work, and also how it measures up as regards supervision, fellow employees, chance for advancement, and other factors which could not be gauged in advance. If it measures up to his standards of a satisfactory job on all counts, he gradually makes a firmer mental commitment to stay with it. If it does not measure up, he begins to cast around for other possibilities in the way described earlier, and perhaps eventually quits the job and starts looking again.

It is this process which accounts for a large proportion of the voluntary quits among short-service employees. Some of the voluntary turnover is due to personal instability of individual workers, some is due to faulty selection and assignment to work by employers, and some to other managerial inadequacies which could be corrected with sufficient effort. A large part of it, however, is unavoidable in a situation where individual capacities and tastes have to be matched with job characteristics by a process of experiment. It follows that absence of voluntary turnover is a sign of economic ill-health rather than the reverse. It indicates that the general demand for labor is so low that workers who have made a mistaken choice must nevertheless stay with the job because they dare not quit. At the other extreme, voluntary turnover can clearly be greater than is necessary or desirable. Somewhere between these extremes there is an optimum rate of turnover which permits workers adequate scope to retreat from undesirable situations. This optimum rate is primarily a function of the worker's ability to make an accurate appraisal of jobs before taking them, and of the employer's ability to make an accurate estimate of the worker's probable performance on the job.

The function of voluntary mobility is thus different from that sometimes attributed to it. There is a tendency to think that, while layoff and discharge connote personal disaster, voluntary quitting connotes deliberate and planned movement to a better opportunity. Voluntary movement does sometimes have this character—witness the 2 per cent of those in Sample 1 who had moved from a satisfactory job to a still better one. In the majority of cases, however, it indicates that the worker has made an error of judgment from which he is obliged to back away and start over again. It is, therefore, something to be minimized rather than maximized. While voluntary movement should be up to the optimum level defined above, this level should itself be as low as possible.

CHAPTER V Occupational Movement

THE movement of workers from one employer to another, analyzed in the last two chapters, may or may not involve a change of occupational status for the workers involved. Moreover, a worker may gain or lose in occupational status without changing employers, through the processes of promotion and demotion within the plant. For the individual, occupational movement is closely identified with personal progress or retrogression. For the economy, it is important that individuals be selected into those occupations in which they make the greatest productive contribution.

The intrinsic importance of occupational movement necessitates a separate chapter on this subject. In the first part of the chapter we shall consider the factors influencing initial choice of occupations—the way in which youngsters get started on one occupational level rather than another. In the latter part of the chapter we shall examine the factors which influence a worker's occupational progress in later life.

ENTRANCE TO THE LABOR MARKET

The way in which a free, informed, and rational individual would choose his occupation was sketched succinctly by Adam Smith, and his analysis has been transmitted with little change through Mill, Marshall, Taussig, and other writers to the present day. At a later date, Cairnes and other writers pointed out that young people may be prevented by economic and social barriers from choosing their careers in this way, and developed theories of "noncompeting groups" or economic classes. The question of how occupational choices are actually made in the United States at present is clearly of great political and social importance; yet there has been remarkably little empirical study of the matter.

The scope of this study limits us to a portion of the subject. We cannot say very much, for example, about the extent to which children of manual workers are able to rise into the professional and mana-

gerial ranks. In order to study this question, one would have to take a cross section of the entire gainfully employed population, examine the origins of the people on different occupational levels, and trace the channels by which they have reached their present positions. Since our samples include only people currently engaged in manual labor, we are limited largely to an examination of mobility within the manual occupations. It will turn out as we proceed, however, that there is considerable scope for occupational progress within the working-class world, and that workers are mainly concerned with this possibility of limited upward movement.

Origins of the Manual Labor Force

More than four-fifths of the people in both of our samples started work in manual occupations. Sixteen per cent of those in Sample 1 and 17 per cent of Sample 2 started out in jobs classified as "clerical and sales"; but most of these were low-grade jobs such as running errands for the corner grocery, and should be ranked below factory production jobs in both skill and earnings. The number who started in professional and managerial occupations was negligible. There does not seem, therefore, to be any marked downward drift into manual labor of people who started out on a higher occupational level.

Taussig and Joslyn discovered[1] that there is a strong tendency for business leaders to be sons of business or professional parents. Is there likewise a tendency for manual workers to be descended from manual workers? The evidence seems to be in the affirmative. Eighty per cent of the people in both samples were children of manual workers, fathers from the agricultural and domestic service groups being counted as manual workers for this purpose. The present manual labor force, then, is drawn predominantly from the children of workers and farmers, and only to a limited extent from other occupational strata.

The fact that manual workers usually have working-class fathers, however, does not demonstrate that working-class fathers produce mainly working-class children. The people in our sample had to be manual workers because of the basis on which the samples were drawn. It is possible, however, that many sisters and brothers from the same families have worked their way up to higher occupational levels, so

[1] F. W. Taussig and C. S. Joslyn, *American Business Leaders* (New York; Macmillan & Co., 1932).

that, looking at all the children of fathers in the previous generation, one would find a marked degree of upward movement. In order to check on this point, we asked for the current occupations of all sisters and brothers of our respondents who had reached working age and were gainfully employed. It was then possible to tabulate the occupational level of the parents of our respondents against the occupational level of all gainfully employed children of these parents. The results for sample A are shown in Table 12.

While these data have certain defects[4] and must be interpreted with caution, they do suggest several tentative conclusions. First, the proportion of children of manual workers who rise to the professional and managerial levels is quite small. Families in which the father is a skilled worker show the largest percentage of children rising to the higher occupations, semiskilled families a lower percentage, and unskilled families a very low percentage indeed. Second, it is easier for children of manual workers to move up to positions in the "sales and clerical" group than it is for them to rise to managerial and professional jobs. Even this movement is not striking, however, amounting to perhaps 10 per cent of all children of manual workers. There is little difference between skilled and unskilled families in the proportion of children going into sales and clerical occupations, possibly because the training required for these occupations is not prolonged or expensive.

Third, the bulk of the children of manual workers remain in manual occupations. If one counts agriculture and service as manual employ-

4 The defects are of three main sorts: (1) The children in the table are classified according to current occupational level. Most women, and some men, are young, and many of them were still quite young at the time of interview. It seems likely that, during the remainder of their lives, more will rise to higher occupational levels than will fall. Thus an occupational distribution of these people at the end of their working lives would probably show larger percentages in the upper occupational groups. (2) The sample of parents is not a cross-section of the entire population since it includes only parents with at least one child in the manual labor force. A large proportion of professional and business families, and even a certain proportion of manual-class families, have all children engaged in nonmanual jobs and hence are excluded by our procedure. The effect of this is an understatement of the proportion of children rising to white-collar occupations. This defect is partly [illegible] for the [illegible] of the table (i.e., business and professional families), [illegible] important for the lower levels, [illegible]. (3) Another difficulty arises from the fact that it was necessary to take the occupational level of the father at one point of time, since many people change occupational levels over their working lives. The reference date selected was the date at which the respondent entered the labor force. This may not be [illegible] of the father's occupational level. [illegible] this bias operates.

that looking at *all* the children of fathers in the previous generation, one would find a marked degree of upward movement. In order to check on this point, we asked for the current occupations of all sisters and brothers of our respondents who had reached working age and were gainfully employed. It was then possible to tabulate the occupational level of the parents of our respondents against the occupational level of all gainfully employed children of these parents. The results for Sample 1 are shown in Table 17.

While these data have certain defects[2] and must be interpreted with caution, they do suggest several tentative conclusions. First, the proportion of children of manual workers who rise to the professional and managerial levels is quite small. Families in which the father is a skilled worker show the largest percentage of children rising to the higher occupations, semiskilled families a lower percentage, and unskilled families a very low percentage indeed. Second, it is easier for children of manual workers to move up to positions in the "sales and clerical" group than it is for them to rise to managerial and professional jobs. Even this movement is not striking, however, amounting to perhaps 10 per cent of all children of manual workers. There is little difference between skilled and unskilled families in the proportion of children going into sales and clerical occupations, possibly because the training required for these occupations is not prolonged or expensive.

Third, the bulk of the children of manual workers remain in manual occupations. If one counts agriculture and service as manual employ-

[2] The defects are of three main sorts: (1) The children in the table are classified according to *current* occupational level. Their working lives, however, are not yet over. Many of them were still quite young at the date of interview. It seems likely that, during the remainder of their lives, more will rise in the occupational scale than will fall. Thus an occupational distribution of these people at the *end* of their working lives would probably show larger percentages in the upper occupational groups. (2) The sample of parents is not a cross section of the entire population, since it includes only parents *with at least one child in the manual labor force.* A large proportion of professional and business families, and even a certain proportion of working-class families, have no children engaged in manual labor and hence are excluded by our procedure. This results, again, in an understatement of the proportion of children entering white-collar occupations. This defect is particularly serious for the first two rows of the table (i.e., business and professional families). It is less important for the lower rows, but still distorts the picture somewhat. (3) Another difficulty arises from the fact that it was necessary to take the occupational level of the father *at some point of time,* since many people change occupational levels over their working lives. The reference date selected was that at which the respondent himself entered the labor force. This may not be an accurate indication of the father's occupational level in earlier years, and it is impossible to tell in which direction this bias operates.

TABLE 17

OCCUPATIONAL LEVEL OF MEMBERS OF SAMPLE 1 PLUS THEIR SISTERS AND BROTHERS, BY OCCUPATIONAL LEVEL OF FATHER

Occupational Level of Father	Total	Occupational Level of Children (Percentage Distribution)								
		Proprietor, etc.	Professional, etc.	Foremen	Skilled	Semiskilled	Unskilled	Clerical and Sales	Service and Domestic	Agriculture
Proprietor, etc.	100	9	4	2	40	28	7	7	3	0
Professional, etc.	100	8	12	4	30	12	14	4	12	4
Foremen	100	13	3	0	43	32	6	3	0	0
Skilled	100	4	5	2	40	25	10	7	5	2
Semiskilled	100	5	0	5	25	43	6	11	4	1
Unskilled	100	2	1	1	26	46	11	8	5	0
Clerical and Sales	100	3	3	0	26	26	16	10	13	3
Service and Domestic	100	3	3	0	19	32	17	14	12	0
Agriculture	100	4	4	2	24	28	18	1	5	14

ments, 82 per cent of the children of skilled workers, 79 per cent of the children of semiskilled workers, and 88 per cent of the children of unskilled and agricultural workers remained in manual labor. It must be remembered, of course, that 60 per cent of the gainfully employed in the area are engaged in manual labor of one sort or another. Even on a random basis, therefore, one would expect three-fifths of the children of manual workers to go into manual occupations. It is only the difference between this figure and the percentages actually encountered which is significant.

The data suggest that, while upward occupational movement is not entirely free, it is still substantial. Movement is greater from the skilled worker and foreman groups than it is from lower laboring groups. There is also more movement into the lower white-collar occupations than into professional and executive positions.

It would be interesting to know more about the *incidence* of this upward movement. Why do some children from some working-class families rise to higher strata while others do not? Is the main factor differences in intelligence, personality, physical stamina, and other characteristics of the children themselves? Or is it difference in the parents—differences in earning power, interest in education, ability to plan for the future, "contacts," and the like? A separate sociopsychological investigation would be necessary to answer these questions.

Occupational transmission *within* the working class does not seem to be strong. It is apparent from Table 17 that the son of a skilled worker has a somewhat better chance of becoming a skilled worker than does the son of a laborer. Conversely, the son of a laborer is more likely to end up a laborer than is the son of a craftsman. The relationship is not very strong, however, particularly in the vast middle ground of semiskilled occupations. The same conclusion is suggested by Table A-16, in which the occupations of our respondents alone are correlated with the occupations of their fathers. There seems no marked tendency for the children of skilled workers to end up in better jobs than children of semiskilled and unskilled workers.

The School System as a Selective Factor

In the complex process of sorting out the maturing adults onto various occupational levels, the most important single mechanism is doubtless the educational system. A specified level of educational achievement is usually required for entrance into nonmanual occupa-

tions and even into the better manual jobs. Moreover, certain types of educational program aim specifically to inculcate vocational skills in the child and to prepare him for a certain type of employment.

A previous study at the Yale Labor and Management Center provides valuable information concerning educational requirements for admission to various occupations in the community. Several hundred employers in every type of industry were interviewed in order to determine their hiring requirements and preferences for different categories of employee.[3] Their preferences in the matter of education may be summarized as follows: *for executive and administrative* positions, more than half the employers preferred college-trained men, and the remainder preferred high school graduation or better. For *routine clerical workers,* more than 90 per cent preferred high school graduation and 50 per cent actually required it for hiring. For *skilled maintenance workers,* 45 per cent of the employers preferred high school graduation, and there was also a marked preference for vocational training. For *production workers,* only one-third preferred high school graduation, although almost all the remainder preferred an eighth-grade education or better. For *common labor,* the great majority either had no educational preference or preferred no more than eighth grade.[4] There is thus a direct relation between educational requirements and the level of the job.

Whether the youngster finishes high school is particularly important for his later progress. If he finishes high school and is able to continue through college, he is a candidate for professional and executive positions. If he goes only through high school, he may still qualify for subprofessional, minor administrative, and routine clerical positions. If he drops out before finishing high school, however, he is usually precluded from anything better than manual work. Even within the field of manual labor he may be handicapped in competing with boys who have a high school diploma.

Short of high school graduation, there does not seem to be a strong relation between the number of years of schooling obtained and the level of the youngsters' first jobs. The analysis of Samples 1 and 2

[3] E. William Noland and E. Wight Bakke, *Workers Wanted* (New York, Harper & Brothers, 1949). A distinction was made in this study between *requirements,* i.e., actual prerequisites to employment, and *preferences,* i.e., characteristics which the employer would like to find if he could. Attention will be paid here principally to preferences, since requirements admittedly fluctuate with the state of the labor market. Employer preferences indicate the criteria which will be used when there is cnough unemployment to permit free selection.

[4] *Ibid.,* pp. 33, 48, 56, 61, 78.

reveals some tendency for workers with less schooling to start out at a lower occupational level, particularly if they have completed less than eight grades. The relation is not as marked, however, as one might have expected. The tabulations on this point may be somewhat misleading because of the fact that the workers in the samples entered the labor market over a period of fifty years, during which employers' educational requirements have doubtless been rising. The fact that workers were able to enter skilled occupations with an eighth-grade education thirty years ago is no indication that they would be able to do so today.

A special commission appointed in 1941 to study the public school system of the area reported that about 65 per cent of the children in the city were completing their schooling with about 35 per cent were dropping out before graduation.[7] Dropouts are concentrated mostly in the ninth and tenth grades and in the 16-to-17 age group; the legal school-leaving age in the state is 16, and two-thirds of those who leave school before graduation do so at this age. These dropouts provide most of the recruits to manual occupations in the area. Since 60 per cent of the jobs in the city are in manual labor, however, the dropout group is not sufficient to fill all manual vacancies, and an increasing number of high school graduates are turning to manual work.[8] If the percentage of students finishing high school continues to rise, as one may expect it to do, an ever-larger percentage of high school graduates will be obliged to take manual jobs, and those who drop out before completion may find themselves crowded down into the poorly paid manual occupations.

Any effort to discover why children are selected into one occupational group rather than another thus leads to an examination of which youngsters drop out of school prematurely and why they do so. Economic pressure to contribute to support of the family is an obvi-

[7] Eliminating the number who moved or transferred to other schools, thirty-five per cent of the pupils in the class of 1939-40 dropped out before finishing high school. Commission Report, p. [illegible]. The proportion in 1942 was about the same as in 1940 and 1941. During the war years, though, the proportion of dropouts was considerably higher, because an unusually large number of youngsters enlisted in the services or entered war industries without waiting to finish high school.

[8] Twenty-one per cent of the workers in Sample 1, and 13 per cent of those in Sample 2, had graduated from high school or gone beyond. The higher percentage in Sample 1 is no doubt due to the fact that this is a younger group, very few of whom left school before [illegible], and to the fact that the proportion of youngsters finishing high school has been rising over the course of time. These figures indicate that, while a substantial and growing proportion of high school graduates are engaged in manual labor, the manual labor force still consists mainly of those who did not finish high school.

reveals some tendency for workers with less schooling to start out at a lower occupational level, particularly if they have completed less than eight grades. The relation is not as marked, however, as one might have expected. The tabulations on this point may be somewhat misleading because of the fact that the workers in the samples entered the labor market over a period of fifty years, during which employers' educational requirements have doubtless been rising. The fact that workers were able to enter skilled occupations with an eighth-grade education thirty years ago is no indication that they would be able to do so today.

A special commission appointed in 1947 to study the public school system of the area reported that about 65 per cent of the children in the city were completing high school, while about 35 per cent were dropping out before graduation.[5] Dropouts are concentrated heavily in the ninth and tenth grades, and in the 16-to-17 age group. The legal school-leaving age in the state is 16, and two-thirds of those who leave school before graduation do so at this age. These dropouts provide most of the recruits to manual occupations in the area. Since 60 per cent of the jobs in the city are in manual labor, however, the dropout group is not sufficient to fill all manual vacancies, and an increasing number of high school graduates are turning to manual work.[6] If the percentage of students finishing high school continues to rise, as one may expect it to do, an ever-larger percentage of high school graduates will be obliged to take manual jobs; and those who drop out before completion may find themselves crowded down into the poorest manual occupations.

Any effort to discover why children are selected into one occupational group rather than another thus leads to an examination of which youngsters drop out of school prematurely and why they do so. Economic pressure to contribute to support of the family is undoubt-

[5] "Eliminating the number who moved or transferred to other schools, thirty-five per cent of the pupils in the class of 1946 dropped out before finishing high school." (*Commission Report*, p. 27). The proportion in 1946 was about the same as in 1940 and 1941. During the war years 1942–45 the proportion of dropouts was considerably higher because an unusually large number of boys enlisted in the services or entered war industries without waiting to finish high school.

[6] Twenty-one per cent of the people in Sample 1, and 32 per cent of these in Sample 2, had graduated from high school or trade school. The higher percentage in Sample 2 is no doubt due to the fact that this is a younger group, very few of whom left school before 1930, and to the fact that the proportion of youngsters finishing high school has been rising over the course of time. These figures indicate that, while a substantial and growing proportion of high school graduates are engaged in manual labor, the manual labor force still consists mainly of those who did not finish high school.

edly an important consideration. Forty-four per cent of the workers in Sample 1, and 35 per cent of those in Sample 2, stated that they had left school before graduation in order to meet the financial needs of their families. Moreover, Table 18 indicates that the proportion leaving school prematurely on this account is strongly correlated with the occupational level of the family.[7] Pressure to leave school early is greatest on children in the lowest occupational groups, and they consequently get off to a poorer educational start. This is probably the most important reason for the tendency toward occupational transmission from one generation to the next which was noted in the preceding section. An unduly large percentage of the children of manual workers remain manual workers because they do not obtain the educational prerequisites for higher occupations.

It is encouraging to note that the severity of economic pressures on the young seems to be diminishing with the passage of time and the continuing rise of living standards. Forty-four per cent of the relatively old group in Sample 1 had left school for financial reasons; 35 per cent of the younger group in Sample 2 had left school on this account; and a study made in the high schools of the area from September to December, 1948, found that only 21 per cent of the dropouts during that period were for economic reasons.[8] Even allowing for the abnormal prosperity of 1948 and the immediately preceding years, it seems almost certain that the trend of dropouts for economic reasons is downward.

School-leaving because of dislike of school shows no tendency to diminish over the years. Twenty-nine per cent of the people in Sample 1 and 28 of those in Sample 2 said that they had left either because they disliked school or, the reverse of the coin, because they had a strong desire to get out and be on their own. The Commission study found that almost half of the dropouts in September-December, 1948, could be attributed to dislike of school. Our interview responses on this point suggest that dislike of school really means failure to achieve a satisfactory and rewarding adjustment to the school environment. This may be due to defects of curriculum, instruction, school facilities,

[7] In this table it is the *relative* size of the percentages for the different occupational groups which is significant, rather than the *absolute* size of each figure. One cannot say, for example, that only 40 per cent of the children of professional families in the area succeed in completing high school, which would be a patently absurb conclusion. It must be emphasized once more that the samples include only those *currently engaged in manual occupations,* a group with a much smaller proportion of high school graduates than one would find in the total population.

[8] *Commission Report, op. cit.,* p. 31.

only an important consideration; forty-four per cent of the workers in Sample 1 and 36 per cent of those in Sample 2 stated that they had left school before graduation in order to meet the financial needs of their families. Moreover, Table 18 indicates that the proportion leaving school prematurely on this account is strongly correlated with the occupational level of the family.[3] Pressure to leave school early is greatest on children in the lowest occupational groups and they consequently get off to a poorer educational start. This is probably the most important reason for the tendency toward occupational transmission from one generation to the next which was noted in the preceding section. Apparently a large proportion of the children of manual workers remain manual workers because they do not obtain the educational prerequisites for other occupations.

It is encouraging to note that the severity of economic pressure on the young seems to be diminishing with the passage of time and the continuing rise of living standards. Forty-four per cent of the relatively old group in Sample 1 had left school for financial reasons; 36 per cent of the younger group in Sample 2 had left school on this account; and a study made in the high schools of the area from September to December, 1948, found that only 24 per cent of the dropouts during that period were for economic reasons.[4] Even allowing for the temporary prosperity of 1948 and the immediately preceding years, it seems almost certain that the trend of dropouts for economic reasons is downward.

School-leaving because of dislike of school shows no tendency to diminish over the years. Thirty-nine per cent of the people in Sample 1 and 28 of those in Sample 2 said that they had left school either because they disliked school or, the reverse of the coin, because they had a strong desire to get out and be on their own. The Commission study found that almost half of the dropouts in September-December, 1948, could be attributed to dislike of school. The interview responses on this point suggest that dislike of school really means failure to achieve a satisfactory and rewarding adjustment to the school environment. This may be due to defects of curriculum, instruction, school facilities,

[3] In this table it is the relative size of the percentages for the different occupational groups which is significant, rather than the absolute size of each figure. The fact, for example, that only 10 per cent of the children of professional families in the area stopped short of completing high school, which would be [illegible] on first consideration, it must be emphasized once more that the Sample includes only those currently engaged in gainful occupations, a group with a much smaller proportion of high school graduates than one would find in the total population.

[4] Commission, [illegible], p. 17.

and other features of the environment. It may also be due to low intelligence, personality characteristics which make it difficult for the youngster to develop good study habits and accept necessary discipline, personal traits which set him off from his fellow students and hamper his social relations with them, poor health and other circumstances of the individual.[a] Any difficulties of adjustment are magnified if the

TABLE [illegible]

[illegible] of [illegible] School [illegible], by Occupational Level of [illegible]

Occupational Level of Parent	Sample I		Sample II	
	Children Leaving School for Financial Reasons (%)	Children Dropping from High School (%)	Children Leaving School for Financial Reasons (%)	Children Graduating from High School (%)
Professional and semiprofessional	[illegible]	[illegible]	[illegible]	[illegible]
Skilled	[illegible]	[illegible]	[illegible]	[illegible]
[illegible]	[illegible]	[illegible]	[illegible]	[illegible]

pupil is retarded beyond the normal age for his grade. Thrown in with smaller and younger children, he is likely to feel inferior, self-conscious, and different in his outside interests. At the same time he sees others of his age who are out earning and spending money, leading that independent life which is so attractive to the adolescent eye. Thus for every year of retardation the probability of the student's dropping out is much increased.

Lack of ability to do school work satisfactorily is probably more important than one would judge from the nominal reasons for school-leaving. It is striking that hardly any of the workers in our samples gave "flunked out" as their reason for leaving. Yet a reading between the lines of what they did say suggests that many of those who talked about "hating school," "fighting with the teacher," "wanting to get away to work" were finding it difficult to pass examinations and meet other criteria of successful performance. The Commission study

[a] Statistical analysis of the characteristics of 700 dropouts and 700 graduates, each in the high schools of the area, revealed a marked difference between the two groups in (1) educational aptitude, as measured by the [illegible] Test; (2) personality ratings by teachers, using such criteria as leadership, resourcefulness, cooperation, industry and reliability; (3) parents' [illegible] [illegible] of [illegible] (4) amount of absence (nonattendance); and (5) retardation in terms of age at the time of [illegible] grade. In all these respects the position of the dropouts was decidedly inferior. (Ibid., p. [illegible].)

and other features of the environment. It may also be due to low intelligence, personality characteristics which make it difficult for the youngster to develop good study habits and accept necessary discipline, personal traits which set him off from his fellow students and hamper his social relations with them, poor health, and other characteristics of the individual.[9] Any difficulties of adjustment are intensified if the

TABLE 18

EXTENT OF PREMATURE SCHOOL-LEAVING, BY OCCUPATIONAL LEVEL OF FATHER

Occupational Level of Father	Sample 1		Sample 2	
	Children Leaving School for Financial Reasons (%)	Children Graduating from High School (%)	Children Leaving School for Financial Reasons (%)	Children Graduating from High School (%)
Professional and Semiprofessional	17	41	14	43
Skilled	39	30	27	36
Unskilled	60	13	61	21

pupil is retarded beyond the normal age for his grade. Thrown in with smaller and younger children, he is likely to feel inferior, self-conscious, and different in his outside interests. At the same time he sees others of his age who are out earning and spending money, leading that independent life which is so attractive to the adolescent eye. Thus for every year of retardation, the probability of the student's dropping out is much increased.

Lack of ability to do school work satisfactorily is probably more important than one would judge from the nominal reasons for school-leaving. It is striking that hardly any of the workers in our samples gave "flunked out" as their reason for leaving. Yet a reading between the lines of what they did say suggests that many of those who talked about "hating school," "fighting with the teacher," "wanting to get away to work" were finding it difficult to pass examinations and meet other criteria of successful performance. The Commission study

[9] Statistical analysis of the characteristics of 700 dropouts and 700 graduating seniors in the high schools of the area revealed a marked difference between the two groups in (1) educational aptitude, as measured by the Iowa Every-Pupil Tests; (2) personality ratings by teachers, using such criteria as leadership, resourcefulness, cooperation, industry, and reliability; (3) parental status—parents living together, separated, or dead; (4) amount of absence from school; and (5) retardation in terms of age while attending eighth grade. In all these respects the position of the dropouts was distinctly unfavorable. (*Ibid.*, p. 31).

reported "low mentality" as the reason for 9 per cent of the dropouts during September-December, 1948, "health" accounted for 7 per cent, and "instability in character" for 11 per cent.

Home and neighborhood influences are important, though more difficult to detect and measure. It makes a difference whether the child's parents are present in the home, whether their relations with the child are good, whether they take an interest in the details of his school work and general progress, whether they urge him to continue in school or to go to work. It makes a difference whether there is sufficient room in the home, or whether it is so crowded that study becomes impossible. The standards and goals of other parents and children in the immediate neighborhood are important. A neighborhood where success is measured in terms of gang leadership places different compulsions on the child from a neighborhood where prestige depends on making the right college. It is significant in this connection that dropouts from high school are much heavier from certain wards of the city than from others.[10] The highest proportion of dropouts come from run-down areas characterized by a large proportion of Negro or first-generation immigrant families, crowded housing conditions, low incomes, poor sanitation, high illness rates, and high rates of juvenile delinquency. The whole milieu in these areas is unfavorable to educational progress, and the child who gets through school needs unusual ability, perseverance, and good luck.

These determinants of school progress do not operate independently, but tend to cooperate and reinforce each other. One frequently finds a combination of low and irregular family income, low parental appreciation of educational opportunities, crowded housing, unsatisfactory neighborhood conditions, poor health, and poor social adjustment of the child to his environment—all conducive to early school-leaving. The opposite conditions also tend to run together and to propel the child on through high school and college. The upshot is a tendency for children born into the lower occupational levels to continue in those levels, and conversely for children born into higher levels.

The School System as a Training Agency

Let us turn now to the subjects studied in high school, and the relation of the youngster's school training to his subsequent employment. The young people emerging from high school in the area in a typical year of the late forties were distributed approximately as

[10] *Ibid.*, pp. 28–29.

follows:[11] graduates of the commercial course, 20 per cent; graduates of the college preparatory course, 18 per cent; graduates of the "general" course (basically academic in character but not designed specifically for college entrance), 16 per cent; graduates of courses in nursing and the arts, 6 per cent; graduates of trade school courses in manual skills, 5 per cent; youths leaving school before graduation, 35 per cent.

Students in the commercial course are enrolled in four basic sequences, in about the following proportions: stenography (45 per cent), selling (30 per cent), bookkeeping (15 per cent), and general clerical (10 per cent). The curriculum emphasizes general education during the first two years, vocational skills during the last two years. About four-fifths of the students are girls, one-fifth boys. The numbers graduating from the various sequences seem to be in reasonably good balance with market requirements. The fact that 20 per cent of these leaving high school are commercial graduates checks remarkably closely with the fact that 20 per cent of the area labor force is employed in the "clerical and sales" category. Over the past several years, commercial graduates have had little difficulty in finding white-collar jobs, usually of the type for which they have been trained. About half the girls graduating from the commercial course get their first jobs through the school placement office. Boys make less use of the office, usually preferring to seek work on their own.

The training offered in the college preparatory and general courses is academic in character, the chief difference being that the general course does not conform so closely to college entrance requirements. Students are assigned to one course or the other on the basis of past scholastic record, intelligence tests, and the professed interest of the student (or his parents!) in going on to college. Virtually all graduates of the general course go to work on graduation, and a considerable number of those in the college preparatory course also end up going to work rather than to college. Thus about a quarter of the youngsters entering the labor market each year come out of school with a good academic background and high occupational hopes but no specific vocational skills.

[11] These figures are based on enrollments in the various types of course, i.e., they assume the same percentage of dropouts before graduation in each course. Moreover, they relate only to high schools in the central city. They would not be greatly altered by inclusion of figures for high schools in adjacent suburban areas. Since residents of these areas are of somewhat higher economic status, however, their inclusion would probably raise somewhat the percentage in college preparatory courses and reduce the percentage of dropouts before graduation.

These youngsters face a problem similar to that faced by graduates of liberal arts colleges. They are supposedly educated—but for what? As regards executive and administrative positions, they are at a disadvantage in competition with college graduates. For clerical jobs requiring a specific skill, commercial high school graduates are usually preferred. Even skilled manual jobs require a trade school course, period of apprenticeship, or other specialized training. The "academic" high school maintains a placement office, but the staff and facilities are too limited to allow it to do more than take calls made by employers on their own initiative. A few of the larger organizations in the city, such as the telephone company, come to the high school each spring to recruit trainees for skilled manual or clerical positions. The bulk of the requests which come into the placement office, however, are for low-skilled and low-paid work: errand boys, stock clerks, grocery helpers, sweepers, and the like.

Graduates of the academic courses naturally aspire to white-collar jobs. The hard fact is, however, that there are not enough white-collar jobs available to take care of nearly all who want them. As realization of this dawns on the new graduates, some of the more alert youngsters decide to undertake specialized trade or technical training. The less alert must seek work as factory operatives or take the nondescript jobs which flow into the placement office.

The gap between the expectations of high school graduates and the job opportunities actually open to them will probably be closed gradually by a readjustment of expectations. As high school graduation becomes more nearly universal and the proportion of high school graduates going into manual jobs increases, one may expect the white-collar aura surrounding the high school to diminish. A powerful force working in this direction is the steady improvement in wages and other terms of employment for manual occupations relative to those for white-collar jobs. As it becomes more widely recognized that many manual jobs pay much better than clerical employment, more and more high school students will be willing to "take the cash and let the credit go."

There will remain, however, the problem of what kind of high school training is appropriate for students of whom at least half are destined for manual labor. The traditional academic curriculum was justified as a sort of vocational training for the learned professions. Can the core of this curriculum be salvaged and justified on grounds of per-

social development and training for citizenship, without any vocational purpose? Or should the high schools undertake to train young people for manual jobs? These questions will have to be examined when we come to discuss practical issues of labor market policy in Chapter X.

The issue is now resolved for about 5 per cent of the high school population by enrollment in a vocational trade school. Students normally enter the school at the end of ninth grade (junior high school graduation), but some enter after eighth grade, after tenth grade, and even (in about 10 per cent of the cases) after high school graduation. The intelligence level of the trade school students is somewhat below that of students enrolled in other high school programs.[9] Graduation from this school does not depend, as in the other high schools, on completion of so many years of study, but simply on attainment of a certain level of trade proficiency. The general education content of the curriculum is quite limited, and students spend the bulk of their time in actual shop work.

The courses offered in this school, and the proportion of the student body enrolled in them in 1948, were as follows: machinists (25 per cent), draftsmen (25 per cent), electricians (14 per cent), automobile mechanics (13 per cent), carpenters (12 per cent), cabinetmakers (6 per cent), and draftsmen (4 per cent). Why are these courses offered rather than others? Apparently on the pragmatic ground that employers are interested in training for these occupations, there is no union opposition to such training, and the equipment required is not too expensive. Courses in plumbing and painting were offered in the twenties, but have not been offered since that time because of union opposition. The number admitted to each course depends mainly on the physical plant of the school, and this is not readily altered because it is difficult to induce the school authorities to undertake large new capital expenditures. In consequence of this, there is a considerable lag between shifts in the demand for different skills and changes in the output from the vocational school.[10] The director of the school is in close touch with the labor market and can tell that certain skills are

9 In the latest period, students enrolled in the college preparatory course had an average I.Q. of 109, students in the commercial high school 98.5, and those in the trade school 94.6. (Carmichael Report, pp. 138–140.)

10 The percentage of students enrolled in each trade in 1948 was almost identical with the percentage in 1940. Over a period of such great social and economic upheaval, there must have been marked shifts in the requirements for the various skills.

sonal development and training for citizenship, without any vocational purpose? Or should the high schools undertake to train young people *en masse* for manual jobs? These questions will have to be examined when we come to discuss practical issues of labor market policy in Chapter X.

The issue is now resolved for about 5 per cent of the high school population by enrollment in a vocational trade school. Students normally enter this school at the end of ninth grade (junior high school graduation); but some enter after eighth grade, after tenth grade, and even (in about 10 per cent of the cases) after high school graduation. The intelligence level of the trade school students is somewhat below that of students enrolled in other high school programs.[12] Graduation from this school does not depend, as in the other high schools, on completion of so many years of study, but simply on attainment of a certain level of trade proficiency. The general education content of the curriculum is quite limited, and students spend the bulk of their time in actual shop work.

The courses offered in this school, and the proportion of the student body enrolled in them in 1948, were as follows: machinists (26 per cent), dressmakers (23 per cent), electricians (14 per cent), automobile mechanics (14 per cent), carpenters (11 per cent), compositors (8 per cent), and draftsmen (4 per cent). Why are these courses offered rather than others? Apparently on the pragmatic ground that employers are interested in training for these occupations, there is no union opposition to such training, and the equipment required is not too expensive. Courses in plumbing and painting were offered in the twenties, but have not been offered since that time because of union opposition. The numbers admitted to each course depend basically on the physical plant of the school, and this is not readily altered because it is difficult to induce the school authorities to undertake large new capital expenditures. In consequence of this, there is a considerable lag between shifts in the demand for different skills and changes in the output from the vocational school.[13] The director of the school is in close touch with the labor market and can tell that certain skills are

[12] In the most recent year, students enrolled in the college preparatory course had an average I.Q. of 109.6, those in the commercial high school 98.5, and those in the trade school 93.8. (*Commission Report, op. cit.*, pp. 139–140.)

[13] The percentage of students enrolled in each trade in 1948 was almost identical with the percentage in 1940. Over a period of such great industrial expansion, however, there must have been marked shifts in the requirements for the various skills.

becoming easier to place and others harder. It is difficult, however, for him to do much about it, particularly in the direction of installing or expanding courses which require expensive new equipment.

The fact that the proportion of youngsters trained for different trades in the vocational school does not correspond closely with the proportions required in the labor market raises no serious problem in practice because the vocational school meets only a small part of the total demand for these skills. The great majority of new compositors, machinists, electricians, and so on continue to be trained by employers on the job. This means that the vocational school is working within large margins of safety on the demand side. If the school system undertook to meet the full demand for various trade skills, there would be a serious problem of detecting shifts in demand and adjusting school facilities to meet them. As matters stand, this problem does not arise because employers take up the slack, training workers at an accelerated rate when demand is high and ceasing to train altogether when demand slackens.

While the vocational school has no formal placement facilities, the instructors in the various courses are in touch with employers in their respective industries. The director of the school also devotes considerable time to developing contacts with employers. During the forties, because of the active demand for skilled labor, employers were eager to hire vocational school students on graduation or even before graduation. The main problem was to keep students from being hired before they were adequately trained. During the years 1944–48, about 75 per cent of those graduating each year obtained jobs with employers who applied at the school. Moreover, the bulk of these students obtained the kinds of jobs for which they had been trained. A study of the 1947 graduating class one year after graduation showed that 62 per cent were working at the trade for which they had been trained, while an additional 27 per cent had jobs utilizing part of their school training. These results reflect a full employment situation, of course, and the showing might not be so favorable in a year of lower employment.

The local office of the State Employment Service has recently begun, with the cooperation of the school system, to register all high school seniors in the city for employment. It also obtains from the school authorities the names of students who drop out during the year and attempts to obtain registrations from these students. While most

students continue to secure jobs on their own or through the school, use of the Employment Service may be expected to grow in the future. There is much to be said, indeed, for centralizing all placement of students in the Employment Service rather than the school system, which can scarcely hope to rival the service in knowledge of local job opportunities and in closeness of contact with employers. This question will be discussed further in Chapter X.

CHOICE OF THE FIRST JOB IN MANUAL LABOR

The general type of work into which a youngster will go is heavily influenced, as we have seen, by the educational level he has attained. Within each broad category of employment, however, are thousands of specific jobs, differing greatly in wage level, prospects of advancement, and general attractiveness. Why does the youngster starting to work go into one of these jobs rather than another? We are concerned here specifically with job choices by youngsters destined for manual labor, and the conclusions should not be taken as applicable to other levels of employment. There is reason to think that job choices at the clerical level are somewhat more careful and deliberate than those at the manual level, and that college graduates going into executive and professional positions show still greater deliberation and foresight.

Our data on this matter are derived from interviews with the workers in Samples 1 and 2. Each worker was asked in some detail about the circumstances surrounding his first job—what it was, how he heard about it, whether he considered other alternatives, how much he knew about the job before he took it, and how it turned out. The answers obtained were better than on most other parts of the questionnaire; people seem to remember a great deal about how they first went to work, even when this was twenty or thirty years in the past. Since the answers were analyzed in a preliminary report,[1] they may be summarized here in a few propositions: most youngsters (and their parents) approached the choice of a first job with no clear conception of where they were going; the great majority of first jobs were found in a very informal way, predominantly through relatives and friends; the great majority of youngsters took the first job they found and did not make comparisons with any other job; their knowledge of the job before they took it was in most cases extremely

[1] Lloyd G. Reynolds and Joseph Shister, *Job Horizons* (New York: Harper & Brothers, 1949), chapter 4.

students continue to secure jobs on their own or through the school, use of the Employment Service may be expected to grow in the future. There is much to be said, indeed, for centralizing all placement of students in the Employment Service rather than the school system, which can scarcely hope to rival the Service in knowledge of local job opportunities and in closeness of contact with employers. This question will be discussed further in Chapter X.

Choice of the First Job in Manual Labor

The general type of work into which a youngster will go is heavily influenced, as we have seen, by the educational level he has attained. Within each broad category of employment, however, lie thousands of specific jobs, differing greatly in wage level, prospects of advancement, and general attractiveness. Why does the youngster starting to work go into one of these jobs rather than another? We are concerned here specifically with job choices by *youngsters destined for manual labor*, and the conclusions should not be taken as applicable to other levels of employment. There is reason to think that job choices at the clerical level are somewhat more careful and deliberate than those at the manual level, and that college graduates going into executive and professional positions show still greater deliberation and foresight.

Our data on this matter are derived from interviews with the workers in Samples 1 and 2. Each worker was asked in some detail about the circumstances surrounding his first job—what it was, how he heard about it, whether he considered other alternatives, how much he knew about the job before he took it, and how it worked out. The answers obtained were better than on most other parts of the questionnaire; people seem to remember a great deal about how they first went to work, even when this was twenty or thirty years in the past. Since the answers were analyzed in a preliminary report,[14] they may be summarized here in a few propositions: most youngsters (and their parents) approached the choice of a first job with no clear conception of where they were going; the great majority of first jobs were found in a very informal way, preponderantly through relatives and friends; the great majority of youngsters took the *first job* they found and did not make comparisons with any other job; their knowledge of the job before they took it was in most cases extremely

[14] Lloyd G. Reynolds and Joseph Shister, *Job Horizons*, (New York, Harper & Brothers, 1949), Chapter 4.

meager; and in most cases the job turned out to be a blind alley which did not lead to anything better. A few words of explanation is required on each of these points.

1. The workers in both Samples 1 and 2 were asked whether, during their school years, either they or their parents had formed any definite plans about what they should do in later life. Moreover, since many of those in Sample 1 were old enough to have children already at work or approaching working age, they were asked whether they had made any occupational plans for their own children. About half of those in both samples said that they had made no occupational plans at all while at school; and a majority in both samples said that their parents had made no definite plans for them. Again, 56 per cent of those in Sample 1 said that they had made no occupational plans for their own children.

Where a definite occupational ambition was reported, this was usually quite unrealistic in view of the family's circumstances. Thus, of the people in Sample 1 who expressed an occupational preference for their children, two-thirds mentioned medicine, law, or some other profession. It was usually clear that this was an aspiration rather than a concrete plan of action, and by comparing family income with educational costs one could predict that in few cases would the aspiration be realized. Very few families had an occupational plan for the child which they were doing something about and which was within the bounds of realization.

A comment on this point in our preliminary report may be repeated here: "The fact that a majority of the group had no definite occupational plans for their children does not mean that they were uninterested in the child's progress. On the contrary, most of them said they wanted the child to 'get ahead,' 'do better than I've done,' and so on. They knew little, however, about job opportunities outside of manual labor—or in some cases even inside manual labor—and about the way in which one has to prepare for various occupations. They were thus not in a position to know how the child could 'get ahead' most effectively or to make specific vocational plans. There seemed to be a general feeling that additional years of schooling would ensure a better job for the child. Many workers said that they cared only that their children should finish school, after which they could do what they liked."[15] This faith in the possibility of advancement through educa-

[15] *Ibid.*, p. 79.

tion was rarely linked up, however, with any coherent educational and vocational program for the child.

2. The way in which the workers in our samples learned about their first jobs is shown in Table 19. The striking thing in both samples is the preponderant importance of parents, relatives, and acquaintances. In more than half the cases the youngster got his first job by going

TABLE 19

METHOD OF LEARNING ABOUT FIRST JOB

Method	Sample 1 (%)	Sample 2 (%)
Through Relatives or Acquaintances: in Same Plant	35	34
Through Relatives or Acquaintances: Not in Same Plant	11	8
Working for Relatives or Acquaintances	9	11
Previous Part-time Work in Plant	9	7
Direct Application	29	29
All Others	7	11
Total	100	100

with a relative or friend to the plant where the latter was working, or using friends to make a contact in some other plant, or going to work for a relative or acquaintance. In a large proportion of these cases, the initiative in getting the job was taken by the parent or relative, and the youngster simply accepted the suggestion.

In some cases the youngster had worked part time for an employer while going to school and continued with the same employer on a full-time basis after graduation.

Where a youngster did not have any of these ready-made contacts, he usually sought work on his own by direct application. The choice of firms at which to apply seems to be made in the same general fashion described in Chapter IV for adult workers. The youngster tends to apply first at plants which are large and conspicuous, or which are near his home, or which he has heard mentioned by friends, or which he simply happens to be passing on the street. The search for work is not guided to any extent by knowledge of comparative wage rates and job opportunities in different plants. The small percentage in the "all others" category indicates that little use was made of formal placement agencies such as the schools, the public employment service, and trade unions.

Many of these workers, particularly those in Sample 1, entered the

labor market before organized placement agencies were in existence. Use of such agencies will no doubt increase as their facilities improve and knowledge of their activities spreads throughout the working-class world. Table 19 suggests, however, that they will have an uphill struggle against the established custom of finding jobs through "contacts" supplemented by haphazard application at plants. It is significant that the workers in Sample 2, most of whom had entered the labor market since 1930, showed little more use of placement agencies than the older workers in Sample 1. Work-seeking customs apparently respond only slowly to the establishment of new channels of placement.

Workers' methods of finding their first job were cross-tabulated by age, sex, years of education, fathers' occupation, level of the first job, and other variables which it was thought might reveal significant relationships. The only clear relation discovered was with the level of the father's occupation. In Sample 1, for example, 44 per cent of the children of skilled parents found their jobs through their father, other relatives, or friends already working in the plant; only 22 per cent had to resort to applying on their own. For children of unskilled parents, these proportions were reversed; only 29 per cent got their first jobs through friends and relatives, while 46 per cent had to resort to direct application. Skilled workers are apparently in a better position than the unskilled to steer children into jobs in the plant where they are working themselves.

3. There is little tendency to shop around, locate alternative opportunities, and compare their merits before accepting a particular job. Ninety per cent of the workers in Sample 1 and 85 per cent of those in Sample 2 said that they took the first job they found after leaving school and did not compare it with any other job. In some cases (about 20 per cent of the total in Sample 1 and 10 per cent of those in Sample 2) the youngster had a preference for a particular line of work and took the first job he found *in that line*. In most cases, however, he literally took the first job he came across.

Cross-tabulation with personal characteristics of the sample members revealed some relation between education level and the deliberateness of job choices. Thus 41 per cent of those in Sample 2 who had more than twelve years of education shopped around before taking their first job, compared with 28 per cent for those with eleven or twelve years, and only 14 per cent for those with five to eight years of education. Similar results were found in Sample 1. It is significant that

occupation was found with the present age of the worker, i.e., with the date at which he entered the labor market. The studies do not seem to have shown any tendency toward an increase in the definiteness of job choices (at the manual labor level) over the course of time.

3. In the small minority of cases where the youngster did compare two or more jobs before reaching a decision, the decision seems to have been based mainly on two factors. The fact that a friend or relative was already employed in a particular plant frequently tipped the scales in favor of that plant. The other factor taken into account was the prospective weekly take-home pay.

4. The youngsters' knowledge of the jobs they were accepting was extremely meager. Seventy per cent of the people in Sample I said that they knew nothing whatever about their first job except the starting wage rate; in a surprising number of cases not even the wage rate was specified. Where the worker did know anything beyond the wage level, this was usually only the general physical characteristics of the job. The prospective duration and stability of employment, and the prospects for advancement, were unknown in virtually all cases.

5. Two-thirds of the workers in Sample I reported that their first jobs were "blind alleys," which did not prepare them for anything better or help them in any way to move up the occupational ladder. The remaining third stated that their first job had contributed to their later advancement, usually in one of the following ways: leading to a better job with the same company; leading to a better job with another company on the basis of experience gained on the first job; or leading to a better job with another company as a result of personal contacts made on the first job.

Altogether, then, workers' initial job choices appear to be singularly uninformed, haphazard, and unrewarding. It is necessary to append to this gloomy picture two comments—one concerning the reasons for the observed behavior, the other concerning its significance for the worker's subsequent progress.

It appears at first glance that the youngsters whose behavior has been described (and their parents) stand convicted of culpable negligence. Further reflection suggests, however, that their behavior is a natural response to the circumstances in which they find themselves. This is not to say that it is inevitable, but simply that changes in it must come from changes in the institutional setting. Admonitions to go and behave more sensibly, in the absence of institutional change, are likely to be ineffective.

no relation was found with the present age of the worker, i.e., with the date at which he entered the labor market. There does not seem to have been any tendency toward an increase in the deliberateness of job choices (at the manual labor level) over the course of time.

In the small minority of cases where the youngster did compare two or more jobs before reaching a decision, the decision seems to have been based mainly on two factors. The fact that a friend or relative was already employed in a particular plant frequently tipped the scales in favor of that plant. The other factor taken into account was the prospective weekly take-home pay.

4. The youngsters' knowledge of the jobs they were accepting was extremely meager. Seventy per cent of the people in Sample 1 said that they knew nothing whatever about their first job except the starting wage rate; in a surprising number of cases not even the wage rate was specified. Where the worker did know anything beyond the wage level, this was usually only the general physical characteristics of the job. The prospective duration and stability of employment, and the prospects for advancement, were unknown in virtually all cases.

5. Two-thirds of the workers in Sample 1 reported that their first jobs were "blind alleys" which did not prepare them for anything better or help them in any way to move up the occupational ladder. The remaining third stated that their first jobs had contributed to their later advancement, usually in one of the following ways: rising to a better job with the same company; moving to a better job with another company on the basis of experience gained on the first job; or moving to a better job with another company as a result of personal contacts made on the first job.

Altogether, then, workers' initial job choices appear to be singularly uninformed, inappropriate, and unrewarding. It is necessary to append to this gloomy picture two comments—one concerning the *reasons* for the observed behavior, the other concerning its *significance* for the worker's subsequent progress.

It appears at first glance that the youngsters whose behavior has been described (and their parents) stand convicted of culpable negligence. Further reflection suggests, however, that their behavior is a natural response to the circumstances in which they find themselves. This is not to say that it is inevitable, but simply that changes in it must come from changes in the institutional setting. Admonitions to go and behave more sensibly, in the absence of institutional changes, are likely to be ineffective.

The circumstances which condition the job choices of young people are, broadly speaking, the same as those which condition the choices of older workers. They include the great difficulty of getting accurate information about the location and characteristics of job vacancies, the tendency of employers to fill vacancies from within their present work force or from acquaintances of present employees, the consequent justified belief among workers that "contacts" are extremely important in getting work, the fact that in depression vacancies are so scarce that it may be quite rational to take the first which presents itself, and the fact that even in good times few workers have sufficient resources to permit a leisurely survey of the market. The very limited job horizon of most workers prevents them from advising their children correctly just as it hampers them in making a wise choice of jobs themselves.

In addition to these general limitations on job choices, certain features of the child's situation make it particularly difficult for him to reach wise job decisions. Intellectual and emotional immaturity, the habit of relying on parents and other adults for key decisions, leads him naturally to accept the initiative of others in getting him a job. In many cases, as was noted earlier, the child's adjustment to school is so poor that he welcomes any chance of release from an uncongenial situation. Again and again in our life histories we found youngsters who fled to any job which offered itself in order to justify leaving school. Finally, the responsibility and income attaching to any sort of full-time job is so exhilarating to an adolescent that for some time he asked nothing better of life. The feeling of independence which comes from earning a wage instead of relying on parents for spending money is so gratifying that the youngster may not be at all interested in the possibility that he might get a higher wage somewhere else.[16]

The significance of the job choices described in this section needs to be qualified in two respects. First, our data relate to choices within one category of employment—manual labor. The more important problem, however, is the allocation of young people *between* broad occupational categories, and particularly between professional or managerial jobs and manual or routine clerical jobs. When we come

[16] It was noted in Chapter IV that young, single people are almost invariably satisfied with their wage regardless of the size of the wage. An obvious reason for this is that the youngster requires very little for self-support at this stage, particularly if he is living at home and does not have the main responsibility for support of the family. The worker's interest in money per se normally begins with marriage, and is sharpened with increasing size of his family.

in Chapter X to discuss methods of ensuring a better allocation of labor among different occupations, we shall need to pay major attention to this broader problem. The second qualification is that the worker's first job is often very short and may be relatively unimportant in his entire occupational history. If the first job proves unsatisfactory, the youngster shifts to another, and may make several changes during the first few years of employment. This "settling down period" involves considerable waste of time, needless effort, and disappointment; but it also serves the constructive purpose of educating the worker to the realities of employment and of clarifying his own abilities and interests. By trial and error he eventually locates a job which, if not ideal, is at least reasonably congenial and within his capacity. The extent to which this process might be shortened and improved through systematic vocational counseling and placement will be considered in Chapter X.

CURRENT OCCUPATIONAL MOVEMENT

In the preceding section we developed the theme that youngsters enter manual labor in a haphazard fashion. Their first jobs typically stand near the bottom of the occupational ladder. We now want to inquire how many of these youngsters make occupational progress in later years, how far they are able to rise, and by what routes. Why do some rise and others not? Is there sufficient upward movement to gratify the ambitions of the more able workers and to ensure that skilled occupations are manned by those best able to fill them? We shall be dealing, by the nature of our material, only with mobility within manual labor. The range of manual occupations is wide, however, and presents great possibilities of occupational progress and retrogression. It is these possibilities which are of practical interest to most workers. Few workers, as we shall see, rate seriously the chance of rising above manual labor altogether.

We shall not try at this point to give a precise definition of what is meant by occupational progress. One can attempt an objective definition by classifying jobs on the basis of skill level, wage rate, or other characteristics. One can, on the other hand, use a subjective definition by which any job change is counted as a "promotion" if the worker himself feels it to be so. We shall have occasion to use both methods at different points in this section. Each presents certain difficulties and neither is fully satisfactory.

in Chapter X to discuss methods of ensuring a better allocation of labor among different occupations, we shall have to pay major attention to this broader problem. The second qualification is that the worker's first job is often very short and may be relatively unimportant in his entire occupational history. If the first job proves unsatisfactory, the youngster shifts to another, and may make several changes during the first few years of employment. This "settling-down period" involves considerable waste of time, needless effort, and disappointment; but it also serves the constructive purpose of educating the worker to the realities of employment and of clarifying his own abilities and interests. By trial and error he eventually locates a job which, if not ideal, is at least reasonably congenial and within his capacity. The extent to which this process might be shortened and improved through systematic vocational counseling and placement will be considered in Chapter X.

LIFETIME OCCUPATIONAL MOVEMENT

In the preceding section we developed the theme that youngsters enter manual labor in a haphazard fashion. Their first jobs typically stand near the bottom of the occupational scale. We have now to inquire how many of these youngsters make occupational progress in later years, how far they are able to rise, and by what routes. Why do some rise and others not? Is there sufficient upward movement to gratify the ambitions of the more able workers and to ensure that skilled occupations are manned by those best able to fill them? We shall be dealing, by the nature of our material, only with mobility *within* manual labor. The range of manual occupations is wide, however, and presents great possibilities of occupational progress and retrogression. It is these possibilities which are of practical interest to most workers. Few workers, as we shall see, take seriously the chance of rising above manual labor altogether.

We shall not try at this point to give a precise definition of what is meant by occupational progress. One can attempt an objective definition by classifying jobs on the basis of skill level, wage rate, and other characteristics. One can, on the other hand, use a subjective definition by which any job change is counted as a "promotion" if the worker himself feels it to be so. We shall have occasion to use both methods at different points in this section. Each presents certain difficulties, and neither is fully satisfactory.

Patterns of Occupational Movement

The work histories obtained from the people in Sample 1 enable us to trace their careers from the time they began work until they were interviewed in 1947.[17] The technique used was to classify each job in the work histories according to the occupational categories of the Census Bureau, using the Dictionary of Occupational Titles as a guide in doubtful cases. It was then possible to prepare summary tabulations, also in terms of the Census Bureau categories. These categories are rather unsatisfactory for the present purpose but, since any attempt at a new classification of occupations would have required much work and carried us far off the main track of our study, we continued to use the accepted classification.[18]

The pattern which emerges from the work histories of Sample 1 may be summarized as follows: the workers in the sample had made relatively few changes of occupational level. Most of them had spent their entire careers either on one occupational level or on two adjacent levels. Such occupational movement as had occurred was confined largely to manual jobs; only about 10 per cent of the workers had spent any time in supervisory, technical, or managerial positions. As

[17] While we shall refer to these as "lifetime work histories," this is not strictly correct, since few of the workers had reached retirement age at the date of interview. Indeed, since the history cuts off at age 30 in some cases and age 65 in other cases, the data are not really comparable. There are, however, two saving features in the situation. First, the average age of the sample (45 years) is quite high, so that we have a long span of work experience in most cases. Second, cross-tabulation of occupational level by age indicates that people aged 60 in our sample have not, on the average, progressed any farther occupationally than those aged 40. Progress, if it comes at all, seems to come fairly early, and these significant early years are included in virtually all of our work histories.

[18] It became clear as the study proceeded that the accepted categories stand in need of thorough rethinking and revision. A few of the difficulties which they present may be noted:

1. The *skilled* category ("craftsmen, foremen, and kindred workers") mixes together members of true craft occupations such as printing or carpentry, skilled maintenance workers in manufacturing, and a wide variety of production workers in manufacturing. These are groups with very different mobility characteristics. Moreover, the Dictionary of Occupational Titles seriously overstates the degree of skill involved in present-day manufacturing operations; the number of production jobs in manufacturing which can properly be called skilled is considerably less than the number so classified in the Dictionary.

2. The *semiskilled* category ("operatives and kindred workers") is much too broad, ranging all the way from virtually unskilled jobs paying about the same as common labor to jobs which pay (on an output basis) more than many craft occupations.

3. The treatment of *service* workers as a separate category rests on an *industrial* rather than an *occupational* distinction. Workers in service industries should be distributed among the skilled, semiskilled, and unskilled categories, depending on the kind of work they do. Most service workers are probably akin to semiskilled workers in manufacturing, and our results indicate that there is extensive interchange between the two groups.

regards advancement, the bulk of those in the Sample had either had no change in occupational level or had followed an oscillating course with no perceptible trend. A minority of about 20 per cent showed appreciable progress over their working lives, while 4 per cent showed marked retrogression. Upward movement thus seems to exceed downward movement. The evidence on each of these points may be briefly reviewed.

Table 20 shows the *number* of different occupational levels on which the members of our sample had worked. Relatively few workers had spent their entire working life on the same level. The commonest

TABLE 20

Extent of Occupational Movement, by Current Occupational Level

(Sample 1)

Number of Levels Worked on	Total (%)	Current Occupational Level		
		Skilled (%)	Semiskilled (%)	Unskilled (%)
1	17	7	25	22
2	45	50	44	42
3	26	30	22	30
More than 3	12	13	9	6
Total	100	100	100	100

situation was for a man to have worked at two levels—his present level and another immediately adjacent to it. A large proportion of the skilled men have worked at semiskilled jobs, while a high proportion of those now on semiskilled jobs have held either skilled or unskilled jobs. Only 12 per cent of those in the sample had worked on more than three levels.

The *types* of occupations at which members of the sample had worked are shown in Table 21. It should be noted that this table shows a distribution of jobs rather than a distribution of individuals. Thus the first column shows that, for workers now at the unskilled level, 48 per cent of the jobs held at other occupational levels were in semiskilled labor, 21 per cent were in skilled labor, and so on. It is clear that people tend most frequently to have worked at other occupations immediately adjacent to their present level. The jobs held in the "service" category, if they could be classified by skill level, would doubtless turn out to be semiskilled in most cases. The jobs reported under "clerical and sales" were usually the worker's first job, and were low-skilled jobs in groceries and the like. About 10 per cent

of the jobs held at other occupational levels fall in the "foremen," "professional and semiprofessional," and "proprietors, managers and officials" categories. Most of these jobs were as foreman, proprietor of a small retail or service establishment, or in some subprofessional occupation. Scarcely any members of the sample had been in the professions or in responsible executive positions. These results confirm our earlier findings that there is much more movement *within* manual labor than *between* manual labor and higher occupational strata.[19]

TABLE 21
JOBS HELD AT OTHER OCCUPATIONAL LEVELS, BY CURRENT OCCUPATIONAL LEVEL
(Sample 1)

Jobs Held at Other Occupational Levels	Total (%)	Current Occupational Level Unskilled (%)	Semiskilled (%)	Skilled (%)
Unskilled	19	—	28	22
Semiskilled	30	48	—	45
Skilled	12	21	22	—
Foremen	3	2	3	3
Clerical and Sales	13	12	15	11
Service, Incl. Domestic	15	9	24	11
Professional and Semiprofessional	2	3	2	2
Proprietors, Managers, and Officials	6	5	6	6
Total	100	100	100	100

Movement is not the same as progress. We must now examine how far the members of the sample had advanced or retrogressed over their working lives. Two indicators of occupational progress were prepared. The first of these, a simple cross-tabulation of the worker's present occupational level against the level of his first job, is presented in Table 22. It is clear that there has been a considerable amount of upward movement. Thirty-eight per cent of those who started in semiskilled jobs have risen to skilled positions, while 67 per cent of those who started as unskilled are now in skilled or semi-

[19] Subject always to the qualification that our samples do not include people who started in manual labor but were in nonmanual occupations at the date of interview. Our samples include people who climbed out of the manual group *and later slipped back*, but they do not include those who "made good." The occupations from which members of our sample had slipped back, however, suggests that most of those who graduate from manual labor go into minor supervisory positions and small proprietorships, while very few go into higher executive positions or the professions.

skilled jobs. There is also evident a certain amount of retrogression. More than a third of those who began as apprentices in skilled trades, for example, have dropped out of the trade and are now in lower occupations.

The other indicator was an "occupational profile," a visual chart showing the level of each job held in chronological order. A separate profile was prepared for each worker, and the results were then

TABLE 22

CURRENT OCCUPATIONAL LEVEL BY OCCUPATIONAL LEVEL OF FIRST JOB (Sample I)

Level of First Job	Total (%)	Current Occupational Level: Skilled (%)	Semiskilled (%)	Unskilled (%)
Apprentice	100	64	26	10
Semiskilled	100	38	50	12
Unskilled	100	[illegible]	32	42
Clerical and Sales	100	42	41	17
Agriculture and other Extractive Industries	100	[illegible]	[illegible]	[illegible]
Total	100	38	37	25

grouped into a few categories.[b] The largest group, almost half of the total, showed a substantially level profile over their working lives, without appreciable progress or retrogression. Some 20 per cent showed a virtually continuous rise in occupational level over their working lives, while 4 per cent showed a downward trend. The remainder of the sample showed irregular patterns with no clear trend—in some cases a rise in earlier life followed by a subsequent decline, in other cases several upward and downward movements forming a zigzag pattern. The results indicate that, while a minority of manual workers are able to make steady upward progress, the majority have

[a] The figures in Table 22 correspond remarkably closely with the results of Davidson and Anderson's study of San Jose, California. (P. E. Davidson and H. D. Anderson, *Occupational Mobility in an American Community*, Stanford University Press, 1937, p. 97.) The chief difference is that, in their study, 57 per cent of those who began as unskilled laborers were still unskilled at the date of interview. This may be due to the importance of agricultural labor and of Mexican and other ethnic groups in the area which is studied.

[b] The "profile" technique, while it requires judgment by the coder and lacks complete quantitative precision, is in some ways more useful than the other. It takes into account the whole work record of the individual rather than simply the first and last jobs, either or both of which may be very brief and unimportant in the total history.

skilled jobs.[20] There is also evident a certain amount of retrogression. More than a third of those who began as apprentices to skilled trades, for example, have dropped out of the trade and are now in lower occupations.

The other indicator was an "occupational profile," a visual chart showing the level of each job held in chronological order. A separate profile was prepared for each worker, and the results were then

TABLE 22

CURRENT OCCUPATIONAL LEVEL AND OCCUPATIONAL LEVEL OF FIRST JOB
(Sample 1)

Level of First Job	Total (%)	Current Occupational Level: Skilled (%)	Semiskilled (%)	Unskilled (%)
Apprentice	100	63	23	14
Semiskilled	100	38	50	12
Unskilled	100	29	38	33
Clerical and Sales	100	32	48	10
Agriculture and Other Extractive Industries	100	57	24	19
Total	100	38	39	23

grouped into a few categories.[21] The largest group, almost half of the total, showed a substantially level profile over their working lives, without appreciable progress or retrogression. Some 20 per cent showed a virtually continuous rise in occupational level over their working lives, while 4 per cent showed a downward trend. The remainder of the sample showed irregular patterns with no clear trend —in some cases a rise in earlier life followed by a subsequent decline, in other cases several upward and downward movements forming a zigzag pattern. The results indicate that, while a minority of manual workers are able to make steady upward progress, the majority have

[20] The figures in Table 22 correspond remarkably closely with the results of Davidson and Anderson's study of San Jose, California. (P. E. Davidson and H. D. Anderson, *Occupational Mobility in an American Community*, Stanford University Press, 1937, p. 95). The chief difference is that, in their study, 57 per cent of those who began as unskilled laborers were still unskilled at the date of interview. This may be due to the importance of agricultural labor and of Mexican and other ethnic groups in the area which they studied.

[21] The "profile" technique, while it requires judgment by the coder and lacks complete quantitative precision, is in some ways more useful than the other. It takes into account the whole work record of the individual rather than simply the first and last job, either or both of which may be very brief and unimportant in the total history.

either an uneventful career on the same general level or a checkered career without appreciable progress.

Why do some move upward and others not? Why do some move down, either steadily or during certain periods in their work history? We have no positive answers to these questions. The degree of occupational progress shows no correlation with the age of the worker, his years of schooling, the occupational level of his father, or any of the other variables measured in this study. It would doubtless show some correlation with intelligence and other psychological characteristics of the individual, but these we did not attempt to measure.

A careful reading of the work histories, however, suggests hypotheses which seem worthy of further study. The youngsters who move upward seem to be those who, at an early stage in their work history, either set themselves to learn a skilled trade or formed a definite attachment to a particular company which offered opportunities for advancement. The indications are that most of the upward movement occurs in the first ten years of the individual's work history[22] and that movement becomes much more difficult after that stage. There are several obvious reasons for this. Employers are reluctant to take on a trainee for a skilled job who is beyond his early twenties; nor is there any need for them to do so, since a new crop of youngsters comes out of school onto the market each year. From the worker's standpoint, training for a new job involves some risk and frequently a temporary loss of earning power. After the worker has married and had a child or two, the need for current income compels him to keep on with whatever he is doing.

This still does not answer the question of why some youngsters set out to train themselves for good jobs during their first few years out of school, while others waste these crucial years moving around among a variety of jobs which lead nowhere, and others actually drop out of apprenticeships or training programs on which they had started. On this point we can do no more than repeat a comment from the preliminary report.[23]

"There is some reason to think that the most influential factors are first, personal characteristics of the worker—intelligence, manual

[22] A special tabulation on this point revealed that 42 per cent of those in Sample 1 moved up at least one step on the occupational ladder during the first five years of their work history. During the next five years, only 24 per cent made an upward move. After this point the rate of upward movement fell off rapidly, and after twenty years of work experience downward moves began to exceed upward moves.

[23] Reynolds and Shister, *op. cit.*, pp. 67–68.

dexterity and other physical characteristics, and perhaps also qualities of temperament and character; and second, factors which may be regarded as accidental—the good fortune of being in the right place when a vacancy occurred, of happening to get in an expanding company with good promotional opportunities, of having strategically located friends and relatives, and so on. How much of the occupational progress observed in this study was due to merit and how much to luck is an intriguing question, but there is unfortunately no way of answering it from the data we have.

Downward movement seems also to result from a combination of personal shortcomings and economic circumstances. Those in our sample who had lost their footing on the economic ladder did so in a number of standard ways: general depression or some special misfortune overtook the company and they were laid off. Technological change eliminated the job in which they were employed. The grocery store, barber shop, or other small business which they had managed to acquire went into bankruptcy—usually, one suspects, because of the limited managerial capacity of the individual. The people displaced in these ways were obliged to seek work with new employers and, as is typically the case with involuntary movement, the new jobs were at a lower level than the old. Some managed eventually to climb back to their previous level, but others did not, and many of our sample had been through this down-and-up cycle a discouraging number of times.

Loss of physical stamina with increasing age is an important reason for downward movement in later life. Beyond a certain age, most men cannot do stevedoring and other heavy labor, and even the operation of high-speed machinery is beyond their capacity. They are obliged to step down to jobs as watchman, janitor, elevator operator, sweepers and oilers, and the like. It is significant that our tabulations show more downward than upward moves after the first twenty years of work experience.

INTERPLANT MOVEMENT: CONTRIBUTING FACTORS

It was noted in Chapter IV that workers have a strong preference for staying on with the same company. When they think of advancement, therefore, they tend to think of opportunities within the establishment where they are currently employed. Moreover, the bulk of actual upward movement is intraplant movement. A change of employers typically means retrogression in the occupational scale. This is notably true of involuntary changes of employment. Even in the

dexterity and other physical characteristics, and perhaps also qualities of temperament and character; and second, factors which may be regarded as accidental—the good fortune of being in the right place when a vacancy occurred, of happening into an expanding company with good promotional opportunities, of having strategically located friends and relatives, and so on." How much of the occupational progress observed in this study was due to merit and how much to luck is an intriguing question, but there is unfortunately no way of answering it from the data we have.

Downward movement seems also to result from a combination of personal shortcomings and economic mischance. Those in our sample who had lost their footing on the economic ladder did so in a number of standard ways. General depression or some special misfortune overtook the company and they were laid off. Technological changes eliminated the job on which they were employed. The grocery store, barber shop, or other small business which they had managed to acquire went into bankruptcy—usually, one suspects, because of the limited managerial capacity of the individual. The people displaced in these ways were obliged to seek work with new employers and, as is typically the case with involuntary movement, the new jobs were at a lower level than the old. Some managed eventually to climb back to their previous level, but others did not, and many of our sample had been through this down-and-up cycle a discouraging number of times.

Loss of physical stamina with increasing age is an important reason for downward movement in later life. Beyond a certain age, most men cannot do stevedoring and other heavy labor, and even the operation of high-speed machinery is beyond their capacity. They are obliged to step down to jobs as watchmen, janitors, elevator operators, sweepers and oilers, and the like. It is significant that our tabulations show more downward than upward moves after the first twenty years of work experience.

Intraplant Movement: Conditioning Factors

It was noted in Chapter IV that workers have a strong preference for staying on with the same company. When they think of advancement, therefore, they tend to think of opportunities within the establishment where they are presently employed. Moreover, the bulk of actual upward movement is intraplant movement. A change of employers typically means retrogression in the occupational scale. This is notably true of involuntary changes of employment. Even in the

case of voluntary changes, however, it was noted in Chapter IV that only a small percentage of such changes represent deliberate movement to better opportunities. The worker typically "climbs the ladder" within an enterprise, then slips back to a greater or less extent if he changes employers. It thus becomes important to explore the factors which determine how much upward movement there will be in a plant and which workers will get first chance at the opportunities which arise.

The extent and incidence of intraplant movement is determined by four main factors: the production setup, which determines the kinds of jobs to be done; employer policies concerning the filling of vacant jobs; the attitudes of the workers toward movement from one job to another; and union contact provisions governing promotions and transfers.

1. The Production Setup

The most important single factor in the situation is the structure of production. This determines the kinds of job available and hence the outside limits of interjob movement. The structure of production, and the consequent array of jobs, varies enormously from one type of industry to another. The discussion which follows relates solely to manufacturing plants, and much of what is said may not apply with equal force to other industries.

One tends to think of the jobs in a manufacturing plant as forming a continuous hierarchy from completely unskilled to very highly skilled, and of vertical mobility as going on all the way from the bottom to the top of this hierarchy. This is not a correct view of the situation. The labor force of a typical manufacturing plant divides into three distinct categories: production workers, usually machine operatives, who form the bulk of the labor force; skilled maintenance and service workers; and unskilled workers—heavy laborers, sweepers, oilers, hand truckers, janitors, elevator operators, and the like. There is little vertical movement from one of these categories to the next. Skilled maintenance workers require a special background of training and experience, and must usually be hired from outside the plant. Large plants sometimes find it economical to maintain their own trade schools to train workers for these occupations; but the trainees are normally recruited from outside rather than from present production workers. The unskilled jobs are normally filled either from outside the plant or from present employees who have become incapable of pro-

decline work because of age and physical disability. These jobs tend to serve as a stepping stone down from production work rather than up to it.

Upward occupational movement is most vigorous within the range of production jobs. The extent of this range varies greatly from one plant to the next, depending mainly on: (1) The variety of products manufactured and the number of separate production departments. (2) The frequency of shifts in type of product and the extent of output fluctuations on each product. These variations in types and quantities of output increase the necessity for horizontal transfers of labor from one department to another, and this is likely to open up greater possibilities of vertical movement as well. (3) The processes used in making a particular product. Some products require a very narrow range of skills and all workers in the department are on virtually the same level; other products require everything from the lowest to the finest kinds of work. (4) Size of plant is important insofar as it may involve one of the three previous factors. In general, greater size of plant normally means greater variety of products and greater possibilities of upward movement.

Narrowing the focus to a single production department of a manufacturing plant, one will usually find that the jobs fall within a rather narrow band amounting to, say, three labor grades in the National Metal Trades job evaluation system. In few cases does one job prepare specifically for any other job in the department. On the contrary, the learning time on most jobs is only a few days or at most a few weeks, so that one can move with almost equal ease from any job to any other. The main differences among jobs are not in skill but in degree of physical effort, pleasantness or unpleasantness of the work, responsibility for machinery and materials, and other factors. Natural "ladders" or channels of promotion are rare except on large pieces of equipment requiring a crew of two or more workers. In these cases there are usually senior and junior members of the crew, the latter working in time to become senior members. For the most part, however, each job in the department stands by itself and job transfers may run in any direction.

What is the concrete meaning of promotion under these circumstances? At least six possibilities may be distinguished: (1) Transfer from the third shift to the second or the second to the first is counted as a big step forward, except for the small minority of workers who prefer night work. Many companies indeed make a practice of hiring

duction work because of age and physical disability. These jobs tend to serve as a stepping stone *down* from production work rather than up to it.

Upward occupational movement is most vigorous within the range of production jobs. The extent of this range varies greatly from one plant to the next, depending mainly on: (1) The variety of products manufactured and the number of separate production departments; (2) The frequency of shifts in type of product and the extent of output fluctuations on each product. Great variation in types and quantities of output increases the necessity for horizontal transfers of labor from one department to another, and this is likely to open up greater possibilities of *vertical* movement as well; (3) The processes used in making a particular product. Some products require a very narrow range of skills and all workers in the department are on virtually the same level; other products require everything from the roughest to the finest kinds of work; (4) Size of plant is important insofar as it may involve one of the three previous factors. In general, greater size of plant normally means greater variety of products and greater possibilities of upward movement.

Narrowing the focus to a single production department of a manufacturing plant, one will usually find that the jobs fall within a rather narrow band amounting to, say, three labor grades in the National Metal Trades job evaluation system. In few cases does one job prepare specifically for any other job in the department. On the contrary, the learning time on most jobs is only a few days, or at most a few weeks, so that one can move with almost equal ease from any job to any other. The main differences among jobs are not in skill but in degree of physical effort, pleasantness or unpleasantness of the work, responsibility for machinery and materials, and other factors. Natural "ladders" or channels of promotion are rare except on large pieces of equipment requiring a crew of two or more workers. In these cases there are usually senior and junior members of the crew, the latter aspiring in time to become senior members. For the most part, however, each job in the department stands by itself and job transfers may run in any direction.

What is the concrete meaning of promotion under these circumstances? At least six possibilities may be distinguished: (1) Transfer from the third shift to the second or the second to the first is counted as a big step forward, except for the small minority of workers who prefer night work. Many companies, indeed, make a practice of hiring

all new employees on the second or third shift, and promoting the best of them to the first shift as vacancies occur. (2) Transfer from a job paid on an hourly basis to one paid on an output basis is normally considered a promotion, because it means greater independence and usually higher average earnings. (3) Transfer to a job in a higher labor grade. (4) Transfer to a job which, while in the same labor grade, provides consistently higher earnings because of the "looseness" of time standards on the job. (5) Transfer to another job which, while it affords about the same earnings, is physically easier, more interesting, steadier, has a better foreman, or is pleasanter in some other respect. (6) The receipt of more money for doing the *same* job. A surprising proportion of workers make no distinction between getting more money on the same job and getting more money by moving to a different job.

From a subjective standpoint, then, "promotion" is not a homogeneous thing and is not capable of precise quantitative measurement. A worker may be moved from the second shift to a job on the first shift which, however, is one labor grade below his previous job; or he may be moved from an incentive job in labor grade 10 to an hourly rated job in labor grade 8 which, despite its higher rating, yields lower hourly earnings. Has he been promoted or not? One can find out only by asking him, or by observing whether he is willing to make the proposed change voluntarily. One cannot determine how many promotions he has had simply by tracing his changes of status in the company's personnel records, still less by using such broad occupational categories as "unskilled" or "semiskilled" labor.

All six types of change listed above are movements within the range of semiskilled jobs. Most of the occupational progress experienced by manufacturing workers, indeed, consists of advancement within semiskilled employment. "Semiskilled" has become an omnibus term for virtually all production work in manufacturing, and embraces a very wide range of job opportunities. The tabulations of the last section, then, give a misleadingly low impression of the extent of occupational progress among manual workers. It may be that only 20 per cent of workers succeed in moving from one broad occupational category to another. Many more, however, may be able to make significant progress within a particular category.

2. *Management Practices*

We have already noted that the structure of production places certain compulsions on management in the matter of promotion.

There is little upward movement from unskilled work in the plant to semiskilled production jobs. Able workers are unwilling to remain in unskilled jobs while waiting for a production job to open up. Management tends to recruit for these jobs people who are incapable of production work, and many resign themselves permanently to unskilled labor. There is also a tendency to use light unskilled jobs to take care of present employees whose strength is impaired by age or disability, or who simply want to retire from production work to jobs with a slower tempo. A considerable number of workers who are physically capable of production work prefer to take unskilled hourly rated jobs, the loss in earnings being offset in their minds by a reduction in effort and responsibility. As one employment manager said, "The only way to maintain any stability in the unskilled groups, to keep turnover at an acceptable figure, is to hire selectively for these jobs. We pick up the handicapped, the older, the generally incompetent, for these jobs—people who are physically or temperamentally unsuited for better jobs and who are happy to stay in the bottom ranks." Another plant manager said, "We often use these jobs—sweepers, janitors, material handlers, truckers—as spots for workers in higher skilled production operations who get too old or who can't stand the pace on an incentive job any longer."

There is also little movement from semiskilled production jobs into skilled maintenance and repair work. Most companies either hire skilled men from the outside or bring in youngsters as apprentices for skilled occupations. In-plant training tends to be confined to large plants which have a sufficient number of machinists to make regular training programs feasible. Many even of the larger companies, however, prefer to hire fully trained workers whenever possible, thus avoiding the expense of a training program plus the uncertainty as to whether the apprentice will stay with the company after he has been trained.

Upward movement within the plant, then, takes three main forms: (1) Promotion from one grade to another within a skilled occupation, from Machinist Class C to Class B to Class A, with a corresponding enlargement of tasks and responsibilities; (2) promotion from one semiskilled job to another within a production department; (3) Promotion to supervisory positions. The amount of upward movement at any time is naturally much influenced by the behavior of total employment in the company and the area. If labor is scarce in the area, and if the company is trying to expand its operations, there will be a strong tendency to fill vacancies from inside the plant and the num-

There is little upward movement from unskilled work in the plant to semiskilled production jobs. Able workers are unwilling to remain in unskilled jobs while waiting for a production job to open up. Management tends to recruit for these jobs people who are incapable of production work and must resign themselves permanently to unskilled labor. There is also a tendency to use light unskilled jobs to "take care of" present employees whose strength is impaired by age or disability, or who simply want to retire from production work to jobs with a slower tempo. A considerable number of workers who are physically capable of production work prefer to take unskilled hourly rated jobs, the loss in earnings being offset in their minds by a reduction in effort and responsibility. As one employment manager said, "The only way to maintain any stability in the unskilled groups, to keep turnover at an acceptable figure, is to hire selectively for those jobs. We stick to the handicapped, the older, phlegmatic applicants for those jobs—people who are physically or temperamentally unsuited for better jobs and who are happy to stay in the bottom ranks." Another plant manager said, "We often use those jobs—sweepers, janitors, material handlers, truckers—as spots for workers in higher skilled production operations who get too old or who can't stand the pace on an incentive job any longer."

There is also little movement from semiskilled production jobs into skilled maintenance and repair work. Most companies either hire skilled men from the outside or bring in youngsters as trainees for skilled occupations. Inplant training tends to be confined to large plants which have a sufficient number of vacancies to make regular training programs feasible. Many even of the larger companies, however, prefer to hire fully trained workers whenever possible, thus avoiding the expense of a training program plus the uncertainty as to whether the apprentice will stay with the company after he has been trained.

Upward movement within the plant, then, is of three main sorts: (1) Promotion from one grade to another within a skilled occupation, from Machinist Class C to Class B to Class A, with a corresponding enlargement of tasks and responsibilities. (2) Promotion from one semiskilled job to another within a production department. (3) Promotion to supervisory positions. The amount of upward movement at any time is naturally much influenced by the behavior of total employment in the company and the area. If labor is scarce in the area, and if the company is trying to expand its operations, there will be a strong tendency to fill vacancies from inside the plant and the num-

ber of promotions will be large. If the company's employment is contracting rapidly, demotions will be the order of the day; foremen will become production workers and production workers will sweep floors. If there is a large surplus of labor in the area, but the company is expanding its own employment, there will be some tendency to pick up exceptionally qualified workers from the outside and inplant promotions may decline. It should be remembered, then, that this study was made at a time of high employment when most companies were struggling to maintain or expand their operations. The practices prevailing at the time, and particularly the heavy emphasis on internal promotion, doubtless reflect this situation.

Almost all the companies interviewed stated that their policy was to fill vacancies on production jobs by promotion from within "wherever possible." Further questioning, however, revealed that the proportion of vacancies actually filled from within varied from almost zero in some companies to almost 100 per cent in others.[24] The reasons for this variation are to be found in the occupational structure of the plant, the attitudes and preferences of management, the willingness of workers to change jobs, and the nature of union rules.

In some of the plants visited there was little scope for vertical movement. All the production jobs were at nearly the same level of skill and earnings, and a worker established in one had little incentive to move to another. In these plants the normal practice was to fill all vacancies from the outside and internal transfers were rare.

In most plants there was sufficient occupational spread to make internal promotion feasible. In some cases one found definite promotion "ladders," work on one job in a department normally preparing the worker for advancement to a higher job. Thus in the tirebuilding department of a rubber company in the area, a man can advance from general helper to floor servicer to pan servicer to tire builder. A paper company reported a typical progression from stock booster to feeder to pressman, the latter two jobs having skill breakdowns making possible further steps in promotion.

These definite job hierarchies, however, are the exception rather than the rule. The typical situation is one in which, while no job prepares specifically for any other job, there is sufficient variation in job attractiveness to provide an incentive for movement from one to

[24] We estimate that for the group as a whole the proportion of production vacancies filled from within the plant was between one-half and two-thirds. Since many of the companies were unable to give quantitative information on this point, however, this estimate is only a rough approximation.

another. Moreover, since none of the jobs require prolonged training, workers are highly interchangeable among them. The differences in job attractiveness, which provide a basis for internal mobility, were discussed in Chapter IV. Wage differences are important; personnel officials report that a variation of even five cents per hour in the base rate is regarded as significant by most workers. Apart from this, some jobs are easier than others, have a better supervisor or a more congenial work crew, have loose piece rates which permit higher earnings, have traditionally been regarded in the plant as "better jobs," or have other advantages. When shifts do not rotate, movement to the day shift (or on a better shift) is an important channel of promotion.

Given a choice between hiring from the outside and promotion from within the department, which will management do? There are advantages on either side. If a qualified applicant can be found, hiring from the outside is usually cheaper in the short run. The alternative of internal promotion involves costly retraining which may extend far beyond the original move. If a man is moved from job B to job A, someone else must be transferred from job C to job B, and so on. A determined insistence on internal promotion might mean that each vacancy would cause a dozen transfers. On the other hand, if all vacancies are filled from the outside, there will be bad long-run effects on the morale of the labor force and able workers will leave the company to win promotion elsewhere.

These considerations are weighed differently by different managements. The result is that while almost all will defend promotion from within as the "right" thing to do, some make many more exceptions to the rule than others. Company practice is affected also by the extent to which employment decisions are centralized within the company. If the foreman has a free hand, he will frequently take the easiest way out by recruiting from the outside. Personnel officials and higher management are likely to be more conscious of the long-run advantages of a vigorous promotion policy. If they are able to exercise an effective check on foremen's actions, internal promotion is likely to be more frequent.

3. Worker Attitudes

Even where management prefers to fill vacancies from within the plant, its ability to do so depends on finding workers who will move to the vacant jobs. Again and again in our interviews managers complained of workers' reluctance to change jobs within the plant and

another. Moreover, since none of the jobs require prolonged training, workers are highly interchangeable among them. The differences in job attractiveness which provide a basis for internal mobility were discussed in Chapter IV. Wage differences are important; personnel officials report that a variation of even five cents per hour in the base rate is regarded as significant by most workers. Apart from this, some jobs are easier than others, have a better supervisor or a more congenial work crew, have loose piece rates which permit higher earnings, have traditionally been regarded in the plant as "better jobs," or have other advantages. Where shifts do not rotate, movement to the same job on a better shift is an important channel of promotion.

Given a choice between hiring from the outside and promotion from within the department, which will management do? There are advantages on either side. If a qualified applicant can be found, hiring from the outside is usually cheaper in the short run. The alternative of internal promotion involves costs of retraining which may extend far beyond the original job. When a man is moved from job B to job A, someone else must be transferred from job C to job B, and so on; a determined insistence on internal promotion might mean that each vacancy would cause a dozen transfers. On the other hand, if all vacancies are filled from the outside, there will be bad long-run effects on the morale of the labor force and able workers will leave the company to win promotion elsewhere.

These considerations are weighed differently by different managements. The result is that, while almost all will defend promotion from within as the "right" thing to do, some make many more exceptions to the rule than others. Company practice is affected also by the extent to which employment decisions are centralized within the company. If the foreman has a free hand, he will frequently take the easiest way out by recruiting from the outside. Personnel officials and higher management are likely to be more conscious of the long-run advantages of a vigorous promotion policy. If they are able to exercise an effective check on foremen's actions, internal promotion is likely to be more frequent.

3. *Worker Attitudes*

Even where management prefers to fill vacancies from within the plant, its ability to do so depends on finding workers who will move to the vacant jobs. Again and again in our interviews, managers complained of workers' reluctance to change jobs within the plant and

pointed out cases in which they had been compelled to go outside to fill a vacancy. One manager said, "The fundamental principle of our workers' psychology seems to be never to take any chances; they don't like change, but they always want more money. We've gotten so we hate to try to switch people about, the mortality is so high in such situations; fifty per cent of those who change jobs quit." Another said, "Our long-service people seem to be married to their jobs; only the younger people seem anxious to change. We have to sell a job on which there is a vacancy to an employee before we can get him to move."

The reasons for this reluctance to change jobs within the plant are akin to the reasons noted in Chapter IV for reluctance to change employers. In many ways, indeed, a shift within the plant is the same as a change of employers. It means moving away from friends to a new work group, a new supervisor, and new physical surroundings. It means learning new duties and routines. It may involve financial risk, especially on incentive work where the earnings on the new job cannot be predicted accurately in advance. There is also the risk that you may not make good on the new job, in which case you may be out of work entirely. On incentive work, these risk elements seem to be more important than moderate differences in the base rates of different jobs.

The companies interviewed were asked whether recent reductions in the percentage spread between different labor grades, resulting from equal cents-per-hour increases throughout the plant, had made workers less willing to move from "lower" to "higher" jobs. The replies were almost uniformly in the negative. Only two serious difficulties seemed to exist at the time of the interview. High earnings of certain groups of incentive workers, resulting not from high base rates for the jobs but from the general loosening up of time standards during the war years, were causing considerable grumbling among skilled maintenance workers paid on an hourly basis who frequently found themselves earning less than semiskilled men. In some plants increases in foremen's salaries had not kept pace with increases in piece workers' earnings, and this was contributing to difficulty in recruiting foremen. As regards transfers within semiskilled employment, however, the recent narrowing of percentage wage differentials does not seem to have had any marked effect.

An interesting phenomenon encountered in the study was the unwillingness of many workers to accept promotion to a foremanship.

this attitude was reported to us frequently by management, and its prevalence was confirmed by our discussions with workers in the plant. One reason for it is the serious risk that the worker may not make good at the supervisory level. Even if company policies permit an unsatisfactory foreman to step down to his previous job, this is an unpleasant step to take and many men will quit the company rather than lose face with their associates. Some companies reported that their foremen will usually quit rather than take a demotion to production work even when this is due to a general reduction of force throughout the plant and not to personal shortcomings. Turnover among foremen is high, and a foreman is considerably less secure than a skilled worker with adequate seniority protection. One of the companies interviewed reported, for example, that out of 37 foremen who had been in the plant five years previously, only 2 were still there at the time of our interview.

There are other features of the foreman's job which reduce its attractiveness to many workers. It frequently pays little more than he can earn as a skilled worker, and there are not uncommon instances in which incentive workers with loose time standards are able to earn considerably more than their foremen. It does not provide the feeling of direct accomplishment enjoyed by a master mechanic who can actually see what he has made. It involves responsibility and worry; the foreman finds it harder to leave the shop behind at five o'clock. It means stepping out of the union, which is usually a loss in personal satisfaction as well as economic protection. Accepting a foremanship tends to alienate a man from his former friends and associates. Again and again in our interviews workers explained that "the foreman has no friends," and expressed their repugnance for the "driving" or other traits which they felt were a necessary part of the foreman's job. Even those who would enjoy the exercise of authority point out that the actual authority of the foreman has been eroded by the growth of personnel and production specialists and by union organization. The plight of the foreman caught between the opposing pressures of the union and higher management is a familiar one and many workers

For illustrative quotations from workers on this point see Reynolds and Shister, op. cit., pp. 72-73.

Companies in our sample which maintain a sizable differential between salaries of foremen and the earnings of the workers under them seem to have relatively little difficulty in filling foremanships. This suggests that higher salaries for foremen in other companies might remedy part of the shortage of foreman applicants.

This attitude was reported to us frequently by management, and its prevalence was confirmed by our discussions with workers in the area.[25] One reason for it is the serious risk that the worker may not make good at the supervisory level. Even if company policies permit an unsatisfactory foreman to step down to his previous jobs, this is an unpleasant step to take and many men will quit the company rather than "lose face" with their associates. Some companies reported that their foremen will usually quit rather than take a demotion to production work, even when this is due to a general reduction of force throughout the plant and not to personal shortcomings. Turnover among foremen is high, and a foreman is considerably less secure than a shop worker with adequate seniority protection. One of the companies interviewed reported, for example, that out of 38 foremen who had been in the plant five years previously, only 2 were still there at the time of our interview.

There are other features of the foreman's job which render it unattractive to many workers. It frequently pays little more than one can earn as a skilled worker; and cases are not uncommon in which incentive workers with loose time standards are able to earn considerably more than their foreman.[26] It does not provide the feeling of direct accomplishment enjoyed by a master mechanic who can actually see what he has made. It involves responsibility and worry; the foreman finds it harder to leave the shop behind at five o'clock. It means stepping out of the union, which is usually a loss in personal satisfaction as well as economic protection. Accepting a foremanship tends to alienate a man from his former friends and associates. Again and again in our interviews workers explained that "the foreman has no friends," and expressed their repugnance for the "driving" of other men which they felt was a necessary part of the foreman's job. Even those who would enjoy the exercise of authority point out that the actual authority of the foreman has been eroded by the rise of personnel and production specialists and by union organization. The plight of the foreman, caught between the opposing pressures of the union and higher management, is a familiar one and many workers

[25] For illustrative quotations from workers on this point, see Reynolds and Shister, *op. cit.*, pp. 71–73.

[26] Companies in our sample which maintains a sizeable differential between salaries of foremen and the earnings of the workers under them seem to have relatively little difficulty in filling foremanships. This suggests that higher salaries for foremen in other companies might provide part of the answer to the "foreman problem."

have no wish to get themselves into this position. In consequence, many of the workers best qualified to become foremen are unwilling to do so, while those who push themselves forward for promotion are often unqualified.

4. Union Contract Provisions

Our findings concerning the impact of collective bargaining on intraplant mobility may be summarized briefly, since they merely confirm previous writing on the subject. Most union contracts in the area provide for posting of job vacancies and bidding on these jobs by interested workers in the plant, who must be considered before outsiders are recruited. This type of rule clearly increases the amount of intraplant movement. It establishes promotion from within as a definite policy which foremen are not free to ignore. It also gives workers in the plant a better chance to hear about vacancies which might interest them. While public posting of vacancies is not unknown in nonunion plants, it seems to be the exception rather than the rule.

Most union contracts also provide that length of service shall be considered along with ability in selecting workers for promotion. Seniority is rarely the main criterion, usually coming into play only when ability and training are relatively equal. The unions are pressing for greater emphasis on seniority, however, both in negotiating new contracts and in discussing the filling of particular vacancies.

Unionism thus reinforces the tendency for each company to become a water-tight compartment in the labor market. To the extent that intraplant mobility is accelerated, interplant movement is impaired. Emphasis on seniority places a premium on continued attachment to the same company. Additional service helps one to win promotions and protects one against demotion and layoff. Fluctuations in labor demand are absorbed, not by the less capable workers, but by the short-service workers.

As a result of the combined operation of the factors discussed in this section, promotion from within is now the general rule and is increasing over the course of time. Working in this direction are the growth of centralized employment departments strong enough to control foremen's actions, the increasing belief of employers that internal promotion is proper policy, the increasing reluctance of workers to change employers, and the extension of collective bargaining. The main limitations on internal promotion are the reluctance of many workers to accept transfers to other jobs and the limited oppor-

tunities for promotion in some companies because of the production structure.

INTRAPLANT MOVEMENT: EXTENT AND DIRECTION

We have now examined the factors which determine how many opportunities there will be for promotion and who will get them. What are the consequences in terms of amount of upward movement in industrial plants? What proportion of workers are able to make significant progress during their tenure of employment with a company?

Our first item of evidence on this point comes from the workers in Sample B. Each worker was asked whether he had had any changes of job assignment since coming with his present employer. If the answer was "Yes," he was asked to describe the jobs he had held in the company, indicating in each case whether the change was an improvement or not. These replies give a subjective view of occupational progress. They indicate how many workers in the sample had moved to jobs which seemed better to them.

Sixty-seven per cent of the workers stated that they had had no change of job assignment within their present company. Twenty-eight per cent said that they had moved up to better jobs, while 5 per cent said they had moved to jobs which they regarded as worse than their first jobs. As one would expect, long-service workers showed more upward movement than short-service workers. Forty-three per cent of those with ten to twenty years of service with the same company had moved to better jobs, compared with 35 per cent of those with three to five years of service, and 11 per cent of those with less than one year's service. The worker's chance of advancement is clearly improved by a long period of service with the same employer; but even among long-service employees something like one-half are unable to make significant progress over the years.[4]

The second piece of evidence comes from a case study of intraplant movement in a medium-sized metal-fabricating plant in the area. From the personnel record cards maintained by the company, we selected one-third of those who had been employed continuously since 1941. The year 1941 was chosen because in that year the company installed the National Metal Trades system of job evaluation. From

[4] These percentages refer, of course, only to progress through promotion. A number of those who had had no change of job had doubtless experienced some improvement in terms of [illegible] work content, wage rating, and other factors; and [illegible] progressed markedly in money earnings. It should be noted also that our sample did not include those who had advanced to foremanships or higher supervisory positions.

tunities for promotion in some companies because of the production structure.

Intraplant Movement: Extent and Direction

We have now examined the factors which determine how many opportunities there will be for promotion and who will get them. What are the consequences in terms of *amount* of upward movement in industrial plants? What proportion of workers are able to make significant progress during their tenure of employment with a company?

Our first item of evidence on this point comes from the workers in Sample 1. Each worker was asked whether he had had any changes of job assignment since coming with his present employer. If the answer was "Yes," he was asked to describe the jobs he had held in the company, indicating in each case whether the change was an improvement or not. The replies give a subjective view of occupational progress. They indicate how many workers in the sample had moved to jobs which seemed better to them.

Sixty-seven per cent of the workers stated that they had had no change of job assignment within their present company. Twenty-eight per cent said that they had moved up to better jobs, while 5 per cent said they had moved to jobs which they regarded as worse than their first jobs. As one would expect, long-service workers showed more upward movement than short-service workers. Forty-three per cent of those with ten to twenty years' service with the same company had moved to better jobs, compared with 23 per cent of those with three to five years' service, and 11 per cent of those with less than one years' service. The worker's chance of advancement is clearly improved by a long period of service with the same employer; but even among long-service employees something like one-half are unable to make significant progress over the years.[27]

The second piece of evidence comes from a case study of intraplant movement in a medium-sized metal manufacturing plant in the area. From the personnel record cards maintained by the company, we selected one-third of those who had been employed continuously since 1941. The year 1941 was chosen because in that year the company installed the National Metal Trades system of job evaluation. From

[27] This statement refers, of course, only to progress through a change of job assignment. Some of those who had had no change of job had doubtless made progress *on that job* in terms of shift, work content, wage rating, and other factors; and virtually all had progressed markedly in money earnings. It should be recalled also that our sample did not include those who had advanced to foremanships or higher supervisory positions.

this time on the labor grade of each job held by a worker was entered on his record card, which made it possible to identify each job change as "upward," "downward," or "horizontal."

This material is not directly comparable with the interview information from Sample 1. Only one company is involved, and this company may not be typical of all companies in the area.[28] The data relate, not to the entire work record of the individual, but to an eight-year span from 1941 through 1948. The definition of "progress" is objective, involving a change in N. M. T. A. labor grade, and may differ somewhat from the subjective evaluation of the worker himself.

The workers in the sample had worked, on the average, at three and a half different jobs during the eight years covered by the study. Of all the job changes made during the period, 34 per cent were upward, 26 per cent were downward, 30 per cent were lateral movements involving no change in labor grade or type of compensation, and the remaining 10 per cent were unclassified.[29]

In addition to classifying each job change, it was possible to classify the work record of each individual over the eight-year period. This tabulation revealed that 70 per cent had not improved their position over the period in terms of the labor grade rating of their job. The largest single group, 35 per cent, had had no change of work at all. An additional 11 per cent had changed jobs within the same labor grade, while 24 per cent had moved up and down the occupational scale with no clear trend. It cannot be asserted that these workers have not improved themselves in any respect. Some have doubtless moved to a more desirable shift, others may have increased their earnings by shifting from hourly to incentive work or from a "tight" incentive job to a "loose" one, and others may have gained in working conditions. As regards the rank of their job in the plant hierarchy, however, they have either stood still or moved up and down without trend. Twenty-two per cent of those in the group showed definite advancement—15 per cent by only one labor grade, 7 per cent by more than this. The remaining 8 per cent had moved down one or more

[28] There is reason to think that this company probably has more vertical mobility than the average company in the area. It has frequent changes in product and methods of production, is very competently managed, and encourages inplant promotion both as a matter of policy and because of the provisions of its union contract.

[29] These were moves involving improvement in one respect and retrogression in another, the net effect being uncertain. A movement to a job in a lower labor grade, for example, involving also a shift from hourly to incentive payment, might easily raise the worker's earnings and might be regarded by him either as a promotion or a demotion. One of the most interesting byproducts of this case study was a revelation of how difficult it is to obtain a clear objective definition of occupational progress.

labor grades during the period. It is interesting that these proportions (70, 22, and 8 per cent) are so close to those derived from Sample 1 (67, 28, and 5 per cent) despite differences in the origin of the data.

Both types of data indicate that only a minority of workers are able to move a significant distance up the occupational ladder via intraplant promotions. The main reasons for this have already been discussed. The narrow range of production jobs in many plants leaves little opportunity for advancement. The skilled maintenance and repair jobs are typically walled off from the production jobs by training requirements. Workers are frequently reluctant to change jobs even where vacancies are available. Where there is no union, foremen frequently prefer to hire from the outside rather than move an experienced man from his present job and create a second vacancy. Thus the possibilities of promotion, already narrow enough on technical grounds, are further narrowed by worker attitudes and managerial practice.

Some Consequences of Limited Occupational Movement

These limitations on upward movement raise two main issues. The first issue is that of productive efficiency. Do present promotional arrangements ensure an optimum allocation of the skills and abilities of the labor force among different occupations? Does the "right" man get the "right" job? The second problem is one of worker satisfaction. Are most workers satisfied with the occupational level which they are able to achieve? Or is there a great deal of frustrated ambition which, blocked from its normal outlets, is forced into other directions? A word on these points will form a fitting conclusion to this chapter.

It is clear that present arrangements do not ensure that a vacancy will always be filled by the best qualified worker. This would require a method of pretesting the probable performance of different workers on a vacant job; and it would require that the vacancy be thrown open to all comers, inside and outside the company, selection among them being made strictly according to ability. These conditions do not exist at present, and it is doubtful whether they could be brought into existence. From management's standpoint, an attempt to fill vacancies on a competitive basis would involve costs which might more than cancel out any gains in production efficiency: the cost of an occupational testing program, of advertising vacancies and examining applicants, of delays in production while the search for the "right" man was going on. From the workers' standpoint, competitive

filling of vacancies would doubtless appear unfair and undesirable. Most workers consider it proper that people within the enterprise should have first chance at vacancies, and that attention should be paid to length of service as well as to ability. Even in the absence of a union, management is not entirely free to override these worker attitudes.

The filling of vacancies will probably continue, then, to be rather haphazard from an efficiency standpoint. The effects on production, however, are probably not as harmful as one might think. The requirements of most jobs in modern industry are not very exacting: a minimum level of manual dexterity, reaction-speed, and physical stamina; ability to understand simple instructions; and such personal traits as punctuality, attentiveness, and ability to adjust to personal contacts with fellow workers and supervisors. Given these traits, all but a small percentage of manual jobs can be learned quickly and performed competently. This amounts to saying that for most jobs there are a great many "right" men, and that which of these men gets the job is a matter of indifference from a production standpoint.

The answer to the second question posed above is less encouraging. There seem to be many industrial workers who would like to move up to a better job but are unable to do so. Of the workers in Sample 1 who were planning to stay with their present employer, 40 per cent said that they preferred to continue doing their present job, 15 per cent wanted to move up and expected to do so, and 45 per cent wanted to move up but did not expect to do so.[30] The commonest reason given for inability to work up was the obvious one—lack of vacancies. Another large group said that they lacked the necessary skill and training for higher jobs, and did not feel able to acquire it at their present age. They were not willing to face the risks and the temporary loss of income involved in training for a more skilled job.

It should be noted that the typical worker's conception of "promotion" is a very limited one. This was pointed out repeatedly by management officials, and our worker interviews confirm their opinion. Few workers aspire to office jobs in the company, or to foremanships, or even to skilled maintenance work. Their aspirations are focussed on a job which is on a better shift, or in the next higher labor grade, or is pleasanter in some other respect.

Where even this modest ambition is frustrated, as it very frequently

[30] The percentage of workers in Sample 2 who felt unable to secure promotion was considerably smaller, probably because this group included only young, short-service workers. For a fuller discussion of worker attitudes on this point, see Reynolds and Shister, *op. cit.*, pp. 70–75.

is, the worker tends to concentrate on bettering his position on his present job. This drive takes many forms—getting the newest and best machine in the department or a convenient work location or slightly more intricate and varied products, or some other advantage which sets him slightly above the others in his work group. It also takes the form of getting more money for doing the same job. To many workers, indeed, more money is virtually the whole meaning of occupational progress. Our first interview schedule contained the question, "Have you had any promotions since you started work here?" This question had later to be rephrased, because a large proportion of workers answered it by saying, "Oh yes, I've had three raises since I came with the company."

More money may be obtained in a variety of ways. It may come from plant-wide wage increases; it may come from a personal loosening of time standards on an incentive job. It may come through promotion from Class C to Class B to Class A on the same job. Some companies maintain a classification of this sort even on semi-skilled production jobs. The classification is sometimes justified by differences in work content. We also found cases, however, in which a so-called three-level classification was maintained even though the work content was indistinguishable. This maintenance of an artificial hierarchy enables management to gratify the worker's desire for progress without actually changing the nature of his work. Where there is a rate range of 10 to 20 cents an hour for each labor grade, the worker can progress by individual increases within the rate range. The desire of workers for frequent indications of progress in the form of higher earnings drives unions to press for automatic "escalation" of workers' pay rates at specified intervals until the top of the rate range is reached. After the top has been reached, there is continued pressure on the union to "boost the rate" for the job so that earnings can continue to climb with no change of job assignment.

It is wrong to attribute this drive toward higher earnings simply to a desire for more money to spend. It is also partly (or mainly) a desire for occupational progress, under conditions in which the only possible evidence of progress is higher earnings.

A different, less realistic, form which workers' ambitions assume is the urge to escape from manual employment altogether into business or professional work. The workers in both Samples 1 and 2 were asked what kind of work they would most like to do if they had a free choice of occupation. A majority, including 50 per cent in Sample 1 and 70 per cent in Sample 2, answered that they would keep on doing

is, the worker tends to concentrate on bettering his position on his present job. This drive takes many forms—getting the newest and best machine in the department or a convenient work location, or slightly more intricate and varied products, or some other advantage which sets him slightly above the others in his work group. It also takes the form of getting more money for doing the same job. To many workers, indeed, more money is virtually the whole meaning of occupational progress. Our first interview schedule contained the question: "Have you had any promotions since you started work here?" This question had later to be rephrased, because a large proportion of workers answered it by saying "Oh yes, I've had three raises since I came with the company."

More money may be obtained in a variety of ways. It may come from plant-wide wage increases. It may come from a gradual loosening up of time standards on an incentive job. It may come through promotion from Class C to Class B to Class A on the same job. Some companies maintain a classification of this sort even on semiskilled production jobs. The classification is sometimes justified by differences in work content. We also found cases, however, in which a two- or three-level classification was maintained even though the work done was indistinguishable. This maintenance of an artificial hierarchy enables management to gratify the worker's desire for progress without actually changing the nature of his work. Where there is a rate range of 10 to 20 cents an hour for each labor grade, the worker can progress by individual increases within the rate range. The desire of workers for frequent indications of progress in the form of higher earnings drives unions to press for automatic "escalation" of workers' pay rates at specified intervals until the top of the rate range is reached. After the top has been reached, there is continued pressure on the union to "bust the rate" for the job so that earnings can continue to climb with no change of job assignment.

It is wrong to attribute this drive toward higher earnings simply to a desire for more money to spend. It is due partly to a continuing desire for occupational progress, under conditions in which the only possible evidence of progress is higher earnings.

A different, less realistic, form which workers' ambitions assume is the urge to escape from manual employment altogether into business or professional work. The workers in both Samples 1 and 2 were asked what kind of work they would most like to do if they had a free choice of occupation. A minority, including 30 per cent in Sample 1 and 20 per cent in Sample 2, answered that they would keep on doing

what they were presently doing. The most significant difference here was between the responses of skilled workers and others. A good majority of the skilled workers in both samples preferred to continue in their present occupations, while the proportion of semiskilled and unskilled workers expressing this preference was much smaller. Another sizeable group, consisting of 16 per cent in Sample 1 and 25 per cent in Sample 2, aspired to learn a skilled trade. About 40 per cent in both samples expressed a desire for sales and service work, professional work, or management of their own businesses. Many workers expressed a desire to set up their own retail store, filling station, construction or building repair business, or some other type of small enterprise.

The workers were asked also why they would like this particular type of work. The reason most frequently given was the desire for interesting work, i.e., work which provides variety, an opportunity for contact with people, and for full use of one's skills. The desire for greater independence ranked second. These two factors account for 57 per cent of the answers in Sample 1 and 58 per cent of those in Sample 2. The desire for interesting work seems to be strongly correlated with amount of education. Thus, of workers in Sample 1 with four years of schooling or less, only 19 per cent indicated a desire for interesting work, compared with 54 per cent of the workers with more than twelve years of schooling. Similar results were obtained for Sample 2. This recalls our earlier conclusion that the growing proportion of young people finishing high school is creating a marked discrepancy between job aspirations and the job opportunities actually available.

It should be added that most of the workers interviewed took a realistic view of their chances of getting into the desired kind of work. Thus, only 26 per cent of those in Sample 1 who wanted skilled jobs thought that they would actually get them, and only 9 per cent of those who wanted professional or semiprofessional positions thought there was any chance for them. The most optimistic group were those who wanted to set up their own businesses, of whom half thought they would be able to do so. In few cases was the worker taking any concrete steps to get into the desired occupation, and in most cases the professed desire for higher work seemed to be more nearly a day dream than a program of action. Speculation about pleasant possibilities for the future helps to console the worker for the shortcomings of his present employment.

CHAPTER VI Determination of the Plant Wage Level

IN THE four preceding chapters we have examined the characteristics of labor mobility, taking the wage structure of the area as given. We must now examine how the wage structure itself is determined, and what part labor mobility plays in the process. In this chapter we shall consider the factors which management and union officials in the area take into account in reaching wage decisions. In the next chapter we shall present statistical data on the evolution of the area wage structure over the years 1940–1948.

The limited focus of this chapter needs to be emphasized. The discussion is limited to a single area. Wage changes in any local area are obviously a response to inflationary or deflationary processes in the national economy, but we shall not inquire into the origin of these processes. This amounts to saying that we are interested, not in the average rate of change in the area wage level, but in differences in the rate of wage increase in particular companies. Why, in a particular year, does one company give a wage increase of 5 cents an hour while another company gives an increase of 15 cents an hour? Why does one find, at a particular point of time, one company offering a starting rate of 75 cents an hour while another offers a starting rate of $1.15?

The discussion is further limited to manufacturing industry. Since we could not hope to do a comprehensive analysis of the area in the time available, it was decided to concentrate on manufacturing in the collection of both wage and mobility material. The manufacturing companies also have better wage data than most other industries in the area.

Also, decisions on the general wage level of the plant are only one type, though usually the most important type, of wage decision. Other significant decisions relate to relative wage levels for different jobs in the plant, the structure and administration of incentive systems, and the size of supplementary or "fringe" payments.

Because of these numerous dimensions of wage structure, the size

CHAPTER VI Determination of the Plant Wage Level

IN THE four preceding chapters we have examined the characteristics of labor mobility, taking the wage structure of the area as given. We must now examine how the wage structure itself is determined, and what part labor mobility plays in the process. In this chapter we shall consider the factors which management and union officials in the area take into account in reaching wage decisions. In the next chapter we shall present statistical data on the evolution of the area wage structure over the years 1940–1948.

The limited focus of this chapter needs to be emphasized. The discussion is limited to a single area. Wage changes in any local area are obviously a response to inflationary or deflationary processes in the national economy, but we shall not inquire into the origin of these processes. This amounts to saying that we are interested, not in the average rate of change in the area wage level, but in differences in the rate of wage increase in particular companies. Why, in a particular year, does one company give a wage increase of 5 cents an hour while another company gives an increase of 15 cents an hour? Why does one find, at a particular point of time, one company offering a starting rate of 75 cents an hour while another offers a starting rate of $1.15?

The discussion is further limited to manufacturing industry. Since we could not hope to do a comprehensive analysis of the area in the time available, it was decided to concentrate on manufacturing in the collection of both wage and mobility material. The manufacturing companies also have better wage data than most other industries in the area.

Also, decisions on the general wage level of the plant are only one type, though usually the most important type, of wage decision. Other significant decisions relate to relative wage levels for different jobs in the plant, the structure and administration of incentive systems, and the size of supplementary or "fringe" payments.

Because of these numerous dimensions of wage structure, the size

of plant-wide wage increases is not a very precise indicator of the movement of either workers' earnings or employers' labor costs over the course of time. It remains, however, the most important single determinant, and we shall concentrate on it for the remainder of this chapter. We shall consider first the main criteria which management uses in judging the proper wage level for the plant at a particular time, and then proceed to consider union wage objectives and bargaining strategy. In nonunion plants, which formed about half of our sample, wage decisions are made by management and the criteria used by management are thus of decisive importance. Under union conditions, management determines only its own position at the bargaining table, and the actual wage results from an interplay of union and management positions. The criteria which management uses in judging proper wage behavior, however, seem to be essentially the same in both cases. The difference is that under unionism management is sometimes forced to do things which it regards as "uneconomic" and which would not be done voluntarily.

MANAGEMENT CRITERIA IN WAGE SETTING

The term "criteria" in this context does not mean the *ex post facto* rationalizations which management people give of their wage decisions, still less the arguments which they use in negotiations with the union. It means rather the mental process through which they go in arriving at a decision. Criteria become interesting and significant only when defined in this operational sense. The difficulty is that criteria in this sense are very difficult to determine. While our discussions with management people were extensive, and were conducted soon after each "round" of wage increases, we were still served up generous portions of rationalization and argument in many cases. The attempt to read between the lines, to penetrate back from rationalizations to reasons, was doubtless only partially successful. The results, while suggestive, cannot claim any high degree of precision.

The drift of the evidence may be summarized briefly as follows: For companies in this area during the years 1946–1948, the dominant considerations were the profit prospects of the company and the wage changes currently being made by other companies in the area. Where these two criteria conflicted, the tendency of the nonunion companies was to follow ability to pay, even if this meant lagging behind area wage movements. Wage changes by firms in the same industry in other areas seem to have had less influence on management thinking.

In unionized plants, of course, increases being won by the union in other parts of the industry had considerable effect on the settlements made in this area. This was due, however, to union pressure rather than to management's acceptance of industry patterns as a valid criterion for wage settlements. In the remainder of this section these findings will be elaborated and the supporting evidence presented in some detail.

"Keeping Up With the Area"

When we first visited the cooperating companies to discuss their wage policies, almost everyone said that his company was paying at least as much as "the area wage level." When we came to examine wage statistics for these companies, however, wide differences in wage levels appeared. The explanation of this paradox is partly that management people wanted to believe that they were paying the prevailing wage for the area because this is the respectable thing to do. A more important point, however, is that "the area wage level" is an ambiguous concept, capable of being defined and interpreted in a variety of ways. This makes it possible for any management to convince itself that it is "keeping up with the area" in one sense or another.

"Keeping up with the area" may be interpreted in terms of either wage levels at a point of time or rates of change of wages over a period of time. Management officials in the area seem mainly to follow the latter interpretation. A company is keeping up with the area if its general wage increases in a particular year are about equal to the average of the general increases granted by other companies. It may still be below the area wage level in absolute terms, but at least it has maintained its relative standing.

Management recognizes that there are many possible reasons for differences in the absolute wage levels of different plants in the area. A particular plant may have unusually high wage rates because it is large, technically progressive, or relatively sheltered from competition and so can afford high wages; or because it uses few women workers; or because it employs an unusually high ratio of skilled workers; or because its work is unusually heavy and requires additional compensation for this reason; or because the plant was recently established and has needed a high wage scale in order to build its labor force; or because the industry to which it belongs has a high general wage level. Other plants may have unusually low earnings for the opposite reasons. Over the course of time these differences

In unionized plants, of course, increases being won by the union in other parts of the industry had considerable effect on the settlements made in this area. This was due, however, to union pressure rather than to management acceptance of industry patterns as a valid criterion for wage settlements. In the remainder of this section, these findings will be elaborated and the supporting evidence presented in some detail.

"Keeping Up With the Area"

When we first visited the cooperating companies to discuss their wage policies, almost everyone said that his company was paying at least as much as "the area wage level." When we came to examine wage statistics for these companies, however, wide differences in wage levels appeared. The explanation of this paradox is partly that management people want to believe that they are paying the prevailing wage for the area because this is the respectable thing to do. A more important point, however, is that "the area wage level" is an ambiguous concept, capable of being defined and interpreted in a variety of ways. This makes it possible for any management to convince itself that it is "keeping up with the area" *in one sense or another*.

"Keeping up with the area" may be interpreted in terms of either wage levels at a point of time or rate of change of wages over a period of time. Management officials in the area seem mainly to follow the latter interpretation. A company is keeping up with the area if its general wage increases in a particular year are about equal to the average of the general increases granted by other companies. It may still be below the area wage level in absolute terms, but at least it has maintained its *relative* standing.

Management recognizes that there are many possible reasons for differences in the absolute wage levels of different plants in the area. A particular plant may have unusually high wage rates because it is large, technically progressive, or relatively sheltered from competition and so can afford high wages; or because it uses few women workers; or because it employs an unusually high ratio of skilled workers; or because its work is unusually heavy and requires additional compensation for this reason; or because the plant was recently established and has needed a high wage scale in order to build up its labor force; or because the industry to which it belongs has a high general wage level. Other plants may have unusually low earnings for the opposite reasons. Over the course of time these differences

in plant wage levels become recognized and customary. Individual managements do not strive to eliminate them and achieve absolute equality with other plants; they strive rather to protect their established position in the wage hierarchy of the area.

While the dominant emphasis is upon rates of wage change, absolute comparisons are also of some importance. These comparisons may be made in terms of: (1) Average weekly earnings. This sort of comparison is quite significant because many workers think of "wages" mainly in terms of weekly take-home pay. (2) Average plant-wide hourly earnings. This sort of comparison, while significant, is difficult to interpret. Average hourly earnings in a plant may vary considerably without any change in base rates, because of changes in the amount of overtime work, changes in the kind of work passing through the plant (where an incentive wage system is used), changes in the composition of the labor force, and other well-known factors. (3) Starting rates for probationary employees. This is a particular strategic comparison, since the practice of hiring all new employees at the starting rate is still widespread in the area. (4) Base rates for comparable jobs above the plant minimum. This sort of comparison is significant for hourly rated jobs, less significant for incentive jobs because of variations in the "looseness" of time standards from one plant to another. It is also difficult to make except among plants performing very similar operations.

All these types of comparisons are used in the area, some managements placing more weight on one and some on another. On the whole, comparisons (3) and (4) seem to be regarded as more important than the first two. Comparisons of *rate of wage increase*, as was noted earlier, are considered most significant of all.

Management has reasonably adequate data on wage rates and wage changes in the area. Periodic wage surveys are conducted by the telephone company, the Chamber of Commerce, and the National Metal Trades Association. In addition, there is a good deal of informal interchange of wage information, particularly on starting rates, rates for individual jobs, and recent or prospective general increases. The city is sufficiently small that the principal employers are well known to each other. Leading officers of the larger manufacturing companies meet weekly for luncheon. Their seconds-in-command meet weekly in a separate group. The personnel managers have their own association, which meets once a month. These gatherings provide ample opportunity for discussion of wage and hiring problems. The larger com-

panies whose wage changes tend to affect other firms in the area regard it as an act of courtesy to inform their colleagues of impending wage increases some time before these are announced publicly. There is no evidence, however, of systematic wage leadership by the larger companies.

When employers talk about "keeping up with the area," they frequently mean keeping up with certain other plants in the area which they regard as close to themselves for wage-setting purposes. The two main grounds for regarding another plant as close to one's own seem to be similarity of products and, therefore, of productive operations in the plant, and close geographical location, which involves competition for the labor available in the neighborhood. The two criteria sometimes coincide. Certain plants feel close to each other from a wage standpoint both because of similarity of production processes and because they draw on the same labor supplies.

Why does management want to "keep up with the area," or at least with certain other companies in the area? The most important considerations seem to be (1) a widespread opinion that management is morally obligated to pay prevailing wages, and that failure to do so is a confession of managerial failure; (2) a belief that failure to match wage increases made by other plants will lead to a lowering of employee morale and productivity; and (3) a belief that, over the long run, substandard wages will hamper the company in recruiting a satisfactory labor force. Each of these considerations deserves a word of comment.

The belief that "keeping up with the area" is the fair thing to do was impressed so frequently in our interviews that it cannot be dismissed as sheer rationalization. One manager, for example, explained that it would not be fair for this company to base its wage rates on the company's current ability to pay. "Your profit margin doesn't influence what you pay for materials. Why should it influence what you pay for labor? We pay what we ought to, and then go ahead and try and stay in business." Another manager said substantially the same thing: "We try to pay what is right; then we go out and try to improve through technical progress and good management."

In several cases managers explained that they felt responsible for maintaining the real purchasing power of their workers. Since the cost of living was rising during 1946–1948, they felt obliged in fairness to raise wages, regardless of union pressures or developments elsewhere in the area. Numerous other companies explained that they

panies, whose wage changes tend to affect other firms in the area, regard it as an act of courtesy to inform their colleagues of prospective wage increases some time before these are announced publicly. There is no evidence, however, of systematic wage leadership by the larger companies.

When employers talk about "keeping up with the area," they frequently mean keeping up with *certain other plants* in the area, which they regard as close to themselves for wage-setting purposes. The two main grounds for regarding another plant as close to your own seem to be similarity of products and, therefore, of productive operations in the plant, and close geographical location, which involves competition for the labor available in the neighborhood. The two criteria sometimes coincide. Certain plants feel close to each other from a wage standpoint *both* because of similarity of production processes and because they draw on the same labor supplies.

Why does management want to "keep up with the area," or at least with certain other companies in the area? The most important considerations seem to be (1) a widespread opinion that management is morally obligated to pay prevailing wages, and that inability to do so is a confession of managerial failure; (2) a belief that failure to match wage increases made by other plants will lead to a lowering of employee morale and productivity; and (3) a belief that, over the long run, subnormal wages will hamper the company in recruiting a satisfactory labor force. Each of these considerations deserves a word of comment.

The belief that keeping up with the area is the fair thing to do was expressed so frequently in our interviews that it cannot be dismissed as sheer rationalization. One manager, for example, explained that it would not be fair for this company to base its wage rates on the company's current ability to pay. "Your profit margin doesn't influence what you pay for materials. Why should it influence what you pay for labor? We pay what we ought to, and then go ahead and try and stay in business." Another manager said substantially the same thing: "We try to pay what is right; then we go out and stay in business through technical progress and good management."

In several cases, managers explained that they felt responsible for maintaining the real purchasing power of their workers. Since the cost of living was rising during 1946–1948, they felt obliged in fairness to raise wages, regardless of union pressures or developments elsewhere in the area. Numerous other companies explained that they

felt obliged to raise hourly rates when hours of work were reduced, in order to cushion the decline in workers' weekly incomes.

These statements were, of course, made during a prosperity period in which most managements had little financial difficulty in paying "fair" wages. Wage increases which managers ascribed to their own sense of fairness may really have been induced by high profit margins. The real test of how firmly management clings to ethical norms in wage setting would perhaps come during a depression, when maintenance of wage levels might involve operating losses.

Ethical considerations cut in both directions. From the standpoint of relations with workers, it is not ethical to pay too low a wage. From the standpoint of relations with other employers, however, it is not ethical to pay too high a wage. As one employer remarked, "In a city like this, you can't compete with other companies for labor on the basis of wages. If you do, you will end up in the same position as the gasoline stations who indulge in excessive price cutting. After all, we have to live with the people in the other companies." Another employer said that he did not feel he could go more than 15 per cent above the average wage level of similar companies without stirring up trouble.

Another reason for keeping in step with other plants is to minimize worker discontent. While workers do not seem to know much about wage levels in other plants, they are somewhat sensitive to news of wage *changes* in other plants. This is particularly true during a period of rising prices. The worker is under pressure for more money to meet the family budget; he feels that he is losing ground day by day. If on top of this he hears that other companies are raising wages, he will feel that it is only elementary justice for his employer to raise wages also.

One employer explained the problem in this way: "It isn't so much that people leave you. It's mainly that they start muttering around the shop. The word comes back very fast—'Gee, did you hear about so-and-so? They gave a ten-cent increase.' Pretty soon the word goes all over the shop—'We are going to get an increase too.' The pressure builds up inside the shop, and unless the increase comes through, you have trouble on morale and production." Another nonunion employer explained a substantial wage increase in the spring of 1946 in this way: "This increase was just about forced on us. It was going to spread everywhere and so we had to do it. The workers knew what

was happening, even though they didn't come in and ask us for the increase. Call it good business if you will."

The problem which faces the employer who lags behind an upward wage movement is not mainly one of labor turnover. Workers, particularly those who have several years' service with the company, will rarely leave it for wage reasons alone. The problem is rather that they become increasingly dissatisfied where they are. Without quitting the job, they can make their discontent felt in the quantity and quality of their output and in their personal relations with supervisors. Quite apart from the loss of productive efficiency, it is unpleasant for management and supervisors to come into the plant every morning and meet an atmosphere of general resentment. When the tension becomes great enough, a general wage increase may be called for to reduce it.

Related to reduction of worker discontent is avoidance of unionization. Most of the larger nonunion plants in the area have been subjected to several organizing campaigns in recent years. They have been conscious that failure to follow a general wage movement in the area would provide additional arguments for the union organizer. In several cases a general wage increase was directly connected with an actual or prospective organizing campaign. It is interesting to note that a wage increase does not always have the desired effect. In two cases which came to our attention, a substantial wage increase was followed by unionization of the plant within a few weeks.

A considerable number of employers stated that it is necessary to keep up with the area wage level in order to ensure a reasonable quantity and quality of labor. It is significant that the strongest expressions of opinion on this point came from companies with relatively low wage levels. Their opinion seems to have been based, not on the fact that they were actually paying the area level, but rather that they were underpaying and were suffering in consequence.

There is little evidence that a high wage level causes more workers to apply at a particular plant; for, as was noted in Chapter IV, most workers know very little about comparative wage levels in various plants. The main advantage of a high wage level is in persuading those who do apply to accept employment with the company. If the company's wage level is very low, most applicants will find that the rates offered them are below their previous earnings and, if times are good and job openings numerous, they will reject the offer and try again

was happening, even though they didn't come in and ask us for the increase. Call it good business, if you will."

The problem which faces the employer who lags behind an upward wage movement is not mainly one of labor turnover. Workers, particularly those who have several years' service with the company, will rarely leave it for wage reasons alone. The problem is rather that they become increasingly dissatisfied *where they are.* Without quitting the job, they can make their discontent felt in the quantity and quality of their output and in their personal relations with supervisors. Quite apart from the loss of productive efficiency, it is unpleasant for management and supervisors to come into the plant every morning and meet an atmosphere of general resentment. When the tension becomes great enough, a general wage increase may be made to reduce it.

Related to reduction of worker discontent is avoidance of unionization. Most of the larger nonunion plants in the area have been subjected to several organizing campaigns in recent years. They have been conscious that failure to follow a general wage movement in the area would provide additional arguments for the union organizer. In several cases a general wage increase was directly connected with an actual or prospective organizing campaign. It is interesting to note that a wage increase does not always have the desired effect. In two cases which came to our attention, a substantial wage increase was followed by unionization of the plant within a few weeks.

A considerable number of employers stated that it is necessary to keep up with the area wage level in order to attract an adequate quantity and quality of labor. It is significant that the strongest expressions of opinion on this point came from companies with relatively low wage levels. Their opinion seems to have been based, not on the fact that they were actually paying the area level, but rather that they were underpaying and were suffering in consequence.

There is little evidence that a high wage level causes more workers to *apply* at a particular plant for, as was noted in Chapter IV, most workers know very little about comparative wage levels in various plants. The main advantage of a high wage level is in persuading those who do apply to accept employment with the company. If the company's wage level is very low, most applicants will find that the rates offered them are below their previous earnings and, if times are good and job openings numerous, they will reject the offer and try again

somewhere else. If the company's wage level is high, on the other hand, most applicants who are offered jobs will be willing to accept them. This enables the company to set high hiring standards and accept only the most desirable applicants. It also enables management to weed out during the probationary period any workers who fail to live up to expectations, with full assurance that they can replace them from new applicants. A low-wage plant is forced to accept low-quality applicants and to hang on to them as long as possible. One employer, for example, explained that when his rates get too far below the going rates he has great difficulty with discipline in the plant. The foremen are reluctant to enforce discipline because they are afraid that the workers will quit and that it may not be possible to replace them.

A high wage level has other advantages. Many companies have frequent short-term layoffs arising from irregular fluctuations of demand. If the company's wages and working conditions are good, workers will wait for recall to their former jobs instead of seeking work elsewhere. If wages are low, on the other hand, the labor force tends to evaporate as soon as it is laid off and the company cannot get people back when it needs them.

Several employers stressed the fact that over the course of the years a company develops a general reputation in the community as a good or poor place to work. The company's wage level is only one element in the situation. Steadiness of employment, size of the plant, lightness or heaviness of the work, physical working conditions, the type of worker employed, the quality of supervision, and numerous other factors influence the general reputation of the firm. Wages are important, however, and if the company loses too much ground in this respect, its standing in the community will suffer. A good reputation is important not merely for labor recruitment but also, one suspects, for the gratification of management itself. It is much more satisfying to be running "the best place in town" than to be known as the manager of "a cheap shop."

Ability to Pay

The period in which this study was conducted was not the best possible one for testing the effect of ability to pay on company wage policies. Ability to pay was generally high, elastic (in the sense that product prices were not raised as much as they could have been on the basis of short-run demand curves), and in many companies did not

somewhere else. If the company's wage level is high, on the other hand, most applicants who are offered jobs will be willing to accept them. This enables the company to set high hiring standards and accept only the most desirable applicants. It also enables management to weed out during the probationary period any workers who fail to live up to expectations, with some assurance that they can replace them from new applicants. A low-wage plant is forced to accept low-quality applicants, and to keep workers on as long as possible. One employer, for example, explained that when his rates get too far below the going rates, he has great difficulty with discipline in the plant. The foremen are reluctant to enforce discipline because they are afraid that the workers will quit and that it may not be possible to replace them.

A high wage level has other advantages. Many companies have frequent short-term layoffs arising from irregular fluctuations of demand. If the company's wages and working conditions are good, workers will wait for recall to their former jobs instead of seeking work elsewhere. If wages are low, on the other hand, the labor force tends to evaporate as soon as it is laid off and the company cannot get people back when it needs them.

Several employers stressed the fact that over the course of the years a company develops a general reputation in the community as a good or poor place to work. The company's wage level is only one element in the situation. Steadiness of employment, size of the plant, lightness or heaviness of the work, physical working conditions, the type of worker employed, the quality of supervision, and numerous other factors influence the general reputation of the firm. Wages are important, however, and if the company loses too much ground in this respect its standing in the community will suffer. A good reputation is important not merely for labor recruitment but also, one suspects, for the gratification of management itself. It is much more satisfying to be known as "the best place in town" than to be known as the managers of "a cheap shop."

Ability to Pay

The period in which this study was conducted was not the best possible one for testing the effect of ability to pay on company wage policies. Ability to pay was generally high; elastic (in the sense that product prices were not raised as much as they could have been on the basis of short-run demand curves); and in many companies did not

serve as an effective limiting factor on wage increases. In other companies, however, it was sufficiently important that we were able to obtain some clues to management thinking on the matter.

There are two starting points for management reasoning on ability to pay. The first is the conception of a "normal" or "fair" rate of profit. This is invariably expressed as a percentage of sales, but the percentage regarded as normal varies with the circumstances of the industry. An industry which turns over its capital more rapidly, i.e., has a higher ratio of annual sales to capital investment, can afford to be content with a smaller profit percentage. The rate of return on capital thus enters indirectly into businessmen's conceptions of a normal profit.

The other starting point is the income statement for the most recent accounting period, usually a calendar quarter. Some attention is paid also to earlier periods in order to determine the general trend of sales and profits, and there is some tendency to assume that the trend will continue in its present direction. If the fourth quarter of 1948 was better than the third quarter of 1948, the most probable estimate is that the first quarter of 1949 will be better than the fourth quarter of 1948.

The next step in estimating the impact of a wage change is to compute the probable addition to payroll costs. Management says "This increase will cost us $50,000 a month," or whatever the figure may be. By inserting this figure into the most recent income statement (or the projection for the next quarter) it is possible to estimate the effect on the profit margin. The result may be to reduce the margin below what is regarded as a normal or safe level. The next question which arises, then, is how the profit margin can be restored to a proper level. In management parlance, "Where is the money (to pay the wage increase) coming from?" Can it be obtained from greater physical volume of sales, or higher prices, or both?

The estimate of prospective sales volume is particularly strategic. A marked drop in volume can very quickly push a plant below its break-even point. On the other hand, an appreciable increase in volume may enable the company to absorb a wage increase without change in selling prices. It is very difficult, however, to estimate prospective sales with any degree of precision. Some of the larger companies in the area set up sales and production budgets for a year in advance, but little reliance is placed on figures beyond the quarter immediately ahead. When conditions are changing rapidly, estimates may have to be revised even within the quarter. Most of the smaller

serve as an effective limiting factor on wage increases. In other companies, however, it was sufficiently important that we were able to obtain some clues to management thinking on the matter.

There are two starting points for management reasoning on ability to pay. The first is the conception of a "normal" or "safe" rate of profit. This is invariably expressed as a percentage of sales, but the percentage regarded as normal varies with the circumstances of the industry. An industry which "turns over its capital" more rapidly, i.e., has a higher ratio of annual sales to capital investment, can afford to be content with a smaller profit on sales. The rate of return on *capital* thus enters indirectly into businessmen's conceptions of a normal profit.

The other starting point is the income statement for the most recent accounting period, usually a calendar quarter. Some attention is paid also to earlier periods in order to determine the general trend of sales and profits, and there is some tendency to assume that the trend will continue in its present direction. If the fourth quarter of 1948 was *below* the third quarter of 1948, the most probable estimate is that the first quarter of 1949 will be *below* the fourth quarter of 1948.

The next step in estimating the impact of a wage change is to compute the probable addition to payroll costs. Management says "This increase will cost us $150,000 a month," or whatever the figure may be. By inserting this figure into the most recent income statement (or the projection for the next quarter), it is possible to estimate the effect on the profit margin. The result may be to reduce the margin below what is regarded as a normal or safe level. The next question which arises, then, is how the profit margin can be restored to a proper level. In management parlance, "where is the money (to pay the wage increase) coming from?" Can it be obtained from greater physical volume of sales, or higher prices, or both?

The estimate of prospective sales volume is particularly strategic. A marked drop in volume can very quickly push a plant below its "break-even point." On the other hand, an appreciable increase in volume may enable the company to absorb a wage increase with no change in selling prices. It is very difficult, however, to estimate prospective sales with any degree of precision. Some of the larger companies in the area set up sales and production budgets for a year in advance, but little reliance is placed on figures beyond the quarter immediately ahead. When conditions are changing rapidly, estimates may have to be revised even within the quarter. Most of the smaller

companies do not even attempt systematic budgeting or forecasting. They rely on current reports from salesmen in the field, trade gossip, the tone of voice which their customers use in placing orders, and other straws in the wind which they interpret on the basis of past experience.

A similar uncertainty attaches to the future course of prices. This may be uncertainty as to how prices themselves will behave (in industries which are subject to strong price competition), or uncertainty as to whether higher prices will mean a reduction in sales volume (in industries where prices are relatively well controlled). Altogether, then, prospective ability to pay is highly uncertain, though the degree of uncertainty varies with the general business situation. It was much greater, for example, in the midst of the 1949 recession than it had been during 1946–1948.

Uncertainty has a twofold effect on management's conception of a proper wage policy. First, most managers believe that you should not try to pay wages as high as you *might* be able to pay on the basis of budget forecasts, for if these forecasts prove erroneous you may be in a bad situation. This amounts to weighting the possibility that your revenue estimates are too high more heavily than the possibility that they are too low. The effect is to reduce the present worth of anticipated future profits. As one employer said, "We try to be very conservative in calculating our ability to pay. We want to have enough safety margin so that we know any increase we make can be maintained." Another company said, "We have always followed a conservative financial policy. We want to make absolutely sure where the money is coming from before we start handing it out. Unless we have rather definite assurance about future income, we won't even consider an increase in wages." Still another management man said, "It's a very dangerous thing to try to anticipate your financial returns. The safe thing is to make your profits first and then hand them out, instead of trying to hand them out in advance. We figured on a twelve million dollar business last year. It turned out to be a lot less than that. If we had made our wage increases on the basis of this twelve million dollar figure, we would now be out of business."

The second effect of uncertainty on management's wage policy is to produce a desire for flexibility. The time horizon of most businesses seems to be quite short. Production and sales plans are rarely viewed with much confidence for more than three months ahead. Businessmen therefore dislike committing themselves on wages for a

year in advance; and, if they must commit themselves for a year, they are reluctant to make as large a commitment as they would make for a shorter period. As one employer remarked, "I would have made a larger increase last spring if I could have reconsidered it after three months. But with the union, any increase I make is with me for at least a year. So I had to play safe."

So much for what management thinks it ought to do. What does it actually do? Are estimates of ability to pay a governing consideration in wage changes? The situation differs materially in union and nonunion plants. In union plants many managements were obliged during 1946–1948 to raise wages faster than they considered wise on economic grounds. Again and again one encountered the statement, "Well, we gave an increase—but we shouldn't have done it," or "There wasn't any economic basis for the increase we gave." In the spring of 1949 profits were declining and uncertainty was so great that many managements believed wages should actually be reduced as a safety measure. This conviction did not extend to the point of being willing to stand a shutdown, however, and in most cases contracts were renewed at the same wage level. It is important to note that when management gives an increase larger than it should give, it is not concerned merely over the reduction of prospective profits; it is concerned also with the reduction in the company's safety margin. The union does not allow as large a discount for uncertainty as management would like. Union pressure on the wage structure, in other words, forces managers to assume a greater degree of risk than they would be willing to assume voluntarily.

What of the nonunion firms? How far are they guided by ability to pay as compared with movements in the area wage level? In some cases there is no conflict between the two criteria. If the firm's profits are high enough, it can readily keep up with the area level and may even try to get a little ahead of the area. As one company explained, "At the present time, our profit position is not very good, but we have to make increases anyway in order to keep up with the area level. I call this a defensive tactic. When our profits are high, on the other hand, we will give increases regardless of what others are doing and try to get ahead of the area level. This is an offensive tactic. Getting ahead of the area increases the firm's margin of safety for future years. If profits should decline, the firm can afford to stand still for a while even though the area level continues to rise."

Difficulties arise, however, when the area wage level is rising and

year in advance and, if they must commit themselves for a year, they are reluctant to make as large a commitment as they would make for a shorter period. As one employer remarked, "I would have made a larger increase last spring if I could have reconsidered it after three months. But with the union, any increase I make is with me for at least a year. So I had to play safe."

So much for what management thinks it *ought* to do. What does it actually do? Are estimates of ability to pay a governing consideration in wage changes? The situation differs materially in union and nonunion plants. In union plants, many managements were obliged during 1946–1948 to raise wages faster than they considered wise on economic grounds. Again and again one encountered the statement, "Well, we gave an increase—but we shouldn't have done it," or "There wasn't any economic basis for the increase we just gave." In the spring of 1949 profits were declining and uncertainty was so great that many managements believed wages should actually be reduced as a safety measure. This conviction did not extend to the point of being willing to stand a shutdown, however, and in most cases contracts were renewed at the same wage level. It is important to note that when management gives an increase larger than it "should" give, it is not concerned merely over the reduction of prospective profits; it is concerned also with the reduction in the company's safety margin. The union does not allow as large a discount for uncertainty as management would like. Union pressure on the wage structure, in other words, forces managers to assume a greater degree of risk than they would be willing to assume voluntarily.

What of the nonunion firms? How far are they guided by ability to pay as compared with movements in the area wage level? In some cases there is no conflict between the two criteria. If the firm's profits are high enough, it can readily keep up with the area level and may even try to get a little ahead of the area. As one company explained, "At the present time, our profit position is not very good, but we have to make increases anyway in order to keep up with the area level. I call this a defensive tactic. When our profits are high, on the other hand, we will give increases regardless of what others are doing and try to get ahead of the area level. This is an offensive tactic." Getting ahead of the area increases the firm's margin of safety for future years. If profits should decline, the firm can afford to stand still for a while even though the area level continues to rise.

Difficulties arise, however, when the area wage level is pressing hard

against the firm's ability to pay. Management is then faced with a dilemma: Should it give a wage increase which the company "can't afford" in order to keep up with the area level, or should it hold firm on wages and drop below the area level? Management opinion on this point was by no means unanimous. At one extreme a few companies said firmly that they would not give an increase until they felt able to afford it. At the other extreme some companies said they would try to keep up with the area even if profit forecasts were unfavorable. One manager explained, "You have to take a risk sometimes. Business consists of taking risks, and this is just another one of them." Another company, which gave a substantial increase in 1946 in spite of a poor financial position explained, "We have to be ready to take losses sometimes, because a business is not operating just for one year. We simply go on producing because we have faith in the future and because we feel we have an obligation to our employees to provide them with work." Another manager argued, "If the company is unable to pay, that's management's fault. The company ought to pay the going rates and management should go out and find the money somehow."

Taking the nonunion group as a whole, one gets the impression that during the 1946–1948 upswing wage decisions were influenced more heavily by the short-run profit position of each company than by area wage movements. This is suggested also by the marked dispersion in the size of wage increases given by various companies, a point which will be documented in Chapter VII.

Wages of other Firms in the Industry

The role of industry comparisons in collective bargaining will be considered in the next section. We are concerned here only with the weight which nonunion firms give to the wage levels of companies outside the area which compete with them in product markets. There was a surprising unanimity of testimony that this factor is of minor importance in wage setting. The only exceptions were a few plants in industries characterized by severe price competition and a high ratio of labor costs to total costs. Many companies said that they had little knowledge of the wages being paid by their competitors. Even those which had information on wage rates of competitors seemed to use this mainly as a test of management performance rather than as a basis for wage setting. Many managers feel that unless they can pay wage rates reasonably in line with the rest of the industry and still stay in business there must be something wrong with their own

efficiency. One manager, after stating that his company tries to maintain the highest wage level in the industry, said: "Our company is the largest company in the industry. In fact, we are known as the Tiffany of the ____ industry. We should pay the highest wages, because the other companies in the industry look to us for leadership."

There are several reasons why wage decisions of firms in this area do not seem to be much affected by the wage levels of other firms in their respective industries. First, a surprising number of plants have few close competitors. This is due partly to the fact that many plants in the area make small, specialized parts which go into producers' goods rather than consumers' goods. In some cases the product of a particular plant is unique, being built to the specifications of a single customer. In other cases, even though there are rival producers, each has well-established contacts with a few large customers who buy on long-term established contracts. The primary basis of competition in these cases seems to be quality, speed of delivery, or something other than price. Second, even where there is active price competition, company wage levels often play a minor role in this competition. The most important factor seems to be modernness of plant equipment and production techniques. Next to this comes efficiency of supervision and the degree of effort obtained from workers in the plant. Differences among competing firms in these respects seem to be more important than moderate differences in wage levels, except in industries such as foundry which have a very high labor cost ratio.

Other Factors in Wage Policy

Wage decisions are influenced from time to time by a variety of other considerations, many of them unique to particular situations and not susceptible of generalization. Two factors, however, were encountered frequently enough to deserve a word of comment. These are the length of the work week and changes in the length of the work week, and whether wages are paid on a time or output basis.

Decisions about wages and hours of work are necessarily interrelated, since the worker judges the adequacy of his wage partly on the basis of his weekly pay check. A reduction in weekly take-home is regarded as a "wage cut" and a company which makes such a reduction is likely to have serious discontent among its labor force. Moreover, it must keep its weekly take-home reasonably comparable with that of other companies in order to stay in competition for the available labor supply. One of the techniques which companies with low hourly

efficiency. One manager, after stating that his company tries to maintain the highest wage level in the industry, said: "You see, we are the largest company in the industry. In fact, we are known as the Tiffany of the ______ industry. We should pay the highest wages, because the other companies in the industry look to us for leadership."

There are several reasons why wage decisions of firms in this area do not seem to be much affected by the wage levels of other firms in their respective industries. First, a surprising number of plants have few close competitors. This is due partly to the fact that many plants in the area make small, specialized parts which go into producers' goods rather than consumers' goods. In some cases the product of a particular plant is unique, being built to the specifications of a single customer. In other cases, even though there are rival producers, each has well-established contacts with a few large customers who buy on long-term established contracts. The primary basis of competition in these cases seems to be quality, speed of delivery, or something other than price. Second, even where there is active price competition, comparative wage levels often play a minor role in this competition. The most important factor seems to be modernness of plant, equipment, and production techniques. Next to this comes efficiency of supervision and the degree of effort obtained from workers in the plant. Differences among competing firms in these respects seem to be more important than moderate differences in wage levels, except in industries such as clothing which have a very high labor cost ratio.

Other Factors in Wage Policy

Wage decisions are influenced from time to time by a variety of other considerations, many of them unique to particular situations and not susceptible of generalization. Two factors, however, were encountered frequently enough to deserve a word of comment. These are the length of the work week and changes in the length of the week; and whether wages are paid on a time or output basis.

Decisions about wages and hours of work are necessarily interrelated, since the worker judges the adequacy of his wage partly on the basis of his weekly pay check. A reduction in weekly take-home is regarded as a "wage cut," and a company which makes such a reduction is likely to have serious discontent among its labor force. Moreover, it must keep its weekly take-home reasonably comparable with that of other companies in order to stay in competition for the available labor supply. One of the techniques which companies with low hourly

rates use to recruit and retain a labor force is to offer forty-five or fifty hours of work per week. A certain number of workers are attracted by the weekly take-home from these plants, apparently without reflecting that they could earn as much in other plants for forty hours' work.

Wage increases in the area during 1946–1948 were definitely influenced by the gradual reduction of the work week from wartime levels to a general level of forty hours by early 1949. In a tight labor market, with active union organizing under way and with living costs rising, most managements considered it unwise to allow a marked drop in weekly take-home. A cut in hours, therefore, was usually accompanied by a roughly offsetting increase in hourly wage rates. The type of reasoning used may be illustrated by two examples of wage increases made in the spring of 1946. One company, operating at fifty hours a week, calculated that if it came down to forty hours and gave the 18½-cent increase which steel and certain other industries were giving at this time, the result would be a 17 per cent reduction in its workers' take-home pay. It decided, therefore, to cut hours only to forty-five and to give a 12-cent wage increase, which reduced take-home pay only 3 per cent.

Another company, in view of the general pattern of wage increases developing around the country, concluded that a 15 per cent increase was the least it could do without having an adverse psychological effect on its workers. It would have preferred at the same time to reduce the work week from forty-eight to forty hours, but this would have produced too large a drop in weekly take-home. It therefore set the work week at forty-two and one-half hours, which reduced weekly take-home only about 2 per cent. In both cases, maintenance of a work week longer than the "normal" forty-hour week served as an alternative to granting a larger increase in hourly rates.

By the spring of 1949 the psychological climate in the area had changed considerably. There was considerable unemployment and short-time work, and many workers were concerned for the future security of their jobs. Reductions in hours at this time were interpreted as a sign of business depression, which workers took to mean that it was an unpropitious time to press for wage increases. Under these circumstances, some companies were able to reduce hours to forty with no increase in hourly rates. The fact that the cost of living had been declining for several months also had something to do with the situation.

Payment on the basis of output introduces additional dimensions

into the wage structure and complicates the meaning of wage changes. An increase in base rates (minimum hourly guarantees) may have little effect on workers' earnings unless piece rates are also adjusted, and this adjustment may be carried out in a variety of ways. On the other hand, earnings may be raised or lowered considerably without any change in base rates by means of a general loosening or tightening of work standards. Incentive workers who have been following the almost universal practice of output restriction can, and frequently do, increase their hourly output when weekly hours of work are reduced, so that weekly take-home is maintained without any adjustment of wage rates. In consequence of these variable factors, "a wage increase" does not have the same unambiguous meaning under incentive work that it does under day work; nor can one assume that "a ten-cent wage increase" in a plant operating under incentive is equivalent to "a ten-cent wage increase" in a day-work plant. It is unfortunate that economists have concentrated so largely on the economic theory of hourly wage rates and have failed to penetrate into the complex phenomena of incentive payment systems.

UNION OBJECTIVES AND TACTICS

The nature of union wage policies cannot be adequately explored in a study limited to one area. In manufacturing industries, at least, the key wage decisions are usually made at national union headquarters, and one would have to go there to study them. We are able to say something, however, about the way in which national decisions are interpreted and applied at the local level.

The nonunion plant, as we have seen, looks principally to wage developments within the area. The characteristic feature of unionism is that it looks beyond the area to wage levels and wage changes in other parts of the country. The scope of these geographical comparisons varies with the type of industry and the stage of development of collective bargaining. From an area standpoint, three types of situations may be distinguished: (1) Cases in which the wage rate of firms in the area is determined by regional or national bargains; (2) genuine local bargains; (3) bargains which, while local in form, are actually influenced by national union policies and by bargains already reached with other firms in the industry. This may be termed "pattern" local bargaining, or "implicit" industry-wide bargaining, and is perhaps the commonest situation in manufacturing industries.

The wages of many workers in the area are determined by bargains

into the wage structure and complicates the meaning of wage changes. An increase in base rates (minimum hourly guarantees) may have little effect on workers' earnings unless piece rates are also adjusted, and this adjustment may be carried out in a variety of ways. On the other hand, earnings may be raised or lowered considerably *without* any change in base rates by means of a general loosening or tightening of time standards. Incentive workers who have been following the almost universal practice of output restriction can, and frequently do, increase their hourly output when weekly hours of work are reduced, so that weekly take-home is maintained without any adjustment of wage rates. In consequence of these variable factors, "a wage increase" does not have the same unambiguous meaning under incentive work that it does under day work; nor can one assume that "a ten-cent wage increase" in a plant operating under incentives is equivalent to "a ten-cent wage increase" in a day-work plant. It is unfortunate that economists have concentrated so largely on the economic theory of hourly wage rates and have failed to penetrate into the curious phenomena of incentive wage systems.

UNION OBJECTIVES AND TACTICS

The nature of union wage policies cannot be adequately explored in a study limited to one area. In manufacturing industries, at least, the key wage decisions are usually made at national union headquarters, and one would have to go there to study them. We are able to say something, however, about the way in which national decisions are interpreted and applied at the local level.

The nonunion plant, as we have seen, looks primarily to wage developments within the area. The characteristic feature of unionism is that it looks beyond the area to wage levels and wage changes in other parts of the country. The scope of these geographical comparisons varies with the type of industry and the stage of development of collective bargaining. From an area standpoint, three types of situations may be distinguished: (1) Cases in which the wage rate of firms in the area is determined by regional or national bargains; (2) genuine local bargains; (3) bargains which, while local in form, are heavily influenced by national union policies and by bargains already reached with other firms in the industry. This may be termed pseudo-local bargaining or incipient industry-wide bargaining, and is perhaps the commonest situation in manufacturing industries.

The wages of many workers in this area are determined by bargains

made on a broader basis. Wages of railroad employees are determined through a system-wide agreement with the company. Wages of telephone workers are also determined on a system-wide basis. The local transit company operates throughout the state, and there is a single state-wide agreement between it and the union. The teamsters' union negotiates a single agreement covering Connecticut, Rhode Island, and southern Massachusetts, though there are occasional deviations from this agreement to meet the financial necessities of a particular employer. Wages in the unionized shirt shops in the area are governed by a national bargain between the Institute of Shirt Manufacturers and the Amalgamated Clothing Workers of America. The dress shops in the city work on contract for jobbers in New York City, and are members of the New York Contracting Association. Their wage scale is governed by an agreement negotiated in New York between the jobbers and the New York Joint Dress Board of the International Ladies' Garment Workers' Union.

Local bargaining is found in such industries as retail trade, cleaning and dyeing, hospitals and educational institutions, building construction and repair, and newspaper printing. Even in these cases, however, the position taken by the unions may be influenced by wage developments in other areas. The building trades, for example, compare their rates with those of other cities in the state and try to keep pace with what is happening in these cities. Again, the Typographical Union tries to win the same increase from newspapers in this area as from newspapers in New York City. The chain of events in this case is as follows: The union tries to win the same increase from the commercial printers in New York City as from the newspapers there; but there are commercial printers in this area which compete with the New York City printers, so that the union must try to obtain the same increase for them; finally, in order to maintain equity within this area, it tries to win the same increase from the newspapers as from the commercial printers here. The fact that bargaining is decentralized, then, does not necessarily mean that it is influenced only by local considerations.

Bargaining in manufacturing, while nominally on a local basis, is heavily influenced by the program of the national union as expounded by its field representatives. In form, there is wide scope for local autonomy. The local union meets, elects its bargaining representatives, and formulates its demands. There is no constitutional requirement that these demands must be uniform from one local to the next. There is no requirement that the national representative for the area be

made on a broader base. Wages of railroad employees are determined through a system-wide agreement with the company. Wages of telephone workers are also determined on a system-wide basis. The local transit company operates throughout the state and there is a single state-wide agreement between it and the union. The teamsters' union negotiates a single agreement covering Connecticut, Rhode Island, and southern Massachusetts, though on rare occasions deviations from this agreement to meet the unusual needs of a particular employer. Wages in the unionized shirt shops in the area are governed by a national bargain between the Institute of Shirt Manufacturers and the Amalgamated Clothing Workers of America. The dress shops in the city work on contract for jobbers in New York City and are members of the New York Contracting Association. Their wage scale is governed by an agreement negotiated in New York between the jobbers and the New York Joint Dress Board of the International Ladies' Garment Workers' Union.

Local bargaining is found in such industries as retail trade, cleaning and dyeing, hospitals and educational institutions, building construction and repair, and newspaper printing. Even in these cases, however, the decision taken by the unions may be influenced by wage developments in other areas. The building trades, for example, compare their rates with those of other cities in the state and try to keep pace with what is happening in these cities. Again, the Typographical Union tries to win the same increases from newspapers in this area as from newspapers in New York City. The chain of events in this case is as follows: The union tries to win the same increase from the commercial printers in New York City as from the newspapers there; but there are commercial printers in this area which compete with the New York city printers, so that the union must try to obtain the same increase for them. Finally, in order to maintain equity within this area, it tries to win the same increase from the newspapers as from the commercial printers here. The fact that bargaining is decentralized, then, does not necessarily mean that it is influenced only by local considerations.

Bargaining in manufacturing, while nominally on a local basis, is heavily influenced by the policies of the national unions, as expounded by its field representatives. In form, there is wide scope for local autonomy. The local union meets, elects its bargaining representatives, and formulates its demands. There is no constitutional requirement that these demands must be uniform from one local to the next. There is no requirement that the national representative for the area be

included in the bargaining committee. The local membership is free to accept or reject any settlement which the bargaining committee may reach with the employer, though the national union frequently requires that the agreement be ratified by national headquarters as well.

In practice, however, the national representative is normally a member of the bargaining committee. He almost always participates in the preliminary discussion of local demands. He expounds the program of wage and other demands which the national union has decided to push in a particular year, and this program is usually ratified by the membership. Each employer is confronted, therefore, with substantially the same demands. These have already been presented to the leading firms in the industry. Companies in the area are inclined to wait until negotiations with the "big fellows" have been concluded and the "pattern" for the year has been established. Thus the union tries to ensure that both initial demands and ultimate results will be substantially uniform from one firm to the next. If the Auto Workers demanded 25 cents an hour from the leading auto companies and got 15 cents, all unionized auto companies in this area will be confronted with an initial demand for 25 cents and an actual demand of 15 cents. The Steelworkers look to the U. S. Steel settlement, the Electrical Workers to General Electric and Westinghouse, the Automobile Workers to General Motors, and so on.

Despite this emphasis on national uniformity there have been frequent deviations in the settlements reached in this area. The general wage changes made by companies operating under contract with the Steelworkers, Rubber Workers, UE, and UAW during the years 1946–1948 are presented in Table 43, and compared with the industry patterns for those years. It will be noted that in no year did as many as half of the local agreements conform precisely to the industry pattern, and that the degree of conformity in 1948 was less than in 1946 or 1947.

The national pattern is thus only a starting point, a target at which to shoot. The local union rarely settles for more than this, but frequently settles for less. This raises the question of what determines the degree of departure from the national pattern. Under what conditions will the national representative agree to step down to a lower figure, and what determines how low he will go? The main factors which determine how far local settlements will depart from the national pattern are, first, the economic position of the company as judged by the union; and second, the strength of organization in the plant and

included in the bargaining committee. The local membership is free to accept or reject any settlement which the bargaining committee may reach with the employer, though the national union frequently requires that the agreement be ratified by national headquarters as well.

In practice, however, the national representative is normally a member of the bargaining committee. He almost always participates in the preliminary discussion of local demands. He expounds the program of wage and other demands which the national union has decided to push in a particular year, and this program is usually ratified by the membership. Each employer is confronted, therefore, with substantially the same demands as have already been presented to the leading firms in his industry. Contracts in the area are timed so that they will expire after negotiations with the "big fellows" have been concluded and the "pattern" for the year has been established. Thus the union tries to ensure that both initial demands and actual results will be substantially uniform from one firm to the next. If the Rubber Workers demanded 25 cents an hour from the leading tire companies and got 11 cents, all unionized rubber companies in this area will be confronted with a nominal demand for 25 cents and an actual demand for 11 cents. The Steelworkers look to the U. S. Steel settlement, the Electrical Workers to General Electric and Westinghouse, the Automobile Workers to General Motors, and so on.

Despite this emphasis on national patterns, there have been frequent deviations in the settlements reached in this area. The general wage changes made by companies operating under contract with the Steelworkers, Rubber Workers, UE, and UAW during the years 1946–1948 are presented in Table 23, and compared with the industry patterns for those years. It will be noted that in no year did as many as half of the local agreements conform precisely to the industry pattern, and that the degree of conformity in 1948 was less than in 1946 or 1947.

The national pattern is thus only a starting point, a target at which to shoot. The local union rarely settles for more than this, but frequently settles for less. This raises the question of what determines the degree of departure from the national pattern. Under what conditions will the national representative agree to step down to a lower figure, and what determines how low he will go? The main factors which determine how far local settlements will depart from the national pattern are, first, the economic position of the company as judged by the union, and second, the strength of organization in the plant and

the willingness of the local leadership and membership to stand a strike. These two points deserve brief comment.

Our discussions with national union representatives in the area suggest that they are highly conscious of economic limitations on wage

TABLE 23

General Wage Increases by Companies under Contract with Selected Unions, 1946–48*

(Cents per hour)

Union	1946	1947	1948
United Steelworkers:			
National Pattern	18½	12½	13
Company A	18½	12½	13
Company B	18	10	0
Company C	10	15	15
United Rubber Workers:			
National Pattern	18½	11½	11
Company A	18½	11½	11
Company B	11	11½	9
Company C	10	12	6
Company D	18½	8	0
United Electrical Workers:			
National Pattern	18½	12½	12
Company A	15	10	6
Company B	4	11½	8
Company C	18½	12½	8
Company D	(not organized)	(not organized)	10
United Automobile Workers:			
National Pattern	18½	12½	11
Company A	13	3	5½

* Figures in this table represent increases in basic wage rates rather than the so-called "package" increase, which includes pensions, vacations, group insurance, and other fringe items. Inclusion of fringe items would not, however, alter the general conclusions. Most companies in the area during 1946–1948 undershot the national patterns on fringe items as well as on base rate increases.

demands. When convinced that they have exhausted the company's ability to pay they will stop, even if this means a settlement below the national pattern. As one union official said, "In bargaining with employers, we use the national pattern as a guide and try to adjust to the particular conditions of the plant. We have some idea of how far the plant will go in offering concessions by the orders on hand, by the prices they are charging, by activity in the plant, and sometimes we even manage to get hold of financial statements—don't ask me how." Another official said, "The national pattern is something to shoot at, but we always take into account how far the employer can go. If we feel that he cannot pay the national pattern, we will settle for less. In

all cases it is the economic ability of the company plus the degree of unity among the workers which decides how far we can go."

How do union leaders judge the employer's capacity to pay? In the case of large companies, the research staff of the international union is able to furnish the local with analyses of published financial statements. For smaller companies, cruder methods have to be used. Considerable reliance is placed on reports from workers concerning the degree of activity in the plant. In commercial printing, for example: "No matter what the employers or the composing room say, so long as the presses are going full blast we know that they must be making money. Once the presses start slowing down and they start laying off men, then we know that things aren't so hot and we take that into account when we negotiate."

Where the union official trusts the man with whom he is dealing, he may simply take his word concerning the state of business. As one union representative said, "I rely a lot on the candidness of the man with whom I'm dealing. If I've found in the past that he has been truthful and have already accepted that he is speaking honestly, I'm ready to place a lot of faith in his statements."

A good indication of ability to pay is the degree of resistance which the employer puts up in the bargaining negotiations. Union representatives develop remarkable shrewdness in judging when an employer is simply saying 'No' and when he really means it. As one man said, "I can tell how far guys will go just watching them at times. We were negotiating at the X Company and weren't getting anywhere. I finally told them the company could afford ten cents and would give ten cents just like the other companies in town. After a while the old man started pacing the floor, up and down. That's when I knew his resistance had given out. You see, in all our previous negotiations the same thing happened. Every time that he was about ready to break he would get up, start pacing the floor, mumble a little bit, and then turn around to us and say, 'Well, let's see if we can't get together on this thing.' And then we'd get the settlement all cleared up.... I just seem to know how far they'll go and when they say no sometimes I feel that they will go further, and other times when they say no I just sense that they won't go any further and if we want it we will have to ..."

In the last resort, the threat of a strike may be used to obtain a final appraisal of management's position. As another union representative said, "And then of course we rely on pressure as a test of

all cases it is the economic ability of the company plus the degree of unity among the workers, which decides how far we should go."

How do union leaders judge the employer's capacity to pay? In the case of large companies, the research office of the national union is able to furnish the local with analyses of published financial statements. For smaller companies, cruder methods have to be used. Considerable reliance is placed on reports from workers concerning the degree of activity in the plant. In commercial printing, for example, "No matter what is happening in the composing room, so long as the presses are going full blast we know that they must be making money. Once the presses start slowing down and they start laying off men, then we know that things aren't so hot and we take that into account when we negotiate."

Where the union official trusts the man with whom he is dealing, he may simply take his word concerning the state of business. As one union representative said, "I rely a lot on the personality of the man with whom I'm dealing. If I've found in the past that he has been truthful and has really accepted the union wholeheartedly, I'm ready to place a lot of faith in his statements."

A good indicator of ability to pay is the degree of resistance which the employer puts up in the bargaining negotiations. Union representatives develop remarkable shrewdness in judging when an employer is simply saying "No" and when he really means it. As one man said, "I can tell how far guys will go by just watching their actions. We were negotiating at the X Company and weren't getting anywhere. I finally told them the company could afford ten cents and would give ten cents, just like the other companies in town. Mr._______ got up and started pacing the floor, up and down. That's when I knew his resistance had given out. You see, in all our previous negotiations the same thing happened. Every time that he was about ready to break he would get up, start pacing the floor, mumble a little bit, and then turn around to us and say, 'Well, let's see if we can't get together on this thing.' And then we'd get the settlement all cleared up. . . . I just seem to know how far they'll go and when they say no sometimes I feel that they will go further, and other times when they say no I just sense that they won't go any further and if we want more we'll have to strike."

In the last resort, the threat of a strike may be used to obtain a final appraisal of management's position. As another union representative said, "And then of course we rely on pressure as a test of

how far management will go. We don't give in to management until the last day of the negotiations and then when we threaten a strike and management is willing to accept a strike, we feel that probably management cannot give any more. There was this company which claimed that they couldn't give more than five cents, for otherwise they would go out of business. I threatened to strike unless they offered more. At that point the company asked for an extension of negotiations for two weeks, which we granted. At the end of the two weeks, they gave us ten cents. You see, there was a case of a fellow whom I never really did trust, and so I had to sound him out through a threat."

The other factor which the national representative has to gauge is the sentiment of the local membership, and whether they will strike to back up a wage demand. Unionism in the manufacturing industries of the area is still relatively weak. This is due in some cases to sheer newness of the union organization. One national representative, in explaining why he had made a settlement below the national pattern, said "We only have about half the people organized down there. We can't push them into a strike, because if we did we might lose the plant altogether." Another said: "After fourteen months of organization, the members still can't do a thing by themselves. We're not really strong down there—only sixty per cent organized, and those aren't real union members. All they want is the returns. They are not very intelligent. They act like a bunch of kids. Get them a wage increase and it is like a new toy. Soon they get tired of the toy and want a new one. So we get them seniority. And as soon as we stop giving them new toys, they'll quit."

Even where a local has been in existence for several years, the members and local leaders are frequently unwilling to push for the full national pattern. The reader should recall in this connection what was said in Chapter I concerning the predominantly immigrant character of the labor force, the paternalistic and nonunion tradition of the community, the lack of aggressiveness and independence among the workers, and the small scale of industry which is conducive to unusually close worker-employer relations. Even when the national representative is convinced that a company can afford to give a certain increase, he frequently has trouble convincing the members and local leaders that they should hold out for this amount.

In one case, for example, the local negotiating committee recommended that the members accept a six-cent increase in the face of a national pattern of twelve cents. The national representative explained

this to us by saying that the local committee was made up of "stooges for the company." Actually, the committee seems merely to have been responsive to the sentiment of the members, who were fearful of a strike. Another local of the union in a nearby city had just been through a severe strike involving much personal hardship. The members of the local in this plant believed that the company would face a strike rather than go above six cents, and they simply did not want to strike.

In another case, the company stood firm at a maximum increase of eight cents despite a national twelve-cent pattern. The national representative, fortified with financial statements, was convinced that the company could pay more and recommended a strike. When a vote was taken, however, the strike proposal was defeated. The national representative explained that the workers had such a strong attachment to the company that they would not even consider striking. In addition, "the local leaders are too conciliatory toward the company—they aren't real unionists."

In some of the smaller plants there are close personal relations between management and union officials. One national representative attributed the low settlements in a particular company to the fact that he was never called into the negotiations, apparently because the president of the local union was a brother of the plant superintendent. "Why those guys up there don't know what's going on. Why do you know that almost seventy-five per cent of them can't read or write. . . . What's more, they're scared. You see, it's like this. The local president tells them all they can get is so much and they believe it because they fear authority. What's more, they point out that if they kick against the local president, why they'll get fired from their jobs because the president is the brother of the big shot in the plant. . . . What can you do?"

There are thus two main reasons for settlements below the national pattern. First, the employer may not be able to pay and may be able to convince the national union representative of this fact. Second, the local leaders may undershoot the mark, and the national representative may be unable to persuade local leaders and members to hold out for as much as the company could pay. While the first factor is doubtless of primary importance, the second factor should not be ignored.

A careful examination of collective bargaining in this area suggests that the gains won by the unions from a few giant companies do not

have as much binding force over negotiations with smaller companies as has sometimes been assumed. It suggests also that union estimates of a company's wage-paying ability play a significant role in the bargaining process. This is evident from the way in which the wage increase demanded of a company in a particular year is tempered to the financial position of the company. It is evident also from the extent to which unions have been willing to allow certain companies to remain at a permanently lower wage level than other companies because of differences in wage-paying ability. A silver company which, because of old-fashioned production methods and relatively small production volume, is at a cost disadvantage compared with larger rivals, has been allowed to maintain a somewhat lower wage level. When an automobile parts company in the area was first organized in the early forties, the union asserted its intention of raising wage rates to the Detroit level. It gradually became convinced of the impracticability of this objective, however, and has left the plant substantially below Detroit. No effort is made to force manufacturers of rubber sundries in the area up to the wage level of the tire companies. Instances of this sort could be multiplied. Taken as a whole, they suggest that union leaders take considerable account of economic calculations.

MANAGEMENT REACTION TO WAGE CHANGES

We have considered up to this point only the forces bearing on the *determination* of the plant wage level. A limited amount of information was obtained also about the *consequence* of wage changes, and particularly the consequences for employment in the plant.

The data at our disposal are defective in several respects. First, they represent only the opinions of business managers in the area, obtained by the interview method. It would have been desirable to go behind these opinions into the accounts of each company, and to trace the movements of labor costs, total costs, prices, profit margins, output, and employment over the course of the years. This time-consuming sort of investigation was not possible within the budget of the present study. It is obvious, however, that interview material is not as reliable as detailed case studies using accounting material, such as were conducted a decade ago by the Temporary National Economic Committee.[1]

Second, the economic situation during the years 1946–1948 was

[1] Douglass V. Brown, John T. Dunlop, Edwin M. Martin, and John A. Brownell, *Industrial Wage Rates, Labor Costs, and Price Policies,* T.N.E.C. Monograph No. 5 (Washington, Government Printing Office, 1940).

distinctly unusual. Demand for most products was in excess of productive capacity, most plants were operating at or near capacity, and most companies were earning substantial profits. The primary concern of most manufacturers was to get enough labor and materials to meet the orders from their regular customers, and to carry through programs of plant renovation and expansion. Cost increases were readily translated into price increases. Not until 1949 did cost increases impinge on profits, and this was due to falling sales volume rather than to rising prices of labor and materials. Third, only manufacturing companies were studied, and most of these had between two hundred and one thousand employees. The procedures and policies of these companies may differ considerably from those of companies in other industries and other size-groupings.

The questions in section C of Schedule A (see Appendix B) were asked of fifty-four manufacturing companies in the area. These included virtually all manufacturing companies with two hundred or more employees, and a small sampling of companies with less than two hundred workers. Attention was focused on the larger companies because the greater uniformness of their procedures and the higher average quality of their managements made systematic information easier to obtain.

The effects of wage increases on labor supply and worker effort (questions C.1 and C.2) seem to have been small. The effect of wage increases on production volume (question C.3) seems also to have been small during the years 1946–1948. A few plants attempted to lower labor costs by reducing the amount of overtime worked. This usually did not mean any reduction in weekly output, however, but rather a more efficient scheduling of production so as to avoid the necessity of overtime in bottleneck departments. A few other plants stated that they had changed the composition of their output by reducing the production of low-margin items and increasing the output of high-margin items. This did not, however, mean any appreciable change in total employment.

The companies interviewed were next asked (question C.4): "Did the wage increase cause you to make a special effort to reduce costs by raising the efficiency of production, reducing the use of indirect labor, eliminating certain operations, or making other changes in methods?" During the years 1946–1948 the answers to this question were almost uniformly in the negative. The main reason seems to be that during these years cost increases were fully offset by price in-

distinctly unusual. Demand for most products was in excess of productive capacity, most plants were operating at or near capacity, and most companies were earning substantial profits. The primary concern of most manufacturers was to get enough labor and materials to meet the orders from their eager customers, and to carry through programs of plant renovation and expansion. Cost increases were readily translated into price increases. Not until 1949 did costs encroach seriously on profits, and this was due to falling sales volume rather than to rising prices of labor and materials. Third, only manufacturing companies were studied, and most of these had between two hundred and one thousand employees. The procedures and policies of these companies may differ considerably from those of companies in other industries and other size-brackets.

The questions in Section C of Schedule 4 (see Appendix B) were asked of fifty-four manufacturing companies in the area. These included virtually all manufacturing companies with two hundred or more employees, and a small sampling of companies with less than two hundred workers. Attention was focussed on the larger companies because the greater definiteness of their procedures and the higher average quality of their managements made systematic information easier to obtain.

The effects of wage increases on labor supply and worker effort (questions C.1 and C.2) seem to have been small. The effect of wage increases on production volume (question C.3) seems also to have been small during the years 1946–1948. A few plants attempted to lower labor costs by reducing the amount of overtime worked. This usually did not mean any reduction in weekly output, however, but rather a more efficient scheduling of production so as to avoid the necessity of overtime in bottleneck departments. A few other plants stated that they had changed the composition of their output by reducing the production of low-margin items and increasing the output of high-margin items. This did not, however, mean any appreciable change in total employment.

The companies interviewed were next asked (question C.4), "Did the wage increase cause you to make a special effort to reduce costs by raising the efficiency of direct labor, reducing the use of indirect labor, eliminating certain operations, or making other changes in methods?" During the years 1946–1948 the answers to this question were almost uniformly in the negative. The main reason seems to be that during these years cost increases were fully offset by price in-

creases and did not encroach on profit margins. It is a *shrinkage in the profit margin,* rather than a wage increase per se, which calls forth emergency efforts to lower costs. Such a shrinkage in margins is most likely to occur during recession, when the manufacturer is squeezed between falling income from sales and a rigid wage level. During the recession of 1949 we found for the first time a considerable number of companies who were "making a drive on costs."

What is involved in "making a drive on costs"? This does not usually mean an intensification of the normal research, methods-improvement, engineering, and cost control work of the company. This work is going on continuously and cannot be speeded up without an increase of personnel in the departments concerned, which is not regarded as desirable at a time of shrinking profits. The normal procedure seems to be a straight reduction in the budgets of the various operating departments. The general manager calls the department heads into his office and says "John, I want five thousand dollars out of your department next month; Charlie, I want four thousand out of yours," and so on down the line.

It is easier to give such instructions than to ensure that they will be carried out. When the pressure gets great enough, however, costs will be forced down by one method or another. Among the most vulnerable cost items seem to be expenditure for indirect factory labor, factory supervision, clerical help, and general administrative overhead. We found a few cases in which management had economized on direct factory labor by such methods as reducing the use of helpers on machines or increasing the size of machine assignments. There were many more cases, however, in which the office staff had been weeded out, foremen had been demoted to production work, painting and other maintenance work had been deferred, and men engaged in indirect plant labor had been laid off or transferred to production operations. When companies were asked in the spring of 1949 what they were doing to offset falling margins, the commonest answer was "We're making a drive on overhead," i.e., on indirect wage and salary expense. It seems likely that this type of expense shows a marked countercyclical movement, tending to creep up gradually during prosperous periods and to be cut back during depression.

The companies interviewed were asked also about capital-labor substitution (question C.5): "Did you, as a result of the wage increase, put in any new labor-saving machinery which you wouldn't have put in otherwise?" In the course of discussing this question, we ranged

beyond the immediate objective in an effort to discover the influences and considerations which affect management decisions to install new equipment. The information obtained, while qualitative and fragmentary, is quite suggestive and agrees in general with the results of other empirical studies.

We must distinguish at the outset between equipment installed to produce a new product or an improved quality of product, and equipment installed to reduce the cost of producing an existing product. While the former is quantitatively very important, it is only with the latter that we are concerned here. The decision whether to install a cost-reducing improvement starts from a calculation of the prospective savings from the new equipment. This usually means savings in direct labor cost. While this avoids the complexities of overhead cost accounting, it tends to weight the scales against new equipment, since savings in nonlabor costs are ignored. Even the calculation of savings in direct labor cost is not as easy as might be supposed. One plant manager, for example, reported that the engineers' estimates of prospective savings are invariably too optimistic, since they assume that the machine will run continuously at peak efficiency and without breakdowns. In order to correct for this excessive optimism, he customarily reduces the engineering estimates by 50 per cent before passing them on to higher management.

The next step is to divide the prospective monthly savings into the cost of the machine in order to determine the "pay-out period." This is then used as an index of the desirability of the improvement, other things equal, a piece of equipment with a short pay-out period is preferable to one with a longer period. The conception of a proper pay-out period varies greatly from one company to another, within the same company from time to time, and from one type of equipment to another. Large and costly machines are usually allowed a longer pay-out period than less expensive machines. A standard type of machine is usually allowed a longer period than a novel piece of equipment on which the risk of obsolescence is greater. A machine which has already been adopted by most of the industry, and which the company feels obliged to adopt in order to remain in competition, will be allowed a longer pay-out period than one on which the company itself is pioneering.

The pay-out periods which managers require in order to adopt a

See in particular Ruth P. Mack, *The Flow of Business Funds and Consumer Purchasing Power* (New York, Columbia University Press, 1941).

beyond the immediate objective in an effort to discover the main considerations which affect management decisions about installing new equipment. The information obtained, while qualitative and fragmentary, is quite suggestive and agrees in general with the results of other empirical studies.[2]

We must distinguish at the outset between equipment installed to produce a new product or an improved quality of product, and equipment installed to reduce the cost of producing an existing product. While the former is quantitatively very important, it is only with the latter that we are concerned here. The decision whether to instal a cost-reducing improvement starts from a calculation of the prospective savings from the new equipment. This usually means savings in *direct labor only*. While this avoids the complexities of overhead cost accounting, it tends to weight the scales against new equipment since savings in nonlabor items are ignored. Even the calculation of savings in direct labor is not as easy as might be supposed. One plant manager, for example, reported that his engineers' estimates of prospective savings are invariably too optimistic, since they assume that the machine will run continuously at peak efficiency and without breakdowns. In order to correct for this excessive optimism, he customarily reduces the engineering estimates by 50 per cent before passing them on to higher management.

The next step is to divide the prospective monthly saving into the cost of the machine in order to determine its "pay-out period." This is then used as an index of the desirability of the improvement; other things equal, a piece of equipment with a short pay-out period is preferable to one with a longer period. The conception of a proper pay-out period varies greatly from one company to another, within the same company from time to time, and from one type of equipment to another. Large and costly machines are usually allowed a longer pay-out period than less expensive machines. A standard type of machine is usually allowed a longer period than a novel piece of equipment on which the risk of obsolescence is greater. A machine which has already been adopted by most of the industry, and which the company feels obliged to adopt in order to remain in competition, will be allowed a longer pay-out period than one on which the company itself is pioneering.

The pay-out periods which managers require in order to adopt a

[2] See in particular Ruth P. Mack, *The Flow of Business Funds and Consumer Purchasing Power* (New York, Columbia University Press, 1941).

new piece of equipment impress one at first glance as surprisingly short. Many types of heavy equipment are required to pay out within two or three years, and small tools must usually pay out in a year or less. This apparently conservative policy is due mainly to considerations of risk. Management is highly conscious of the danger that the machine may become obsolete in a few years, or that the product which it was designed to produce may become obsolete, or that even if these things do not happen the machine may stand idle part of the time because of cyclical fluctuations in demand. The rate of discount applied to future items of expected income because of their uncertainty is very high—so high that it dwarfs the effect of moderate variations in wage rates, interest rates, and machinery prices.[3]

In some of the smaller companies each proposed equipment purchase is considered *ad hoc* on its own merits. The larger companies, however, usually prepare a program of capital expenditures for the coming year, the size of which and all major items in which must be approved by the board of directors. Funds for this purpose come primarily from depreciation allowances and reinvestment of earnings, supplemented in some cases by sale of old equipment, reduction of working capital, and borrowing. In general, however, borrowing is frowned on in the conservative financial atmosphere of the area, and is scarcely ever used except for major plant expansions.

The decision on a particular item thus depends on whether, when ranked in its proper order on a priority list of desirable projects, it comes within the over-all equipment budget approved by the directors. The size of the budget determines the cut-off point on the list, and the lowest ranking projects have to be dropped. This means, among other things, that the cut-off point is much lower in a prosperous year when a good deal of money is available for reinvestment than in a year of depression. In a good year, the funds available may enable management to go down the list to projects with a pay-out period of five years; in bad times, projects with a pay-out period of two years may be rejected as submarginal.

During the years 1946–1948, perhaps because of the deferral of equipment purchases and the wearing out of old equipment during the War years, most companies had more opportunities for profitable investment than they could finance from the funds available to them.

[3] This point has been noted by economists concerned with the theory of business planning. See particularly the discussion in J. R. Hicks, *Value and Capital* (London, Oxford Press, 1939), Chapter XVII.

The cut-off points on their priority lists were relatively high. In examining equipment recently installed in plants throughout the area, I was constantly impressed by its technical superiority over the equipment which it had replaced. I saw many machines which were two or three hundred per cent more productive than their predecessors, and few which were only twenty or thirty per cent more productive. During these years at least, management did not seem to be installing machines which had been pushed barely over the margin of profitability as a result of wage increases.

The wage increases of 1946–1948 seem to have had remarkably little effect on the pace of mechanization, except insofar as they may have altered the amount of earnings available for reinvestment. We did not find a single change in the annual investment program of any company which could be attributed directly to an increase in its wage level. This was perhaps to be expected, since a wage increase of 5 or 10 per cent was not large compared with other elements in management calculations, notably the risk element already mentioned, and since the wage increases were offset by a roughly proportionate rise in the price of new machinery.

It would be undesirable to minimize the importance of wage changes over longer periods of time. Over a period of decades, the normal tendency is for money wage rates to rise more rapidly than commodity prices, including machinery prices. This steadily reduces the pay-out period of new equipment. As one manager remarked, "It gives the engineers more to play with." A relative rise in wages must, therefore, be favorable to mechanization; but one should not expect to see appreciable results from small wage increases or over short periods of time.

The clearest and strongest effect of wage increases in the communities studied was upon product prices (question 5(b)). Wage and price increases went on hand-in-hand throughout the period. One cannot say in every case that a wage increase caused a price increase. In some cases the price increase came first and might have been made even had wages remained stable. In any event, the possibility of price increases combined with high rates of output enabled wage increases to be absorbed with little difficulty until the latter part of 1948. There was little immediate effect on output or employment, for demand was sufficiently high that most firms could sell all they could produce, even at increased prices. The wage and price levels reached by various industries during this period, however, will affect their ability to maintain sales in future periods of more normal demand. There seems no

The cut-off points on their priority lists were relatively high. In examining equipment recently installed in plants throughout the area, I was constantly impressed by its technical superiority over the equipment which it had replaced. I saw many machines which were two or three hundred per cent more productive than their predecessors, but few which were only twenty or thirty per cent more productive. During these years, at least, management did not seem to be installing machines which had been pushed barely over the margin of profitability as a result of wage increases.

The wage increases of 1946–1948 seem to have had remarkably little effect on the pace of mechanization, except insofar as they may have altered the amount of earnings available for reinvestment. We did not find a single change in the annual investment program of any company which could be attributed directly to an increase in its wage level. This was perhaps to be expected, since a wage increase of 5 or 10 per cent was not large compared with other elements in management calculations, notably the risk element already mentioned; and since the wage increases were offset by a roughly proportionate rise in the price of new machinery.

It would be undesirable to minimize the importance of wage changes over longer periods of time. Over a period of decades, the normal tendency is for money wage rates to rise more rapidly than commodity prices, including machinery prices. This clearly reduces the pay-out period of new equipment. As one manager remarked, "It gives the engineers more to play with." A relative rise in wages must, therefore, be favorable to mechanization; but one should not expect to see appreciable results from small wage increases or over short periods of time.

The clearest and strongest effect of wage increases in the companies studied was upon product prices (question C.6). Wage and price increases went on hand-over-hand throughout the period. One cannot say in every case that a wage increase caused a price increase. In some cases the price increase came first, and might have been made even had wages remained stable. In any event, the possibility of price increases combined with high rates of output enabled wage increases to be absorbed with little difficulty until the latter part of 1948. There was little immediate effect on output or employment, for demand was sufficiently high that most firms could sell all they could produce even at increased prices. The wage and price levels reached by various industries during this period, however, will affect their ability to maintain sales in future periods of more normal demand. There seems no

reason to doubt, therefore, that differing rates of wage-price increase during 1946–1948 will eventually affect relative employment levels in different firms and industries.

The concept of a sloping labor demand curve for the individual firm or industry thus contains an important element of truth. It needs, however, to be qualified in at least three respects. First, the elasticity of demand for labor rests mainly on shiftability of consumer purchases rather than on shiftability of production techniques. A relative increase in the wage level of an industry tends to cause a relative decline in employment mainly because wages react on prices, which in turn react on sales, output, and employment. While there may also be a decline of employment via capital-labor substitution, this is likely to be of quite secondary importance. Second, the tendency holds only for substantial increases in wages. The wage-price relation is sufficiently loose jointed that a small wage increase may be lost in the interstices of company accounting. Third, the tendency is operative only over a period of one or more business cycles. During a cyclical upswing, the general upsurge of demand may prevent any immediate effect of wage-price increases on output and employment. The effects are likely to reveal themselves only during the subsequent recession.

It is desirable to emphasize this element of validity in the labor demand curve concept because in Chapter VIII I shall argue that the concept of a labor supply curve to the firm has little meaning or usefulness. At that point it may seem to the reader that I am conducting a general onslaught on marginal analysis and urging that it be abandoned in toto. This is not so. My basic viewpoint is that the usefulness of marginal analysis varies enormously from one area of economic life to another. It is wrong to reject it in areas where it does serve an explanatory purpose. It is equally wrong to insist on purely logical grounds that it *must* be useful even in areas where its assumptions are demonstrably inaccurate.

reason to doubt, therefore, that differing rates of wage-price increase during 1946–1949 will eventually affect relative employment levels in different firms and industries.

The concept of a sloping labor demand curve for the individual firm or industry thus contains an important element of truth. It needs, however, to be qualified in at least three respects. First, the elasticity of demand for labor rests mainly on variability of consumer purchases rather than on variability in production techniques. A relative increase in the wage level of an industry tends to cause a relative decline in employment mainly because wages react on prices, which in turn react on sales, output, and employment. While there may also be a decline of employment via capital-labor substitution, this is likely to be of quite secondary importance. Second, the tendency holds only for substantial increases in wages. The wage-price relation is sufficiently loose jointed that a small wage increase may be lost in the interstices of company accounting. Third, the tendency is operative only over a period of one or more business cycles. During a cyclical upswing, the general upsurge of demand may prevent any immediate effect of wage-price increases on output and employment. The effects are likely to reveal themselves only during the subsequent recession.

It is desirable to emphasize this element of validity in the labor demand curve concept because in Chapter VIII I shall argue that the concept of a labor supply curve to the firm has little meaning or usefulness. At that point it may seem to the reader that I am conducting a general onslaught on marginal analysis and urging that it be abandoned in toto. This is not my view. My viewpoint is that the usefulness of marginal analysis varies enormously from one area of economic life to another. It is wrong to reject it in areas where it does serve an explanatory purpose. It is equally wrong to insist on purely logical grounds that it must be useful even in areas where its assumptions are demonstrably inaccurate.

CHAPTER VII The Evolution of the Area Wage Structure

THIS chapter is an extended statistical footnote to Chapter VI. Its purpose is to trace changes in the structure of manufacturing wage rates in the area over the years 1940–1948.[1] Most studies of wage structure are on an industry rather than an area basis and are cross sections at a point of time. For the purpose of relating wage structure to labor mobility, however, the area is probably the most significant unit of study; and, since economic adjustments take time, such studies gain in value by being extended over a considerable period. Even the period 1940–1948 is shorter than would be desirable. Few manufacturers in the area had a systematic wage structure before 1940, however, and ready-made wage statistics scarcely exist before that year. For earlier years it would have been necessary to reconstruct each company's wage structure directly from payroll records, which would have become a major undertaking in itself.

The material to be presented falls into four parts: (1) A comparison of the general wage levels of manufacturing companies in the area, and an analysis of changes in interplant wage relations over the period. This material will supplement the discussion in Chapter VI of how plant wage levels are determined, and will be especially pertinent to the question of how far individual companies actually succeed in "keeping up with the area." (2) Changes in relative wage rates for skilled and unskilled work in each company. (3) The characteristics of wage incentive systems in the area and the effect of these systems on the behavior of earnings. (4) The size of pension, vacation, and other supplementary wage payments. A key question here is whether companies with low wage rates offset this by offering workers more in "fringe" benefits.

[1] Our wage studies were confined to manufacturing for two reasons: (1) In most nonmanufacturing industries of the area establishments are numerous, small, and have poor personnel records. Reliable and representative wage information would have been difficult or impossible to obtain. (2) A primary purpose of gathering wage data was to relate these to data on labor turnover and mobility, company wage and hiring policies, and so on. Since we had these latter types of data only for manufacturing, it seemed most useful to concentrate the wage survey on manufacturing also.

INTERPLANT DIFFERENCES AND THE PATTERN OF WAGE CHANGE

Information on the wage structure of twenty-eight manufacturing companies in the area over the years 1940–1948 was obtained by a special survey. The questionnaire used and some of the difficulties encountered are discussed in Appendix B. The sample is strongly biased in the direction of large companies.[2] We attempted to work farther downward in the size scale, but found that most of the small plants did not maintain records which would enable them to complete our questionnaire. The sample covers about half of the manufacturing employment of the area and is homogeneous throughout the period, except for a few companies which were unable to provide information before 1941 or 1942.

On what basis should one compare the wage levels of different companies? The best basis would be wage rates or average hourly earnings on identical jobs in different plants. There are several reasons, however, why such a comparison is not feasible. The industry of the area is highly diversified and many jobs are found in only one or a few plants. Even where the same job title occurs in numerous plants, considerable study would be necessary to determine the comparability of job content. Finally, the ranking of plants with respect to one job would differ from their ranking with respect to any other job, and the outcome would depend on which job was selected for comparison.[3]

For companies which use the same system of job evaluation, one can compare the rates paid by different companies for the same "labor grade," even though the jobs included in this grade may be completely different in each plant. Twenty-one of the twenty-eight plants studied were using the job evaluation plan of the National Metal Trades Association in 1948, and this provides a basis for comparing their 1948 wage levels. Since these companies had installed the N.M.T.A. system at varying dates over the period, however, it is not feasible to use it as a basis for earlier years.

[2] Twelve of the companies surveyed had more than five hundred employees (out of a total of sixteen plants in the area in this category); ten had between two hundred and five hundred employees (out of a total of twenty-five in this group); and six had between fifty and two hundred employees. No plant with less than fifty employees was included, although there are four hundred and eleven such plants in the area.

[3] These considerations suggest that the whole concept of a "plant wage level" may not make much sense. Perhaps the only valid comparisons which can be made are for specific jobs. Still, one feels that there is some meaning in the commonsense statement that "A is a higher-wage plant than B," and one would like to find a way of testing such statements.

For the most part, therefore, we shall have to fall back on two less satisfactory indicators of the plant wage level. The first is the plant's hiring rate for new employees. While this does not have a homogeneous meaning in terms of job content, it is the wage which is normally offered to all applicants at the plant, except skilled workers who can demonstrate their right to immediate classification at a higher rate on the basis of previous work experience. It is thus a particularly strategic figure from the standpoint of labor recruitment. A second and less satisfactory measure is average hourly earnings for the plant as a whole. This is a very ambiguous figure, which is affected not only by basic wage rates but also by the occupational composition of the plant, the looseness or tightness of incentive rates (if these are used), the amount of overtime being worked, and numerous other factors. Despite these imperfections, we shall use average hourly earnings[4] on occasion as a crude indicator of where a plant stands in the area wage structure.

The survey data enable us to say something about the following questions: (1) How great was the dispersion in the wage levels of manufacturing firms in 1948? (2) What happened to the degree of dispersion over the period 1940–1948? The most plausible hypothesis which comes to mind is that, since these were years of labor shortage during which plants had to compete actively in recruiting labor, the dispersion of plant wage levels should have decreased over the period. (3) What happened to the ranking of different plants over the period? Did they retain about the same relative standing, or were there significant shifts? (4) How uniform were the general wage increases given by different companies during the three postwar "rounds" of increases in 1946, 1947, and 1948? To the extent that differing increases were given, what factors seem to have been responsible? The data on each of these points will be presented in the order listed.

1. The dispersion of plant wage levels in July, 1948, on three different bases of comparison, is shown in Table 24. The degree of dispersion at this time seems quite large when one considers that the measurement was made at the end of a long period of high employment and that the companies included were a rather homogeneous

[4] An attempt was made to adjust *gross* hourly earnings, which was all most of the companies could supply, to a straight-time basis by using an adjustment factor. Because overtime was in most plants very unevenly distributed over the labor force, these adjustments proved so unreliable that we eventually abandoned them. The inclusion of overtime is not too serious for comparisons of 1940 and 1948, since little overtime was worked in either year. It should be noted that when we refer to the period 1940–1948, this means strictly July 1, 1940—July 1, 1948, since companies were asked to supply wage information for the payroll period closest to July 1st in each year.

group—relatively large companies, three-fourths of them engaged in metalworking, employing predominantly male labor, and recruiting this labor in the same area. It is surprising that starting rates could have varied from a low of 69 cents per hour to a high of $1.185 cents per hour, and that the minimum rate for labor grade ten ranged from

TABLE 24

DISPERSION OF PLANT WAGE LEVELS, JULY, 1948, ON THREE BASES OF COMPARISON

Dollars per hour	Average Hourly Earnings	Starting Rate	Minimum of the Rate Range for Labor Grade 10*
Range, Lowest to Highest	0.88–1.69	0.69–1.185	0.66–1.07
Median (M)	1.27	0.80	0.80
Interquartile Range ($Q_3 - Q_1$)	0.205	0.15	0.12
$\frac{Q_3 - Q_1}{M}$ (per cent)	16.1	18.9	15.0

* For the twenty-one plants using the N.M.T.A. job evaluation system. Grade 10 is the lowest labor grade for male employees; it is roughly equivalent to, but more precise than, the so-called "common labor rate."

66 cents to $1.07 per hour. If the smaller companies in the area had been included, the range from top to bottom of the wage structure would have been even greater. In the spring of 1949, when none of the large companies had a starting rate below 75 cents per hour, some of the small companies were still trying to recruit labor at 60 cents.

The fact that we can compare companies on three different bases enables us incidentally to check on the reliability of these bases themselves. A check was made on this point, using ten plants for which all three measures are available. The ranking based on the rate paid for N.M.TA. labor grade ten is believed to be most reliable, for reasons already noted. The ranking on the basis of starting rates conforms quite closely to the N.M.T.A. ranking; the average amount by which a company's rank on one basis differs from that on the other is only 1.4 points. The ranking on the basis of average hourly earnings shows a much poorer correspondence with the N.M.T.A. ranking; the average deviation in a company's rank on the two bases is 3.2 points (compared with a maximum possible deviation of 5.0 points). The inference is that ranking by starting rate is considerably more reliable than ranking by average hourly earnings, and we shall therefore use the former method of comparison wherever possible.

The actual starting rates of individual companies as of July 1, 1948, are shown in Table 25. What accounts for these marked differences in

group—relatively large companies, three-fourths of them engaged in metalworking, employing predominantly male labor, and recruiting their labor in the same area. It is surprising that starting rates could have varied from a low of 69 cents per hour to a high of $1.05 cents per hour, and that the minimum rate for labor grade ten ranged from

TABLE 14

DISPERSION OF HOURLY WAGE RATES, JULY 1948, ON DIFFERENT BASES OF COMPARISON

* [illegible]

96 cents to $1.07 per hour. If the smaller companies in the area had been included, the range from top to bottom of the wage structure would have been even greater. In the spring of 1949, when none of the large companies had a starting rate below 75 cents per hour, some of the small companies were still trying to recruit labor at 65 cents.

wage level? An examination of the listing against the background of our knowledge of each company suggests that several factors are at work: the industry in which the firm is engaged, intensity of competition in the industry, and the wage levels of rival producers, the nature of the work and the kind of labor force required, the presence

TABLE [illegible]

RANKING OF COMPANIES BY STARTING RATE, [illegible]

Company Rank	Starting Rate (Cents per hour)
1	[illegible]
2	[illegible]
3	[illegible]
4	[illegible]
5	[illegible]
6	[illegible]
7	[illegible]
8	[illegible]
9	[illegible]
10	[illegible]
11	[illegible]
12	[illegible]
13	[illegible]
14	[illegible]
15	[illegible]
16	[illegible]
17	[illegible]
18	[illegible]
19	[illegible]
20	[illegible]
21	[illegible]
22	[illegible]
23	[illegible]
24	[illegible]
25	[illegible]

a Under union contract.

or absence of unionism, the efficiency of plant and equipment; and in some cases the efficiency of management. The relevance of these factors need not be labored. The importance of union organization is suggested, though not demonstrated conclusively, by the listing in the table. It will be noted that eleven of the twelve highest-wage plants are under union contract, while only three of the thirteen lowest-wage plants are unionized.

It may be interesting to say something about the characteristics of the companies at the top and bottom of the wage structure. Company 1

wage level? An examination of the listing against the background of our knowledge of each company suggests that several factors are at work: the industry in which the firm is engaged, intensity of competition in the industry, and the wage levels of rival producers; the nature of the work and the kind of labor force required; the presence

TABLE 25

RANKING OF COMPANIES BY STARTING RATE, JULY, 1948

Company Rank	Starting Rate (Cents per hour)
1*	118.5
2*	104
3*	100
4*	93
5*	91
6*	90
7*	90
8	88
9*	87
10*	85
11*	85
12*	83
13	80
14	80
15	80
16	80
17*	80
18	77
19	75
20*	75
21	72
22	70
23	70
24	69
25	69

* Under union contract.

or absence of unionism; the efficiency of plant and equipment; and in some cases the efficiency of management. The relevance of these factors need not be labored. The importance of union organization is suggested, though not demonstrated conclusively, by the listing in the table. It will be noted that eleven of the twelve highest-wage plants are under union contract, while only three of the thirteen lowest-wage plants are unionized.

It may be interesting to say something about the characteristics of the companies at the top and bottom of the wage structure. Company 1

is a branch plant of a large steel company, operating under union contract, and its wage level is geared to decisions made in Pittsburgh. Apart from this there are some unpleasant features of the work which might help to explain a relatively high wage level: heavy materials which make the work very strenuous, a great deal of noise, rotating shifts, and considerable irregularity of employment.

Company 2 is engaged in the paper industry, which is a relatively high-wage industry on a national basis. It is the largest company in its branch of paper manufacture, and has traditionally regarded itself as the wage leader for this branch. Company 3 underwent a sensational expansion during the war, in the course of which it grew from a few hundred workers to a peak of approximately five thousand; wages were raised rapidly to aid in the recruitment of labor, and the company has not been able to climb down from this high wage level since the war. Company 4 makes small components for a much larger machine. Demand is almost completely inelastic and there are few rival suppliers. The company operates under contract with a CIO union which tries to follow national wage patterns. Company 5 is a tire producer which is tied, through the union, to the high wage level of the Akron companies.

At the bottom of the list, Company 21 is a small metalworking plant making parts which are sold to a few large manufacturers. Competition with rival suppliers is keen, and labor costs form between 50 and 60 per cent of total costs. The monopsonistic character of the product market and the high ratio of labor costs combine to exert downward pressure on wage rates. Company 22 is engaged in a branch of garment production and employs a high proportion of women workers, so that it is natural that its rates should be below those for men in heavier types of industry. Company 23 is a small and not very modern plant in a highly competitive industry. It has little influence over product prices, and labor costs form between 40 and 50 per cent of total costs.

Company 24 is a large metalworking plant which, in spite of its size, tends to lag behind wage movements in the area rather than to lead them. Its low rank in terms of starting rates is somewhat misleading, since it ranks near the midpoint of the companies studied in terms of average hourly earnings. It follows a conservative policy of keeping starting rates low, even though job rates and actual earnings are reasonably comparable with other leading manufacturers. In spite of low starting rates it is able to attract sufficient labor because of

its sheer size and conspicuousness in the area, because it is willing to hire Negroes who have few employment opportunities in other manufacturing plants in the area, and because its great age and stability of operations have created a tradition that employment with it constitutes a lifetime career. Company 25 produces a variety of light consumer goods. A high proportion of its products are sold on contract to a large retail chain which [illegible] drives a rather hard bargain. The work is relatively light and low skilled, and the proportion of women workers is higher than in most of the nearby plants. The union is new and quite weak and has not been able to alter the company's relative wage position in the area.

A full explanation of each firm's position in the wage structure would require a much more intensive analysis of its costs, earnings, and competitive situation. The comments just made, however, provide some clues to the forces at work. They suggest that the major factor is difference in the companies' wage-paying ability, plus in some cases the presence of a union which forces a company closer to the limit of its ability to pay. Labor supply considerations seem to be somewhat less important, for reasons which will be elaborated in the next chapter.

Table 25 suggests that when companies state that they are trying to "keep up with the area," this means maintaining their customary position rather than trying to reach the average wage level of the area. Over the years some companies find themselves able to pay more than the area average, while others are resigned to the fact that they cannot pay as much as the average. Instead of engaging in a futile attempt to climb to a higher rank, they content themselves with keeping in approximate step with wage changes in other companies.

2. The next question to be considered is how the dispersion of plant wage levels changed over the period 1940–1948. Since few companies used the NMTA job evaluation system in 1940, and since average hourly earnings figures are not a very reliable index, it seems best to use starting rates for this comparison. Table 26 shows the dispersion of starting rates in the companies surveyed in 1940, 1947, 1948, and 1949.

The most significant part of the table is the last line, which shows the interquartile range as a percentage of the median. This is an abstract measure of dispersion which is not affected by changes in the absolute wage level. It will be noted that there was little change in the dispersion of plant wage levels over the period as a whole. There

its sheer size and conspicuousness in the area, because it is willing to hire Negroes who have few employment opportunities in other manufacturing plants in the area, and because its great age and stability of operations have created a tradition that employment with it constitutes a lifetime career. Company 25 produces a variety of light consumer goods. A high proportion of its products are sold on contract to a large retail chain, which doubtless drives a rather hard bargain. The work is relatively light and low skilled, and the proportion of women workers is higher than in most of the metalworking plants. The union is new and quite weak, and has not thus far been able to alter the company's relative wage position in the area.

A full explanation of each firm's position in the wage structure would require a much more intensive analysis of its costs, earnings, and competitive situation. The comments just made, however, provide some clues to the forces at work. They suggest that the major factor is difference in the companies' wage-paying ability, plus in some cases the presence of a union which forces a company closer to the limit of its ability to pay. Labor supply considerations seem to be somewhat less important, for reasons which will be elaborated in the next chapter.

Table 25 suggests that when companies state that they are trying to "keep up with the area," this means maintaining their *customary position* rather than trying to reach the *average wage level* of the area. Over the years some companies find themselves able to pay more than the area average, while others get used to the fact that they cannot pay as much as the average. Instead of engaging in a futile attempt to climb to a higher rank, they content themselves with keeping in approximate step with wage changes in other companies.

2. The next question to be considered is how the dispersion of plant wage levels changed over the period 1940–1948. Since few companies used the N.M.T.A. job evaluation system in 1940, and since average hourly earnings figures are not a very reliable index, it seems best to use starting rates for this comparison. Table 26 shows the dispersion of starting rates in the companies surveyed in 1940, 1942, 1945, and 1948.

The most significant part of the table is the last line, which shows the interquartile range as a percentage of the median. This is an abstract measure of dispersion which is not affected by changes in the absolute wage level. It will be noted that there was little change in the dispersion of plant wage levels over the period as a whole. There

was a slight reduction in dispersion during the war years 1942–1945. This is readily explicable on the basis of wartime wage controls[5] plus the very high level of demand for labor. After the end of controls in early 1946, the dispersion of wage levels increased once more and by 1948 had returned almost to the prewar level. An important factor

TABLE 26

Dispersion of Plant Starting Rates, 1940, 1942, 1945, and 1948*

Dollars Per Hour	1940	1942	1945	1948
Range, Lowest to Highest	0.35–0.625	0.35–0.78	0.50–0.78	0.69–1.185
Median (M)	0.43	0.55	0.60	0.80
Interquartile Range $(Q_3 - Q_1)$	0.087	0.11	0.10	0.15
$\frac{Q_3 - Q_1}{M}$ (per cent)	20.3	20.0	16.7	18.9

* Data are as of July 1st in each year. The sample for 1940 is not strictly comparable with that for later years, since only fifteen of the twenty-five companies were able to furnish data as far back as 1940. A tabulation using these fifteen companies only, however, showed the same tendencies over the years 1940–1948 as does Table 26.

here was the incomplete unionization of manufacturing industry in the area. The wage levels of unionized plants rose considerably more from 1945 to 1948 than did those of nonunion plants, and this produced an increase in interplant wage differences, both in absolute and percentage terms.

The data thus do not support our initial hypothesis that interplant wage differences tend to become narrower during a period of high employment. In July, 1948, after eight years of a tight labor market, interplant differences were about as great percentage-wise as they had been in July, 1940. Yet the low-wage firms were still able to hire and retain enough labor to meet their production schedules. How they were able to do this is an interesting problem which we shall have to explore further in the next chapter.

3. Although there has been little change in the over-all dispersion of plant wage levels, there has been considerable change in the relative

[5] The policies of the National War Labor Board had the effect of freezing the wage levels of high-wage companies rather firmly, while increases in the wage levels of low-wage plants were permitted on several bases: elimination of "substandard" conditions of living, elimination of interplant "inequities" within the area, and in some cases the necessity of manning a plant for war production. Our work sheets reveal that five of the highest-wage companies in 1942 made no increase in starting rates between July 1, 1942, and July 1, 1945. The lowest-wage companies in 1942, on the other hand, came up very substantially, in most cases by something like 15 cents per hour. Companies which were medium-wage companies in 1942 tended to raise their starting rates by 5 to 10 cents an hour over the period.

was a slight reduction in dispersion during the war years 1942–1945. This is readily explicable on grounds of wartime wage controls plus the very high level of demand for labor. After the end of controls in early 1946, the dispersion of wage levels increased once more and by 1948 had returned almost to the prewar level. An important factor

TABLE 3

Dispersion of Plant Starting Rates, 1940, 1942, 1945, and 1948

Dollars Per Hour	1940	1942	1945	1948
Range, Lowest to Highest	0.45–0.62	0.55–0.78	0.59–1.01	1.05–1.37
Median (Q2)	0.55	0.75	0.86	1.30
Interquartile Range (Q3 – Q1)	0.09	0.11	0.10	0.18
$\frac{Q_3 - Q_1}{Q_2}$ (Percent)	16.1	14.7	[illegible]	13.9

[illegible]

tor was the incomplete unionization of manufacturing industry in the area. The wage levels of unionized plants rose considerably more from 1945 to 1948 than did those of nonunion plants, and this produced an increase in interplant wage differences, both in absolute and percentage terms.

The data thus do not support our initial hypothesis that interplant wage differences tend to become narrower during a period of high employment. In July, 1948, after eight years of a tight labor market, interplant differences were about as great percentagewise as they had been in July, 1940. Yet the low-wage firms were still able to hire and retain enough labor to meet their production schedules. How they were able to do this is an interesting question which we shall have to explore further in the next chapter.

3. Although there has been little change in the over-all dispersion of plant wage levels, there has been considerable change in the relative

The policies of the National War Labor Board had the effect of freezing the wage structure. [illegible] increases in the wage level of low-wage plants [illegible] permitted on several bases [illegible] "substandard" [illegible] of hiring [illegible] production [illegible] highest-wage companies in 1940 made no increase in starting rates [illegible] 1942 and July 1, 1945. The lowest wage companies in 1940, on the other hand, [illegible] substantially [illegible] cents per hour. Companies which were medium-wage companies in 1942 tended to raise their starting rates by 5 to 10 cents an hour over the period.

position of individual firms. In Table 47 the rank order of firms in 1948 is compared with their rank in 1942, this year being used instead of 1940 because of the larger number of firms for which 1942 data are available. It will be seen that there have been substantial changes in the ranking of most firms. Seven of the twenty-two experienced a gain

Table 47

[illegible]

Company No.	Rank, July 1, 1948	Rank, July 1, 1942
1	1	1
6	[illegible]	[illegible]
[illegible]	[illegible]	[illegible]
[illegible]	[illegible]	[illegible]
[illegible]	[illegible]	[illegible]
17	[illegible]	[illegible]
15	[illegible]	[illegible]
4	[illegible]	[illegible]
[illegible]	9	[illegible]
[illegible]	10	10
[illegible]	11	11
21	12	[illegible]
[illegible]	13	[illegible]
2	14	[illegible]
14	[illegible]	[illegible]
[illegible]	[illegible]	[illegible]
[illegible]	17	[illegible]
[illegible]	18	[illegible]
16	19	19
20	20	20
18	21	[illegible]
12	22	22

or loss of ten points or more, and the median shift for all firms was four points. Some of these shifts are not very significant when one takes into account also the behavior of job rates and average hourly earnings in the companies concerned.[a]

Where the shifts seem to be of genuine significance, it can usually be linked up either with the wartime experience of the company or with unionization. Companies which were not able to convert to war

[a] Some companies, including Nos. 6 and 7, which have moved up on the basis of starting rates, have moved down the scale of average hourly earnings. Other companies, including Nos. 4 and 21 which have moved down in terms of starting rates, have moved up in terms of average hourly earnings. Such discrepancies arise partly because some companies in the area follow a conservative policy of keeping starting rates down even when job rates are rising; other plants raise starting rates as fast as or even faster than job rates when labor is scarce. The numerous factors other than job rates which affect the behavior of average hourly earnings have already been noted.

position of individual firms. In Table 27 the rank order of firms in 1948 is compared with their rank in 1942, this year being used instead of 1940 because of the larger number of firms for which 1942 data are available. It will be seen that there have been substantial changes in the ranking of most firms. Seven of the twenty-two experienced a gain

TABLE 27

RANKING OF COMPANIES BY STARTING RATE, 1942 AND 1948

Company No.	Rank, July 1, 1948	Rank, July 1, 1942
1	1	1
2	2	6
3	3	7
4	4	4
5	5	19
6	6	15
7	7	22
8	8	8
9	9	9
10	10	13
11	11	14
12	12	21
13	13	3
14	14	2
15	15	11
16	16	17
17	17	18
18	18	16
19	19	20
20	20	10
21	21	5
22	22	12

or loss of ten points or more, and the median shift for all firms was four points. Some of these shifts are not very significant when one takes into account also the behavior of job rates and average hourly earnings in the companies concerned.[6]

Where the shift seems to be of genuine significance it can usually be linked up either with the wartime experience of the company or with unionization. Companies which were not able to convert to war

[6] Some companies, including Nos. 6 and 7, which have moved up on the basis of starting rates, have moved *down* the basis of average hourly earnings. Other companies, including Nos. 14 and 21, which have moved *down* in terms of starting rates, have moved *up* in terms of average hourly earnings. Such discrepancies occur partly because some companies in the area follow a conservative policy of keeping starting rates down even when job rates are rising; other plants raise starting rates as fast as, or even faster than, job rates when labor is scarce. The numerous factors other than job rates which affect the behavior of average hourly earnings have already been noted.

production from 1941–1945 tended to lose ground in the area wage structure relative to plants in war industries, and many of them have not been able to recover this ground since the war. Again, unionized companies, particularly in the steel, rubber, and paper industries, have had their wages pushed up more rapidly in the postwar years than have the nonunion companies.

4. The course of events during the postwar inflation is shown in Table 28, which presents the general wage increases granted by each company over the period July 1, 1945, to July 1, 1948.[7] It will be noted that different companies gave very different aggregate increases over the period, varying from 0 to 46.5 cents per hour. There was a slight positive correlation between the wage level of a plant at the beginning of the period and the size of the increases given during the period. On the average, plants which were at the top of the wage structure in 1945 gave increases which were larger, both absolutely and percentage-wise, than those given by companies at the bottom of the wage structure. This checks with our earlier finding that the dispersion of plant wage levels increased over the period 1945–1948. There was a slight negative relation between the size of wage increases and the rate of change of employment in the company. The coefficient of rank correlation is —0.29.

The clearest relation which emerges from the table is between size of wage increase and the union or nonunion status of the company. The average general wage increase granted by unionized companies over the period was 32 cents, compared with 19 cents for nonunion plants. A separate calculation of increases in starting rates in the two groups of companies gives the same general result. The average increase in starting rates was 28 cents for the union plants, compared with 18 cents for the unonunion plants.

The impetus to wage changes in this area since 1945 seems definitely to have come from the negotiations between national union leaders and such leading manufacturers as United States Steel, General Motors, and General Electric. While manufacturers in the area are

[7] While most wage increases during these years were applied uniformly "across-the-board," different increases were given in some cases to different departments, different labor grades, etc. In this case the plant-wide *average* increase, as reported to us by the company, was used in preparing Table 28. While companies were asked to report only the change in basic wage rates, excluding fringe payments, some companies reported the total "package" and we are not certain that we have managed to exclude fringe payments entirely. Another minor problem is that a few companies in the area had not yet made their "third-round" increases by July 1, 1948, and did make increases later in the year. Inclusion of these increases, however, would not change the picture very much.

production from 1941–1945 tended to lose ground in the area wage structure relative to plants in war industries, and many of them have not been able to recover this ground since the war. Again, unionized companies, particularly in the steel, rubber, and paper industries, have had their wages pushed up more rapidly in the postwar years than have the nonunion companies.

4. The course of events during the postwar inflation is shown in Table 72, which presents the general wage increases granted by each company over the period July 1, 1945 to July 1, 1948. It will be noted that different companies gave very different general increases over the period, varying from 21 to 46.5 cents per hour. There was a slight positive correlation between the wage level of a plant at the beginning of the period and the size of the increases given it during the period. On the average, plants which were at the top of the wage structure in 1945 gave increases which were larger, both absolutely and percentagewise, than those given by companies at the bottom of the wage structure. This checks with our earlier finding that the dispersion of plant wage levels increased over the period 1945–1948. There was a slight negative relation between the size of wage increases and the rate of change of employment in the company. The coefficient of rank correlation is −.029.

The clearest relation which emerges from the table is between size of wage increase and the union or nonunion status of the company. The average general wage increase granted by unionized companies over the period was 32 cents, compared with 19 cents for nonunion plants. A separate calculation of increases in starting rates in the two groups of companies gives the same general result. The average increase in starting rates was 29 cents for the union plants, compared with 18 cents for the nonunion plants.

The impetus to wage changes in this area since 1945 seems definitely to have come from the negotiations between national union leaders and such leading manufacturers as United States Steel, General Motors, and General Electric. The manufacturers in the area are

While most wage increases during these years were applied uniformly "across-the-board," different increases were made in some cases to different departments, different labor grades, etc. In this case the plant-wide average increase, as reported to us by the company, was used in preparing Table 72. While the companies were asked to report only the change in basic wage rates, excluding fringe payments, some companies reported the total "package" and we are not certain that we have managed to exclude fringe payments entirely. Another minor problem is that several plants in the area had made their third-round increases by July 1, 1948, and so did not make increases later in the year. Inclusion of these increases, however, would not change the picture very much.

reluctant to be tied tightly to the national "pattern" for their respective industries, they recognize it as a factor which must be taken into account. In recent years both union and management officials in the

TABLE 26

General Wage Increases in Manufacturing Companies, Jan. 1, 1946, to July 1, 1949

Company	Total Increase, 1946–1949 (Cents per hour)	Starting Rate, Jan. 1, 1949 (Cents per hour)	Change in Employment, 1945–1949 (%)
A	18.5	78.0	−21.6
B	20.3	66.3	+ 2.0
C	17.1	70.0	**
D	25.0	*	*
E	20.5	77.0	− 3.2
F	18.5	*	+ 1.1
G	22.0	70.5	18.7
H	[illegible]	80.0	+ 1.5
I	17.0	80.0	14.5
J	17.0	75.0	+20.1
K	20.5	69.5	+10.2
L	20.0	80.0	−22.8
M	24.9	65.0	− .5
N	20.0	70.0	−20.0
O	18.[illegible]	**	**
P	22.5	75.0	+24.8
Q	22.0	75.0	+11.3
R	22.0	65.0	9.55
S	22.0	75.0	[illegible]
T	21.5	60.0	+17.6
U	19.0	65.0	+15.4
V	15.0	65.0	+ 2.4
W	8.0	60.0	[illegible]
X	15.0	78.0	+40.0
Y	18.0	50.0	−20.8
Z	11.5	65.0	−15.0
AX	10.0	65.0	− 3.0
BY	20.0	60.0	−10.0

* [illegible]
** [illegible]

area, by mutual consent, have timed the expiration of contracts so that their negotiations will come after the national negotiations. Employers are reluctant to make any move until they have seen "what the big fellows are going to do."

Most of the wage negotiations in the area occur between March 1 and July 1. There seems to be little consultation among local unions in the area either on the size or timing of wage demands. Each follows

reluctant to be tied rigidly to the national "pattern" for their respective industries, they recognize it as a factor which must be taken into account. In recent years both union and management officials in the

TABLE 28

GENERAL WAGE INCREASES IN MANUFACTURING COMPANIES, JULY 1, 1945, TO JULY 1, 1948

Company	Total Increase 1945–1948 (Cents per hour)	Starting Rate, July 1, 1945 (Cents per hour)	Change in Employment, 1945–1948 (%)
A*	46.5	78.0	−24.6
B*	46.5	66.5	+ 2.0
C*	41.0	70.0	**
D*	38.0	**	**
E*	36.5	57.0	−34.2
F*	35.5	**	+ 2.1
G*	35.0	70.0	−10.7
H	35.0	70.0	+41.5
I*	32.0	60.0	+34.6
J*	31.0	55.0	+20.7
K*	30.5	60.0	+16.8
L	30.0	50.0	+28.8
M*	28.0	65.0	−35.4
N*	28.0	60.0	−59.0
O	28.0	**	**
P	27.5	55.0	+92.8
Q*	25.0	75.0	+11.5
R	22.0	60.0	−88.6
S	22.0	65.0	+14.0
T*	21.5	60.0	+47.8
U	19.0	65.0	+15.6
V*	15.0	60.0	+20.6
W	15.0	60.0	−26.8
X	15.0	55.0	+40.3
Y	15.0	50.0	+94.8
Z	14.5	55.0	+51.0
AA	10.0	65.0	− 5.0
BB	0.0	65.0	+16.0

* Under union contract
** Not available.

area, by mutual consent, have timed the expiration of contracts so that their negotiations will come after the national negotiations. Employers are reluctant to make any move until they have seen "what the big fellows are going to do."

Most of the wage negotiations in the area occur between March 1 and July 1. There seems to be little consultation among local unions in the area either on the size or timing of wage demands. Each follows

the path marked out by its own international headquarters. Each demands the "package" which has already been secured from "the big fellows," though actual settlements sometimes run considerably below the national pattern for reasons noted in the previous chapter. After the unionized plants in the area have set the general tone for the year, the nonunion plants come along with increases which are generally smaller in amount and less regular in timing. Most of the union plants gave an increase every year from 1946 through 1948, and some gave more than three increases because of wage reopening clauses in their contracts. Many of the nonunion plants, on the other hand, skipped one or more of the postwar wage "rounds," and, when increases were given they averaged less than those in the unionized plants.

Much the largest manufacturing plant in the area is a nonunion plant which, because of its size, might be expected to act as a wage leader.[8] There is no evidence, however, that the company actually plays this role. The company usually does not move on wages until it is reasonably sure how events are shaping up in the unionized plants, both within the area and elsewhere. It made a wage increase in the spring of 1941, no general increases during the war, a substantial increase in the spring of 1946, no increases in 1947 or 1948, and a "catching-up" increase in the spring of 1949. It tends to wait until substantial wage increases have occurred elsewhere, and then to make an increase which seems large enough to stabilize its own situation for some time to come. Other nonunion companies in the area do not seem to follow the large company's lead at all closely. In 1946, to be sure, the large company's increase was matched almost immediately by five other important nonunion companies. In 1947–1948, however, most of the nonunion companies made at least one increase even though the large company did not move, apparently because of the pressure put on them by successive rounds of wage increases in the union plants.

The way in which manufacturing wage rates in the area seem to rise may be summed up as follows. The size of the wage increases granted by major manufacturing companies outside the area establishes the general tempo for a particular year. There is, however, a marked tapering off of these patterns in the course of their impact on the area. Unions in the area tend to settle for somewhat less than the national patterns, and nonunion plants in the area raise wages less than the

[8] This company had an employment of about 5300 workers in mid-1948, or about 12 per cent of total manufacturing employment in the area. The next largest plant in the area had less than 2000 employees.

union plants. The result is that the advance of wages in the area is conditioned both in timing and amount. The average size of the national pattern influences the average size of wage increases in the area, but has no binding effect on the course of events in individual companies.

THE STRUCTURE OF OCCUPATIONAL RATES

In addition to shifts in the relative wage levels of different companies over the period 1940–1948, there have been important changes in the internal wage structure of each company, notably a reduction in the percentage differential between the highest and lowest jobs.[15] In an effort to measure the extent of this reduction, each company included in the wage survey was asked to report its hourly rate for the lowest paid job and the highest paid job in the plant for each year from 1940 through 1948. The percentage which the lowest rate formed of the highest was then calculated, providing a rough indicator of the effective rate range for the plant.[16]

The median ratio for the surveyed companies in 1940 was 48.9 per cent; i.e., on the average, the base rate for the lowest rated job in the plant was a little less than half of that for the highest job. This percentage rose to 53.7 in 1943, 58.9 in 1945, and 60.9 in 1948, indicating a marked reduction in the percentage spread between high- and low-paid jobs. On an absolute basis, the spread increased from an average of 62.1 cents per hour in 1940 to 62.7 cents per hour in 1948.

These figures understate the reduction in occupational differentials over the period, for two reasons. First, they refer to base rates of pay only. The great majority of the low-rated production jobs, however, are paid on an output basis, while the top jobs are usually maintenance

[15] This has, of course, been a general tendency in manufacturing throughout the United States over the past twenty years. See on this point Harry Ober, "Occupational Wage Differentials," *Monthly Labor Review*, August 1948, pp. 127–134.

[16] This measure is somewhat ambiguous since the specific jobs which have the highest and lowest rates may change over the years. It is not, therefore, a measure of changes in the spread between two specific jobs (say, common and skilled) which remain identical over time. It is merely a measure of the range of effective job rates in the plant, regardless of the addition or discontinuance of jobs, [illegible] of new jobs, and shifts in the relative ranking of existing jobs. It should be noted, however, that the same problem arises with respect to any other means of calculation, such as the ratio of a company's rate for a [illegible] labor grade [illegible] to its rate for labor grade [illegible]. Moreover, most companies have no jobs classified in labor grades [illegible], so that ratios for these [illegible] 'plant' rates. [illegible] tries to avoid this by taking the [illegible] in which there actually is a job [illegible] class 1, and gives a measure similar to the one we have used. This measure is not strictly comparable between companies, or within the same company over time, but it seems to be the best that is available.

union plants. The result is that the advance of wages in the area is quite uneven both in timing and amount. The average size of the national patterns influences the average size of wage increases in the area, but has no binding effect on the course of events in individual companies.

THE STRUCTURE OF OCCUPATIONAL RATES

In addition to shifts in the relative wage levels of different companies over the period 1940–1948, there have been important changes in the internal wage structure of each company, notably a reduction in the percentage differential between the highest and lowest jobs.[9] In an effort to measure the extent of this reduction, each company included in the wage survey was asked to report its hourly rate for the lowest paid job and the highest paid job in the plant, for each year from 1940 through 1948. The percentage which the lowest rate formed of the highest was then calculated, providing a rough indicator of the effective rate range for the plant.[10]

The median ratio for the surveyed companies in 1940 was 48.3 per cent; i.e., on the average, the base rate for the lowest rated job in the plant was a little less than half of that for the highest job. This percentage rose to 55.7 in 1942, 55.9 in 1945, and 60.9 in 1948, indicating a marked reduction in the *percentage* spread between high- and low-paid jobs. On an *absolute* basis, the spread increased from an average of 48.1 cents per hour in 1940 to 62.4 cents per hour in 1948.

These figures understate the reduction in occupational differentials over the period, for two reasons. First, they refer to base rates of pay only. The great majority of the low-rated production jobs, however, are paid on an output basis, while the top jobs are usually maintenance

[9] This has, of course, been a general tendency in manufacturing throughout the United States over the past twenty years. See on this point Harry Ober, "Occupational Wage Differentials," *Monthly Labor Review*, August, 1948, pp. 127–134.

[10] This measure is somewhat ambiguous since the specific jobs which have the highest and lowest rates may change over the years. It is not, therefore, a measure of changes in the spread between two specific jobs (say, toolmaker and laborer) which remain identical over time. One is measuring rather the range of effective job rates in the plant, regardless of disappearance of jobs, appearance of new jobs, and shifts in the relative ranking of existing jobs. It should be noted, however, that the same problem arises with respect to any other basis of calculation, such as the ratio of a company's rate for N.M. T.A. labor grade 10 to the rate for labor grade 1. Moreover, most companies have no jobs classified in labor grades 1 or 2, so that rates for these grades are "phantom rates." If one tries to avoid this by taking the highest grade in which there actually is a job classified, one gets a measure similar to the one we have used. This measure is not strictly comparable between companies, or within the same company over time; yet it seems to be the best that is available.

and repair jobs paid on a time basis. The low-rated workers normally earn considerably more than their base rates, and this excess of earnings over base rates has tended to increase throughout the period because of a general loosening up of time standards. In 1947 and 1948 it was not unusual to find production workers in labor grades 8 or 9 who were taking home more money than maintenance men in grades 3 or 4. Second, there was a marked tendency during this period for low-skilled jobs to be upgraded. Work which should have been classified in labor grade 10 was frequently put in labor grade 9 or 8 in order to hire and hold labor in unattractive jobs.

Reduction of occupational differentials has thus been due partly to deliberate management policy in a tight labor market, in which workers tended to flee the less attractive occupations and had to be held in them by special inducements. In part, however, it has been a product of the growing practice of making general wage increases on a uniform cents-per-hour basis. If one continues year after year to grant the same number of cents "across-the-board" to all occupational levels, the result must be a shrinkage of the percentage differentials between occupations.

Almost all the management officials interviewed were of the opinion that across-the-board changes should be made on a uniform percentage basis rather than a uniform cents-per-hour basis. Three main reasons were given for this view: (1) Percentage changes will maintain a "fair differential" between low-skilled and high-skilled work, and will provide necessary encouragement for low-skilled men to work up to higher jobs as vacancies occur. (2) Skilled workers are accustomed to a higher standard of living than unskilled workers. In a period of rising prices, the skilled men need a larger cents-per-hour increase in order to maintain the same relative standard of living. (3) A larger increase for the skilled workers is justified by the fact that they make a greater contribution to the final product. It is only fair that their greater contribution should be recognized in terms of wages and, if this is not done, the skilled men will become discouraged.

The unions in manufacturing industry usually, though not invariably, favor equal cents-per-hour increases for all workers in the plant. A few AFL locals in the area bargain for percentage increases, and even in plants organized by CIO unions we found cases in which a local had accepted larger increases for the top labor grades than for the lower grades, or differing increases for different departments of the

plants. For the most part, however, equal cents-per-hour increases are the accepted union policy.

Workers are divided on this matter, though tending to favor equal cents-per-hour increases. The workers in Sample I were asked the following question: "Suppose wages are being raised in your plant. Here are two men, one getting $1.00 an hour, another $1.50 an hour. Should both get 10 cents an hour, or should the low man get 10 cents and the high man 15 cents?" Fifty-four per cent of the workers favored an equal cents-per-hour increase, 42 per cent favored an equal percentage increase, while 4 per cent were undecided.

The reasons which workers gave for these preferences have been discussed elsewhere.[14] It is interesting to note, however, that there is little correlation between a man's attitude on this matter and his own wage level. On the basis of economic self-interest, one would expect high-paid workers to favor percentage increases and low-paid workers to prefer cents-per-hour increases. This turns out not to be the case. The wage distribution of those favoring percentage increases is almost identical with that of those favoring cents-per-hour increases.

Actual practice in the area has varied. A large majority of the unionized plants gave equal cents-per-hour increases during 1940–1948, though this was contrary to the wishes of most managements. A few union plants, however, consistently gave equal percentage increases, and some of those which normally gave cents-per-hour increases departed from this on occasion. In the nonunion plants, the situation is reversed. Most of the large nonunion plants still use percentage increases, though a few have swung over to cents-per-hour increases. In many of the smaller nonunion plants there are no general increases of any sort, wage adjustments being made entirely on an individual basis. This was the general practice in the area before 1940 and, while it has now been abandoned in the larger plants, it lingers on in the smaller establishments.

The net effect of these varying practices has been, on the average, to reduce the percentage differential between the higher and lower occupations. Since many employers object to this reduction on the ground that it reduces the incentive to learn skilled occupations, we asked each company whether it had actually experienced any difficulty in getting workers to accept promotion to higher jobs. The answers

[14] Lloyd G. Reynolds and Joseph Shister, *Job Horizons*, New York: Harper & Brothers, 1949, pp. 79–80.

plant. For the most part, however, equal cents-per-hour increases are the accepted union policy.

Workers are divided on the matter, though tending to favor equal cents-per-hour increases. The workers in Sample 1 were asked the following question: "Suppose wages are being raised in your plant. Here are two men, one getting $1.00 an hour, another $1.50 an hour. Should both get 10 cents an hour, or should the low man get 10 cents and the high man 15 cents?" Fifty-four per cent of the workers favored an equal cents-per-hour increase, 42 per cent favored an equal percentage increase, while 4 per cent were undecided.

The reasons which workers give for these preferences have been discussed elsewhere.[11] It is interesting to note, however, that there is little correlation between a man's attitude on this matter and his own wage level. On the basis of informed self-interest, one would expect high-paid workers to favor percentage increases and low-paid workers to prefer cents-per-hour increases. This turns out not to be the case. The wage distribution of those favoring percentage increases is almost identical with that of those favoring cents-per-hour increases.

Actual practice in the area is mixed. A large majority of the unionized plants gave equal cents-per-hour increases during 1945–1948, though this was contrary to the wishes of most managements. A few union plants, however, consistently gave equal percentage increases, and some of those which normally gave cents-per-hour increases departed from this on occasion. In the nonunion plants, the situation is reversed. Most of the large nonunion plants still use percentage increases, though a few have swung over to cents-per-hour increases. In many of the smaller nonunion plants there are no general increases of any sort, wage adjustments being made entirely on an individual basis. This was the general practice in the area before 1940 and, while it has now been abandoned in the larger plants, it lingers on in the smaller establishments.

The net effect of these varying practices has been, on the average, to reduce the percentage differential between the higher and lower occupations. Since many employers object to this reduction on the ground that it reduces the incentive to learn skilled occupations, we asked each company whether it had actually experienced any difficulty in getting workers to accept promotion to higher jobs. The answers

[11] Lloyd G. Reynolds and Joseph Shister, *Job Horizons* (New York, Harper & Brothers, 1949), pp. 29–30.

were overwhelmingly in the negative. While workers sometimes resist job transfers for the reasons noted in Chapter V, this resistance is due mainly to factors other than the structure of job rates. Only two of the companies interviewed cited specific instances in which workers had refused transfer to higher jobs primarily on grounds of earnings.

It appears, therefore, that the narrowing of occupational differentials has not yet become a serious barrier to movement up the occupational ladder. This is not surprising, since the higher occupations usually have marked nonwage advantages. They are lighter, more secure, carry greater responsibility and prestige, are more varied, permit greater independence of action, and give greater scope for the display of personal excellence. Many workers would doubtless choose them for these reasons, even if they carried no wage premium.

INCENTIVE WAGE SYSTEMS, OUTPUT, AND EARNINGS

Most manufacturing workers in the area are paid on an incentive basis. Most companies use straight piece rates, under which workers' earnings vary directly and proportionately with output. Through discussions with employers and examination of wage records, we learned a good deal about the operation and consequences of these systems. Little will be said on this matter here because the problems are endemic throughout manufacturing rather than specific to this area, and because there is a large literature on the subject which the interested reader can consult. It may be useful, however, to comment briefly on the general significance of incentive systems for the study of wages.

1. An incentive system permits workers' earnings and, under certain types of incentive formula, unit labor costs of production as well, to fluctuate considerably without any change in "wages," i.e., in hourly base rates of pay. There is a tendency, if piece rates are left unchanged, for workers' output and earnings to rise gradually over the course of time through the accretion of minor improvements in production methods. During a period of labor shortage, a company may find it expedient to allow this process to go on unchecked, or even to accelerate it by deliberately setting "loose" piece rates which permit workers to make abnormally high earnings.

Much of the interplant competition for labor in this area during World War II seems to have been carried on, not by raising base rates, but by setting piece rates so high that workers could earn much more than their nominal wage. The accepted principle in the area is to set piece rates so that they will yield a worker of average efficiency about

25 per cent more than his base rate. Yet in 1947 we found numerous plants which reported that incentive earnings for the plant as a whole were averaging 50, 60, or even 80 per cent above base rates. On individual jobs, earnings were sometimes double the base rate of pay. These plants had thus given large indirect wage increases, amounting in some cases to as much again as the direct increases in base rates.

During depression, on the other hand, labor costs may be reduced by cutting piece rates which have been allowed to get too loose, and by making sure that new rates are set accurately; by tightening up on quality standards and inspection methods, so that workers are paid only for good work; by reevaluating jobs which have been allowed to get out of line; by rescheduling production so as to eliminate overtime and night-shift work and to minimize the number of machine shut-downs during the day; by tightening up on promotions and individual merit increases; by a better selection of personnel and more vigorous supervision; by requiring workers to put in a full day instead of knocking off early; and numerous other techniques. The existence of these variables permits flexibility of labor costs in spite of a fixed (downward) rigidity in basic wage rates. There is a close analogy here with commodity pricing. There is a well-known tendency toward a "softening" of price structures during a period of falling demand—concealed price cuts, better discounts and allowances, improved quality, more favorable terms of sale, and so on—even where the basic price structure is frozen by monopolistic agreement. The same thing is true, and perhaps in even larger measure, of the pricing of labor.

It is doubtless more difficult for management to attain downward flexibility of labor costs under unionism than under nonunion conditions, but it is by no means impossible. If management can convince the union that falling revenues necessitate a reduction in unit labor costs, union leaders will probably prefer to let management effect this reduction by "whittling around the edges" rather than by a general wage cut, which would be an open defeat for the union. Even during the prosperous years 1946 and 1947 we found several cases in which the union, in return for an increase in base rates, permitted management to tighten up loose piece rates, reduce the amount of "wash-up time" and other waste time, and make other cost-reducing adjustments. The same kinds of concession might be necessary during depression simply to maintain the wage structure intact.

2. We have already noted the tendency for piece rates to "loosen up" gradually over the course of time. Even if management makes no

25 per cent more than his base rate. Yet in 1947 we found numerous plants which reported that incentive earnings for the plant as a whole were averaging 30, 40, or even 50 per cent above base rates. On individual jobs, earnings were sometimes double the base rate of pay. These plants had thus given large indirect wage increases, amounting in some cases to as much again as the direct increase in base rates.

During depression, on the other hand, labor costs may be reduced by cutting piece rates which have been allowed to get too loose, and by making sure that new rates are set accurately; by tightening up on quality standards and inspection methods, so that workers are paid only for good work; by reevaluating jobs which have been allowed to get out of line; by scheduling production so as to eliminate overtime and night-shift work, and to minimize the number of machine shutdowns during the day; by tightening up on promotions and individual merit increases; by a better selection of personnel and more rigorous supervision; by requiring workers to put in a full day instead of "knocking off early"; and numerous other techniques. The existence of these variables permits flexibility of labor costs in spite of marked (downward) rigidity in basic wage rates. There is a close analogy here with commodity pricing. There is a well-known tendency toward a "softening" of price structures during periods of falling demand—via concealed price cuts, better discounts and allowances, improved quality, more favorable terms of sale, and so on—even where the basic price structure is frozen by monopolistic agreement. The same thing is true, and perhaps in even larger measure, of the pricing of labor.

It is doubtless more difficult for management to attain downward flexibility of labor costs under unionism than under nonunion conditions; but it is by no means impossible. If management can convince the union that falling revenues necessitate a reduction in labor costs, union leaders will probably prefer to let management effect this reduction by "nibbling around the edges" rather than by a general wage cut which would be an open defeat for the union. Even during the prosperous years 1946 and 1947 we found several cases in which the union, in return for an increase in base rates, permitted management to tighten up loose piece rates, reduce the amount of "wash-up time" and other waste time, and make other cost-reducing adjustments. The same kinds of concession might be necessary during depression simply to maintain the wage structure intact.

2. We have already noted the tendency for piece rates to "loosen up" gradually over the course of time. Even if management makes no

change in materials, equipment, or work methods, the workers themselves discover shortcuts which enable them to do the job faster. These small changes in method are usually not reported to the foreman or the time-study department. Even if the foreman learns about them, he is usually inclined to sympathize with the workers and to feel that it will not make much difference to the company if they earn a few more cents per hour.

This "creeping-up of earnings" is uneven from one job to the next. Some jobs afford greater opportunity for shortcuts than others and since time study has not attained complete precision, some rates may have been set looser than others to begin with. It is therefore unsafe to conclude that if a plant has given 30 cents in across-the-board increases over a period of years, the earnings on each job in the plant will also have increased by 30 cents.[12] Examination of wage data may show that earnings on one job have risen 25 cents an hour, on another 40 cents an hour, and on still another 50 cents an hour. It is also unsafe to take the ranking of jobs in terms of base rates as an indication of how these jobs compare in actual earnings. A job with a low base rate may stand much higher in terms of earnings, and vice versa.

A time-study engineer might argue that these things need not happen if management keeps close check on incentive earnings and revises piece rates often enough to ensure that the workers on each job never average much more than the normal premium over their base rates. The remedy for loose rates is to tighten them. It is easy enough for a staff official to say this; but the foreman and other line supervisors must face the aggrieved workers, to whom anything which reduces the size of their pay check is a "rate cut." Revision of piece rates is

[12] It may be noted in passing that the meaning of a general wage increase is much more ambiguous under incentive payment than under time payment. A "general increase" of, say, 10 cents per hour may be applied to an incentive system in several different ways, with quite different effects on workers' earnings. To take only a few examples: (1) The increase may be added to base rates without any revision of piece rates. This will have little direct effect on earnings. (2) The increase may be added to base rates, and piece rates may then be recalculated to yield the usual premium—say, 25 per cent—over base rates. This will mean an increase in earnings of about 12½ cents per hour. (3) The increase may be incorporated directly in the piece rates, with or without a revision of base rates. This should yield an increase of 10 cents an hour in earnings. (4) The workers' incentive earnings may be computed on the basis of the old piece rates, and the 10-cents-per-hour increase may then be added "on the side." This will also increase earnings 10 cents an hour.

The effects of differing policies are actually even more complicated than this comparison suggests; for an alteration in the spread between incentive earnings and the guaranteed base rate, such as would occur in cases 1, 3, and 4 above, will probably have some effect on worker effort and therefore on output and earnings.

certainly the most controversial issue in wage administration, and possibly in personnel administration as a whole.

Who is to say that a piece rate is "too loose"? In other words, who is to say that the men are not working fast enough on a particular job? Suppose earnings have been creeping up. How does one know that this is not due simply to greater effort on the part of the workers, the fruits of which they should certainly be entitled to retain? Or, if the higher earnings result from production shortcuts which the workers have discovered, why should they not be allowed to keep the benefits of their ingenuity? A substantial change in equipment or methods, introduced by management, is generally regarded as a legitimate reason for retiming a job and setting new standards. But what about cases in which management, convinced that earnings or a particular job are out of line and that the situation must be corrected, attempts to "sneak up on the job" by a minor or unnecessary change in methods, which is then used to justify a new time study? Is this a legitimate tactic? How can one distinguish bona fide methods changes from changes which are merely a subterfuge for rate reductions?

The emotional tension surrounding this issue is so great that many managements, particularly in unionized establishments, hesitate to take any step which will reduce workers' earnings, except in connection with major methods changes whose legitimacy is self-evident. Rather than face the worker unrest and union pressures arising from a charge of "rate cutting," they prefer to live with a loose rate until the job is eliminated or undergoes a major transformation or until the workers on the job can be transferred to other work and new workers brought in at revised piece rates. The latter solution is inferior to the former, for workers often do not like to be transferred, and the new men may learn that piece rates have just been cut and be resentful on this account.

Once a loose rate has developed, in short, the only easy solution is elimination of the job. We encountered numerous cases in which management got along with a loose rate for five to ten years before anything could be done about it. In addition, many of the smaller establishments leave their piece rates unchanged year after year simply because they have no systematic time-study and rate-setting facilities. Rates are set by the foreman on a hit-or-miss basis, and are not changed until they are clearly and drastically out of line.

3. A general accompaniment of incentive payment is systematic

restriction of output by workers. The existence of output restriction is indicated by such things as: (1) marked uniformity of output rates within a work group despite differences in individual ability; (2) marked uniformity in the amount of work turned in by the same individual day after day; (3) the practice of accumulating a "kitty" to tide the worker over periods of unexpectedly low production due to machine shutdown or other reasons; (4) idling or obviously slow pace of work during part of the day; (5) maintenance of the same weekly output despite variations in weekly hours of work. We encountered cases in which a reduction of five or six hours in the work week failed to produce any drop in the output of certain groups of incentive workers.[13]

It is interesting to note that general wage increases seem to have little effect on the extent of output restriction. One might expect that when workers are paid more for each piece produced they will either step up production to take advantage of the higher rates or trade income for leisure by decreasing their rate of output. If these tendencies exist at all, they appear to cancel out on a plant-wide basis. Data obtained from individual companies on average plant-wide earnings of incentive workers reveal that earnings normally rise by about the extent of a general rate increase. The established norms of "proper" output and work speed on each job seem to continue undisturbed; workers pocket the extra money but do not adjust output rates as one might expect on the basis of individualistic reasoning.

INDIRECT AND SUPPLEMENTARY WAGE PAYMENTS

In this area, as throughout the country, indirect and supplementary wage payments have increased greatly in importance during recent years. Paid vacations, paid holidays, differentials for work on the second and third shifts, and group life, health, and accident insurance plans are now in general use by the larger companies in the area. In

[13] It is well known that on many operations workers will produce as much in a week of 45 or 48 hours as they will in a week of 60 hours. The explanation usually given is that when they work fewer hours they become less fatigued and their efficiency rises on this account. Our observations suggest an alternative explanation. One need assume only that they were producing below full capacity at the longer work week, and that they have become accustomed to a certain level of weekly earnings which they are determined to maintain. When this level of earnings is threatened by a reduction of working hours, the men simply work closer to their hourly capacity and produce and earn as much per week as before. There is a limit, of course, to what they can safely do in this respect. They may "get by" with turning out as much in 40 hours as they did in 48. If they still continued to turn out the same amount in 32 hours, however, their hourly earnings would be so far above their base rate that they would be very vulnerable to a rate cut.

addition, many companies provide one or more of the following: retirement pensions; year-end bonus; paid wash-up time, rest periods, or lunch periods; severance pay; and miscellaneous items such as cafeterias, athletic programs, picnics, and other benefit activities. In July, 1948, the aggregate cost of these supplementary payments ranged from 3.5 cents per man-hour in the lowest company to 25.0 cents per man-hour in the highest, with a median cost of 11.[illegible] cents. The cost of supplementary payments averaged a little less than 10 per cent of the cost of direct wage payments in the surveyed companies.

The size and variety of fringe payments is greater in the larger companies than in the smaller ones, and is somewhat greater in union than in nonunion plants. The main pressure for establishment and liberalization of fringe benefits has come from the unions. Many nonunion plants have gone along with the trend, but on the average they have not yet gone as far as the union plants. It is interesting to note also that there is a slight positive relation between the total size of fringe payments provided and the wage level of the plant, whether measured by starting rates or by average hourly earnings. The coefficient of rank correlation between average hourly earnings and size of fringe payments is [illegible]. Using starting rates, the coefficient becomes [illegible].

addition, many companies provide one or more of the following: retirement pensions; year-end bonus; paid wash-up time, rest periods, or lunch periods; severance pay; and miscellaneous expenditure for cafeterias, athletic programs, picnics, and other benefit activities. In July, 1948, the aggregate cost of these supplementary payments ranged from 5.5 cents per man-hour in the lowest company to 28.0 cents per man-hour in the highest, with a median cost of 11.4 cents. The cost of supplementary payments averaged a little less than 10 per cent of the cost of direct wage payments in the surveyed companies.

The size and variety of fringe payments is greater in the larger companies than in the smaller ones, and is somewhat greater in union than in nonunion plants. The main pressure for establishment and liberalization of fringe benefits has come from the unions. Many nonunion plants have gone along with the tide, but on the average they have not yet gone as far as the union plants. It is interesting to note also that there is a slight *positive* relation between the total amount of fringe benefits provided and the wage level of the plant, whether measured by starting rates or by average hourly earnings. The coefficient of rank correlation between average hourly earnings and size of fringe payments is 0.17. Using starting rates, the coefficient becomes 0.15.

PART II

LABOR MARKET THEORY AND POLICY

CHAPTER VIII Wages and Mobility: the Strength of Competitive Forces

WE must now attempt to focus the material of Chapters II–VII on the central issues raised at the beginning of this book. To what extent are the processes of labor mobility and wage determination interrelated? To what extent, and in what terms, can one conceive of "a labor market"?

The concept of a competitive market for labor is attractive because it succeeds in fusing mobility and wage determination into a single problem. In considering mobility, one finds the wage structure as a major determinant of movement among occupations, firms, and areas. When one turns to examine the wage structure, one finds it shaped by actual and potential mobility of labor. One moves around a closed circle of predictable relationships and results.

The realism of labor market concepts has been subject to frequent challenge, however, and this issue has become inextricably involved with that of the economic consequences of trade unionism. Those who believe that competitive forces are inherently strong tend to conclude that wage bargaining has unfavorable effects on the structure of prices and output. Conversely, those who feel that union activities are desirable often discount the effectiveness of market forces, or even dismiss competitive theory as useless and misleading. At this point discussion frequently ends in a fog of mutual recrimination between labor economists and economic theorists.

We shall try here to avoid the emotional overtones of this ancient controversy and to seek a reasonable balance between extreme views. No one would assert that competitive forces have no influence on the movement and pricing of labor; nor would anyone assert that they completely dominate the scene. The problem is to choose a defensible position between these poles.

A proper test of competitive labor market theory would require factual evidence sufficient to test the key assumptions of this theory. One should have quantitative data on all major points, drawn from a considerable number of areas at different points of time. We actually

CHAPTER VIII Wages and Mobility: The Strength of Competitive Forces

WE must now attempt to focus the material of Chapters II–VII on the central issues raised at the beginning of the book. To what extent are the processes of labor mobility and wage determination interrelated? To what extent, and in what terms, can one conceive of "a labor market"?

The concept of a competitive market for labor is attractive because it succeeds in fusing mobility and wage determination into a single problem. In considering mobility, one finds the wage structure as a major determinant of movement among occupations, firms, and areas. When one turns to examine the wage structure, one finds it shaped by actual and potential mobility of labor. One moves around a closed circle of predictable relationships and results.

The realism of labor market concepts has been subject to frequent challenge, however, and this issue has become inextricably involved with that of the economic consequences of trade unionism. Those who believe that competitive forces are inherently strong tend to conclude that wage bargaining has unfavorable effects on the structure of prices and outputs. Conversely, those who feel that union activities are desirable often doubt the effectiveness of market forces, or even dismiss competitive theory as useless and misleading. At this point discussion frequently ends in a fog of mutual recrimination between labor economists and economic theorists.

We shall try here to avoid the emotional overtones of this ancient controversy and to seek a reasonable balance between extreme views. No one would assert that competitive forces have no influence on the hiring and pricing of labor; nor would anyone assert that they completely dominate the scene. The problem is to choose a defensible position between these poles.

A proper test of competitive labor market theory would require factual evidence sufficient to test the key assumptions of this theory. One should have quantitative data on all major points, drawn from a considerable number of areas at different points of time. We actually

have only material for one area at one time, and this material is unsatisfactory in many respects. Some important variables are not susceptible of quantitative measurement, and even the quantitative data are usually susceptible of differing interpretations. We must be careful, therefore, to distinguish between hypothesis and proof, and to hold our zeal for generalization within the bounds of the evidence.

This chapter is concerned with the "supply side of the market," and we shall say nothing about the factors determining how much labor an employer will be willing to hire at given wage rates. Discussion of this matter would lead us into the dynamics of the firm and industry, a subject which has been little studied at either the theoretical or empirical level. In any event, it is not necessary to understand the determinants of labor demand in order to analyze supply reactions.[1]

THE MEANING OF A COMPETITIVE LABOR MARKET

We need spend no time in flogging the dead horse of the "perfect labor market." It is doubtful whether any major theorist has taken this as more than a point of departure. Marshall and Pigou, for example, took great pains to indicate some of its realistic shortcomings. Recent discussion of labor markets, as of product markets, has run increasingly in terms of "workable" though "imperfect" competition.

What does competitive theory, conceived in this way, have to say about wage determination and its relation to labor mobility? The main characteristics of a competitive labor market may be summarized under three headings: the nature of workers' job choices, the nature of employers' hiring strategy, and the characteristics of the wage structure. The first two points deal with structural prerequisites of the market, while the third relates to consequences of its operation.

1. Workers have some knowledge of jobs other than that on which they are currently engaged, have some freedom of choice among employers, and make some calculation of the relative attractiveness of alternative jobs. This calculation need not be based solely, or even primarily, on wage considerations. The worker may take into account any aspect of a job which he considers relevant. It is not necessary that workers have full knowledge of job opportunities or that all workers make careful comparisons; competition may operate effec-

[1] The concept of a downward sloping labor demand curve for a particular firm or industry is probably essentially correct, particularly over extended periods of time. If, that is to say, the wage level of a firm or industry rises over the long run more rapidly than the wage level of rival firms, there will be some tendency toward a relative contraction of employment in that firm or industry.

tively despite the ignorance or inertia of the majority. This is as true in labor markets as in product markets.

Within limits set by their knowledge and other structural features of the market, workers will choose better jobs in preference to poorer ones. Voluntary movement of labor will thus be from less desirable to more desirable jobs. Employers whose jobs are particularly desirable will have a surplus of applicants for work, while employers at the other end of the scale will encounter labor shortages.

2. It follows that an employer who wishes to retain a constant share of the area labor force must keep the over-all attractiveness of his jobs in line with the attractiveness of jobs offered by other employers. This does not, of course, imply any specific structure of relative wage rates in the area. If nonwage considerations are very important to workers, one may find wide differences in the wages offered by different companies for similar work, these differences being offset by attractive nonwage conditions in the low-wage plants. The employer may have some latitude in selecting ingredients for the package of employment conditions which he offers. He is bound, however, by the requirement that the package as a whole must be as attractive as that offered by other employers.

3. In consequence of this behavior of workers and employers, there is a tendency toward equalization of the net attractiveness of all jobs in the area. The concept of "equal net attractiveness" is easy to define if one assumes that all workers in the area have identical preferences as between money income, physical effort, job interest, hours of work, and other job characteristics. The concept becomes more complicated if one assumes variation of individual preferences, but is still clear in principle.

This tendency toward equalization of net attractiveness requires time to become operative. It would be fully effective only if each employer in the area desired to retain the same proportion of the area labor force in perpetuity. An employer whose employment is expanding relative to the area may need to offer more attractive terms than other firms until he has raised employment to the desired level. Conversely, an employer whose business is contracting can offer poorer terms of employment than other companies, terms which will cause him to lose labor at just the right rate. Differences in the quality of labor also enter in as a balancing factor. An employer may be able to offer relatively poor terms of employment provided he is willing to hire low-quality workers.

tively despite the ignorance or inertia of the majority. This is as true in labor markets as in product markets.

Within limits set by their knowledge and other structural features of the market, workers will choose better jobs in preference to poorer ones. Voluntary movement of labor will show a drift from less desirable to more desirable jobs. Employers whose jobs are particularly desirable will have a surplus of applicants for work, while employers at the other end of the scale will encounter labor shortages.

2. It follows that an employer who wishes to retain a constant share of the area labor force must keep the over-all attractiveness of his jobs in line with the attractiveness of jobs offered by other employers. This does not, of course, imply any specific structure of relative wage rates in the area. If nonwage considerations are very important to workers, one may find wide differences in the wages offered by different companies for similar work, these differences being offset by attractive nonwage conditions in the low-wage plants. The employer may have some latitude in selecting ingredients for the "package" of employment conditions which he offers. He is bound, however, by the requirement that the package as a whole must be as attractive as that offered by other employers.

3. In consequence of this behavior of workers and employers, there is a tendency toward equalization of the net attractiveness of all jobs in the area. The concept of "equal net attractiveness" is easy to define if one assumes that all workers in the area have identical preferences as between money income, physical effort, job interest, hours of work, and other job characteristics. The concept becomes more complicated if one assumes variation of individual preferences, but is still clear in principle.

The tendency toward equalization of job attractiveness requires time to become operative. It would be fully effective only if each employer in the area desired to retain the same proportion of the area labor force in perpetuity. An employer whose employment is expanding relative to the area may need to offer more attractive terms than other firms until he has raised employment to the desired level. Conversely, an employer whose business is contracting can offer poorer terms of employment than other companies, terms which will cause him to lose labor at just the right rate. Differences in the quality of labor also enter in as a balancing factor. An employer may be able to offer relatively poor terms of employment provided he is willing to hire low-quality workers.

With these qualifications, one can regard the terms of employment in an area as an interrelated system. Since wages are an important element in job choices, the wage structure of the area forms part of this larger system. A change in any wage in the system must call forth appropriate changes in wage rates *or in nonwage terms of employment* on other jobs. One can allow for moderate ranges of indeterminacy, but these should become smaller the longer the period of time considered.

This seems to me a fair, though obviously far from complete, statement of the tendencies which one would expect in a strongly competitive labor market. To what extent are these expectations borne out with respect to this area over the years 1945–1948?

THE NATURE OF WORKERS' JOB CHOICES

This matter is of basic importance, since on it rests the entire superstructure of labor market theory. If workers do not make a reasonably informed and systematic choice among jobs, then employers need not compete for labor, the wage structure no longer forms an interrelated system, and the market mechanism breaks down. To put the point drastically, if workers were distributed among vacant jobs by lot, and if they remained thereafter in those jobs regardless of wages and other terms of employment, one could no longer assume a tendency toward equalization of either wage rates or total job attractiveness. One would have a completely noncompetitive situation. The actual pattern of job choices lies somewhere between this pole and the pole of perfect economic calculation. Our problem is to locate actual worker behavior along this axis.

It was noted in Chapter IV that most workers in the area have a firm attachment to their present employer. This attachment, of course, may well result from rational calculation. Workers with considerable seniority on their present jobs tend to reason that known conditions and some measure of security are too valuable to throw over for the hypothetical possibility of a better job elsewhere. Others may stay where they are from sheer inertia. In any event, the workers with a strong company attachment are not really in the general labor market. There is no indication that their attachment can be weakened by moderate variations in the wage rates of other companies in the area.

A mobile minority of even 10 per cent, however, might be sufficient

With these qualifications, one can regard the terms of employment in an area as an interrelated system. Since wages are an important element in job choices, the wage structure of the area forms part of this larger system. A change in any wage in the system must call forth appropriate changes in wage rates or in nonwage terms of employment on other jobs. One can allow for moderate ranges of indeterminacy, but these should become smaller the longer the period of time considered.

This seems to me a fair, though obviously far from complete, statement of the tendencies which one would expect in a strongly competitive labor market. To what extent are these expectations borne out with respect to this area over the years 1940–1948?

THE NATURE OF WORKERS' JOB CHOICE

This matter is of basic importance, since on it rests the entire superstructure of labor market theory. If workers do not make a reasonably informed and systematic choice among jobs, then employers need not compete for labor, the wage structure no longer forms an interrelated system, and the market mechanism breaks down. To put the point drastically, if workers were distributed among vacant jobs by lot, and if they remained thereafter in those jobs regardless of wages and other terms of employment, one could no longer assume a tendency toward equalization of either wage rates or total job attractiveness. One would have a completely noncompetitive situation. The actual pattern of job choices lies somewhere between this pole and the pole of perfect economic calculation. Our problem is to locate actual worker behavior along this scale.

It was noted in Chapter IV that most workers in the area have a firm attachment to their present employer. This attachment, of course, may well result from rational calculation. Workers with considerable seniority on their present jobs tend to reason that known conditions and some measure of security are too valuable to throw over for the hypothetical gains in [illegible] of a better job elsewhere. Others may stay where they are from sheer inertia. In any event, the workers with a strong company attachment are not really in the general labor market. There is no indication that their attachment can be weakened by moderate variations in the wage rates of other companies in the area.

A mobile minority of even 10 per cent, however, might be sufficient

to bring about the marginal adjustments contemplated in economic theory, provided that shifts in individual employers' demands for labor are not too large, and provided that the workers involved choose their new jobs on the basis of reasonably adequate information. The behavior of the workers who are in process of changing jobs at any time is of decisive importance for labor market functioning.

The effective labor supply at any time seems to include three main groups: new entrants to the market, laid off and discharged workers, and workers who have become sufficiently dissatisfied with their jobs to quit of their own accord. During a period of full employment a dissatisfied worker can sometimes find a new job before leaving his old one. The more usual procedure, however, is to quit the job and then start a serious search for new employment.

The way in which unemployed workers find jobs was described in Chapter IV. Main reliance is placed on tips received from relatives and friends, and on direct application at plant employment offices. The criteria used in selecting a plant at which to apply have little to do with terms of employment at the plant, which are usually unknown to the worker until he visits it. A minority of workers use the facilities of the State Employment Service. For the most part, however, the job hunting methods used are no more likely to lead the worker to a good job than a poor one. Convinced that good jobs are scarce, the worker usually accepts the first job he finds which meets his minimum standards. It does not occur to him to continue the search until he finds the best job available in the area. Moreover, he is behaving quite rationally. Jobs come into the market and are filled so rapidly that a worker who pursues the bird in the bush too diligently may find himself permanently unemployed.

There are clear indications that workers have a minimum supply price, a fairly definite conception of what constitutes reasonable terms of employment. This conception of reasonable terms affects the worker's behavior in several ways. When he is unemployed, he will not consider a job offer unless it measures up to his minimum standards as regards type of work and prospective earnings. After he takes a job he will quit after a short time unless it measures up to his standards as regards working conditions, supervision, fairness of treatment, and other important matters. Long-service employees who are reluctant to quit their jobs can still express their resentment at what they consider unfair treatment by deliberate reduction of efficiency on

to bring about the marginal adjustments contemplated in economic theory, provided that shifts in individual employers' demands for labor are not too large, and provided that the workers involved choose their new jobs on the basis of reasonably adequate information. The behavior of the workers who are in process of changing jobs at any time is of decisive importance for labor market functioning.

The effective labor supply at any time seems to include three main groups: new entrants to the market, laid off and discharged workers, and workers who have become sufficiently dissatisfied with their jobs to quit of their own accord. During a period of prosperity, a dissatisfied worker can sometimes line up a new job before leaving his old one. The more usual procedure, however, is to quit the job and then start a serious search for new employment.

The way in which unemployed workers hunt jobs was described in Chapter IV. Main reliance is placed on tips received from relatives and friends, and on direct application at plant employment offices. The criteria used in selecting a plant at which to apply have little to do with terms of employment at the plant, which are usually unknown to the worker until he visits it. A minority of workers use the facilities of the State Employment Service. For the most part, however, the job-hunting methods used are no more likely to lead the worker to a good job than a poor one. Convinced that good jobs are scarce, the worker usually accepts the first job he finds which meets his minimum standards. It does not occur to him to continue the search until he finds the best job available in the area. Here, too, he is behaving quite rationally. Jobs come into the market and are filled so rapidly that a worker who pursues the bird in the bush too diligently may find himself permanently unemployed.

There are clear indications that workers have a minimum supply price, a fairly definite conception of what constitutes reasonable terms of employment. This conception of reasonable terms affects the worker's behavior in several ways. When he is unemployed, he will not consider a job offer unless it measures up to his minimum standards as regards type of work and prospective earnings. After he takes a job, he will quit after a short time unless it measures up to his standards as regards working conditions, supervision, fairness of treatment, and other important matters. Long-service employees who are reluctant to quit their jobs can still express their resentment at what they consider unfair treatment by deliberate reduction of efficiency on

the job.[2] This possibility of "striking without quitting" exerts pressure on employers to maintain acceptable employment standards.

The wage component of workers' minimum standards is of special interest at this point. The worker's family status, his accustomed standard of living, and the trend of retail prices have an important influence on his wage expectations. When unemployed workers in the area were asked how low a wage they would accept, the commonest answer was, "Well, I guess we'd need about _______ dollars a week to get by on." The worker's earnings on his last previous job are important, since he tends to assume that another job in the same line of work should pay at least as much as he has been earning. This is the main way in which prevailing wage rates in the area influence the worker's supply price. He does not know much about the area wage structure as a whole; but he does know what he has been making, and perhaps what some of his friends have been making, and he uses this knowledge in judging whether a particular employer's offer is reasonable. For employed workers, wage rates on other jobs in the same plant are of considerable importance. For unemployed workers, the weekly income available from unemployment compensation or relief tends to set a lower limit to the acceptable wage. Altogether, then, the worker's minimum supply price turns out to be a rather complex concept.

It was noted in Chapter IV that the worker is usually not in the position of choosing between two or more alternative jobs. For the employed worker, the problem is usually "Is my present job so unsatisfactory that I should quit it and take a chance on finding another?" The unemployed worker, if he locates a job opening, must usually accept or reject it on the spot without waiting to canvass other possibilities. The decision to take or to keep a job usually depends on a comparison between the characteristics of the job and the worker's minimum standards, rather than on a comparison of the job with other known alternatives. The decision is also affected by the worker's estimate—usually a bearish estimate—of the probable demand for his skills; and by his willingness to take risks, which is influenced by his family status and personal temperament.

[2] In one of the plants studied, for example, management told us that the workers in a particular department had stayed "on strike" on the job for about nine months because they believed piece rates had been unfairly set. During this whole period they produced the bare minimum necessary to earn their base rates, rather than their normal output of 30 to 40 per cent above the base level. Why did management tolerate this situation? Partly because of the existence of union organization, but partly also because it was not feasible to replace all workers in the department.

When a worker is confronted with a choice between two jobs, the choice is strongly influenced by economic considerations. Prospective weekly earnings are particularly important in the choice of a new job. Given two jobs which differ in earnings, the worker usually chooses the higher-paid job. Where he does not do so, there is usually an obvious reason for his choice. Thus we encountered cases in which a worker moved to a lower-wage plant in order to avoid rotating shifts, or heavy work, or marked irregularity of employment. There were also numerous cases in which elderly workers gladly stepped down to lower-paid and less strenuous jobs in the same plant. Within limits set by his knowledge and the objective chances afforded by the market, the worker pursues a self-interested course.

The limitations on workers' knowledge and freedom of choice, however, are formidable in the extreme. Workers are confronted by the elaborate structure of employer hiring preferences described in Chapter III, and also by the antipirating policy which prohibits recruitment of workers currently employed elsewhere. Their knowledge of wage and nonwage terms of employment in other companies is very meager. There is no mechanism for transmitting this sort of information rapidly and accurately to all workers in the area. Information is obtained by gossip and rumor, and much of what workers purport to know about other companies is inaccurate.

Further analysis of the interview schedules enables us to add a footnote to what was said about workers' knowledge in Chapter IV. It will be recalled that all workers interviewed were asked whether they regarded their wage as fair or unfair and for what reasons. In the course of the discussion, many workers volunteered statements that their company's wage level compared favorably or unfavorably with wage rates in other plants. The information obtained from the wage survey makes it possible to check the actual rank of a plant in the area wage structure against the opinions expressed by workers in that plant.

The replies on fairness of wage rates show no correlation at all with the actual wage level of the plant. The percentage of workers in the low-wage plants who regarded their wage as fair was just as large as in the high-wage plants. There is a slight correspondence between workers' statements about the relative wage level of their company and the actual situation. Thus for companies in the top half of our wage ranking, 77 per cent of the workers said that the plant wage

When a worker is confronted with a choice between two jobs, the choice is strongly influenced by economic considerations. Prospective weekly earnings are particularly important in the choice of a new job. Given two jobs which differ in earnings, the worker usually chooses the higher paid job. Where he does not do so, there is usually an obvious reason for his choice. Thus we encountered cases in which a worker moved to a lower-wage plant in order to avoid rotating shifts, or heavy work, or marked irregularity of employment. There were also numerous cases in which elderly workers gladly stepped down to lower paid and less strenuous jobs in the same plant. Within limits set by his knowledge and the objective characteristics of the market, the worker pursues a self-interested course.

The limitations on workers' knowledge and freedom of choice, however, are formidable in the extreme. Workers are confronted by the elaborate structure of employer hiring requirements described in Chapter III, and also by the antipirating policy which prohibits recruitment of workers currently employed elsewhere. Their knowledge of wage and nonwage terms of employment in other companies is very meager. There is no mechanism for transmitting this sort of information rapidly and accurately to all workers in the area. Information is obtained by gossip and rumor, and much of what workers purport to know about other companies is inaccurate.

Further analysis of the interview schedules enables us to add a footnote to what was said about workers' knowledge in Chapter IV. It will be recalled that all workers interviewed were asked whether they regarded their wage as fair or unfair, and for what reasons. In the course of the discussion, many workers volunteered statements that their company's wage level compared favorably or unfavorably with wage rates in other plants. The information obtained from the wage survey makes it possible to check the actual rank of a plant in the area wage structure against the opinions expressed by workers in that plant.

The replies on fairness of wage rates show no correlation at all with the actual wage level of the plant. The percentage of workers in the low-wage plants who regarded their wage as fair was just as large as in the high-wage plants. There is a slight correspondence between workers' statements about the relative wage level of their company and the actual situation. Thus for companies in the top half of our wage ranking, 95 per cent of the workers said that the plant wage

level compared favorably with other plants. For companies in the lower half of the ranking, only 80 per cent of the workers said that the company's wages were higher than rates elsewhere.[3]

While the knowledge of most workers in the area is extremely limited, it should be noted that some workers are better informed than others. Skilled workers in craft unions use the union as a source of information about terms of employment and availability of jobs. The unions of manufacturing workers seem to perform this function much less adequately. This may be due not only to the newness of most of these unions but also to the greater heterogeneity of jobs and complexity of rate structures in manufacturing. In addition to this difference, workers accustomed to regular use of the State Employment Service probably obtain more adequate job information than workers who do not use the Service. As was noted in Chapter III, however, the Service does not yet provide a thoroughgoing labor exchange and it is doubtful how far it can do so. The adequacy of a worker's labor market information is also strongly influenced by his length of residence in the area and by how many relatives and friends he has. Since general job information and knowledge of specific vacancies come largely through personal contacts, the worker with a wide network of acquaintances is in a superior position.

The actual movement of labor in the area during 1946 and 1947 was not predominantly toward higher paid jobs. The workers in Sample 1 who had changed jobs since the end of the war were asked about earnings on their last previous job, and their earnings at the time of leaving the previous job were compared with their initial earnings on the new job. The comparison presented here is in terms of weekly earnings because this is what seems really significant to most workers. A tabulation in terms of hourly earnings, however, would look similar. A few of those in the sample gained in hourly earnings but lost in weekly earnings because they moved to a job with a shorter work week, but there were not enough such cases to change the picture appreciably.

In interpreting the results, it should be remembered that about one-

[3] The detail of these tabulations is quite interesting. The plant which ranked lowest in our wage survey received an almost perfect score from its employees. On the other hand, the plant which had the largest percentage of its employees convinced that their wages were below other companies actually stood exactly in the middle of the area wage structure. This company is organized by a left-wing union with which its relations have been somewhat acrimonious from the outset. It may be that workers who are generally resentful against management conclude that management must be unfair on wages as on other matters, while workers who are generally satisfied with their situation conclude that wages are good regardless of the objective situation.

quarter of the job-changers had lined up a new job before quitting the old one. Thirty-five per cent had quit their previous job without lining up a new one, while 40 per cent had been laid off or discharged. The experience of these three groups was as follows:

Circumstances of Job Change	Total (%)	Gross Weekly Earnings on New Job, Compared with Previous Job		
		Higher	Same	Lower
		(%)	(%)	(%)
Quit with New Job Lined up	100	60	6	34
Quit without New Job Lined up	100	25	9	66
Laid off or Discharged	100	17	7	76
Total	100	26	8	66

These findings, while obviously not conclusive as regards motivation, are still of some interest. Much the best results were obtained by those who had lined up a new job before leaving the old one. Sixty per cent of this group gained in earnings, which suggests that where a worker has a direct choice between two jobs earnings will be a major factor in the choice. The members of this group who lost in earnings may have misjudged the prospective wage on the new job, may have wanted a shorter work week, may have taken a low starting rate in the hope of working up to something better, or may have regarded some nonincome characteristics as decisive. Among those who quit and then started looking for work, two-thirds ended up with lower earnings. Those who were laid off or discharged did even less well. This was perhaps to be expected during a period of postwar industrial demobilization in which many high-paid jobs were being eliminated. It should also be remembered that the amount of overtime work was declining during this period, and that even workers who continued on the same job typically lost in weekly earnings (see Chart 4, Chapter I).

Much of the movement within the shiftable segment of the labor force seems to represent retrogression rather than progress. This is notably true of involuntary movement; but even voluntary movement fails to show any strong drift toward better jobs. This is because most voluntary movement is not direct from one job to another which is known in advance and deliberately chosen as better. The usual pattern is to quit an unsatisfactory job, spend some time in unemployment, and then locate a new job by highly imperfect methods.

It should be emphasized that the findings summarized in this section were obtained at a time of unusually high demand for labor. It is a truism that workers' freedom of choice among jobs is largely suspended in recession and depression periods. The riskiness of job changes increases sharply at such times, and even dissatisfied workers cling to their jobs rather than take their chances in the market. Prolonged unemployment forces workers' supply prices down to a point where they no longer exert any compulsion on the wage structure. The tendency to grasp the first job offered, almost regardless of terms, becomes overwhelming.

EMPLOYERS' RIVALRY FOR LABOR

It was noted in Chapter III that employers in the area do not engage in aggressive competition for labor. Employers do not approach workers in other plants and solicit their services. Even if the worker takes the initiative and applies for work at another plant, he will usually not be considered for employment unless his present employer is willing to relinquish him.

The more significant meaning of competition, however, is impersonal rivalry, in which each employer establishes terms of employment designed to attract the number and types of worker he wants. It thus becomes important to inquire how far labor supply considerations influence management decisions about wage rates and other terms of employment.

Some of the most important nonwage terms of employment cannot be varied at will. Regularity of employment, physical nature of the job, intrinsic interest of the job, and opportunities for advancement in skill within the plant are heavily influenced by the nature of the industry and the physical setup of production. The agreeableness of individual supervisors is related only loosely to the policies of top management. Company welfare activities, personnel procedures, and fringe benefit payments are more subject to deliberate control, and company policy on these matters is undoubtedly shaped partly by the need to attract and retain an adequate labor force.

Employers certainly *use* attractive nonwage conditions of employment as inducements in labor recruitment. An employer in an unusually stable industry, or an employer whose production processes are light, clean, or interesting does not hesitate to tell workers about these advantages. This is different, however, from saying that these conditions are *determined* by considerations of labor recruitment. Many of them

are determined on other grounds, and the employer then uses them as "talking points" with workers.

Wage rates are doubtless the most flexible element which can be varied to secure the amount of labor required. Use of wages as a compensative device would require that each employer reach an independent decision on the desirable wage level for his plant, and that each employer consider labor supply a function of wages and act accordingly.

The first requirement is substantially met in this area. There is naturally a good deal of discussion among employers about recent economic developments, how union demands are shaping up both locally and nationally, and what is a "reasonable" position for employers to take. The larger companies are conscious that their wage actions will affect other employers in the area and take some account of this factor. In the end, however, each company works out its own salvation; there is no binding agreement to follow a common course. In addition to the general testimony of employers on this point, the divergent movement of wage levels in different companies (Chapter VII) testifies eloquently to the lack of a common policy.

The evidence on the second point is less clear. When questioned directly, employers are reluctant to admit that labor supply has much influence on wage decisions, possibly because the notion of competition for labor is abhorrent to them. At the same time, they emphasize the importance of "keeping up with the area." While this policy is usually explained in terms of ethical and prestige considerations, one judges from various side remarks that it also has something to do with getting and keeping workers.

What is the basis for employer concern about labor supply? What is likely to happen to an employer who fails to "keep up with the area"? A priori reasoning suggests several things which might happen. Which of these are actually significant in practice?

First, a plant which lagged too far behind the area level might have an unusually high rate of voluntary quits. In order to check on this point, we correlated the voluntary quit rates of the twenty-five plants included in our wage survey with two indexes of wage level—the plant starting rate and plant-wide average hourly earnings. The wage data were taken as of July 1 each year, while the quit rates were annual averages for the year. Calculations were made for the years 1947, 1948, and 1949. The rank correlation coefficients ranged from 0.18 to 0.22, indicating only a slight relation between the two variables.

are determined on other grounds, and the employer then uses them as "talking points" with workers.

Wage rates are doubtless the main flexible element which can be varied to secure the amount of labor required. Use of wages as a competitive device would require that each employer reach an independent decision on the desirable wage level for his plant, and that each employer consider labor supply a function of wages and act accordingly.

The first requirement is substantially met in this area. There is naturally a good deal of discussion among employers on current economic developments, how union demands are shaping up both locally and nationally, and what is a "reasonable" position for employers to take. The larger companies are conscious that their wage actions will affect other employers in the area and take some account of this factor. In the end, however, each company works out its own salvation; there is no binding agreement to follow a common course. In addition to the general testimony of employers on this point, the divergent movement of wage levels in different companies (Chapter VII) testifies eloquently to the lack of a common policy.

The evidence on the second point is less clear. When questioned directly, employers are reluctant to admit that labor supply has much influence on wage decisions, possibly because the notion of competition for labor is abhorrent to them. At the same time, they emphasize the importance of "keeping up with the area." While this policy is usually explained in terms of ethical and prestige considerations, one judges from various side remarks that it also has something to do with getting and keeping workers.

What is the basis for employer concern about labor supply? What is likely to happen to an employer who fails to "keep up with the area"? *A priori* reasoning suggests several things which might happen. Which of these are actually significant in practice?

First, a plant which lagged too far behind the area level might have an unusually high rate of voluntary quits. In order to check on this point, we correlated the voluntary quit rates of the twenty-five plants included in our wage survey with two indicators of wage level—the plant starting rate and plant-wide average hourly earnings. The wage data were taken as of July 1 each year, while the quit rates were annual averages for the year. Calculations were made for the years 1942, 1945, and 1948. The rank correlation coefficients ranged from 0.18 to 0.27, indicating only a slight relation between the two variables.

These results are obviously not conclusive. The quit rate is affected by many things other than wages. The small size of the sample and the nonmeasurable character of some of the relevant variables made it impossible to separate them out in our analysis. There may still, therefore, be an underlying relation between quit rates and wage levels which is blurred by the presence of other factors.[4] Again, the quit rate may be related, not to present wage levels, but to the rate of change of wages over some past period. The average quality of the workers quitting may also differ from plant to plant. A low-wage firm, even though it does not lose any more workers, may lose better workers than a high-wage firm. The most one can say, therefore, is that there are no surface indications of a strong relation between quit rate and wage level.

Second, a low-wage plant might find itself with fewer applicants for work than a high-wage company. We found little evidence, however, that this is actually the case. Complaints that too few qualified workers were coming into the employment office, or that vacancies were remaining unfilled too long, were received about as frequently from high-wage as from low-wage companies. The reason is doubtless the meager information which workers have about relative wage rates in the area and the haphazard character of their job hunting. Their search for employment is so nearly random (from a wage standpoint) that they are almost as likely to wander into a low-wage plant as a high-wage one.

Third, even though a low-wage plant gets as many *applicants,* it may get fewer *acceptances* of jobs than a high-wage plant. Applicants may come in, discover that rates are low, and go away again. This point is of considerable importance. Most unemployed workers have some conception of a wage rate below which they will not work. If a plant's wage level is very low, it will fall below the supply price of most of the unemployed, so that few applicants will be willing to take the jobs offered. This consideration is more important, of course, during prosperity than during depression. It was noted in Chapter IV that workers' supply prices tend to fall as their period of unemployment lengthens. When there has been large-scale unemployment for twelve or eighteen months, workers' supply prices will have fallen so low that they can be recruited even into very low-wage plants. The importance of a

[4] One such interfering factor is size of plant. The smaller plants in the sample tend to have lower voluntary quit rates than the larger plants. They also have lower wage levels. This factor thus operates to produce a *positive* relation between wage level and quit rate instead of the negative relation which one might expect.

These results are obviously not conclusive. The quit rate is affected by many things other than wage levels. The small size of the sample and the nonmeasurable character of some of the relevant variables made it impossible to separate these out in our analysis. There may still, therefore, be an underlying relation between quit rate and wage level which is blurred by the presence of other factors.[4] Again, the quit rate may be related, not to present wage levels, but to the rate of change of wages over some past period. The average quality of the workers quitting may also differ from plant to plant. A low-wage firm, even though it does not lose any more workers, may lose better workers than a high-wage firm. The most one can say, therefore, is that there are no surface indications of a strong relation between quit rate and wage level.

Second, a low-wage plant might find itself with fewer applicants for work than a high-wage company. We found little evidence, however, that this is actually the case. Complaints that too few qualified workers were coming into the employment office, or that vacancies were remaining unfilled too long, were received about as frequently from high-wage as from low-wage companies. The reason is doubtless the meager information which workers have about relative wage rates in the area and the haphazard character of their job hunting. Their search for employment is so nearly random (from a wage standpoint) that they are almost as likely to wander into a low-wage plant as a high-wage one.

Third, even though a low-wage plant gets as many applicants, it may get fewer acceptances of jobs than a high-wage plant. Applicants may come in, discover that wages are low, and go away again. This point is of considerable importance. Most unemployed workers have some conception of a "fair wage" below which they will not work. If a plant's wage level is very low, it will fall below the supply price of most of the unemployed, so that few applicants will be willing to take the jobs offered. This consideration is more important, of course, during prosperity than during depression. It was noted in Chapter IV that workers' supply prices tend to fall as their period of unemployment lengthens. When there has been large-scale unemployment for twelve or eighteen months, workers' supply prices will have fallen so low that they can be recruited even into very low-wage plants. The importance of a

[4] Including interference of size of plant. The smaller plants in the sample tended to have lower voluntary quit rates than the larger plants. They also have lower wage levels. This factor thus operates to produce a positive relation between wage level and quit rate instead of the negative relation which one might expect.

high wage level also depends on the size of the turnover (hiring) problem. It is more important for expanding plants than for those whose employment is stationary or declining; and it is more important for plants with a high retirement or quit rate than for plants whose turnover is low.

Fourth, the workers who are willing to take jobs in low-wage plants may be of relatively low quality. Even in the tight labor market of 1946–1948 all employers in the area seemed able to hire workers of one sort or another. One suspects, however, that plants with a starting rate of 60 cents an hour were not getting as good recruits as those with starting rates of $1.00 an hour. While we were not able to devise any statistical tests for this point,[1] the qualitative evidence obtained supports the following hypotheses: (1) There is some tendency for workers to get sorted out according to quality, poor workers going to low-wage plants and vice versa. (2) This tendency is most noticeable particularly at the extremes of the area wage structure; it is less noticeable among the middle two-thirds or three-quarters of the plants studied. (3) The difference in average quality of work force in different plants is considerably less than the difference in their wage levels, so that the low-wage plants are still getting a "better buy," i.e., labor is costing them less per efficiency unit than it is costing the high-wage firms.[2]

Fifth, failure to keep up with wage movements in the area may adversely affect the morale and efficiency of the company's present employees. They may respond not by quitting but by grumbling, putting out less work, and making things generally unpleasant for their supervisors. This consideration seems to be quite important in

[1] Quality of labor turns out to be remarkably difficult to measure, or even to define, especially when one considers that the relative efficiency of different workers will vary with the type of work in question. Women may be best for light manufacturing work, men for longshore work, and older men for night watchman's jobs. While no quite satisfactory index is available, one might use the percentage of workers in a plant meeting company standards of "normal" effort as a rough index of quality of the labor force. This would work only for incentive jobs, however, and would require that the standards be similarly determined in all the plants compared.

[2] In the spring of 1949, when the starting rates of the larger manufacturing plants in the area ranged between $1.25 and $1.40 per hour, some small employers were still sending orders to the Employment Service for workers at $.80 an hour. We asked the Employment Service interviewers how these plants were able to hold their workers, and were told that many workers in these plants were older people who stayed where they were because they felt they would have difficulty getting new jobs in the face of the employer preference for younger people. These older workers are presumably somewhat below the average level of efficiency. These plants also seem to get an undue share of marginal applicants. The Employment Service, for example, tends to refer to these plants workers who have irregular work records, or a fair number of very young workers who are judged to be unacceptable to the better companies in the area.

high wage level also depends on the size of the firm's recruiting problem. It is more important for expanding firms than for those whose employment is stationary or declining; and it is more important for plants with a high retirement or quit rate than for plants whose turnover is low.

Fourth, the workers who are willing to take jobs in low-wage plants may be of relatively low quality. Even in the tight labor market of 1946–1948, all employers in the area seemed able to hire workers of one sort or another. One suspects, however, that plants with a starting rate of 60 cents an hour were not getting as good recruits as those with starting rates of $1.00 an hour. While we were not able to devise any statistical tests on this point,[5] the qualitative evidence obtained supports the following hypothesis: (1) There is some tendency for workers to get sorted out according to quality, poor workers going to low-wage plants, and vice versa. (2) This tendency is noticeable particularly at the extremes of the area wage structure,[6] less noticeable among the middle two-thirds or three-quarters of the plants studied. (3) The difference in average quality of work force in different plants is considerably less than the difference in their wage levels, so that the low-wage plants are still getting a "better buy," i.e., labor is costing them less *per efficiency unit* than it is costing the high-wage firms.

Fifth, failure to keep up with wage movements in the area may adversely affect the morale and efficiency of the company's present employees. They may respond, not by quitting, but by grumbling, putting out less work, and making things generally unpleasant for their supervisors. This consideration seems to be quite important in

[5] "Quality" of labor turns out to be remarkably difficult to measure or even to define, especially when one considers that the relative efficiency of different workers varies with the type of work in question. Women may be best for light manufacturing, young men for longshore work, and older men for night watchmen or janitors. Within manufacturing, one might use the percentage of workers in a plant meeting time-study standards of "normal" effort as a rough index of quality of the labor force. This would work only for incentive jobs, however, and would require that time standards be similarly determined in all the plants compared.

[6] In the spring of 1949, when the starting rates of the larger manufacturing plants in the area ranged between $0.75 and $1.10 per hour, some small employers were still sending orders to the Employment Service for workers at $.60 an hour. We asked the Employment Service interviewers how these plants were able to hold their workers, and were told that many workers in these plants were older people who stayed where they were because, if they quit, they would have difficulty getting new jobs in the face of employer preference for younger people. These older workers are probably somewhat below the average level of efficiency. These plants also seem to get an adverse selection of new applicants. The Employment Service, for example, tends to send out to these jobs workers who have proven unable to hold a job anywhere for very long, or who are judged to be unacceptable to the better companies in the area.

practice. It should be noted that the compulsion on the firm is not to pay the *same* rates as other employers but to keep pace with *wage changes* by other employers. Considerable difference in the wage levels of different firms may be accepted by workers if they have existed long enough to be regarded as natural. It is changes in established differentials which cause unrest and difficulty.

Sixth, a nonunion plant which fails to keep reasonably close to the wage level of unionized plants may find itself faced with a successful organizing campaign. This seems to have been an important consideration with some of the larger nonunion plants in the area.

There is thus considerable pressure on an employer to keep his wage rates above some minimum level, and this minimum is influenced by the rates which other employers in the area are paying. There is, to be sure, no strong tendency toward voluntary and deliberate movement of workers from low-wage to high-wage firms. Other types of competitive pressure, however, are present—notably the fact that an unemployed worker's earnings on previous jobs influence his current supply price. If previous employers have paid him a certain rate, he will be reluctant to work elsewhere for much less than this rate.

THE INTERRELATEDNESS OF THE AREA WAGE STRUCTURE

Under strongly competitive conditions one would expect a tendency toward equalization of the total attractiveness of different jobs. One would expect also that a wage change by one employer would call forth offsetting changes in wage rates or other terms of employment by other employers. The area wage structure would constitute an interrelated system, each part showing a high degree of stability relative to other parts, and the whole structure tending to move in lockstep. To what extent are these expectations confirmed by the present study?

The meaning of "equal job attractiveness" depends on the nature of workers' preferences among different elements of a job. It is worth noting, therefore, that the preference systems of workers in this area seem to be broadly similar. The workers interviewed tended to mention the same job elements and to give them about the same relative weight. A "fair wage," moderate physical effort, some degree of interest in the work, and "a good boss" stood out consistently as the prime requisites of a satisfactory job. Indirect confirmation is provided by the fact that employers in the area show little tendency to "differen-

ated" their jobs for purposes of competition in the labor market, as one would expect them to do if there was great variation in workers' preferences. On the contrary, they tend to do about the same thing at the same time, following trends in the literature of personnel management and in the demands of the national trade unions. The tendency is toward uniformity rather than differentiation of policies on nonwage matters.

The meaning of a "good job" is thus reasonably uniform throughout the area. Given complete information about any two jobs, most workers would express the same preference between them. How do different jobs in the area compare in over-all attractiveness, judged by the criteria which workers themselves apply? There is, of course, wide variation in company wage levels. Within manufacturing alone, the starting rate for inexperienced workers varied in June, 1948, from about $0.[illegible] per hour in the lowest plants to $1.[illegible] per hour in the highest plant in the area. Average plant-wide hourly earnings varied from about $[illegible] per hour to $[illegible] per hour. It should be noted, however, that there was some concentration of companies toward the middle of the distribution. Thus, twenty-two of the twenty-five larger companies from whom wage data were obtained had starting rates between $0.99 and $1.14 per hour; only three large unionized plants were above this range, and only a scattering of small plants were below it. Moreover, there is reason to believe that wage differences are offset, to a limited extent, by differences in quality of worker, and that this is true particularly at the two extremes of the wage structure.

While dispersion of company wage levels is thus less than appears on the surface, it is still very substantial. These wage differences, moreover, seem to be accentuated rather than offset by differences in nonwage terms of employment. It was noted in Chapter VII that there is a positive correlation between a plant's wage level and the size of its supplementary or "fringe" payments to workers. While conditions of work cannot be measured with the same precision, our visits to plants throughout the area left a strong impression that the larger plants (which tend also to be the high-wage plants) have better physical conditions than most of the small plants. The larger plants also have more adequate personnel procedures and exercise greater care in selection and training of supervisors, though these may be partly offset by the more informal atmosphere and closer personal relationships in a small plant. For the most part, then, the company which can afford a high wage level can also afford to make the job pleasanter in

tiate" their jobs for purposes of competition in the labor market, as one would expect them to do if there was great variation in workers' preferences. On the contrary, they tend to do about the same thing at the same time, following trends in the literature of personnel management and in the demands of the national trade unions. The tendency is toward uniformity rather than differentiation of policies on nonwage matters.

The meaning of a good job is thus reasonably uniform throughout the area. Given complete information about any two jobs, most workers would express the same preference between them. How do different jobs in the area compare in over-all attractiveness, judged by the criteria which workers themselves apply? There is, of course, wide variation in company wage levels. Within manufacturing alone, the starting rate for inexperienced workers varied in mid-1948 from about $0.60 per hour in the lowest plants to $1.18 per hour in the highest plant in the area. Average plant-wide hourly earnings varied from about $0.75 per hour to $1.70 per hour. It should be noted, however, that there was some concentration of companies toward the middle of the distribution. Thus, twenty-two of the twenty-five larger companies from whom wage data were obtained had starting rates between $0.69 and $0.94 per hour; only three large unionized plants were above this range, and only a scattering of small plants were below it. Moreover, there is reason to believe that wage differences are offset to a limited extent by differences in quality of worker, and that this is true particularly at the two extremes of the wage structure.

While dispersion of company wage levels is thus less than appears on the surface, it is still very substantial. These wage differences, moreover, seem to be accentuated rather than offset by differences in nonwage terms of employment. It was noted in Chapter VII that there is a positive correlation between a plant's wage level and the size of its supplementary or "fringe" payments to workers. While conditions of work cannot be measured with the same precision, our visits to plants throughout the area left a strong impression that the larger plants (which tend also to be the high-wage plants) have better physical conditions than most of the small plants. The larger plants also have more adequate personnel procedures and exercise greater care in selection and training of supervisors, though there may be some offset to this in the more informal atmosphere and closer personal relationships in a small plant. For the most part, then, the companies which can afford a high wage level can also afford to make the job pleasanter in

other ways. Their superior financial ability expresses itself both in the wage structure and in other terms of employment.

As regards occupational differences, the skilled jobs in the area not only pay much more than the unskilled but are in general more secure, more interesting, and carry greater prestige. Nor is this offset to any important extent by the time required to learn these occupations. A trainee for a skilled occupation usually starts at a rate which is little, if any, below the rate for unskilled labor, and in the latter part of his training earns considerably more than the unskilled rate.

Nonwage terms of employment thus tend to accentuate wage differentials rather than to offset them. Instead of equality of job attractiveness, one finds wide dispersion. The top jobs are attractive from almost every standpoint, while the lowest jobs have scarcely anything to recommend them. The more attractive jobs have a large surplus of candidates who can be drawn into them by simply opening the doors. They are rationed out among those who want them, partly on the basis of merit, partly in accordance with seniority and other union rules, partly on the basis of "contacts," accident, and sheer propinquity of a man to a vacancy. Those who are not able to get into the best jobs are forced down to lower levels and, except during brief periods of peak prosperity, even the lowliest jobs find an adequate labor supply.

Even though a cross-section view of employment at a point of time shows wide differences in job attractiveness, these differences may tend to shrink over the course of time through the operation of competitive processes. The existence of such a tendency is not confirmed by the present study. Interplant dispersion of wage levels was almost precisely the same in 1948 as in 1940, and there is no reason to think that differences in nonwage terms of employment were reduced. There was some reduction of the percentage spread between skilled and unskilled wage rates in manufacturing; but this seems to have been due mainly to the spread of unionism in the area and to union insistence on equal cents-per-hour increases for all categories of labor.

While the dispersion of plant wage levels changed very little between 1940 and 1948, some firms rose appreciably in the area wage structure while others suffered a relative decline. Whether one considers the entire period 1940–1948 or only the postwar years, one finds that wage levels in some plants rose much more than in others, with consequent marked changes in the relative ranking of plants. It must be remembered that this was a period of sharp inflation, and that such periods are always characterized by marked dispersion of price and

wage movements. Over a longer and more stable period, the dispersion of wage movements might be considerably smaller.

It is difficult to draw precise conclusions about the factors which influenced the rate of wage increase in each company. Our observation of individual companies suggests that the most important factors were probably: (1) changes in the profitability of the industry in which the company is engaged, and in the wage levels of other firms in the industry; (2) changes in the competitive position of the company within its industry; (3) the degree of union pressure for wage increases (it will be recalled from Chapter VII that unionized companies in the area gave substantially larger increases than nonunion companies over the years 1945–1948); (4) the magnitude of the company's labor recruitment problem, and the wage level considered necessary to meet it.

It is interesting to note, however, that there was virtually no correlation between the rate of wage increase and the rate of change of employment in individual companies over the period 1940–1948.[7] This suggests that demand conditions and union pressures were the main active forces engaged in reshaping the wage structure, with labor supply playing a relatively passive role.

THE MARKET SCHEMA IN RETROSPECT

This study, like any empirical study, has revealed conflicting tendencies at work. Competitive forces are certainly present, though they operate through somewhat different channels than one might have assumed a priori. On the other hand, these forces seem to be weaker and less effective than they are in most commodity markets. What general conclusion can one draw, then, about the usefulness of competitive reasoning in discussing the hiring and pricing of labor? What remains of the labor market schema?

The findings of this study touch the demand side of the labor market only tangentially. My judgment would be that traditional economic reasoning remains quite useful in analyzing labor demand conditions—the wage-paying ability of a firm or industry, the number

7 What this proves is not at all clear. If unskilled workers were plentiful and if wages were raised only when necessary to recruit labor, one would expect a positive correlation between the rate of change of wages and of employment in individual companies. If, on the other hand, the labor demand curves of all companies tended to rise at the same rate, while the presence of union pressures caused wages to rise more rapidly in some companies than in others, one would expect a negative correlation between the rate of change of wages and employment. Both tendencies may be at work and may have cancelled each other out in the observed results.

wage movements. Over a longer and more stable period, the dispersion of wage movements might be considerably smaller.

It is difficult to draw precise conclusions about the factors which influenced the rate of wage increase in each company. Our observation of individual companies suggests that the most important factors were probably (1) changes in the profitability of the industry in which the company is engaged, and in the wage levels of other firms in the industry; (2) changes in the competitive position of the company within its industry; (3) the degree of union pressure for wage increases (it will be recalled from Chapter VII that unionized companies in the area gave substantially larger increases than nonunion companies over the years 1945–1948); (4) the magnitude of the company's labor recruitment problem, and the wage level considered necessary to meet it.

It is interesting to note, however, that there was virtually no correlation between the rate of wage increase and the rate of change of employment in individual companies over the period 1940–1948.[7] This suggests that demand conditions and union pressures were the main active forces engaged in reshaping the wage structure, with labor supply playing a relatively passive role.

THE MARKET SCHEMA IN RETROSPECT

This study, like any empirical study, has revealed conflicting tendencies at work. Competitive forces are certainly present, though they operate through somewhat different channels than one might have assumed *a priori*. On the other hand, these forces seem to be weaker and less effective than they are in most commodity markets. What general conclusion can one draw, then, about the usefulness of competitive reasoning in discussing the hiring and pricing of labor? What remains of the labor market schema?

The findings of this study touch the demand side of the labor market only tangentially. My judgment would be that traditional economic reasoning remains quite useful in analyzing labor demand conditions—the wage-paying ability of a firm or industry, the number

[7] What this proves is not at all clear. If unionism were absent, and if wages were raised only when necessary to recruit labor, one would expect a *positive* correlation between the rate of change of wages and of employment in individual companies. If, on the other hand, the labor demand curves of all companies remain constant or rise at the same rate, while the presence of unionism causes wages to rise more rapidly in some companies than in others, one would expect a *negative* correlation between the rate of change of wages and employment. Both tendencies may be at work and may have cancelled each other out in the observed results.

of workers who will be employed at alternative wage levels, and the repercussions set in motion by wage changes. This is only an impression, however, and cannot be confirmed or denied on the basis of the data now before us.

On the supply side, my judgment would be that competitive reasoning is more useful for normative than for descriptive purposes and that, within the normative realm, it is more useful as regards labor mobility than as regards wage determination. To take the second point first, competitive reasoning is clearly helpful in defining what one means by an optimum matching of individual abilities and job requirements, and in exploring techniques by which this optimum might be more nearly approached in practice. Our discussion of ideal mobility conditions in Chapter X will draw heavily on competitive theory. In the field of wages, however, we face the fact that wage structures are being shaped increasingly by collective bargaining, plus other deep-seated problems which would exist in the absence of trade unionism. While it is possible in principle to define what is meant by "a competitive wage structure," there seems to be no way of determining how far a particular wage structure deviates from the competitive norm. The concept thus seems to have little operational usefulness for public policy. This matter will also be explored more fully in Chapter X.

When it comes to description and prediction of concrete events, one is faced with a dilemma. Competitive reasoning may be used in such a general way that its results, while broadly correct, are almost self-evident and not very useful. Alternatively, one may try to obtain more precise results—for example, by assuming continuous labor supply curves and imputing certain shapes to these curves. As the theory becomes more precise, however, it is likely also to become more misleading as a guide to actual labor market behavior. This is true, I think, of many of the conclusions commonly deduced from the supply-curve apparatus—for example, that labor is redistributed among firms and occupations primarily through variations in terms of employment, that changes in wage differentials will set up movements of labor, or that expansion of employment in a firm usually involves a rising cost of labor per efficiency unit. There is an element of truth in such statements; but the qualifications are so numerous and important that in many cases they outweigh the proposition which they were supposed to modify.

This does not mean that we should discard competitive reasoning out of hand. It does mean that we should work toward a more general

and more flexible kind of analysis which, while incorporating pecuniary motivation as one element in the situation, is able also to take full account of nonpecuniary motives, the nature of union and management organizations, and irremovable defects of labor market structures. The hypotheses set forth in Chapter 10 are intended as a first step in this direction.

THE RISING LABOR SUPPLY CURVE

The main task of this chapter has now been completed. It seems desirable, however, to add a theoretical footnote on one concept which has gained wide currency in recent years, viz. the forward sloping supply curve of labor to the individual firm. I propose to argue that this concept is more misleading than helpful and that if one wants to think in supply-curve terms it is much more plausible to regard the labor supply curve to the firm as horizontal.*

It has become customary recently to say that the individual firm is faced, because of "labor market imperfections," with a rising labor supply curve. It can recruit additional workers only by raising wages or by improving its nonwage terms of employment. This construction raises serious difficulties even at a conceptual level. Consider first the problem of defining the units on the vertical and horizontal axes of the supply diagram. If the vertical axis is defined in terms of wage rates, one is forced either to ignore or to hold constant all nonwage terms of employment. We know, however, that nonwage terms of employment are both important to workers and quite variable over the course of time, so that a construction which holds them constant is quite unrealistic. The most obvious way out of this difficulty is to enlarge the concept of the "price" of labor to include nonincome characteristics of the job, and to define the vertical axis of the supply diagram as measuring the total satisfactions, monetary and nonmonetary, which the job yields.

This is nevertheless, I think, an unwise course. It leads in the direction of tautologous reasoning, under which anything the worker may do constitutes "economic" behavior.† More serious, it fails to yield a determinate equilibrium level of wages—which was presumably the

* For a more extended discussion see my papers on "The Supply Curve of Labor to the Firm," *Quarterly Journal of Economics*, June 1946, and "Toward a Short-Run Theory of Wages," *American Economic Review*, June 1948.

† This is the same route by which it is possible to demonstrate that, whatever a business man may do, he is by definition [illegible] For a critical comment on the usefulness of this kind of reasoning see Robert A. Gordon, "Short-period Price Determination," *American Economic Review*, June 1948.

and more flexible kind of analysis which, while incorporating informed pecuniary motivation as one element in the situation, is able also to take full account of nonpecuniary motives, the nature of union and management organizations, and irremovable defects of labor market structure. The hypotheses set forth in Chapter IX are intended as a first step in this direction.

THE RISING LABOR SUPPLY CURVE

The main task of this chapter has now been completed. It seems desirable, however, to add a technical footnote on one concept which has gained wide currency in recent years, viz., the forward sloping supply curve of labor to the individual firm. I propose to argue that this concept is more misleading than helpful and that if one wants to think in supply-curve terms it is much more plausible to regard the labor supply curve to the firm as horizontal.[8]

It has become customary recently to say that the individual firm is faced, because of "labor market imperfections," with a rising labor supply curve. It can recruit additional workers only by raising wages or by improving its nonwage terms of employment. This construction raises serious difficulties even at a conceptual level. Consider first the problem of defining the units on the vertical and horizontal axes of the supply diagram. If the vertical axis is defined in terms of wage units, one is forced either to ignore or to hold constant all nonwage terms of employment. We know, however, that nonwage terms of employment are both important to workers and quite variable over the course of time, so that a construction which holds them constant is quite unrealistic. The most obvious way out of this difficulty is to enlarge the concept of the "price" of labor to include nonincome characteristics of the job, and to define the vertical axis of the supply diagram as measuring the total satisfactions, monetary and nonmonetary, which the job yields.

This is nevertheless, I think, an unwise course. It leads in the direction of tautologous reasoning, under which anything the worker may do constitutes "economic" behavior.[9] More serious, it fails to yield a determinate equilibrium level of wages, which was presumably the

[8] For a more extended discussion, see my papers on "The Supply-curve of Labor to the Firm," *Quarterly Journal of Economics,* June, 1946; and "Toward a Short-run Theory of Wages," *American Economic Review,* June, 1948.

[9] This is the same route by which it is possible to demonstrate that, whatever a businessman may do, he *must* by definition be equating marginal revenue and marginal cost! For a critical comment on the usefulness of this sort of reasoning, see Robert A. Gordon, "Short-period Price Determination," *American Economic Review,* June, 1948.

main purpose of the supply-curve concept. We can no longer say, in concrete terms, what constitutes a "competitive wage structure" for an area, nor can we predict the consequences of altering one or more rates in the structure. I suggest, therefore, that an attempt to salvage the supply-curve concept in this way succeeds only in stripping it of any empirical usefulness.

A usable supply curve, then, probably has to run in terms of wage units. This still leaves a problem, however, of what unit is appropriate. Should labor supply be treated as a function of starting rates, job rates, or actual earnings? If earnings, are hourly or weekly earnings more relevant? Actually, workers respond both to hourly rates and to weekly take-home, which might require one to show labor supply in a third dimension.

The horizontal axis is usually defined in terms of "efficiency units of labor." This procedure appears to blend and confuse at least three different things: (1) the effect of wage variations on the effort expended by *present* employees; (2) the effect on the number of new employees who can be recruited; (3) the effect on the *quality* of new recruits. Moreover, since these three things may be markedly affected by changes in nonwage conditions, the supply curve is subject to large and sudden shifts.

Another technical difficulty is that one cannot assume that each firm will set its wage level independently of possible reactions by other firms in the area. Fellner and others have argued that the concept of a demand curve for the product of an oligopolist is self-contradictory.[10] Precisely the same reasoning applies to the purchase of labor by large employers. The leading employers in an area cannot assume that they are free to vary wages without compensating variations by other companies. On the contrary, they must assume that their actions will have some effect on what other firms do. Thus one cannot determine a supply curve for company A without knowing the reactions of company B; but these reactions *depend* in part on the supply curve for company A, so that one becomes involved in circular reasoning.

A third difficulty is that the supply of labor to a firm depends, not simply on the firm's relative wage position at the moment, but also on *the route by which that position was attained.* Suppose, for example, that the wage level of company A declines 10 per cent relative to that

[10] W. Fellner, *Competition Among the Few* (New York, Knopf, 1949), Ch. 1; also O. Morgenstern and J. von Neumann, *The Theory of Games and Economic Behavior* (Princeton, Princeton University Press, 1944).

of other companies in the area. If what has happened is a wage cut of 10 per cent by company A, the wages of other companies remaining unchanged, there will certainly be serious dissatisfaction in the plant, probably some quits, possibly a spontaneous work stoppage. If, on the other hand, Company A has raised wages 10 per cent while other companies were raising theirs 20 per cent, it may have little trouble either with its present employees or in recruiting new employees. Prediction of results in a dynamic situation requires more elaborate assumptions than those used in constructing an instantaneous supply curve.

The basic objection to the rising labor supply curve, however, is that it conveys a misleading impression of reality. It implies that a company can expand employment only by raising wages or other terms of employment. In actuality, an employer can usually expand and contract employment at will without altering his terms of employment. The main reason is the existence in most urban areas of a pool of unemployed which is continuously replenished by layoffs from declining companies, migration from rural areas, and population increase. Underemployment is a normal phenomenon in our economy and shows no tendency to disappear over the long run.

The composition of the unemployed group usually differs somewhat from the pattern of labor demand. An employer may not be able to hire workers already trained for his operations or who meet his preferences in the matter of age, sex, color, education, and so on. Many of these hiring requirements, however, have little relation to productive efficiency, and by reasonable modification of them the employer can usually expand his labor supply as much as he needs to. Nor need the employer face a rising supply curve because the unemployed people whom he hires are less efficient than his present employees. Where layoffs are made largely on a seniority basis, so that the unemployed are predominantly the young, it is reasonable to expect that the new employees after a brief breaking-in period will be about as efficient as those already on the staff.[11]

[11] In addition to including a disproportionate number of people under 25, the unemployed group contains a disproportionate number of people over 50. Older workers displaced by company failure, company movement to another area, or similar causes have marked difficulty in securing new jobs because of employers' age limits on hiring. The unemployed group also contains many people whose efficiency is reduced by physical or mental handicaps and who are chronically unemployed. These people could be hired (1) by companies which, because of relatively low wage rates or poor working conditions, cannot maintain strict hiring requirements, and (2) by all companies for special jobs—watchmen, janitors, elevator operators, etc.—which can be done adequately by such people.

of other companies in the area. If what has happened is a wage cut of 10 per cent by company A, the wages of other companies remaining unchanged, there will certainly be serious disaffection in the plant, probably some quits, possibly a spontaneous work stoppage. If, on the other hand, company A has raised wages 10 per cent while other companies were raising them 20 per cent, it may have little trouble either with its present employees or in recruiting new employees. Prediction of results in a dynamic situation requires more elaborate assumptions than those used in constructing an instantaneous supply curve.

The basic objection to the rising labor supply curve, however, is that it conveys a misleading impression of reality. It implies that a company can expand employment only by raising wages or other terms of employment. In actuality, an employer can usually expand and contract employment at will without altering his terms of employment. The main reason is the existence in most urban areas of a pool of unemployed which is continuously replenished by layoffs from declining companies, migration from rural areas, and population increase. Underemployment is a normal phenomenon in our economy and shows no tendency to disappear over the long run.

The composition of the unemployed group usually differs somewhat from the pattern of labor demand. An employer may not be able to hire workers already trained for his operations or who meet his preferences in the matter of age, sex, color, education, and so on. Many of these hiring requirements, however, have little relation to productive efficiency, and by reasonable modifications of them the employer can usually expand his labor supply as much as he needs to. Nor need the employer face a rising supply curve because the unemployed people whom he hires are less efficient than his present employees. Where layoffs are made largely on a seniority basis, so that the unemployed are primarily the young, it is reasonable to expect that the unemployed, after a brief training period, will be at least as efficient as those already on the staff.[11]

[11] In addition to including a disproportionate number of people under 25, the unemployed group contains a disproportionate number of people over 50. Older workers displaced by company failure, company movement to another area, or technical change have marked difficulty in securing new jobs because of employers' age limits on hiring. The unemployed group also contains many people whose efficiency is reduced by physical or mental handicaps and who are chronically unemployed. These people tend to be hired (1) by companies which, because of relatively low wage rates or poor working conditions, cannot maintain strict hiring requirements; and (2) by all companies for special jobs—watchmen, janitors, elevator operators, etc.—which can be done adequately by older people.

It is no doubt true that the maximum number of workers *potentially* available to a company is an increasing function of its wage level, because of the differing supply prices of the unemployed. The number *potentially* available is of little importance, however, since it is usually far in excess of actual company requirements. The situation is illustrated graphically in Chart 6. This chart assumes that there is a lower

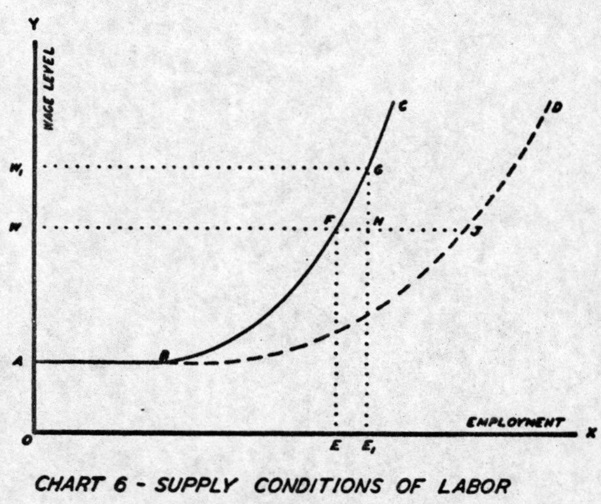

CHART 6 - SUPPLY CONDITIONS OF LABOR TO THE FIRM

limit (*OA*) to the wage level of the firm, set perhaps by a minimum wage law or by unemployment compensation rates. *BC* shows the number of workers which would be available to the firm at various wage levels if there were full employment in the area. *BD* shows the number of workers actually available; it assumes a specified level of unemployment in the area and a given set of employer hiring requirements. It will shift to the right with an increase of unemployment or a relaxation of hiring requirements, and will shift to the left for the opposite reasons. If the company's labor force is a small percentage of total area employment, *BD* will actually lie much farther to the right of *BC* than is shown here.

Suppose now that the company is operating at the point *F*, employing *OE* workers at a wage rate *OW*. (*F* is placed on the full-employment supply curve *BC* solely for purposes of exposition; under unemployment, there is no reason why it need lie on *BC*.) The company decides to increase employment to OE_1. Under the usual reasoning, it would raise wages to OW_1 to attract the necessary labor. In actu-

dling, however, the company simply accepts more of the day-to-day applicants for work without changing its wage rate, i.e., it moves from F to H instead of G. At its present wage rate, indeed, it could go all the way to J, and by relaxing its hiring requirements it could go even farther.

The relevant supply curve, then, is FJ rather than FG. FJ is horizontal, not because of perfect mobility of the employer's labor force, but because of the existence of unemployment. This seems to me an accurate representation of the situation of most companies at most times and places. Only in the event of abnormally low unemployment arising from war and postwar inflation, or in the case of firms near the bottom of the area wage structure, will FJ lie so close to FG that expansion of employment may require wage increases.

I suggest, therefore, that the concept of a rising labor supply curve to the firm be abandoned as technically defective, conveying a false impression of reality, and serving no useful purpose in wage analysis. All that needs to be said about the influence of labor supply on company wage policies and the possible difficulties of low-wage employers can be said without resorting to a device whose apparent simplicity conceals a host of difficulties.

ality, however, the company simply accepts more of the day-to-day applicants for work without changing its wage rate, i.e., it moves from *F* to *H* instead of *G*. At its present wage rate, indeed, it could go all the way to *J*, and by relaxing its hiring requirements it could go even farther.

The relevant supply curve, then, is *FJ* rather than *FC*. It is horizontal, not because of perfect mobility of the *employed* labor force, but because of the existence of unemployment. This seems to me an accurate representation of the situation of most companies at most times and places. Only in the event of abnormally low unemployment arising from war and postwar inflation, or in the case of firms near the bottom of the area wage structure, will *BD* lie so close to *BC* that expansion of employment may require wage increases.

I suggest, therefore, that the concept of a rising labor supply curve to the firm be abandoned as technically defective, conveying a false impression of reality, and serving no useful purpose in wage analysis. All that needs to be said about the influence of labor supply on company wage policies and the possible difficulties of low-wage employers can be said without resorting to a device whose apparent simplicity conceals a host of difficulties.

CHAPTER IX Toward a Revision of Labor Market Theory

IT WAS suggested in the last chapter that competitive labor market theory needs to be considerably revised and enlarged if it is to give an adequate account of reality. Such a revision is already well under way as a result of the studies of Dunlop, Kerr, Lester, Myers, Palmer, Ross, Slichter, Woytinsky, and numerous other scholars.

I propose in this chapter to set forth a series of propositions which, with enough testing and modification by subsequent research, might add up to a theory of the allocation and pricing of labor. These propositions are not intended as inductive generalizations, which would obviously be premature at this stage. They are, I believe, in general accord with the findings of previous studies, but their testing and refinement will require much additional work.

This chapter, in short, is a prologue to further research rather than a body of settled conclusions. The kinds of research required to test each proposition are not set forth explicitly, but will be readily apparent to readers who have worked on these problems.

THE DETERMINATION OF MONEY WAGE RATES

1. Changes in plant wage levels occur in waves—one plant raises wages when other plants are raising them. These waves are set off by forces exogeneous to the firm or area, viz., price and output changes in the national economy. These are the active factors in the situation; wages play a relatively passive role, adjusting themselves with some lag to price and profit levels. The main reason why the wage levels of different plants tend to move together is neither the existence of unionism nor interplant movements of labor, but rather the fact that the wage-paying ability of most firms is moving in the same direction at the same time. In a semiunionized economy, to be sure, the impact of price and profit changes on wages is *mediated* through the demands of powerful trade unions; and it is possible that unionism causes wage adjustments to be faster and more uniform than they otherwise would be. This is an intricate question, however, and the answer is by no means as clear as is sometimes supposed.

CHAPTER IX

Toward a Revision of Labor Market Theory

IT WAS suggested in the last chapter that competitive labor market theory seems to be considerably revised and enlarged if it is to give an adequate account of reality. Such a revision is already well under way as a result of the studies of Dunlop, Kerr, Lester, Myers, Palmer, Ross, Slichter, Woytinsky, and a number of other scholars.

I propose in this chapter to set forth a series of propositions which, with enough testing and modification by subsequent research, might add up to a theory of the allocation and pricing of labor. These propositions are not intended as inductive generalizations, which would obviously be premature at this stage. They are, I believe, in general accord with the findings of previous studies, but their testing and refinement will require much additional work.

This chapter is short, is a program for further research rather than a body of settled conclusions. The kinds of research required to test each proposition are not set forth explicitly, but will be readily apparent to readers who have worked in these problems.

THE DETERMINATION OF MONEY WAGE RATES

1. Changes in plant wage levels occur in waves—one plant raises wages when other plants are raising them. These waves are set off by large movements in the flow of area, wage, price and output changes in the general economy. In general, the active factors in the situation wages play a relatively passive role, adjusting themselves with some lag to price and profit levels. The main reason why the wage levels of different plants tend to move together is neither the existence of unionism nor interplant movements of labor, but rather the fact that the wage-paying ability of most firms is moving in the same direction at the same time. In a commercialized economy, to be sure, the impact of price and profit changes on wages is mediated through the demands of powerful trade unions; and it is possible that unionism causes wage adjustments to be faster and more uniform than they otherwise would be. This is an intricate question, however, and the answer is by no means as clear as is sometimes supposed.

The level of unemployment has nothing directly to do with the time at which wage increases begin or with the speed of the advance. This is determined mainly by the commodity pricing mechanism, i.e., the extent to which increases in aggregate money demand are translated into price increases rather than output increases. In an economy whose structure permitted output to rise to the full employment level without price increases, wage increases would be quite moderate. At the other extreme, if increases in money demand were always fully reflected in prices, even at high levels of unemployment, then wages would climb very rapidly with prices. The behavior of agricultural prices, as I have argued elsewhere,[1] is especially strategic for wage movements.

2. The size of the wage increases given by different firms tends to be uniform within clusters of firms whose limits are defined by (1) interplant rivalry for markets, and (2) interunion rivalry for members. Firms which are close rivals in product markets, particularly oligopoly groups with tacit price agreements, are likely to give similar wage increases even if they are organized by different unions or are unorganized. Again, unions in close rivalry for membership are likely to demand and receive similar increases even though the firms involved are not in direct competition. Pressure for uniformity of increases is at a maximum where the two types of boundary coincide, where there is both interplant and interunion rivalry.

Beyond these boundaries uniformity gives way to marked dispersion of wage movements, even as regards unionized companies, and particularly as regards nonunion companies. This dispersion is much less, however, over periods of twenty or thirty years than over periods of two or three years. During brief periods of marked inflation or deflation, interplant and interindustry wage relationships are frequently disrupted. Over a longer period company wage levels tend to move together again. This is probably due in large measure to labor supply considerations. The disparate movement of wage rates during a period such as 1945–1948 leaves some firms stranded below the lower limit of the "wage band" (see 4 below), within which it is feasible for them to operate over the long run. At some later time, therefore, they must try to climb back into the range of feasible wage rates.

3. Narrowing our focus to a particular company, let us look first at management objectives and policies. The most important distinction here is between companies near the top of the area wage structure

[1] See my paper "Wage Bargaining, Price Changes, and Employment," in *Proceedings of the Industrial Relations Research Association*, 1949, pp. 12–30.

The level of unemployment has nothing directly to do with the time at which wage increases begin or with the speed of the advance. This is determined mainly by the commodity pricing mechanism, i.e., the extent to which increases in aggregate money demand are translated into price increases rather than output increases. In an economy whose structure permitted output to rise to the full employment level without price increases, wage increases would be quite moderate. At the other extreme, if increases in money demand were always fully reflected in prices, even at high levels of unemployment, then wages would climb *pari passu* with prices. The behavior of agricultural prices, as I have argued elsewhere,[1] is especially strategic for wage movements.

2. The size of the wage increases given by different firms tends to be uniform within clusters of firms whose limits are defined by (1) interplant rivalry for markets, and (2) interunion rivalry for members. Firms which are close rivals in product markets, particularly oligopoly groups with tacit price agreement, are likely to give similar wage increases even if they are organized by different unions or are unorganized. Again, unions in close rivalry for membership are likely to demand and receive similar increases even though the firms involved are not in direct competition. Pressure for uniformity of increases is at a maximum where the two types of boundary coincide, where there is *both* interplant and interunion rivalry.

Beyond these boundaries uniformity gives way to marked dispersion of wage movements, even as regards unionized companies, and particularly as regards nonunion companies. This dispersion is much less, however, over periods of twenty or thirty years than over periods of two or three years. During brief periods of marked inflation or deflation, interplant and interindustry wage relationships are violently disrupted. Over a longer period company wage levels tend to draw together again. This is probably due in large measure to labor supply considerations. The disparate movement of wage rates during a period such as 1945–1948 leaves some firms stranded below the lower limit of the "wage band" (see 4. below) within which it is feasible for them to operate over the long run. At some later time, therefore, they must try to climb back up into the range of feasible wage rates.

3. Narrowing our focus to a particular company, let us look first at management objectives and policies. The most important distinction here is between companies near the top of the area wage structure

[1] See my paper "Wage Bargaining, Price Changes, and Employment," in *Proceedings of the Industrial Relations Research Association,* 1949, pp. 38–50.

and those near the bottom. The puzzling thing about the high-wage firms is why they continue to be so. It would seem that they could slip back somewhat in the area wage structure and still maintain an adequate labor force. Why do they not do so? Why do they not pay the lowest wage at which they could "get by"? There appear to be several answers to this question:

a. The high-wage companies have unusually high wage-paying ability resulting from unusual efficiency of plant or management, secure monopoly or oligopoly control of product markets, or a favorable trend of demand. They can afford the luxury of being "good employers."[2] They are usually members of industries whose general wage level is high, so that the company may be in line with its industry even though out of line with the local area.

b. A relatively high wage level has many advantages to the firm. It simplifies the recruitment problem. Even though the company might be able to get enough workers at a lower wage level, it can get them faster and with less persuasion at higher wages. It can also establish strict hiring specifications designed to fill the plant with "a nice class of worker." Workers who are young, well-educated, attractive, and cooperative are nice to have around, even if their efficiency is only average. The company may also be able to insist on better-than-average efficiency, so that higher wages do not produce a proportionate increase in unit labor costs. A high wage level also gives the company a margin of safety against a possible weakening of its position in later years. If it should run into one or two bad years, it can rest on its oars without falling too low in the area wage structure. This is one of the numerous types of safety margin which business firms try to build into their current operations. Most managers doubtless enjoy the good repute which they gain by paying high wages, both with their own employees and in the community generally. A high wage level also has public

[2] See in this connection Sumner H. Slichter, "Notes on the Structure of Wages," *Review of Economics and Statistics*, February, 1950, Vol. XXXII, pp. 80–91. Working with industry averages compiled by the N. I. C. B., Slichter found, among other things, that "the average hourly earnings of male unskilled labor tends to be high where the net income after taxes is a high percentage of sales. The coefficient of rank correlation in 1939 was .6969. The high correlation between sales margins and the average hourly earnings of common labor . . . . reinforces the view that wages, within a considerable range, reflect managerial discretion, that where managements can easily pay high wages they tend to do so, and that where managements are barely breaking even they tend to keep wages down."

Slichter also found that common labor wage rates tend to be high where the ratio of payrolls to income from sales is low. The coefficient of rank correlation in 1939 was .7228. This also suggests that managerial policy is an important element in the determination of wage levels.

relations value for the firm. Critics have a point [illegible] making a case if the company has a high wage level, satisfied employees, perhaps even a satisfied union.

The potential gains from a lower wage level may be quite uncertain, particularly in oligopoly situations. Only under conditions of competition can one assume that a change in the firm's wage level will be fully reflected in profits, and that the firm can select its wage level independently of competitors. Where competitors are few, it may be necessary for each firm to accept wage and price levels which are acceptable to the group as a whole, and which yield satisfactory (though not maximum) profits.

d. It is not too easy for a firm to slip down substantially from its customary position in the area wage structure, even if it wishes to do so. If there is a union in the plant, the union will [illegible] try to make the company at least keep pace with the average rate of wage increase in the area. Even if there is no union, a company which lags behind a general wage movement risks dissatisfaction among its employees, for the reasons noted in Chapter VI.

A high-wage company thus tends to maintain its position as long as it can afford to, because the position confers positive advantages, because the possible gains from a lower wage level are quite uncertain, and because the transition to a lower wage level would be difficult and unpleasant.

The low-wage companies are in a quite different situation. They are squeezed between low wage-paying ability and the minimum wage necessary to recruit new workers. They do have a labor supply problem, arising not so much from losses of labor to high-wage firms as from the difficulty of inducing unemployed workers to accept their jobs. It is this pressure from the supply side which keeps the lower range of the area wage structure moving upward over the course of time.

4. One finds in any area, then, a range or band of feasible wage levels at which a firm may operate. A firm has difficulty in moving rapidly from one level to another; but once established for some time at any level, its position is stable in the sense that it can continue indefinitely to recruit as many workers as it needs. Under such conditions the top of the band appears to be determined not by the highest wage which the most prosperous firm in the area could afford to pay, but rather by the maximum which it can pay without being considered "unethical" by other employers. The lower limit of the band is partly

relations value for the firm. Critics have a harder time making a case if the company has a high wage level, satisfied employees, perhaps even a satisfied union.

c. The potential gains from a lower wage level may be quite uncertain, particularly in oligopoly situations. Only under atomistic competition can one assume that a change in the firm's wage level will be fully reflected in profits, and that the firm can select its wage level independently of competitors. Where competitors are few, it may be necessary for each firm to accept wage and price levels which are acceptable to the group as a whole, and which yield satisfactory (though not maximum) profits.

d. It is not too easy for a firm to slip down substantially from its customary position in the area wage structure, even if it wishes to do so. If there is a union in the plant, the union will certainly try to make the company at least keep pace with the average rate of wage increase in the area. Even if there is no union, a company which lags behind a general wage movement risks disaffection among its employees for the reasons noted in Chapter VI.

A high-wage company thus tends to maintain its position as long as it can afford to because the position confers positive advantages, because the possible gains from a lower wage level are quite uncertain, and because the transition to a lower wage level would be difficult and unpleasant.

The low-wage companies are in a quite different situation. They are squeezed between low wage-paying ability and the minimum wage necessary to recruit new workers. They do have a labor supply problem, arising not so much from losses of labor to high-wage firms as from the difficulty of inducing unemployed workers to accept their jobs. It is this pressure from the supply side which keeps the lower fringe of the area wage structure moving upward over the course of time.

4. One finds in any area, then, a range or band of feasible wage levels at which a firm may operate. A firm has difficulty in moving rapidly from one level to another; but once established for some time at any level, its position is stable in the sense that it can continue indefinitely to recruit as many workers as it needs. Under nonunion conditions the top of the band appears to be defined, not by the highest wage which the most prosperous firm in the area could afford to pay, but rather by the maximum which it can pay without being considered "unethical" by other employers. The lower limit of the band is partly

a function of the upper limit. A company which falls too far below the level of the higher-wage companies will encounter the labor supply difficulties noted in Chapter VIII. The lower limit is also importantly influenced by minimum wage legislation and the level of unemployment compensation benefits.

The entire band moves irregularly upward over the course of time. The main force propelling it on is the growth in wage-paying ability of the more prosperous firms. As the top of the wage structure moves upward on this account, the bottom is pulled up after it by a revision of workers' conceptions of a "reasonable" wage, which raises the supply price of the unemployed. This is in general accord with competitive reasoning, though one must allow for considerable indeterminacy and considerable time lags in the adjustment. Upward revision of legal minimum wages, unemployment compensation benefits, and other social security benefits will also tend to raise the lower limit of the wage structure.

The range of feasible wage levels seems to be quite wide in most areas, though perhaps not as wide as one would judge from basic wage rates alone. Numerous corrections and adjustments would have to be made in order to get a true picture. These adjustments do not all run in the same direction. On the one hand, supplementary wage payments and physical conditions of work seem to be positively correlated with wage level, thus tending to make the differentials in aggregate return from the job larger than the differentials in wage rates alone. The main factor working in the opposite direction is quality of labor. The high-wage plants almost certainly get somewhat better workers than the low-wage plants, so that differences in the cost of labor per efficiency unit are less than the differences in hourly wage rates.

While the net result cannot be measured with any precision, it would appear that there remain substantial difference in labor cost per efficiency unit and even larger differences in job attractiveness. Nor is there much reason to think that these differences tend to diminish over the long run. What does happen is that individual companies rise and fall in the area wage hierarchy over the course of time. Marked expansion of a company's business tends to be accompanied by a rise in its relative wage level, mainly because of higher wage-paying ability. An unusually aggressive union may also push a company gradually upward against its will.

Firms whose wage-paying ability is declining tend to sink gradually toward the bottom of the wage structure. A major effect of this down-

ward plasticity of relative wages is greatest in precisely the weaker portions of declining businesses. As a company's relative wage level falls, it encounters growing "sales resistance" in persuading workers to take its jobs, the quality of new recruits tends to decline, and there may be dissatisfaction among its long-service workers. It may hang on for a remarkably long time, however, particularly during periods of substantial unemployment. The companies at the lower edge of the area wage band at any time are those whose low profitability forces them involuntarily to test how little they can pay and still get labor. Eventually, unless their situation improves, they are forced below the feasible wage range and pass from the scene. A union may hasten the death agonies by refusing to allow the company's relative wage level to sink below a certain point. This action has frequently to be taken by officials of the national union, however, over the protests of members who are anxious to keep their jobs even at low wage rates.

Under nonunion conditions, then, the wage structure of an area is shaped mainly by the labor demand curves of firms in the area. The supply situation is such that each firm, instead of being faced with a market wage rate, is faced with a considerable range of possible wage levels. Depending on the height of its demand curve, it can select a higher or lower position in the area wage structure and can shift this position gradually over the course of time.

The plasticity of wage levels *over the course of time* does not mean that the wage level of a particular firm *at a point of time* is indeterminate over the whole width of the wage band. If, for example, the lowest firm in the area is paying $1.00 an hour for a particular job and the highest firm $1.50, this does not mean that the top firm could also pay $1.00 if it wanted to and that its workers are receiving $0.50 per hour as a sheer bonus. It is more likely that the top company would be obliged in any event to pay, say $1.35 per hour, because of its high hiring requirements, the morale of its labor force, and the expectations generated by the fact that it has customarily been a high-wage firm. The (economically) unexplained bonus is thus only $0.15 per hour instead of $0.50. Each firm in the area has its own wage minimum, which for most firms will lie somewhat above the lowest wage in the area. The amount of genuine indeterminacy in wage differentials is thus considerably less than might appear at first glance.

7 That is, the ability of an employer to accept a stated reduction in his wage standing in the area and still recruit as much labor as he needs. Any judgment of a firm's wage level is, of course, quite difficult even under nonunion conditions.

ward plasticity of relative wages[3] is greatly to prolong the death agonies of declining businesses. As a company's relative wage level falls, it encounters growing "sales resistance" in persuading workers to take its jobs, the quality of new recruits tends to decline, and there may be disaffection among its long-service workers. It may hang on for a remarkably long time, however, particularly during periods of substantial underemployment. The companies at the lower edge of the area wage band at any time are those whose low profitability forces them involuntarily to test how little they can pay and still get labor. Eventually, unless their situation improves, they are forced below the feasible wage range and pass from the scene. A union may shorten the death agonies by refusing to allow the company's relative wage level to sink below a certain point. This action has frequently to be taken by officials of the national union, however, over the protests of members who are anxious to keep their jobs even at low wage rates.

Under nonunion conditions, then, the wage structure of an area is shaped mainly by the labor demand curves of firms in the area. The supply situation is such that each firm, instead of being faced with a market wage rate, is faced with a considerable range of possible wage levels. Depending on the height of its demand curve, it can select a higher or lower position in the area wage structure and can shift this position gradually over the course of time.

The plasticity of wage levels *over the course of time* does not mean that the wage level of a particular firm *at a point of time* is indeterminate over the whole width of the wage band. If, for example, the lowest firm in the area is paying $1.00 an hour for a particular job and the highest firm $1.50, this does not mean that the top firm could also pay $1.00 if it wanted to and that its workers are receiving $0.50 per hour as a sheer bonus. It is more likely that the top company would be obliged in any event to pay, say, $1.35 per hour, because of its high hiring requirements, the quality of its labor force, and the expectations generated by the fact that it has customarily been a high-wage firm. The (economically) unexplained bonus is thus only $0.15 per hour instead of $0.50. Each firm in the area has its own wage minimum, which for most firms will lie somewhat above the lowest wage in the area. The amount of genuine indeterminacy in wage setting is thus considerably less than might appear at first glance.

[3] That is, the ability of an employer to accept a *relative* decline in his wage standing in the area and still recruit as much labor as he needs. Any reduction of *absolute* wage level is, of course, quite difficult even under nonunion conditions.

5. To what extent is the situation altered by the appearance of trade unionism and collective bargaining? The top of the area wage band is now determined, not by employers' estimates of how high they can go without being "unethical," but by the highest wage level which any union in the area is impelled to demand and able to enforce. One might expect that this would push the top plants in the area farther above the bottom ones and widen the interplant differences in wage levels. This probably does happen during periods of marked wage-price inflation, because the unions take the initiative in forcing wage increases, while increases in nonunion plants tend to lag both in size and timing. Over longer periods, however, it is by no means clear that union wage rates rise any faster, on the average, than nonunion rates.[4] Even if the statistical evidence were more satisfactory than it is, it could scarcely be conclusive, for one can never separate out the changes in wage structure which would have occurred in the absence of trade unionism from those which one sees occurring under unionism.

By assuming that union leaders behave like monopolistic sellers of a commodity, one can argue that unionism *must* tend to increase the dispersion of plant wage levels. There are other *a priori* reasons, however, for thinking that unionism may not have much effect on the width of the area wage band. Unions probably do not push the top of the band up as fast as might be expected from strictly economic reasoning; and the bottom of the wage band moves up in response to increases in the top rates so that, even if certain unions try to pull away from the remainder of the area, they may not succeed in so doing.

Union leaders probably follow the principle of economy of effort in pressing for wage increases. There is no indication that they try to get much above the minimum which they judge necessary to keep the members satisfied with the union and its present leadership. There is no indication that they try to maximize the wage level, the wage bill, or any other quantity. The reason may be that, as the size of the wage demand increases, employer resistance grows steadily while the added advantages *to the union as an organization* diminish. Union leaders must make an implicit marginal calculation of the point at which they should stop; but the variables involved in this calculation are not

[4] For a recent discussion of this issue see John T. Dunlop, "Productivity and the Wage Structure," in *Income, Employment, and Public Policy* (New York, W. W. Norton, 1948); Joseph W. Garbarino, "A Theory of Interindustry Wage Structure Variation," *Quarterly Journal of Economics,* May, 1950, pp. 282–305; Arthur M. Ross, *Trade Union Wage Policy* (Berkeley and Los Angeles, University of California Press, 1948), pp. 113–133; Arthur M. Ross and William Goldner, "Forces Affecting the Interindustry Wage Structure," *Quarterly Journal of Economics,* May, 1950, pp. 254–281.

those which would be involved in an attempt to maximize the wage bill. Both the average size of union wage demands and the variation in demands from one union to the next are almost certainly less than they would be if maximization of wage bills were the central objective of union policy.

The other consideration is that as the top rates are pushed up by union pressure, the bottom of the area must be pushed up also. Workers revise their notions of an acceptable wage, and the supply price of the unemployed increases. Employers make some effort on their own account to keep pace with the general upward movement. Legal minimum wages, unemployment compensation rates, and other social insurance benefits are revised upward to reflect the higher wage structure. These processes take some time to become effective. Over periods of a decade or more, however, they seem to be tolerably effective to prevent the top of the wage structure from running away from the bottom.

Even if collective bargaining has little effect on the width of the area wage band, it doubtless has an effect on the relative ranking of firms within this band. Since unions are fairly independent of each other and show some variation of objectives, it would be surprising if one did not find that the wage structure was different from that which would have existed in the absence of collective bargaining. It is unfortunately very difficult to draw any conclusions on this point from statistical data. Though the wage levels of different firms and industries are constantly changing for a variety of reasons,[13] When we observe that the wage levels of certain unionized firms have risen more than others one can never be sure of how much, if any, of the differential movement has been due to union pressure. The observed changes may be due largely to factors which would have been operative in any event. A still more perplexing problem is that even if one could demonstrate that a particular change in relative wage levels was due to union pressure, one could not be certain whether the change represented a movement toward or away from "the competitive pattern of wages." In the absence of a highly competitive labor market, we have no way of knowing what that proper relation between wage rates in different firms and industries is.

6. We have been dealing thus far with the general wage level of the firm. It remains to note that the rates for specific jobs in the plant are determined, within rather broad limits, by managerial discretion or

[13] On this point [illegible] Lindblom, op. cit.

those which would be involved in an attempt to maximize the wage bill. Both the average size of union wage demands and the variation in demands from one union to the next are almost certainly less than they would be if maximization of wage bills were the central objective of union policy.

The other consideration is that as the top rates are pushed upward by union pressure the bottom of the area wage band also rises. Workers revise their notions of an acceptable wage, and the supply price of the unemployed increases. Employers make some effort on their own account to keep pace with the general upward movement. Legal minimum wages, unemployment compensation rates, and other social insurance benefits are revised upward to reflect the higher wage structure. These processes take some time to become effective. Over periods of a decade or more, however, they seem to be sufficiently effective to prevent the top of the wage structure from running away from the bottom.

Even if collective bargaining has little effect on the width of the area wage band, it doubtless has an effect on the relative ranking of firms within this band. Since unions bargain independently of each other and show some variation of objectives, it would be surprising if one did not come out with a wage structure rather different from that which would have existed in the absence of collective bargaining. It is unfortunately very difficult to draw any conclusions on this point from statistical data. The relative wage levels of different firms and industries are constantly changing for a variety of reasons.[5] When one observes that the wage levels of certain unionized firms have risen more than others one can never be sure of how much, if any, of the differential movement has been due to union pressure. The observed changes may be due largely to factors which would have been operative in any event. A still more perplexing problem is that even if one could demonstrate that a particular change in relative wage levels was due to union pressures, one could not be certain whether the change represented a movement toward or away from "the competitive pattern of wages." In the absence of a highly competitive labor market, we have no way of knowing what is a proper relation between wage rates in different firms and industries.

6. We have been dealing thus far with the general wage level of the firm. It remains to note that the rates for specific jobs in the plant are determined, within rather broad limits, by managerial discretion or

[5] See on this point John T. Dunlop, *op. cit.*

union-management negotiation. A job rate is an administered price *par excellence.*

There is obviously a lower limit to the size of occupational differentials; below a certain point, workers would not be willing to undergo training for more skilled positions. There is reason to think, however, that the wage differentials required to induce upward movement are quite small. This is suggested by the fact that most skilled jobs are more attractive than unskilled jobs on nonwage grounds, and also by statistical evidence from other countries. In Sweden, for example, skilled workers frequently earn only 15 or 20 per cent more than unskilled workers in the same industry.[6] In France, the governmentally determined wage rates for unskilled workers stood in 1947 very close to the rates for skilled workers in the same industries.[7]

In the United States, on the other hand, occupational wage differentials seem to have been considerably larger than would be required to induce upward movement of labor. A careful historical study of how this situation came into existence would be extremely interesting and fruitful. The other interesting question is why the large differential between skilled and unskilled labor was not eroded by the operation of competitive forces. Economic reasoning would lead one to expect that even if abnormally large wage differentials (i.e., larger than necessary to induce upward occupational movement of labor) should somehow come into existence, they would gradually be narrowed down to the economic minimum for two reasons: the supply of unskilled labor would be reduced by workers' efforts to climb to the more remunerative skilled jobs, while the demand for unskilled labor would rise because of employers' efforts to substitute cheap labor for dear. Why have these forces not operated with the strength which one might have expected?

The possibility of substituting workers at one occupational level for those at another is narrowly limited at any moment by fixity of production methods. Over the course of time technical changes do alter the composition of the plant labor force, but it is unlikely that these changes are much influenced by the ratio of skilled to unskilled wage rates. The result is that substitution of unskilled for skilled labor occurs mainly through interindustry competition in product markets. A decline in the relative wage level of unskilled workers means a relative expansion in sales of products embodying a high proportion of

[6] Paul H. Norgren, *The Swedish Collective Bargaining System* (Cambridge, Harvard University Press, 1941), pp. 105–109.

[7] See on this point a discussion in the *Monthly Labor Review,* August, 1947, Vol. 65, No. 2, pp. 149–157.

unskilled labor, and this provides a certain amount of competition between labor of various grades. Competition is less effective, however, than it would be if substitution were also possible *within* individual plants and industries.

On the supply side, large occupational differentials will doubtless make many unskilled workers wish to train themselves for higher occupations; but this does not say that they will be able to do so. The great bulk of occupational training in American industry is on-the-job training rather than preemployment training. A worker does not get an opportunity to learn a job until a vacancy develops. Adaptation of labor supplies follows and is induced by changes in demand, rather than the reverse. There is little chance of an excess of trained workers building up and "breaking" the rate for a job. As far as labor supply is concerned, therefore, any established set of occupational differentials is quite stable. If the differentials are larger than required to induce enough workers to transfer to the higher occupations, this simply means that vacancies in these occupations have to be rationed among those who want them. The existence of job rationing—on the basis of seniority, efficiency, personal favoritism, or some combination of these—is one of the most familiar facts of industrial employment.

There is still a problem of why employers have continued, decade after decade, to pay skilled wage rates well above the level necessary to induce upward mobility. An individual employer, of course, cannot do much about this situation. Some consensus among all employers, or at least the leading employers, in an area would be required. It would have been fairly easy, however, for employers *as a group* to have narrowed the skilled-unskilled differential gradually over the years. Since the secular trend of money wage rates was upward, this would not have required that anyone's wages be cut, but simply that unskilled rates be raised relatively faster than skilled rates.

Failure to do this seems to indicate an established belief among employers that skilled workers *ought* to be paid much more than the unskilled. This belief does not seem to be based mainly on competitive reasoning but on a variety of other considerations: acceptance of the fact that skilled workers (many of whom are at least second- or third-generation Americans) have customarily had a markedly higher standard of living than the unskilled (many of whom are of recent immigrant stock), and a belief that this difference in living standards should be perpetuated; a feeling that wages should be related to *specific productivity*, under technological conditions in which the gap

between the specific productivity of skilled and unskilled workers cannot be closed by substitution of one for the other; a feeling that skill and training are meritorious in themselves and should be rewarded (*vide* the heavy weight given to these factors in most management-sponsored job evaluation systems); a recognition that the skilled workers are natural leaders of the labor force and are also potential foreman and supervisors, and a consequent desire to strengthen their loyalty to the company; and the fact that in most manufacturing enterprises a high rate for skilled labor costs the company relatively little, since the bulk of the labor force is concentrated near the bottom of the wage structure.

THE MOVEMENT OF LABOR

1. Discussion of this subject suffers from lack of an adequate terminology. There is a tendency to use the terms "movement" and "mobility" interchangeably. It seems better, however, to use mobility to describe willingness or *propensity to move.* Opportunity must be added to willingness before any actual *movement* will occur. Moreover, both movement and propensity to move turn out on close inspection to be heterogeneous concepts embracing a variety of motives and activities.

It is tempting to define propensity to move as responsiveness to known differences in terms of employment. This is not very useful, however, for cases in which a worker moves directly from one job to another *the availability of which and the terms of which are known with complete certainty* constitute a very small part of total movement. It is probably necessary, as a minimum, to distinguish three kinds of propensity:

a. Propensity to move to an apparently more attractive job whose terms and whose permanence are not known with certainty. The determinants of this propensity are the degree of knowledge of the new job and the individual's willingness to assume the risks arising from imperfect knowledge. Willingness to assume risks is probably conditioned mainly by the age and family responsibilities of the individual, his length of service and apparent security on his present job, and his temperamental characteristics.

b. Propensity to quit a job which has proved unsatisfactory without having a new job in sight. This is influenced by the worker's willingness to assume risks and by his ability to adjust to unpleasant physical

between the specific productivity of skilled and unskilled workers cannot be closed by substitution of one for the other; a feeling that skill and training are precious in themselves and should be rewarded (note the heavy weight given to these factors in most management-sponsored job evaluation systems); a recognition that the skilled workers are natural leaders of the labor force and are also potential foremen and supervisors, and a consequent desire to strengthen their loyalty to the company; and the fact that, in most manufacturing enterprises, a high rate for skilled labor costs the company relatively little since the bulk of the labor force is concentrated near the bottom of the wage structure.

THE MOVEMENT OF LABOR

1. Discussion of this subject suffers from lack of an adequate terminology. There is a tendency to use the terms "movement" and "mobility" interchangeably. It seems better, however, to use mobility to describe willingness to move or *propensity to move*. Opportunity must be added to willingness before any actual movement will occur. Moreover, both movement and propensity to move turn out on close inspection to be heterogeneous concepts embracing a variety of motives and activities.

It is tempting to define propensity to move as responsiveness to known differences in terms of employment. This is not very useful, however, for cases in which a worker moves directly from one job to another, the desirability of which and the terms of which are known with certainty, constitute a very small part of total movement. It is probably necessary, as a minimum, to distinguish three kinds of propensity:

a. Propensity to move to an apparently more attractive job whose terms and whose permanence are not known with certainty. The determinants of this propensity are the degree of knowledge of the new job and the individual's willingness to assume the risks arising from imperfect knowledge. Willingness to assume risks is probably conditioned mainly by the age and family responsibilities of the individual, his length of service and greater security on his present job, and his temperamental characteristics.

b. Propensity to quit a job which one finds unsatisfactory without having a new job in sight. This is influenced by the worker's willingness to assume risks and by his ability to adjust to unpleasant physical

conditions or personal relationships. It is also influenced very significantly by the general level of employment, which affects the worker's estimate of the chances of finding a new job.

c. Propensity of an unemployed worker to change his usual occupation, industry, or place of residence in order to secure employment. Most workers outside the skilled crafts show only moderate resistance to a change of occupation or industry. There is greater resistance to a change of residence, though this varies markedly within the labor force. The propensity to geographical movement seems to be greater for men than for women, for young single people than for older people, and for craftsmen than for factory operatives. Up to a certain point, increasing unemployment in an area probably lowers workers' resistance to interarea movement. If workers become convinced that unemployment is general, however, that things are just as bad there as they are here, their resistance to movement may be reinforced. The propensity to geographical movement is also significantly influenced by whether the individual has friends and relatives in other areas.

2. Movement is quite different from propensity to move. A great deal of movement is involuntary, resulting from layoff or discharge, and worker propensities do not enter the picture at all. Even voluntary movement is not a matter of worker propensities alone. Willingness to move is ineffectual until translated into action by a concrete opportunity.

Voluntary movement, moreover, is not a homogeneous concept. Different types of movement require different sorts of decision by the worker and occur for quite different reasons. The most interesting types of movement are probably those between employing units, occupations, and geographical areas. It is desirable to comment briefly on the distinguishing characteristics of each type.

The most important thing to be said about *interplant movement* is that most of it is not really interplant movement at all. It does not typically involve a comparison of two opportunities to which the worker has simultaneous access and between which he makes a deliberate choice. The worker is normally propelled out of one company by layoff, discharge, or dissatisfaction which leads him to quit the job. He then looks about for a new job; but the significant comparison which he makes is between a specific job offer and continued unemployment, rather than between the new job and the old.

One should not expect, therefore, and one does not actually find that

interplant movement normally improves the worker's position.[8] On the contrary, interplant movement typically involves a reduction in the worker's earnings. This is most strikingly true of laid-off and discharged workers, but it seems also to be true on balance for those who left their last jobs voluntarily. An important reason is that workers entering a new company are usually required to start in the less attractive jobs, the better jobs being filled mainly by intraplant promotion. Interplant movement is quite likely to mean a change of occupation or industrial attachment or both.

There is a good deal of involuntary movement between *occupations*, resulting from elimination of jobs or forced changes of employer, and this movement is typically lateral or downwards. Most occupational movement, however, is upward and is a voluntary response to more attractive opportunities. Upward occupational movement seems to occur mainly within the same firm or at least within the same industry. The laborer becomes a skilled machine operator, the carpenter becomes a building contractor, the retail clerk becomes a store manager, and so on.

Movement between *areas,* like movement between employers, typically has a negative origin. It stems from a lack of adequate economic opportunity in one's present location. For farm boys, this means primarily lack of opportunity to own or rent a farm. For urban workers, it means primarily unemployment. Once an individual's attachment to his home area has been disrupted in this way, his *direction of movement* seems to be determined largely by distance, by personal relationships, and by availability of jobs. If Ford or Goodyear send emissaries out into small towns in the South and Midwest, one will find people from these areas moving toward Detroit or Akron. If California fruit growers distribute handbills throughout Oklahoma, farm workers will start driving westward. Apart from such influences, people tend to move to places in which they have relatives or acquaintances, provided the reports sent back by their friends are reasonably favorable. Distance is also an important consideration, the volume of short-range migration greatly exceeding the amount of long-range migration.[9]

[8] See on this point the data presented in Chapter VIII. See also Charles A. Myers and W. Rupert Maclaurin, *The Movement of Factory Labor* (New York, John Wiley and Sons, 1943), Chapter 3; and the numerous studies of the experience of factory workers displaced by plant shutdowns or technological change.

[9] The most thorough quantitative investigation of geographical movement which I have seen is H. Makower, J. Marschak, and H. W. Robinson, "Studies in the Mobility

2. The distinction between movement and propensity to move is important, both in defining how much movement is desirable in an economy and in explaining the amount of movement which actually occurs. It is frequently said that we should have a more effective labor market if workers were "more mobile." Does this mean ... it is desirable for workers to be more responsive than they are to known differences in terms of employment? Or does it mean that their knowledge of such differences needs to be improved? Or does it mean that there should be more actual movement? If so, what types of movement need to be increased? The problem of defining an optimum amount of movement will be left until the next chapter, since it forms a natural prelude to discussion of labor market policy. It is desirable, however, to say something at this point about what determines the amount of movement which actually occurs.

The irreducible minimum of movement is determined mainly by the behavior of labor demand—the size of general cyclical fluctuations, shifts in the location of industry, shifts in employment among individual companies and industries arising from changes in technology and consumer preferences, and the extent to which technical change is eliminating certain occupations and creating new ones. The necessity for geographical movement is influenced also by the pattern of birth and death rates. To the extent that the location of net increments to the labor force fails to correspond with the location of net increments in labor demand, there must be movement of workers or changes in industrial location or both.

The extent to which actual movement exceeds the irreducible minimum depends mainly on the adequacy of labor market institutions—the facilities which workers have for learning about vacant jobs, the adequacy of their information about terms of employment on these jobs, and the adequacy of employers' techniques for appraising the worker's probable performance and methods of hiring. If workers

of Labor," *Oxford Economic Papers*, October, 1938, pp. 83-123; May, 1939, pp. 70-97; and September, 1940, pp. 39-62. The authors found that differentials in migration into Oxford of expanding industries from other areas of Great Britain could be largely explained on the basis of (1) the relation between the unemployment rate in Oxford and in the area in question, and (2) the distance of the area from Oxford. Counties for which net migration differed markedly from the migration predicted on this ground could be explained in part by the degree of similarity between the industrial structure of the area and that of Oxford. Counties whose industrial composition was most similar to that of Oxford tended to show higher rates of migration. It was found also that the general level of migration into Oxford from all counties varied directly with the general level of prosperity in Britain, rising in good years and falling in poor years.

3. The distinction between movement and propensity to move is important both in defining how much movement is desirable in an economy and in explaining the amount of movement which actually occurs. It is frequently said that we should have a more effective labor market if workers were "more mobile." Does this mean that it is desirable for workers to be more responsive than they are to known differences in terms of employment? Or does it mean that their knowledge of such differences needs to be improved? Or does it mean that there should be more actual movement? If so, what types of movement need to be increased? The problem of defining an optimum amount of movement will be left until the next chapter, since it forms a natural prelude to discussion of labor market policy. It is desirable, however, to say something at this point about what determines the amount of movement which actually occurs.

The irreducible minimum of movement is determined mainly by the behavior of labor demand—the size of general cyclical fluctuations, shifts in the location of industry, shifts in employment in individual companies and industries arising from changes in technology and consumer preferences, and the extent to which technical change is eliminating certain occupations and creating new ones. The necessity for geographical movement is influenced also by the pattern of birth and death rates. To the extent that the location of net increments to the labor force fails to correspond with the location of net increments in labor demand, there must be movement of workers or changes in industrial location or both.

The extent to which actual movement exceeds the unavoidable minimum depends mainly on the adequacy of labor market institutions—the facilities which workers have for learning about vacant jobs, the adequacy of their information about terms of employment on these jobs, and the adequacy of employers' techniques for appraising the worker's probable performance in advance of hiring. If workers

of Labor," *Oxford Economic Papers*, October, 1938, pp. 83–123, May, 1939, pp. 70–97, and September, 1940, pp. 39–62. The authors found that differentials in migration into Oxford, an expanding industrial area, from other areas of Great Britain could be largely explained on the basis of (1) the relation between the unemployment rate in Oxford and in the area in question, and (2) the distance of the area from Oxford. Counties for which actual migration differed markedly from the migration predicted on these two grounds could be explained in part by the degree of similarity between the *industrial structure* of the area and that of Oxford. Counties whose industrial composition was most similar to that of Oxford tended to show higher rates of migration. It was found also that the general level of migration into Oxford from all counties varied directly with the general level of prosperity in Britain, rising in good years and falling in poor years.

and employers have inadequate facilities for locating each other and for appraising what the other has to offer, there is bound to be both an unnecessary amount of job hunting and an unnecessary amount of turnover resulting from errors of judgment.

The amount of movement, then, is determined basically by circumstances external to the worker rather than by workers' average propensity to move. *Differences* in the propensities of individual workers, however, help to determine the *incidence* of movement. Movement tends to be concentrated among those who have relatively high willingness to take risks and set less store by security, who have unusually well-developed career plans, who are of better-than-average ability, or who are temperamentally unstable and incapable of remaining in any job for very long. These personal characteristics help to determine *who* will move into a particular vacancy; but they have little influence on *how many* vacancies there will be or on the total amount of movement.

4. The necessity for movement arises from changes in the availability of jobs in particular companies, occupations, and localities. People move out of situations where jobs have been destroyed by declining demand or technical change; or where, as in the case of rural areas with very high birth rates, there are too many competitors for the opportunities available. They move to places where new jobs are opening up and rivalry for these jobs is less intense.

The view that workers can be redistributed only by changes in wage differentials seems to be mistaken. They are redistributed much more directly and forcefully by differentials in the availability of jobs. There is certainly no difficulty in getting workers out of places where they are no longer needed; they are simply laid off. In order to get them into places where they are needed it is usually necessary only to place a "Help wanted" sign on the plant gate.

Consider, for example, a town with only two sources of employment. Plant A has average earnings of $1.50 per hour, while plant B has average earnings of only $1.20 per hour. The industry to which plant A belongs, however, is contracting while the business of plant B is expanding. Workers will thus be laid off from plant A and, doubtless with a good deal of delay, grumbling, and discontent, will take jobs in plant B. Reallocation will go on just as it would if both plants paid the same wage rate or if plant B's rates were higher than plant A's. The wage levels of the two plants will, of course, have some effect on the number of workers which plant A finds it profitable to release and

plant *B* finds it profitable to absorb the transfer between the plant wage levels will also affect the amount of grumbling and discontent accompanying the transfer. There is no reason to think, however, that the transference of labor will be blocked.

5. Differentials in opportunity can thus produce movement even in the absence of wage differentials. The converse proposition, however, does not hold. The mere existence of known interplant differences in wage levels is incapable of producing movement unless vacancies exist in the higher-wage plants.

This is as true of interarea as of intra-area movement. Differences in the wage levels of different areas will induce movement only under the following conditions: (a) The difference must be large enough to overcome attachment to the home community. For satisfactorily employed workers, this will usually mean a substantial difference in probable weekly earnings; for unemployed workers, no differential at all may be necessary. (b) The differential must become known through newspapers, report sent back by friends already in the new area, or in some other way. (c) Most important, there must be reasonable certainty that there will be jobs available at the quoted wage. A high wage in a labor market where there are few vacancies has little attractive power. Given these three conditions, the money costs of movement are probably not as serious a deterrent to migration as has sometimes been imagined. The large volume of interstate migration during the bad years 1932–1935, and even during prosperous peacetime years, seems to indicate that workers can somehow save or borrow money to finance a move when work is available.

Internal migration in the United States has typically been from low-wage areas to higher-wage areas (e.g., from less urbanized to more urbanized areas). It does not follow, however, that wage differentials have been the reason for this movement. It is more accurate to regard both geographical movement and geographical wage differentials as joint products of certain underlying forces, notably differences in birth rates between rural and urban areas and between different regions of the country, and differences in the rate of economic expansion in different communities and regions. The metropolitan centers, and in some cases entire regions such as the Pacific Coast, have experienced a rate of expansion which both generated high wage levels and at the same time required heavy immigration of labor. There is no direct connection, however, between the two phenomena. Heavy migration would have occurred even in the absence of wage differentials in order to

plant B finds it profitable to absorb. The relation between the plant wage levels will also affect the amount of grumbling and discontent accompanying the transfer. There is no reason to think, however, that transference of labor will be blocked.

5. Differentials in opportunity can thus produce movement even in the absence of wage differentials. The converse proposition, however, does not hold. The mere existence of known interplant differences in wage levels is incapable of producing movement unless vacancies exist in the higher-wage plants.

This is as true of interarea as of intra-area movement. Differences in the wage levels of different areas will induce movement only under the following conditions: (a) The difference must be large enough to overcome attachment to the home community. For satisfactorily employed workers, this will usually mean a substantial differential in probable weekly earnings; for unemployed workers no differential at all may be necessary. (b) The differential must become known through reports passed back by friends already in the new area or in some other way. (c) Most important, there must be reasonable certainty that there will be jobs available at the stated wage. A high wage *at which not to work* has little attractive power. Given these three conditions, the money costs of movement are probably not as serious a deterrent to migration as has sometimes been imagined. The large volume of interstate migration during the war years 1942–1945, and even during prosperous peacetime years, seems to indicate that workers can somehow save or borrow money to finance a move when work is available.

Internal migration in the United States has typically been from low-wage areas to higher-wage areas i.e., from less urbanized to more urbanized areas. It does not follow, however, that wage differentials have been the *reason* for this movement. It is more accurate to regard both geographical movement and geographical wage differentials as joint products of certain underlying forces, notably differences in birth rates between rural and urban areas and between different regions of the country, and differences in the rate of economic expansion of different communities and regions. The metropolitan centers, and in some cases entire regions such as the Pacific Coast, have experienced a rate of expansion which both *permitted* high wage levels and at the same time *required* heavy inmigration of labor. There is no direct connection, however, between the two phenomena. Heavy migration would have occurred even in the absence of wage differentials in order to

correct the discrepancy between the location of new births and the location of new jobs.[10]

6. Movement and potential movement of labor seems inadequate to prevent large and persistent differences in aggregate job attractiveness. Some jobs are very much better than others, and vacancies on these jobs are rationed among a chronic surplus of applicants. Those unable to get into the better jobs must perforce take poorer ones. Nor is this merely a temporary situation. Individual companies and jobs rise and fall in the wage hierarchy over the course of time because of technological and demand shifts affecting the profitability of particular firms and industries, the vagaries of union-management negotiations, and a multitude of other factors. There is no clear tendency, however, for the *dispersion* of job attractiveness to narrow over the long run.

It is often said that this situation is due to "imperfect mobility" of labor, to the limitations on free and informed choice of jobs described in Chapters III and IV above. While this doubtless plays some part in the situation, it does not seem to play the major role. Imperfect choice of jobs by itself could greatly *delay* the tendency toward equalization of job attractiveness, but it is difficult to see how it could prevent it altogether.[11] The reasoning of neo-classical writers on this point seems to me essentially correct. A more important factor in the situation is chronic underemployment of labor,[12] which means that expanding

[10] This is not to deny that wage differentials influence the volume of migration via their effect on labor demand. If wages in region A are lowered relative to those in region B, the prices of goods produced in region A will undergo a relative decline. Assuming free interregional trade, the number of jobs available in region A will increase, the number in region B will diminish, and there will be forced migration from B to A. It will be noted that these effects run in a rather paradoxical direction. A relative rise in the wage level of one region induces movement out of the region rather than into it.

I do doubt the strength of the supply effects frequently presumed to exist. I do not think that people will move on account of wage differentials regardless of availability of work, i.e., that they prefer to be unemployed in a high-wage area rather than a low-wage area.

[11] The most important effect of imperfect choice of jobs is one which tends to be overlooked by people preoccupied with the wage structure. It is the failure to get anything like an optimum adjustment between individual abilities and preferences, on the one hand, and the requirements of individual jobs on the other; and the undue delay and cost involved in such matching as does occur. What can be done as a practical matter to improve this situation will be considered in Chapter X.

[12] I am aware that some economists are annoyed by this sort of statement. In support of it I would point out that, except for war and immediate postwar years, the rate of *full-time* unemployment among manual workers has typically been in excess of 5 per cent; that the amount of *part-time* unemployment probably approximates the amount of full-time unemployment in most years; that there are many additional workers who would enter (or remain in) the labor force if jobs were available to them; that there is a large chronic surplus of workers in agriculture, as well as much disguised unemployment in relatively unproductive urban occupations. When one considers all these things, it is amazing that anyone should deny the prevalence of underemployment. The enormous

correct the discrepancy between the location of new births and the location of new jobs.[18]

6. Movement and potential movement of labor seem inadequate to prevent large and persistent differences in relative job attractiveness. Some jobs are very much better than others, and vacancies in these jobs are rationed among a chronic surplus of applicants. Those unable to get into the better jobs must perforce take poorer ones. Nor is this merely a temporary situation. Individual companies and jobs rise and fall in the wage hierarchy over the course of time because of technological and demand shifts affecting the profitability of particular firms and industries, the vagaries of union-management negotiations, and a multitude of other factors. There is no clear tendency, however, for the differences in job attractiveness to narrow over the long run.

It is often said that this situation is due to "imperfect mobility" of labor, to the limitations on free and informed choice of jobs described in Chapters III and IV above. While this doubtless plays some part in the situation, it does not seem to play the major role. Imperfect choice of jobs by itself could certainly delay the tendency toward equalization of job attractiveness, but it is difficult to see how it could prevent it altogether. The reasoning of neo-classical writers on this point seems to me essentially correct. A more important factor in the situation is chronic underemployment of labor,[19] which means that expanding

[18] This is not to deny that wage differentials influence the volume of migration via their effect on labor demand. If wages in region B are raised relative to those in region A, the prices of goods produced in region A will undergo a relative decline. Assuming free interregional trade, the number of jobs available in region A will increase, the number in region B will diminish, and there will be forced migration from B to A. It will be noted that these effects run from a higher regional differential [illegible] a [illegible] of [illegible], movement out of the region rather than into it.

It is doubtful the strength of the supply effect frequently presumed to exist. I do not think that people ordinarily move on account of wage differentials regardless of availability of work, i.e., that they prefer to be unemployed in a high-wage area rather than a low-wage one.

The most important effect of imperfect choice of jobs, and one which tends to be overlooked by people preoccupied with the wage structure, is the failure to get anything like an optimum adjustment between individual abilities and preferences, on the one hand, and the requirements of individual jobs on the other, and the undue delay and cost involved in such adjustment as does occur. What can be done as a practical matter to improve this situation will be considered in Chapter X.

[19] I am aware that some economists are annoyed by this term or its connotation. [illegible] I would point out that, except [illegible] and immediate postwar years, the full-time unemployment among manual workers has normally been in excess of 4 percent; that the amount of part-time unemployment probably approaches the amount of full-time unemployment in most years; that there are many additional workers who would enter (or remain in) the labor force if jobs were available to them; that there is a large amount of [illegible] as well as outright unemployment [illegible] a relatively unproductive [illegible]. When one considers all these things, it is amazing that anyone should deny the prevalence of chronic underemployment. The concept

occupations, areas, or regions need not attract labor from other jobs, but can instead draw it from the unemployed pool or may set about the minimum supply price of the unemployed. The importance of differentials between the wages offered on a particular job and the wages of other employed workers is thus very much reduced, and pressure for equalization of wage differentials becomes much less than it would be in a full-employment situation.

This is still only a necessary and not a sufficient condition of differences in job attractiveness. It permits them to appear and continue, but does not necessarily bring them into existence. We return to the puzzling question of why many employers pay more than they need to pay on recruitment grounds alone. The first point to be noted is that differences in the profitability of different enterprises are much greater than they would be in a static and fully competitive economy. One important reason is restricted access to industrial opportunities—limitations on the ability of new producers to set themselves up in close competition with established producers.[15] Under pure competition, any firm which used temporarily high profits to pay "too high" wage rates would speedily find itself undercut by new firms operating at lower wage levels. Where entrance is impeded, however, a firm may continue indefinitely with a sheltered wage and price level.

The other main element in the situation is dynamic change. Even in a quite competitive industry, a firm which is unusually fertile in developing new products or processes may gain a substantial lead on competition for five or ten years. Unusually competent management—doubtless a scarce resource, and one not fully compensated in terms of salary—may give a company abnormal profits for an even longer period. Eventually, to be sure, the company will be overtaken by competition; but by this time other companies will have forged ahead in their turn. Thus a cross section of industry at any point of time will show wide differences of wage-paying ability.

It is still necessary, however, to ask why high profits tend to be shared with wage earners rather than retained entirely by the company. That they are so shared seems reasonably clear, and one can think of plausible reasons why this should be so. The managers of a business, in addition to being employees of the stockholders, are leaders

---

increase of production during World War II showed that this was accompanied by a moderate increase in [illegible] "overemployment" [illegible] to demonstrate the existence of a labor reserve in [illegible] years.

[15] For an analysis of the ways in which this is accomplished see [illegible] Competition, Monopoly, and Profit," Economica, N.S., Vol. [illegible]

occupations, firms, or regions need not attract labor from other jobs but can instead draw it from the unemployed pool at any rate above the minimum supply price of the unemployed. The importance of differentials between the wages offered on a particular job and the wages of other *employed* workers is thus very much reduced, and pressure for equalization of wage differentials becomes much less than it would be in a full-employment situation.

This is still only a *necessary* and not a *sufficient* condition of differences in job attractiveness. It permits them to appear and continue, but does not necessarily bring them into existence. We return to the puzzling question of why many employers pay more for labor than they need to pay on recruitment grounds alone. The first point to be noted is that differences in the profitability of different enterprises are much greater than they would be in a static and fully competitive economy. One important reason is restricted access to industrial opportunities—limitations on the ability of new producers to set themselves up in close competition with established producers.[18] Under pure competition, any firm which used temporarily high profits to pay "too high" wage rates would speedily find itself undercut by new firms operating at lower wage levels. Where entrance is impeded, however, a firm may continue indefinitely with a sheltered wage and price level.

The other main element in the situation is dynamic change. Even in a quite competitive industry a firm which is unusually fertile in developing new products or processes may gain a substantial lead on competition for five or ten years. Unusually competent management—doubtless a scarce resource, and one not fully compensated in terms of salary—may give a company abnormal profits for an even longer period. Eventually, to be sure, the company will be overtaken by competition; but by this time other companies will have forged ahead in their turn. Thus a cross section of industry at any point of time will show wide differences of wage-paying ability.

It is still necessary, however, to ask why high profits tend to be shared with wage earners rather than retained entirely by the company. That they are so shared seems reasonably clear; and one can think of plausible reasons why this should be so. The managers of a business, in addition to being employees of the stockholders, are leaders

---

increase of production during World War II, granted that this was accompanied by a moderate amount of "overemployment," almost suffices to demonstrate the existence of a large labor reserve in peacetime years.

[18] The best analysis of these obstacles which I have encountered is F. Machlup, "Competition, Pliopoly, and Profit," *Economica*, N.S., Vol. 9.

of a human organization whose loyalty to them can be reinforced by high wages and attractive jobs. Where the two roles conflict one cannot expect management to operate solely in the interest of stockholders whose contact with the business is often quite remote. Too large profits are embarrassing and, moreover, 40 per cent of them go to the government in corporate income taxes. If a higher wage level only costs you 60 cents on the dollar, if it eases recruitment and attracts a superior quality of labor, if it strengthens employee loyalty and wins you good repute in the community, why not do it? It must be remembered also that the good intentions of management are being fortified increasingly by trade union pressures, and that paying as much as you can afford to pay is becoming compulsory rather than merely fashionable.

7. All things considered, then, the processes of wage determination and labor mobility seem to be much less intimately related than one might expect *a priori*. The wage structure is shaped mainly by variations in companies' ability to pay and by variations in the degree to which management chooses (or is forced by union pressure) to pay as much as it can. Labor supply considerations set outside limits to wage differentials, but these limits are surprisingly wide. There is no solid "competitive" floor to the wage structure but rather a feather mattress, into which companies sink to varying depths depending on the force of the downward pressure on their revenues.

When one turns to consider movements of labor, the relation is reversed. Workers move from one occupation, industry, or locality to another mainly because of the appearance and disappearance of jobs. While the wage structure frequently facilitates such movement, it does not play a central or indispensable role. Workers will move uphill in terms of wages if they can, but they will also move downhill if they must.

COLLECTIVE BARGAINING AND THE ALLOCATION OF LABOR RESOURCES

The growing strength of trade union organization has raised a great variety of complex and, thus far, largely unresolved issues of economic analysis and policy. We select for attention here the issue which impinges most directly on the main theme of this book, viz., the effect of unionism and collective bargaining on the allocation of labor among alternative employments.

A preliminary difficulty is that "resource allocation" is a very ambiguous term which can mean at least four different things: (1)

determination of the amount of labor which will be used in each occupation and industry in the economy; (2) determination of the number of workers who will be attached to each occupation and industry; (3) determination of which individuals will be selected for particular jobs, i.e., the personal incidence of employment; (4) determination of the process by which workers move from one job to another, and the amount of movement. It is necessary to examine the effects of collective bargaining on each of these matters. Let it be said at once that empirical evidence on all four points is very deficient; but a clarification of issues may be useful in indicating what kinds of information are needed.

1. Economic theorists have tended to think that collective bargaining over wages will distort the quantities of labor used in particular occupations and industries in an undesirable way. The argument starts from the assumption of reasonably competitive labor and product markets, in which particular wages and prices are approximately correct relative to each other, and resources are distributed among different lines of production so as to achieve a rough maximization of total welfare for the economy. Trade unions now enter on the scene, and begin raising wages in different industries by varying amounts. Wages in some industries become "too high" relative to others. It follows by a familiar chain of reasoning that prices in these industries will also be too high, their output and employment will be too small, and economic welfare will fall short of what it might be.

While this line of reasoning is implicit in a good deal of economic writing, it has rarely been set forth explicitly. The most lucid and penetrating expression of it is to be found in a paper by Henry Simons.[18] Despite the analytical power of the paper, the argument is marred by numerous misconceptions of fact, arising apparently from lack of detailed familiarity with labor markets and with union-management relations. I note particularly the statements concerning the difficulty of training southern farm workers for industrial employment,[19] the dispersion of ability among workers on the same

18 "Some Reflections on Syndicalism," *Journal of Political Economy*, March, 1944, pp. 1-25; reprinted in a volume of Simons' collected essays, *Economic Policy for a Free Society* (Chicago: University of Chicago Press, 1948). Page references following refer to the latter volume.

19 "Southern labor, on the whole, simply is not worth much, by comparison, to the community." (*Ibid.*, p. 132.) This seems particularly unsound in view of the length of time required to train untrained people into competent factory operatives. Available evidence suggests that southern workers, after training and with comparable equipment and supervision, are about as efficient as northern workers; on this point see Richard A. Lester, "Southern Wage Differentials: Developments, Analysis, and Implications," *Southern Economic*

determination of the amount of labor which will be used in each occupation and industry in the economy; (2) determination of the number of workers who will be attached to each occupation and industry; (3) determination of which individuals will be selected to particular jobs, i.e., the personal incidence of employment; (4) determination of the process by which workers move from one job to another, and the amount of movement. It is necessary to separate out the effects of collective bargaining on each of these matters. Let it be said at once that empirical evidence on all four points is very deficient; but a clarification of issues may be useful in indicating what kinds of information are needed.

1. Economic theorists have tended to think that collective bargaining over wages will alter the quantities of labor used in particular occupations and industries in an undesirable way. The argument starts from the assumption of reasonably competitive labor and product markets, in which particular wages and prices are approximately correct relative to each other, and resources are distributed among different lines of production so as to achieve a rough maximization of total welfare for the economy. Trade unions now enter on the scene and begin raising wages in different industries by varying amounts. Wages in some industries become "too high" relative to others. It follows, by a familiar chain of reasoning, that prices in these industries will also be too high, their output and employment will be too small, and economic welfare will fall short of what it might be.

While this line of reasoning is implicit in a good deal of economic writing, it has rarely been set forth explicitly. The most lucid and penetrating expression of it is to be found in a paper by Henry Simons.[14] Despite the analytical power of this paper, the argument is marred by numerous misconceptions of fact, arising apparently from lack of detailed familiarity with labor markets and with union-management relations. I note particularly the statements concerning the difficulty of training southern farm workers for industrial employment,[15] the dispersion of ability among workers on the same

[14] "Some Reflections on Syndicalism," *Journal of Political Economy,* March, 1944, pp. 1–25; reprinted in a volume of Simons' collected essays, *Economic Policy for a Free Society* (Chicago, University of Chicago Press, 1948). Page references cited hereafter are to the latter source.

[15] "Southern labor, on the whole, simply is not worth much, to enterprisers or to the community." (*Ibid.,* p. 137.) This seems seriously to exaggerate the length of time required to turn untrained people into competent factory operatives. Available evidence suggests that southern workers, after training and with comparable equipment and supervision, are about as efficient as northern workers. See on this point Richard A. Lester, "Southern Wage Differentials: Developments, Analysis, and Implications," *Southern Economic*

job,[16] the impossibility of product market competition in a unionized industry,[17] the tendency of union wage rates to rise faster than nonunion rates,[18] and the possible motivation of union leaders.[19] These statements indicate a tendency to confuse what *might* be so on the basis of logical deduction from supposed first principles with what actually *is* so.

The other difficulties which I find with Simons' argument arise mainly from the terminology used. Constant reiteration of the phrase "union monopoly" manages to create simultaneously a remarkable number of wrong impressions—that nonunion wage rates are competitive, that unions are engaged in the sale of labor services, that union officials are interested in maximizing some monetary quantity, and that there is a presumption that bargained wage rates are too high. It is stated repeatedly that unionism prevents free migration of labor.[20] Closer reading reveals that what Simons actually means is that unions, by affecting wage rates, will alter the quantity of labor *demanded* in various industries and occupations. This is very different, surely, from

---

Journal, April, 1947, pp. 386–394; also the other articles by Lester referred to in this summary article.

16 "The best workers are worth several times as much to a firm as are the poorer ones." (*Ibid.,* p. 133.) This statement was presented as an objection to the standard rate and must refer, therefore, to workers assigned to the same job classification. In this sense, the statement is clearly incorrect. Any reasonably efficient management would ensure, through its personnel selection procedures, that workers assigned to a particular job vary only moderately in efficiency. Where such variation is important, moreover, it can be taken into account by payment on an output basis rather than a time basis.

17 "If one big union is a *fait accompli* in, say, the automobile industry, that industry is all through as a competitive sector of our economy—and damned to full cartelization." (*Ibid.,* p. 156.) I suspect that what Simons means here is that unionization of a monopolistic or oligopolistic industry reduces the likelihood of successful antitrust proceedings against it. This is probably true. But would many people seriously suggest that the antitrust approach could (and would) be applied successfully to such industries in the absence of unionism?

18 "Unionism, barring entry into the most attractive employments, makes high wages higher and low wages lower." (*Ibid.,* p. 142.) Simons presents no evidence whatever for this crucial conclusion. Those who have made careful studies of wage statistics are by no means of one mind concerning the impact of collective bargaining. The preponderance of evidence to date, I think, is that unionism has relatively little effect on interindustry wage differentials over extended periods of time; and that, within an industry, collective bargaining tends to narrow the differentials between firms and between occupations, at least on a percentage basis. See on this point the references cited in footnote 4, p. 236.

19 See, for example, the following: "If I were running a union. . . . I should plan gradually to exterminate the industry by excessive labor costs, taking care only to prevent employment from contracting more rapidly than my original constituents disappeared by death and voluntary retirement." (*Ibid.,* pp. 131–132.) This and other judgments concerning possible union policy seem to have been derived entirely by introspection, without any observation of actual behavior.

20 For example, "one may stress the right to bargain collectively or, rather, the right of free occupational migration. In neither case can one sensibly defend both categorically If one is accorded and exercised, the other is curtailed or destroyed." (*Ibid.,* p. 155.)

Journal, April 1947, pp. 286–294; also the other articles by Lester referred to in the preliminary footnote.

[17] "Unionism would be a [illegible]" (*Ibid.*). The whole point of the matter is that industry is all through as a competitive sector of the economy—and therefore a full cartelization (*ibid.*, p. 136). [illegible] what Simons means here is that the unionization of a monopolistic or oligopolistic industry reduces the likelihood of successful antitrust proceedings, but this is questionable also. This would imply that people seriously suggest that the antitrust approach could, and would, be applied successfully to such industries in the absence of unionism.

[20] For example, "One may [illegible] the need to bargain collectively on [illegible] of the occupation [illegible] and [illegible] if [illegible] the other is [illegible] or destroyed" (*Ibid.*, p. 133).

ments that unionism reduces the possibilities of movement for the individual worker. There are vague but alarming references to "disruption of the economy," "intolerable monopoly," "extortion," "violence," "chaos," and so forth, leading apparently toward eventual economic and political breakdown. I am frankly at a loss to understand the basis for these apocalyptic predictions. Misallocation of economic resources, which is apparently the core of the complaint, has been with us for a long time and on a large scale without startling political consequences.

Stripped of these emotional overtones, the problem which Simons is getting at can be reduced to the following propositions:

a. Collective bargaining may produce marked changes in the relative wage levels of different industries (though there is little indication of this in the available evidence).

b. If it does, these changes may be in the wrong direction from the standpoint of the wage structure which would exist in a highly competitive labor market. (They may, on the other hand, be in the right direction.)

c. If changes are produced and if they are in the wrong direction, this may be a permanent tendency which would exist even under comprehensive collective bargaining.[5] (It may, on the other hand, be a transitional tendency, characteristic of a period during which unions are expanding, in competition with each other, to embrace the entire economy.)

d. If the tendency exists and is permanent, we shall have a poorer distribution of labor among alternative uses than we should have otherwise.

I would not contend that fears on this score are entirely groundless, but simply that what collective bargaining has done in the past and what it may be expected to do in the future is still largely an open question. What collective bargaining has already done to the wage structure is a matter for empirical study, not speculation. While deductive reasoning can help us to form plausible expectations for the future, the models of trade union behavior used in such reasoning must be related to reality. They must take account of the institutional role of the union leader, the pressures operating on him from em-

[5] Simons shows a singular unwillingness to analyze the consequences of comprehensive collective bargaining. This possibility is touched on ... apparently as something he contemplates, with such phrases as ... [illegible] ... a "general disorder" ... [illegible] ... the problem of the [illegible] workers would be solved if they ... [illegible] ... only an idea as if ... [illegible] ... what this means, if anything.

saying that unionism reduces the possibilities of movement *for individual workers*. There are vague but alarming references to "disruption of the economy," "intolerable monopoly," "extortion," "violence," "disorder"—all tending, apparently, toward eventual economic and political breakdown. I am frankly at a loss to understand the basis for these apocalyptic predictions. Misallocation of economic resources, which is apparently the gist of the complaint, has been with us for a long time and on a large scale without startling political consequences.

Stripped of these emotional overtones, the problem which Simons is getting at can be reduced to the following propositions:

a. Collective bargaining *may* produce marked changes in the relative wage levels of different industries (though there is little indication of this in the available evidence).

b. If it does, these changes *may* be in the wrong direction, from the standpoint of the wage structure which would exist in a highly competitive labor market. (They may, on the other hand, be in the right direction.)

c. *If* changes are produced, and *if* they are in the wrong direction, this may be a permanent tendency which would exist even under comprehensive collective bargaining.[21] (It may, on the other hand be a transitional tendency, characteristic of a period during which unions are expanding, in competition with each other, to embrace the entire economy.)

d. If the tendency exists and is permanent, we shall have a poorer distribution of labor among alternative uses than we should have otherwise.

I would not contend that fears on this score are entirely groundless, but simply that what collective bargaining has done in the past and what it may be expected to do in the future is still largely an open question. What collective bargaining has already done to the wage structure is a matter for empirical study, not speculation. While deductive reasoning can help us to form plausible expectations for the future, the models of trade union behavior used in such reasoning must be related to reality. They must take account of the institutional role of the union leader, the pressures operating on him from em-

[21] Simons shows a singular unwillingness to analyze the probable results of comprehensive collective bargaining. This possibility is brushed aside, apparently as too horrible to contemplate, with such *dicta* as "Universally applied, it [unionism] gets nowhere except to create disorder," or "and let no one infer that their problem [i.e., the problem of the low-paid worker] would be solved if they too were organized. The monopoly racket . . . works only so long as it is exceptional." (*Ibid.*, p. 143.) Once more, I am at a loss to know what this means, if anything.

ployers as well as the membership, and the fact that wage bargains are only one facet of the complex task of keeping the union running.[22] In particular, it is necessary to break away from the misleading analogy between a union leader and the monopolistic seller of a commodity. Until much more progress has been made along these lines, we cannot speak with any certainty about the net effect of collective bargaining on wage levels, price levels, and use of labor in various industries.

2. In addition to any effects of trade unionism on the quantity of labor *used* in particular industries, it may tend to inflate the number of workers *attached* to certain industries. Suppose that, because of a secular decline in labor demand or because employment opportunities are irregular and unpredictable, more workers have become attached to an industry than can be provided with full-time employment. Unions sometimes react to this situation by insisting on work-sharing devices which spread the available employment equally over all those attached to the industry, thus perpetuating a situation of chronic underemployment. The fact that workers in the industry get less than a full year's work may even be used as an argument for unusually high hourly wage rates, which reduce employment and aggravate the situation still further.[23]

It would be generally agreed that systematic underemployment of labor is undesirable. However, even under nonunion conditions there is a tendency for too many workers to remain attached to casual and declining industries, and this is mainly a reflection of inadequate over-all demand for labor in the economy. At most, present union policies may tend to reinforce maladjustments which would have existed in any event. Nor should one take these policies as necessarily fixed and unalterable. It is at least conceivable that the administrative machinery of a union could be used to speed the exit of redundant labor from an industry and prevent new workers from entering, thus focussing the employment available on a smaller number of full-time workers.

3. It is clear that unionism has an important effect on the personal incidence of employment—on which workers shall get which jobs. One need only call to mind the elaborate body of contract rules concerning preferential hiring, apprenticeship, layoffs, discharges, promo-

[22] On this range of issues, see the very suggestive discussion in Arthur Ross, *Trade Union Wage Policies* (Berkeley and Los Angeles, University of California Press, 1948).

[23] Sumner H. Slichter has termed this "wage-distortion unemployment" in *The Challenge of Industrial Relations* (Ithica, Cornell University Press, 1947), pp. 76–77.

tions, transfers, and other things affecting the individual worker's tenure of employment. It is not correct to say that these rules prevent or even reduce "free movement of labor." There is no such thing as free movement of labor in the sense that any worker can have any job or that individual capacities are somehow automatically matched with job specifications. There is always a selective mechanism at work. Under nonunion conditions this is a blend of rationale—worker efficiency, employers' techniques for judging efficiency, hiring specifications having no relation to efficiency, personal relationships and contacts, and shop politics.

Unionism changes the structure and operation of the selective mechanism. The question whether this increases or decreases economic efficiency and welfare must be determined separately for each type of contract rule on the basis of concrete evidence. One can be certain only that the balance sheet will be a mixed one. Prevention of arbitrary discharges, for example, might turn out to be desirable all round, while enforcement of seniority on promotions might turn out to be undesirable. There has thus far been more speculation than research in this area, and the subject is much too broad and complicated to be considered here. We shall try in Chapter X to define what would be meant by an optimum distribution of individuals among the jobs available in the economy, but we shall not make any judgment as to whether unionism moves us closer to or farther away from this optimum.

4. Finally, unionism affects workers' propensity to move, the amount of actual movement, and the process by which movement occurs.

Unionism almost certainly decreases the propensity to interplant movement. Seniority rules governing layoff and rehiring, for example, probably encourage workers to hold off the market in the hope of recall to their previous jobs. This statement, however, needs to be qualified in three ways. (a) There is a strong tendency in this direction even under nonunion conditions, due to voluntary use of the seniority principle by employers. Unionism thus merely reinforces an existing tendency. (b) This tendency is not entirely undesirable. It is not economically efficient for workers to shift about from plant to plant in response to temporary fluctuations in demand. Transfers from one employer to another should occur only when the reduction in a firm's demand for labor seems likely to continue indefinitely. (c) While seniority may reduce the propensity to move of high-seniority workers, it may increase the mobility of low-seniority workers. If a layoff goes on for ten years, a man with two years' service may well conclude that

tions, transfers, and other things affecting the individual worker's tenure of employment. It is not correct to say that these rules prevent or even reduce "free movement of labor." There is no such thing as free movement of labor in the sense that any worker can have any job or that individual capacities are somehow automatically matched with job specifications. There is always a selective mechanism at work. Under nonunion conditions this is a blend of intrinsic worker efficiency, employers' techniques for judging efficiency, hiring specifications having no relation to efficiency, personal relationships and contacts, and shop politics.

Unionism changes the structure and operation of the selective mechanism. The question whether this increases or decreases economic efficiency and welfare must be determined separately for each type of contract rule on the basis of concrete evidence. One can be certain only that the balance sheet will be a mixed one. Prevention of arbitrary discharges, for example, might turn out to be desirable all round, while enforcement of seniority on promotions might turn out to be undesirable. There has thus far been more speculation than research in this area, and the subject is much too broad and complex to be considered here. We shall try in Chapter X to define what would be meant by an optimum distribution of individuals among the jobs available in the economy, but we shall not make any judgment as to whether unionism moves us closer to or farther away from this optimum.

4. Finally, unionism affects workers' propensity to move, the amount of actual movement, and the process by which movement occurs.

Unionism almost certainly decreases the propensity to interplant movement. Seniority rules governing layoff and rehiring, for example, probably encourage workers to hold off the market in the hope of recall to their previous jobs. This statement, however, needs to be qualified in three ways: (a) There is a strong tendency in this direction even under nonunion conditions, due to voluntary use of the seniority principle by employers. Unionism thus merely confirms an existing tendency. (b) This tendency is not entirely undesirable. It is not economically efficient for workers to skip about from plant to plant in response to temporary fluctuations in demand. Transfers from one employer to another should occur only when the reduction in a firm's demand for labor seems likely to continue indefinitely. (c) While seniority may reduce the propensity to move of high-seniority workers, it may increase the mobility of low-seniority workers. If a layoff goes up to ten years, a man with two years' service may well conclude that

he has little chance of reemployment and set out immediately to seek new work. In the absence of a definite seniority rule, he might be uncertain and wait around the plant.

There are several other ways in which unionism may reduce workers' propensity to change employers. To the extent that unionism reduces differences in wage levels and working conditions among firms in the same industry, the incentive to interplant movement is reduced. The fact that workers, through the grievance procedures written into union contracts, are able to secure redress of grievances which might otherwise cause them to quit the job reduces the inducement to voluntary movement. Our worker interviews suggest also that where a worker holds office in the local union this constitutes another tie binding him to the plant. He occupies a position of prestige and influence over his fellow workers which would be lost if he left the company.

There can be little doubt, then, that the over-all tendency of collective bargaining is to reduce the propensity to interplant movement. It cannot be presumed, however, that this effect is undesirable. A strong psychological identification with a particular plant and a strong expectation of remaining there should result in greater worker satisfaction from the job, greater ease of supervision, and a higher level of productivity. It is interesting to speculate on the problems of managing a plant all of whose workers were continually on the margin of doubt as to whether or not they should leave it and go somewhere else.

A high propensity to move does, to be sure, have two favorable effects. First, it puts pressure on employers to keep their wage rates and terms of employment reasonably well in line with those of other employers. In a partially unionized economy this remains an important function. Second, it facilitates the redistribution of the labor force toward expanding firms, occupations, industries, and areas. This problem is not so serious as is sometimes supposed, however, for firms expand largely by hiring new entrants to the market, unemployed workers, and migrants from agriculture. It does not even seem too difficult to draw workers out of declining localities when work is actually available for them elsewhere.

What is required, clearly, is an "optimum propensity to move" which, while serving the purposes just noted, will avoid the disadvantages of an extremely unstable labor force. Whether unionism is bringing us closer to or farther away from this optimum position is an important subject for study.

Trade unionism reduces the *amount* of interplant movement, both

by reducing workers' propensity to move and in other ways. Seniority rules governing layoffs make for a stabler plant labor force and probably also make for greater care in hiring new workers. The possibility of carrying discharge cases through the grievance procedure doubtless reduces the number of discharges. Rules requiring that present employees be given first chance to bid for vacant jobs clearly reduce the number of opportunities for interplant movement. The amount of intraplant movement, however, is increased by precisely the same amount.

Unionism increased the height of the walls surrounding each firm in the labor market—the firm, not the industry, being the significant unit in most cases. It makes for a situation in which a worker with substantial seniority in a firm is protected against outside competition and can count on staying with the firm throughout his working life, unless the company fails or the worker is disabled. By the same token, his opportunities for occupational advancement are limited to those which the company can provide. The differences between this situation and that found in actual preunion labor markets should not be exaggerated. Workers have always valued security and employers have always paid some attention to seniority; unionism simply strengthens preexisting tendencies. The type of labor market structure which is emerging under unionism places a very high premium on correct choice of occupation and employer in early life. It thus throws heavy responsibilities on the public agencies concerned with vocational training, guidance, and placement of young people. The problems involved in proper discharge of these responsibilities will be considered in Chapter X.

Trade unionism seems to affect the process of movement in another, clearly desirable way. The craft unions, in particular, furnish their members not only with superior knowledge of wages and conditions in different companies but, more important, with quick and accurate information about availability of jobs. Some unions provide an effective central employment service for all members in a particular locality. The scope of the service is limited, of course, to the jurisdiction of the union—usually a single trade or, at most, a single industry. Within this limit, however, the union tends to render movement more informed and more efficient, to save time and effort for both employers and workers.

I have tried, in this brief review of the effects of collective bargaining on resource allocation, to emphasize three main points. First,

by reducing workers' propensity to move and in other ways. Seniority rules governing layoffs make for a stabler plant labor force and probably also make for greater care in hiring new workers. The possibility of carrying discharge cases through the grievance procedure doubtless reduces the number of discharges. Rules requiring that present employees be given first chance to bid for vacant jobs clearly reduce the number of opportunities for interplant movement. The amount of intraplant movement, however, is increased by precisely the same amount.

Unionism increases the height of the walls surrounding each firm in the labor market—the firm, not the industry, being the significant unit in most cases. It makes for a situation in which a worker with substantial experience in a firm is protected against outside competition and can count on staying with the firm throughout his working life, unless the company fails or the worker is disabled. By the same token, his opportunities for occupational advancement are limited to those which the company can provide. The differences between this situation and that found in actual preunion labor markets should not be exaggerated. Workers have always valued security and employers have always paid some attention to seniority; unionism simply strengthens preexisting tendencies. The type of labor market structure which is emerging under unionism places a very high premium on correct choice of occupation and employer in early life. It thus throws heavy responsibilities on the public agencies concerned with vocational training, guidance, and placement of young people. The problems involved in proper discharge of these responsibilities will be considered in Chapter X.

Trade unionism seems to affect the *process* of movement in a generally desirable way. The craft unions, in particular, furnish their members not only with superior knowledge of wages and conditions in different companies but, more important, with quick and accurate information about availability of jobs. Some unions provide an effective central employment service for all members in a particular locality. The scope of the service is limited, of course, to the jurisdiction of the union—usually a single trade or, at most, a single industry. Within this limit, however, the union tends to render movement more informed and more efficient, to save time and effort for both employers and workers.

5. I have tried, in this brief review of the effects of collective bargaining on resource allocation, to emphasize three main points. First,

"allocation" can have many different meanings, and it is important to specify which of these is involved in a particular discussion. Most theoretical writing has centered on allocation in the sense of quantities of labor used in various occupations and industries. This is only one of several related problems, however, and it is not self-evident that it is the most important.

Second, the effects of collective bargaining can be discovered only by patient investigation of concrete situations. *A priori* speculation is a necessary starting point for research but is incapable by itself of yielding conclusive results. If theorists are justifiably impatient with researchers who work without hypotheses, research workers are entitled to be impatient with theorists who feel capable of making judgments of fact and policy without having examined any data.

Third, investigation will doubtless reveal that the record of collective bargaining is very mixed in this respect as in most others. It will turn out that the distribution and use of labor resources has been improved in certain respects and worsened in others. A judgment as to whether the over-all balance sheet is favorable or unfavorable may serve some historical purpose. The important practical problem, however, is to discover the specific points at which the results of collective bargaining are seriously defective, and to consider how far these defects can be remedied through public policy.

CHAPTER X

The Objectives of Labor Market Policy

THIS chapter will comment briefly on the meaning of such concepts as "proper" wage rates, an "ideal" distribution of the labor force among alternative uses, and an "optimum" amount of movement of labor. It is concerned mainly with norms and objectives rather than with institutions or procedures. We shall also have something to say, however, about possible improvements in the public employment service, vocational training and guidance, and other institutions of the labor market.

NORMS FOR WAGE POLICY

We are concerned here only with particular wage rates relative to each other. The behavior of the general level of money wages is a quite different problem, involving simultaneous consideration of wages, prices, monetary policies, and fiscal policies. To enter on this intricate terrain would carry us far beyond the scope of the present volume.

Even as regards relative wage rates, it is premature to speak of "national wage policy" at this time. Government intervenes sporadically and none too consistently in the setting of particular wage rates through minimum wage laws, benefit rates under social insurance legislation, the wage scales of government employees, "prevailing wage" clauses in public contracts, by intervention in specific union-management disputes, and a variety of other ways. The great majority of wage rates, however, are set by management or by union-management negotiation, without direct oversight or influence by government.

As the scope of collective bargaining expands, as it becomes ever clearer that wage setting is an administrative matter, there will doubtless be demands for increased governmental participation in the process. There is already a demand for norms by which one can decide whether a particular wage rate has been properly set. The need for such norms can be demonstrated, I think, without prejudging the issue of government participation in wage setting. Without some criteria of proper relative wages, we have no way of saying whether private collective

CHAPTER X The Objectives of Labor Market Policy

THIS chapter will comment briefly on the meaning of such concepts as "proper" wage rates, an "ideal" distribution of the labor force among alternative uses, and an "optimum" amount of movement of labor. It is concerned mainly with norms and objectives rather than with institutions or procedures. We shall also have something to say, however, about possible improvements in the public employment service, vocational training and guidance, and other institutions of the labor market.

NORMS FOR WAGE POLICY

We are concerned here only with particular wage rates relative to each other. The behavior of the general level of money wages is a quite different problem, involving simultaneous consideration of wages, prices, monetary policies, and fiscal policies. To enter on this intricate terrain would carry us far beyond the scope of the present volume.

Even as regards relative wage rates, it is premature to speak of "national wage policy" at this time. Government intervenes sporadically and none too consistently in the setting of particular wage rates through minimum wage laws, benefit rates under social insurance legislation, the wage scales of government employees, "prevailing wage" clauses in public contracts, *ad hoc* intervention in specific union-management disputes, and a variety of other ways. The great majority of wage rates, however, are set by management or by union-management negotiation, without direct oversight or influence by government.

As the scope of collective bargaining expands, as it becomes ever clearer that wage setting is an administrative matter, there will doubtless be demands for increased governmental participation in the process. There is already a demand for norms by which one can decide whether a particular wage rate has been correctly set. The need for such norms can be demonstrated, I think, without prejudging the issue of government participation in wage setting. Without some criteria of proper relative wages, we have no way of saying whether private col-

lective bargaining is improving or worsening the wage structure. We have no basis for judging whether the unfavorable effects of collective bargaining—if they exist—are sufficiently serious to warrant greater public control of wages. Nor have we any yardsticks for applying public controls where they may prove necessary.

Development of standards or norms for wage setting is thus a logical prerequisite for any appraisal of collective bargaining and for any discussion of public wage policy. It is also a neutral step in that it does not prejudge any of the subsequent issues. A proper set of norms applied to current wage behavior might reveal that collective bargaining is functioning quite adequately and that government should leave well enough alone.

What is a "proper" wage rate? When the United Steelworkers of America and the United States Steel Corporation agree on a starting rate of $1.20 per hour for the lowest category of steel labor, is this rate too high or too low? How can one tell, and how can one observer convince another of the accuracy of his judgment?

We may take as a point of departure the competitive norm of wages, which has been defined very succintly as follows:

> The proper wage in any area or occupational category is the lowest wage which will bring forth an adequate supply of labor in competition with other employment opportunities. . . . In other words, it is the wage which will permit the maximum transfer of workers from less attractive, less remunerative, less productive employments. . . . We imply that any wage is excessive if more qualified workers are obtainable at that wage than are employed—provided only that the industry is reasonably competitive among firms.[1]

A number of possible objections to this standard come immediately to mind. It is necessary, however, to distinguish genuine difficulties from those which are merely superficial. It is no objection to the competitive norm, for example, to say that workers' job choices are influenced by many things other than wage rates. This is true but irrelevant because, given workers' valuations of the nonwage characteristics of a job, Simons' criterion is adequate to yield a determinate wage rate. One need only change the rule to read, "the *net attractiveness* of any job is excessive if more qualified workers are obtainable at that wage than are employed." Net attractiveness can always be reduced sufficiently by lowering the wage rate on the job.[2]

[1] Henry C. Simons, *Economic Policy for a Free Society* (Chicago, University of Chicago Press, 1948) p. 141.

[2] It can also be reduced by lowering the attractiveness of the job in other respects. The situation is still rendered determinate, however, by the principle that the employer

It is not a basic objection to say that the competitive norm is not empirically ascertainable. No one has seen or will ever see a competitively determined wage structure,[4] but this is true of most of the normative concepts used in economics. It is a basic objection to say that in a partially unionized economy the wage structure is so heavily influenced by bargaining power that there is no chance of the competitive norm being approached. The conclusion from this argument might be merely that union power over wages should be removed or regulated by government, and this conclusion has been drawn by some writers.

There are nonetheless genuine difficulties with the competitive norm, which would render it imperfect even in the absence of trade union organization. They are the persistence of chronic underemployment, the reluctance of employed workers to respond to differentials in job attractiveness, and the failure of employers to maximize profits by paying as low wages as possible. These conditions have been described in earlier chapters, but it remains to point out the difficulties which they raise for competitive pricing of labor.

Chronic underemployment cannot be assumed away in any discussion which purports to be relevant for policy. When there is considerable unemployment, the principle that a wage rate should be lowered until it is barely adequate to attract sufficient labor becomes unworkable. Almost any job rate in the economy can be lowered substantially and one will still get enough labor, not by transfer from other jobs, but by recruitment from the unemployed. The principle enunciated by Simons, who assumed full-employment conditions, is compatible under unemployment with a wide variety of wage structures. It no longer yields a determinate solution. The system of wage differentials appropriate to full employment cannot, under unemployment, be approached by any amount of reshuffling of the wage structure. If we reduce the differential between two jobs and still get more than enough labor for the higher-wage job, we cannot be sure whether (1) the change was in the right direction and we should narrow the differential further, or (2) we have made a change in the wrong direction and are moving away from the competitive norm, but have been saved by the presence of unemployment.

We have noted in earlier chapters that employed workers do not

---

will provide just the necessary number of workers to the job. [illegible] If a job is attractive, the employer will lower wages as far as he could or offset them by improving other job characteristics.

It is not a basic objection to say that the competitive norm is not empirically observable. No one has seen or will ever see a "competitively determined wage structure," but this is true of most of the normative concepts used in economics. Nor is it a basic objection to say that in a partially unionized economy the wage structure is so heavily influenced by bargaining power that there is no chance of the competitive norm being approached. The conclusion from this argument might be merely that union power over wages should be removed or regulated by government, and this conclusion has been drawn by some writers.

There are nonetheless genuine difficulties with the competitive norm, which would render it unworkable even in the absence of trade union organization. They are the persistence of chronic underemployment, the reluctance of employed workers to respond to differentials in job attractiveness, and the failure of employers to maximize profits by paying as low wages as possible. These conditions have been described in earlier chapters but it remains to point out the difficulties which they raise for competitive pricing of labor.

Chronic underemployment cannot be assumed away in any discussion which purports to be relevant for policy. When there is considerable unemployment, the principle that a wage rate should be lowered until it is barely adequate to attract sufficient labor becomes unworkable. Almost any job rate in the economy can be lowered substantially and one will still get enough labor, not by transfer from other jobs, but by recruitment from the unemployed. The principle enunciated by Simons, who assumed full-employment conditions, is compatible under unemployment with a wide variety of wage structures. It no longer yields a determinate solution. The system of wage differentials appropriate to full employment cannot, under unemployment, be approached by any amount of reshuffling of the wage structure. If we reduce the differential between two jobs and still get more than enough labor for the higher-wage job, we cannot be sure whether (1) the change was in the right direction and we should narrow the differential further, or (2) we have made a change in the wrong direction and are moving away from the competitive norm, but have been saved by the presence of unemployment.

We have noted in earlier chapters that employed workers do not

---

will try to recruit the necessary number of workers in *the least expensive way*. If a job is too attractive, the employer will lower wages *unless* he could cut costs more by lowering other job characteristics.

stand ready, in any large numbers, to transfer from less attractive to more attractive jobs. Both high- and low-wage companies recruit predominantly from the unemployed. The comparison which the worker typically makes is *not* between hypothetical jobs in companies A, B, and C, but rather between a concrete job offer from company A and continued unemployment. Once he has taken the job and worked at it for some time, he becomes attached to it by habit and by precautionary considerations; and he will usually stay with it even though he should hear of a vacancy elsewhere which *sounds* more attractive and which he *might* be able to secure and retain. The notion that the attractiveness of different jobs should be equalized *through movement* is one which, if workers were capable of understanding it, would be deeply repugnant to them. What they really want is "fair treatment" on their present job *without moving*. They want administrative equalization of job attractiveness rather than equalization through the painful and uncertain processes of mobility.

Nor do employers show a strong tendency to set wages barely sufficient to attract an adequate labor supply. Most employers would regard this as a last resort, appropriate only to an impoverished firm on the way to bankruptcy. The normal policy, where the profitability of the enterprise permits, is to pay wages which are more than adequate by competitive standards. If one defines a monopolistic wage as one which "is so high that workers in large numbers prefer employment here to the alternatives that are open to them,"[3] then employers are doubtless the most numerous class of offenders.

It is wrong, then, to say that "the issue is simply whether wage rates should be determined competitively or monopolistically,"[4] and to identify this issue with a choice between union and nonunion conditions. The fact is that virtually all wages are "monopolistic" in the sense of being deliberately administered and held stable in the face of short-term variations in demand and supply conditions; and many wages are monopolistic in the additional sense of being higher than they need be to attract an adequate labor supply. Collective bargaining obviously changes the mechanism and the results of wage administration. Whether the results of collective bargaining are better or worse than those of unilateral wage administration by employers seems to me basically a problem for empirical study. To assert at the outset

[3] F. Machlup, *Monopolistic Wage Determination* (U.S. Chamber of Commerce, 1947), p. 24.

[4] H. C. Simons, *op. cit.*, p. 155.

tend ready, in any case, to transfer from less attractive to more attractive ones. Both high- and low-wage companies recruit predominantly from the unemployed. The comparison which the worker typically makes is not between hypothetical jobs in companies A, B, and C, but rather between a concrete job offer from company A and continued unemployment. Once he has taken the job and worked at it for some time, he becomes attached to it by habit and by precautionary considerations, and he will normally stay with it even though he should hear of a vacancy elsewhere which appears more attractive and which he might be able to secure and retain. The notion that the attractiveness of different jobs should be equalized by a mobile labor force is one which, if workers were capable of understanding it, would be deeply repugnant to them. What they really want is "fair treatment" in their present job and community. They want administrative equalization of job attractiveness rather than equalization through the painful and uncertain process of mobility.

Nor do employers show a strong tendency to set wages barely sufficient to attract an adequate labor supply. Most employers would regard this as a last-resort approach only to an impoverished firm on the way to bankruptcy. The normal policy, where the profitability of the business permits, is to pay wages which are more than adequate by comparative standards. If "monopolistic wage-setting" is "so fixing the worker's wage that large numbers prefer employment here to the alternatives that are open to them,"[2] then employers are doubtless the most numerous class of offenders.

It is wrong, then, to say that "the issue is simply whether wages should be determined competitively or monopolistically,"[3] and to identify this issue with a choice between union and nonunion conditions. The fact is that virtually all wages are "monopolistic" in the sense of being deliberately administered and held stable in the face of short-run variations in demand and supply conditions, and many wages are monopolistic in the additional sense of being higher than they need be to attract an adequate labor supply. Collective bargaining obviously changes the mechanism and the results of wage administration. Whether the results of collective bargaining are better or worse than those of unilateral wage administration by employers seems to me basically a problem for empirical study. To assert at the outset

[2] [illegible] Management Wage Determination (U.S. Chamber of Commerce, 1949), p. 24.

[3] H. C. Simons, [illegible], p. [illegible].

tant collective bargaining must a priori, we see the wage structure likely to remain one's observation of reality.

This still leaves us with the problem of developing criteria by which a neutral observer can judge the appropriateness of a particular wage, whether set by an employer or by collective bargaining. If market criteria fail us, what can we put in their place? This is obviously an enormous question, and we can do no more here than skim the fringes of it. As a beginning, I would suggest three broad principles: equalization of wages for the same job, extension of job evaluation techniques across industry lines to provide a comprehensive ranking of jobs throughout the economy, and maintaining the wage spread between the bottom and top of this ranking. It will be noted that all of these principles involve intra-job comparisons. I am in full accord with competitive theory that only such comparisons are relevant to wage determination, and that most of the "criteria" usually used in settling points in collective bargaining—the cost of a "decent" standard of living, the profits of the firm or industry, specific productivity and so on—are logically irrelevant.

The first principle, equal pay by different employers for the same job, needs to be qualified in several respects. It does not, I think, call for serious qualification on account of differences in nonwage terms of employment in different companies. There is no reason why nonwage conditions should be taken as data for all time to come and wages treated as the adjustable item. If wages are equalized, this means merely that nonwage conditions will have to do the adjusting, and in a fully competitive situation would have to become equally attractive in all firms.

Wage differences are justified, however, to compensate for differences in the amount of employment which the company provides over the course of a year, perhaps even over the course of a business cycle. Wages should also, I believe, be adjusted to differences in living cost between regions and between different sizes of communities. Real wages, not money wages, should be equalized. This will mean that, on the reasonably realistic assumption of equal worker efficiency in all communities and regions, firms will get a slight bonus for locating in small towns rather than large cities, and for locating in the South rather than the Northeast or Midwest. The differences in money wage levels will not be great, since living costs and, in fact, urban living standards do not vary greatly in different areas. Moreover, I am inclined to think that movement of industry into the South and into small towns

that collective bargaining must, *a priori,* worsen the wage structure is likely to distort one's observation of reality.

This still leaves us with the problem of developing criteria by which a neutral observer can judge the appropriateness of a particular wage, whether set by an employer or by collective bargaining. If market criteria fail us, what can we put in their place? This is obviously an enormous question, and we can do no more here than skirt the fringes of it. As a beginning, I would suggest three broad principles: equalization of wages for the same job; extension of job evaluation techniques across industry lines to provide a comprehensive ranking of jobs throughout the economy; and minimizing the wage spread between the bottom and top of this ranking. It will be noted that all of these principles involve interjob comparisons. I am in full accord with competitive theory that only such comparisons are relevant to wage determination, and that most of the "criteria" usually used as talking points in collective bargaining—the cost of a "decent" standard of living, the profits of the firm or industry, specific productivity and so on—are logically irrelevant.

The first principle, equal pay by different employers for the same job, needs to be qualified in several respects. It does not, I think, call for serious qualification on account of differences in nonwage terms of employment in different companies. There is no reason why nonwage conditions should be taken as data for all time to come and wages treated as the adjustable item. If wages are equalized, this means merely that nonwage conditions will have to do the adjusting and, in a fully competitive situation, would have to become equally attractive in all firms.

Wage differences are justified, however, to compensate for differences in the amount of employment which the company provides over the course of a year, perhaps even over the course of a business cycle. Wages should also, I believe, be adjusted to differences in living costs between regions and between different sizes of community. Real wages, not money wages, should be equalized. This will mean that, on the reasonably realistic assumption of equal worker efficiency in all communities and regions, firms will get a slight bonus for locating in small towns rather than large cities, and for locating in the South rather than the Northeast or Midwest. The difference in money wage levels will not be great, since living *costs,* as distinct from living *standards,* do not vary greatly in different areas. Moreover, I am inclined to think that movement of industry into the South and into small towns

should be encouraged for a variety of reasons, including the relatively high birth rates in those places.

A more serious problem arises from differences in the productive ability of individual workers. How can differing ability be squared with equal pay? The problem can be and is met in part by careful selection and assignment of workers to jobs. If a man's efficiency on a particular job is much below normal, the conclusion is that he should not be doing that job.[5] Thus, while native differences in reaction speed and other physical characteristics are quite wide, the differences among workers *assigned to a particular job* can be held within much narrower limits. Such differences as remain can be taken care of either by payment on the basis of output or, where this is impracticable, by a series of "steps" in the hourly wage rate for the job. These devices, to be sure, are not entirely successful in practice. Incentive systems typically fail to call forth the full capacity of those working under them, and this is particularly true of the fastest workers. Unions are reluctant to permit differentiation of hourly rates to the extent necessary to match actual differences in ability.

A related problem is whether employers should be allowed to pay subnormal wage rates for a limited time while engaged in training new workers. Suppose that it is desirable to establish new industries in rural areas of the Southeastern states. There is much excess labor, but this labor is not trained for factory work and training will take time. Should firms be encouraged to locate in the South and assisted through the initial training period by allowing them to pay less than the standard rate for the first year or two of operation? Again, suppose that technological and labor force trends make it desirable that women should replace men in a particular type of work. Women are not trained for this work, however, and employers are unaccustomed to using them. Should employers be induced to substitute women by allowing a temporary differential between men's and women's rates? It is assumed in both cases that there is no intrinsic difference in ability which would justify a permanent wage differential, and that the differential would be eliminated after it had served its function of inducting a new group into the labor force.

[5] This does *not* mean, as is sometimes assumed, that large numbers of poorer workers must be ruled out of employment by a standard rate. Workers who are inferior on a job requiring fine muscular coordination may well be superior on another job requiring great physical strength and endurance. Workers who turn out to be inferior on all counts will be selected, on the principle of comparative advantage, for jobs in which their disadvantage is least. Those who cannot stand the pace of manufacturing at all can become parking-lot attendants, and a standard rate for parking-lot attendants is still entirely feasible.

The argument for such a policy is essentially the same as the "infant industry" argument for a protective tariff, and there is the same danger that the protection may be perpetuated after it has served its initial purpose. Unions, recognizing this danger, have been reluctant to permit even temporary deviations from the principle of equal pay. Where deviations have been permitted, this has usually been done to save a declining firm from extinction rather than to help new firms establish themselves. It is possible, however, that a judiciously controlled policy of "promotional wage rates" for specific types of labor might work to the benefit of labor as well as the public.

My second suggestion, advanced with some doubts and reservations, is that the technique of job evaluation might be extended across industry lines to provide a comprehensive ranking of jobs throughout the economy. The market is never going to tell us how much a coal miner should earn as compared with a cotton mill weaver or construction laborer. A direct attack on the problem is required.

Job evaluation systems were originally developed to provide a basis for ranking jobs within a particular enterprise. While many practical difficulties have been encountered in administering these systems, and while unions have been quite critical of them, they will probably survive and expand for lack of any practicable alternative. Some of the claims made for job evaluation by its proponents are exaggerated and untenable. It is not possible to "measure" the relative worth of different jobs with the precision and impersonality of a thermometer. The ranking of jobs continues to rest on a multitude of qualitative judgments. Job evaluation does, however, make explicit the criteria of job worth which are being used, increases the amount of information on which judgments are based, and systematizes the process of reaching a final decision. Where people differ on the proper ranking of a job, it is possible to locate the precise sources of disagreement instead of talking generalities.

Ranking of jobs by this technique is still largely limited to individual firms or, at most, individual industries.[1] I suggest that we might well experiment with extending the technique across industry lines to provide a basis for appraising the relative worth of jobs in widely

[1] There has been a tendency in recent years to extend job evaluation to groups of competing firms, frequently with union participation. The outstanding examples are probably the system developed by the Pacific Coast pulp and paper industry [illegible] and in the basic steel industry in the mid-forties. [illegible] the National Metal Trades Association [illegible]

The argument for such a policy is essentially the same as the "infant industry" argument for a protective tariff, and there is the same danger that the protection may be perpetuated after it has served its initial purpose. Unions, recognizing this danger, have been reluctant to permit even temporary deviations from the principle of equal pay. Where deviations have been permitted, this has usually been done to save a declining firm from extinction rather than to help new firms establish themselves. It is possible, however, that a judiciously controlled policy of "promotional wage rates" for specific types of labor might work to the benefit of labor as well as the public.

My second suggestion, advanced with some doubts and reservations, is that the technique of job evaluation might be extended across industry lines to provide a comprehensive ranking of jobs throughout the economy. The market is never going to tell us how much a bituminous coal miner should earn as compared with a cotton-mill weaver or construction laborer. A direct attack on the problem is required.

Job evaluation systems were originally developed to provide a basis for ranking jobs within a particular enterprise. While many practical difficulties have been encountered in administering these systems, and while unions have been quite critical of them, they will probably survive and expand for lack of any practicable alternative. Some of the claims made for job evaluation by its proponents are exaggerated and untenable. It is not possible to "measure" the relative worth of different jobs with the precision and impersonality of a thermometer. The ranking of jobs continues to rest on a multitude of qualitative judgments. Job evaluation does, however, make explicit the *criteria* of job worth which are being used, increases the amount of *information* on which judgments are based, and systematizes the *process* of reaching a final decision. Where people differ on the proper ranking of a job, it is possible to locate the precise sources of disagreement instead of talking generalities.

Ranking of jobs by this technique is still largely limited to individual firms or, at most, individual industries.[6] I suggest that we might well experiment with extending the technique across industry lines to provide a basis for appraising the relative worth of jobs in widely

[6] There has been a tendency in recent years to extend job evaluation to groups of competing firms, frequently with union participation. The outstanding examples are probably the system developed in the Pacific Coast pulp and paper industry in the late thirties, and in the basic steel industry in the mid-forties. It should be noted also that in the area studied here almost all the larger manufacturing companies use the job evaluation system of the National Metal Trades Association, even though many of them are engaged in paper, rubber and other nonmetalworking industries. This may indicate some tendency for job rating systems to be extended across industry lines *within a locality*.

separated parts of the economy. It would be a prodigious task, of course, to rank even a limited number of key jobs throughout American industry. No individual union or management can be expected to undertake the task, since the cost would far exceed any immediate value to the group concerned. Moreover, it is doubtful whether any of the top labor or management federations would venture to undertake it; for the results would almost certainly be embarrassing to sectors of their membership. The job would probably have to be done by government or by university groups.

The main conceptual difficulty is one which arises in ranking jobs within a plant, but which is present here in even greater measure. What factors shall be used in the rating of jobs, and what relative weights shall be assigned to them? The systems in current use within manufacturing give heavy weight to such things as "skill," "responsibility," "educational requirements," "training requirements," and so on. They give a lighter aggregate weight to physical effort, working conditions, job hazards, and other disutility elements of the job. Management prefers this weighting partly because it produces results which agree rather well with traditional wage structures. Most jobs cluster together near the bottom of the range, while a few skilled jobs get much higher point scores. In addition to the obvious saving in wage costs from this arrangement, management prefers it because of a feeling that skill and training are meritorious per se, that people in the more responsible jobs should have a markedly superior status. Trade unions, at least in the mass-production industries, typically insist that physical effort and other disutility elements should receive greater weight than they now do. The pragmatic basis of this policy is that it would yield larger wage increases for more workers than any alternative approach.

I suggest that the unions' line of argument can be supported also on logical grounds, and that any rating system for interindustry job evaluation should give primary weight to disutility elements. This rests on a view that competitive reasoning is useful even where we cannot use the market as an instrument. Competitive reasoning suggests unmistakably that the only factors relevant to job evaluation are those which affect the attractiveness of jobs to *workers;* and that these factors should be weighted according to the relative importance which workers attach to them. The proper basis for wage setting—and here I am in full agreement with Simons as regards *criteria,* though not as regards *instrumentalities*—is the principle of equalizing the net

attractiveness of jobs. A job should receive a positive score for such things as physical effort, uncomfortable conditions, unavoidable hazards, and training costs. It should receive a negative score for intrinsic interest, variety, independence, and other attractive features.

The development of such a rating scale and its application to a variety of jobs throughout the economy should have a beneficial effect on public thinking about wage determination. It is one thing to have a vague feeling that coal miners and railroad engineers are possibly "overpaid," while shirt sewers and cotton spinners may be "underpaid." It is another thing to be able to say that, on the basis of a specified rating scale, job A ranks no higher than job B but is actually getting a 25 per cent higher wage. One should not, of course, expect that such ratings will have much immediate effect on the course of wage bargaining. Where job evaluation has been established in a plant or industry for some years, however, management and union officials usually become increasingly apologetic about proposing or defending "out of line" rates. Similarly, over the course of the years, management and union officials in different industries might be made more apologetic than they now are about defending wage levels which are clearly out of line with a reasonable interindustry evaluation. This seems, at least, to be one possible way of developing greater "social control" over wage bargaining while stopping short of direct wage regulation by government.

A comprehensive ranking of jobs does not by itself give one a wage structure. In the case of interindustry evaluation, as in intraindustry evaluation, it is necessary to make an additional judgment concerning the proper spread between the bottom and top of the wage structure. If the lowest job is to get $0.50 an hour, should the highest job be paid $1.00, or $2.00, or $3.00 an hour? What should be the slope of the wage line along which different jobs are to be located in accordance with their point scores?

It would seem desirable in principle to narrow the wage structure to the point at which it is just possible to recruit sufficient workers for the higher-paid occupations. Since it is probable that occupational wage differentials in the United States are still considerably larger than necessary for recruitment purposes, further narrowing of differentials should be encouraged down to the point at which marked recruiting difficulties begin to appear. There may be, however, some danger in this policy for the reason noted at the beginning of this section. It is strictly applicable only to full employment conditions.

attractiveness of jobs. A job should receive a positive score for such things as physical effort, uncomfortable conditions, unavoidable hazards, and training costs. It should receive a negative score for intrinsic interest, variety, independence, and other attractive features.

The development of such a rating scale and its application to a variety of jobs throughout the economy should have a beneficial effect on public thinking about wage determination. It is one thing to have a vague feeling that coal miners and railroad engineers are possibly "overpaid," while shirt-sewers and cotton spinners may be "underpaid." It is another thing to be able to say that, on the basis of a specified rating scale, job A ranks no higher than job B but is actually getting a 25 per cent higher wage. One should not, of course, expect that such ratings will have much immediate effect on the course of wage bargaining. Where job evaluation has been established in a plant or industry for some years, however, management and union officials usually become increasingly apologetic about proposing or defending "out of line" rates. Similarly, over the course of the years, management and union officials in different industries might be made more apologetic than they now are about defending wage levels which are clearly out of line with a reasonable interindustry evaluation. This seems, at least, to be one possible way of developing greater "social control" over wage bargains while stopping short of direct wage regulation by government.

A comprehensive *ranking* of jobs does not by itself give one a *wage structure*. In the case of interindustry evaluation, as in intraindustry evaluation, it is necessary to make an additional judgment concerning the proper spread between the bottom and top of the wage structure. If the lowest job is to get $0.50 an hour, should the highest job be paid $1.00, or $2.00, or $5.00 an hour? What should be the slope of the wage line along which different jobs are to be located in accordance with their point scores?

It would seem desirable in principle to narrow the wage structure to the point at which it is just possible to recruit sufficient workers for the higher paid occupations. Since it is probable that occupational wage differentials in the United States are still considerably larger than necessary for recruitment purposes, further narrowing of differentials should be encouraged down to the point at which marked recruitment difficulties begin to appear. There is, to be sure, some danger in this policy for the reason noted at the beginning of this section. It is strictly applicable only to full employment conditions

and, where serious underemployment exists, one may unwittingly narrow differentials more than is desirable. Errors of this sort would be revealed, however, if the economy were to operate near full employment for a substantial period, and could readily be corrected.

These three suggestions are intended only to provide a starting point for subsequent discussion. They are not meant as a completed structure, nor are they meant to suggest that we can do nothing toward improving the national wage structure by indirect methods. One constructive step would be to weaken the monopolistic situations in particular product markets which make possible unduly high wage and price levels. This prescription is notoriously difficult to apply, however, and it is clearly more difficult under union than under nonunion conditions. Unionism is not sympathetic toward antitrust policy, and tends to fortify the general drift toward monopolistic pricing of commodities and services throughout the economy.

OPTIMUM MOVEMENT OF LABOR AND EMPLOYMENT SERVICE OPERATIONS

The Objectives of Mobility Policy

Before making any specific proposals concerning employment service operations, it is desirable to explore briefly what we are trying to do. The objectives of public policy in this area are by no means self-evident and may readily be misconstrued.

The objective is not to increase the amount of interjob movement by workers. On the contrary, there is presently a great deal of wasteful and functionless movement which should be eliminated. Nor is the objective to increase mobility in the sense of workers' willingness or propensity to move. Workers are perfectly entitled to prefer a continuing attachment to a particular firm or locality, and alteration of these preferences is not a proper object of public policy. It is legitimate, however, for government to disseminate job information so that workers realize the opportunities which they are foregoing by remaining on their present job. Government may also alter the objective circumstances within which workers' freedom of choice is exercised. It may be quite proper, for example, to say that workers in a declining area or industry who refuse to transfer to other employment will be supported only at a relief level.

The broad objectives of mobility policy appear to be threefold: (1) to reduce movement of labor to the unavoidable minimum; (2)

to improve the personal incidence of necessary movement and thus approach an optimum distribution of individual workers among available jobs; (3) to minimize the cost of necessary movement, to workers and employers. A word on each of these points will form a useful preface to our concrete proposals for improvement of the public employment service.

1. Movement of labor should be held to the minimum necessary to provide for replacement of retiring workers, on the one hand, and long-term shifts in labor demand on the other. Retiring workers should be replaced mainly by hiring new entrants to the labor force. This will involve some geographical movement of young people because of discrepancies between the location of births and the location of jobs. Interplant movement of workers should occur mainly in response to secular expansion or contraction of employment in particular areas and industries.

Two examples may be cited of functionless movement which should be minimized. First, much needless movement results from faulty selection of jobs by workers and faulty selection of workers by employers. Where a serious mistake is made on either side, the worker eventually quits or is discharged and has to seek work elsewhere. Ideally, the adjustment of the worker to the job should be gauged precisely before he is hired and, once hired, he should remain with the company indefinitely.

Second, workers who are laid off during a cyclical or other short-term drop in demand tend after a time to drift away to other jobs. When the company's business revives, these workers must be recalled from their new jobs with disruptive effects on some other employer, or their places must be filled by the costly process of recruiting and training new employees. If there is reasonable assurance that a drop in demand will be of short duration, it would seem more efficient to hold the plant labor force together during the interim. Seniority rules and unemployment compensation provisions which encourage workers to hold off from other jobs are desirable in such cases. Interplant movements of labor should not occur in response to every minor fluctuation in labor demand.

2. Minimizing the amount of movement does not settle which of the new entrants to the market should be hired for a particular job, or which of the workers in a declining firm or industry should transfer to other employment. Here we fall back on a second principle, viz., that the personal incidence of movement should be such as to improve an

to improve the personal incidence of necessary movement and thus approach an optimum distribution of individual workers among available jobs; (3) to minimize the cost of necessary movement to workers and employers. A word on each of these points will form a useful prelude to our concrete proposals for improvement of the public employment service.

1. Movement of labor should be held to the minimum necessary to provide for replacement of retiring workers, on the one hand, and long-term shifts in labor demand on the other. Retiring workers should be replaced mainly by hiring new entrants to the labor force. This will involve some geographical movement of young people because of discrepancies between the location of births and the location of jobs. Interplant movement of workers should occur mainly in response to secular expansion or contraction of employment in particular firms and industries.

Two examples may be cited of functionless movement which should be minimized. First, much needless movement results from faulty selection of jobs by workers and faulty selection of workers by employers. Where a serious mistake is made on either side, the worker eventually quits or is discharged and has to seek work elsewhere. Ideally, the adjustment of the worker to the job should be gauged precisely before he is hired and, once hired, he should remain with the company indefinitely.

Second, workers who are laid off during a cyclical or other short-term drop in demand tend after a time to drift away to other jobs. When the company's business revives, these workers must be recalled from their new jobs with disruptive effects on some other employer, or their places must be filled by the costly process of recruiting and training new employees. If there is reasonable assurance that a drop in demand will be of short duration, it would seem most efficient to hold the plant labor force together during the interim. Seniority rules and unemployment compensation provisions which encourage workers to hold off from other jobs are desirable in such cases. Interplant movements of labor should not occur in response to every minor fluctuation in labor demand.

2. Minimizing the amount of movement does not tell us which of the new entrants to the market should be hired for a particular job, or which of the workers in a declining firm or industry should transfer to other employment. Here we fall back on a second principle, viz., that the personal incidence of movement should be such as to produce an

optimum adjustment between the abilities and preferences of individual workers, on the one hand, and the characteristics of particular jobs on the other.

If one could assume that all workers are equally efficient on a given job, it would not be difficult to define an optimum distribution of individuals among jobs. The starting point is the fact that workers differ in their preferences for different job characteristics. Some value income particularly highly, others (especially in later life) are preoccupied with security, some have a strong preference for physical ease, still others are concerned with possibilities of advancement. More precisely, while all workers will attach some value to each major job characteristic, the weights which they attach to these characteristics—the shapes of their indifference maps—will vary considerably. Given full information and freedom of choice, workers would tend to sort themselves out among employers in such a way that each job would be filled by the person who could derive greatest *relative* satisfaction from it. This is analogous to the process by which productive resources are allocated among competing uses.

It is obvious, however, that workers differ in ability, and that their relative efficiency varies from one job to the next. It is possible, therefore, to define a different sort of optimum distribution of workers, viz., that which would place each worker in the job on which his *relative efficiency* is highest. This is the distribution which would maximize the output of goods and services in the economy. It is also the distribution which employers, given full information and freedom of choice, will try to achieve.

Neither of these optima can be regarded as superior to the other in any absolute sense. The problem is to secure the best balance between them, i.e., the best balance between the satisfaction which people derive directly from their jobs and the satisfaction which they derive, as consumers, from having an abundance of goods available at low prices. The best way to approach a proper balance would doubtless be to turn all workers and employers loose in a central market, with workers cognizant of all the circumstances of each job offered and employers able to appraise workers' abilities with perfect precision. It is clear, however, that complete accuracy of information and complete exposure of all workers to all employers is an impossible ideal. The practical problem is how far it is feasible to move in this direction through the mechanism of the public employment service.

3. Not only should the right workers find their way to the right

optimum adjustment between the abilities and preferences of individual workers, on the one hand, and the characteristics of particular jobs on the other.

If one could assume that all workers are equally efficient on a given job, it would not be difficult to define an optimum distribution of individuals among jobs. The starting point is the fact that workers differ in their preferences for different job characteristics. Some value income particularly highly, others (especially in later life) are preoccupied with security, some have a strong preference for physical ease, still others are concerned with possibilities of advancement. More precisely, while all workers will attach some weight to each major job characteristic, the weights which they attach to these characteristics—the shapes of their indifference maps—will vary considerably. Given full information and freedom of choice, workers would tend to sort themselves out among employers in such a way that each job would be filled by the person who could derive greatest relative satisfaction from it. This is analogous to the process by which productive resources are allocated among competing uses.

It is obvious, however, that workers differ in ability, and that their relative efficiency varies from one job to the next. It is possible, therefore, to identify a different sort of optimum distribution of workers, viz., that which would place each worker in the job in which his relative efficiency is highest. This is the distribution which would maximize the output of goods and services in the economy. It is also the distribution which employers, given full information and freedom of choice, will try to achieve.

Neither of these optima can be regarded as superior to the other in any absolute sense. The problem is to secure the best balance between them, i.e., the best balance between the satisfaction which people derive directly from their jobs and the satisfaction which they derive, as consumers, from having an abundance of goods available at low prices. The best way to approach a proper balance would doubtless be to turn all workers and employers loose in a central market, with workers cognizant of all the circumstances of each job offered and employers able to appraise workers' abilities with perfect precision. It is clear, however, that complete accuracy of information and complete exposure of all workers to all employers is an impossible ideal. The practical problem is how far it is feasible to move in this direction through the mechanism of the public employment service.

3. Not only should the right workers find their way to the right

jobs, but they should get to them as quickly and easily as possible. Workers should spend a minimum of time and money chasing about the area in search of jobs which may or may not exist. Employers should spend a minimum of time and money in recruiting and interviewing applicants for work.

The Improvement of Employment Service Operations

Attainment of these objectives requires not merely better financing and staffing of the public employment services, but also some reorientation of their work and a variety of procedural improvements. The suggestions made below are not directed specifically at the local office in the area studied, which as a matter of fact is already following some of the recommended procedures. I am concerned simply with defining how an ideal employment service office might operate. Some of the state services are doubtless already approaching the standards suggested here. There is great variation, however, in the quality of employment service operations throughout the country. The problem is to bring all of the state services up to the level of the best.

If the employment service is to approach its goal of a comprehensive labor exchange, particular attention needs to be given to the following points: securing notification from employers of all vacancies which are to be filled from outside the plant; securing more adequate information about such vacancies, including prospective earnings, important nonwage conditions, and employers' hiring specifications; encouraging employed workers who wish to better their position to register at the service along with the unemployed; developing systematic arrangements for exposing each employment service registrant to as many jobs as possible, and considering as many workers as possible for each vacancy; drawing a sharper distinction between employment service and unemployment compensation operations, and reforming the present administration of the "suitable work" requirement in several respects. Each of these points requires brief explanation.

1. It was noted in Chapter III that the employment service faces an impasse in trying to expand the scope of its operations. Notification of vacancies by employers, while increasing in volume, is still far from complete. Many workers believe, therefore, that they stand a better chance of finding work by direct search than by frequenting the employment service, and this is particularly true of the more skilled and proficient workers. Employers then complain that the employment

jobs, but they should get to them as quickly and easily as possible. Workers should spend a minimum of time and money chasing about the area in search of jobs which may or may not exist. Employers should spend a minimum of time and money on recruiting and interviewing applicants for work.

The Improvement of Employment Service Operations

Attainment of these objectives requires not merely better financing and staffing of the public employment services, but also some reorientation of their work and a variety of procedural improvements. The suggestions made below are not directed specifically at the local office in the area studied, which as a matter of fact is already following some of the recommended procedures. I am concerned simply with defining how an ideal employment service office might operate. Some of the state services are doubtless already approaching the standards suggested here. There is great variation, however, in the quality of employment service operations throughout the country. The problem is to bring all of the state services up to the level of the best.

If the employment service is to approach its goal of a comprehensive labor exchange, particular attention needs to be given to the following points: securing notification from employers of all vacancies which are to be filled from outside the plant; securing more adequate information about such vacancies, including prospective earnings, important nonwage conditions, and employer hiring specifications; encouraging employed workers who wish to better their position to register at the service along with the unemployed; developing systematic arrangements for exposing each employment service registrant to as many jobs as possible, and considering as many workers as possible for each vacancy; drawing a clearer distinction between employment service and unemployment compensation operations; and reforming the present administration of the "suitable work" requirement in several respects. Each of these points requires brief explanation.

1. It was noted in Chapter III that the employment service faces an impasse in trying to expand the scope of its operations. Notification of vacancies by employers, while increasing in volume, is still far from complete. Many workers believe, therefore, that they stand a better chance of finding work by direct search than by frequenting the employment service, and this is particularly true of the more skilled and proficient workers. Employers then complain that the employment

service does not get the most desirable applicants, and give this as a reason for not referring more vacancies to the service.

The most effective way of breaking through this circle might be to require employers above a certain size in specified industries to notify the employment service of all vacancies requiring recruitment outside the plant. There would be no compulsion on employers to hire workers referred by the service in preference to workers applying directly. The notification procedure would, however, enable the service to have at all times a complete list of vacant jobs in the area. This would encourage workers to seek work primarily through the service, and this in turn would give the service a better choice of workers for referral to employers. The notification procedure would involve some additional paper work for those employers who do not now make full use of the service; but employers as a group would be amply repaid through better referrals from the service and lower expenditures on independent recruitment and screening of applicants.

The employment service can reach its maximum effectiveness only if employers rely on it for initial screening of job applicants, and employers will do this only if they are satisfied with the service they receive. Pressure on employers cannot serve as a substitute for satisfactory performance by the service itself. The limited type of compulsion suggested here, however, would enable the service to "get over the hump" of employer and worker inertia and demonstrate its potential usefulness to everyone's satisfaction.

2. It was noted in Chapter III that the information obtained from the employer about a vacancy is sometimes quite limited. This gives the employment service interviewer little basis for determining whether a particular worker is suitable for the job, and it gives a worker sitting at the interviewer's desk little basis for judging whether the job will prove attractive. The result may be a general misunderstanding and a fruitless referral.

Good service to all concerned requires that the employment service secure at least the following information when a job order is filed: the plant starting rate and probationary period, the base rate for the job to which the worker will probably be assigned and, for incentive jobs, the probable earnings on the job; the physical characteristics of the work, its degree of interest or monotony, promotion possibilities, and other important nonwage characteristics; and employer hiring requirements or preferences which limit the eligibility of particular workers

for the job. Additional effort in securing a full bill of particulars will be more than repaid in more accurate referrals.

3. If only unemployed workers register at the employment service, the employer placing an order with the service is limited to candidates from the unemployed group. There may well be employed workers in the area, however, who would be more suitable for the vacancy in question and who would consider it a distinct improvement over their present jobs. If the true function of the employment service is to work toward an optimum adjustment between the capacities of all workers in the area and the requirements of all jobs in the area, it seems clear that employed workers who want to improve their situation should be encouraged to register and be included in the active file. Probably not more than 20 to 30 per cent of the employed workers in an area would actually register, but even this would greatly increase the adequacy of the service as a central clearing house.

The chief difficulty with this proposal is that it runs counter to the strong employer sentiment against "labor pirating," i.e., the hiring by one company of a worker currently employed in another company. Agreements among employers not to compete for employed workers are clearly undesirable, however, and public policy should aim to weaken them rather than simply accommodate itself to them. It would seem a desirable first step to legitimize the hiring away of employed workers by channeling such transactions through the employment service. If company A then complains to company B that "You have stolen one of our workers," company B can reply: "No, we did not. We simply filed an order with the employment service, and they picked your man as the best person in the area for us." At the beginning, the employment service might be caught in a good deal of crossfire between employers, but this would die down as the new procedure gradually became accepted.

4. Some of the gravest difficulties of employment service operation arise from the conflicts of interest among those using the service. Employers are in competition for the best workers while workers are in competition for the best jobs. What one gets another cannot get. These conflicts are handled, not through a neutral mechanism whose impersonality protects it from attack, but through an administrative procedure which is all too readily blamed for "unfair" treatment. The best course for the employment service in this situation is to reduce deliberate selection by the service to a minimum, and possibly

for the job. Additional effort in securing a full bill of particulars will be more than repaid in more accurate referrals.

3. If only unemployed workers register at the employment service, the employer placing an order with the service is limited to candidates from the unemployed group. There may well be employed workers in the area, however, who would be more suitable for the vacancy in question and who would consider it a distinct improvement over their present jobs. If the true function of the employment service is to work toward an optimum adjustment between the capacities of all workers in the area and the requirements of all jobs in the area, it seems clear that employed workers who want to improve their situation should be encouraged to register and be included in the active file. Probably not more than 20 to 30 per cent of the employed workers in an area would actually register, but even this would greatly increase the adequacy of the service as a central clearing house.

The chief difficulty with this proposal is that it runs counter to the strong employer sentiment against "labor pirating," i.e., the hiring by one company of a worker currently employed in another company. Agreements among employers not to compete for employed workers are clearly undesirable, however, and public policy should aim to weaken them rather than simply accommodate itself to them. It would seem a desirable first step to legitimize the hiring-away of employed workers by channeling such transactions through the employment service. If company A then complains to company B that "You have stolen one of our workers," company B can reply "No, we did not. We simply filed an order with the employment service, and they picked your man as the best person in the area for us." At the beginning, the employment service might be caught in a good deal of cross-fire between employers, but this would die down as the new procedure gradually became accepted.

4. Some of the gravest difficulties of employment service operation arise from the conflicts of interest among those using the service. Employers are in competition for the best workers, while workers are in competition for the best jobs. What one gets another cannot get. These conflicts are mediated, not through a market mechanism whose impersonality protects it from reproach, but through an administrative procedure which is all too readily blamed for "unfair" treatment. The best course for the employment service in this situation is to reduce deliberate selection by the service to a minimum, and to shift

the onus of choice as far as possible to workers and employers, at the same time providing them with the information necessary for effective choice. The objective should be to reproduce by administrative methods, and no doubt in a limited and imperfect way, the conditions of choice which would exist in a thoroughly competitive market.

Complete exposure of *all* available workers to *all* available vacancies is beyond the range of administrative feasibility. Some progress could be made by reducing job orders and worker registrations to punch-card form and using automatic card-sorting equipment to match qualifications and requirements. The expense of installing such equipment, however, would be justified only in the larger local offices. Moreover, even after the "right" worker's card has been located in the office, there remains the problem of getting the worker himself into the office, seeing whether he is interested, and referring him to the employer. This takes time, particularly if it becomes necessary to canvass several workers before making a referral. If the service spends too much time trying to find the "right" worker, the employer will proceed to hire somebody on his own in order to keep production going.

The best that can be done as a practical matter, then, is to expose each applicant to a limited number of appropriate jobs, and each vacancy to a number of reasonably qualified workers. There is already some tendency—at least in the area studied—to tell applicants about more than one job if they request it. There is also some tendency to "deal from the top of the deck," i.e., to present first those jobs which the interviewer thinks will be most attractive to the applicant. These practices should be regularized and extended. Interviewers should be instructed to present each applicant with alternative openings, and to present first the jobs which seem to have greatest over-all attractiveness. This would increase the worker's chance of finding a job which he will be willing to take and keep. It would also put pressure on companies whose jobs are relatively unattractive to improve their terms of employment. This does not, however, constitute "discrimination" by the service against such employers. It merely subjects them to the operation of competitive forces from which they would otherwise be sheltered by imperfections of knowledge.

The converse problem of exposing each vacancy to a number of qualified workers is considerably more difficult. Workers come into the local office irregularly, so that at any time the interviewer has only a few actually before him. Even these have to be interviewed one at a time, and the interviewer must decide whether to refer A to a certain

job without waiting to discover whether others in the office may be better qualified. The "active file" is supposed to provide a running view of all available workers, whether present in the office or not. Many registrants find jobs on their own, however, and fail to notify the service, so that many of the registrations on file at any time are useless. Moreover, it takes some time to send out post cards asking workers to report in to the office, and a vacancy may be filled before the registrant appears. The first difficulty might be met in part by requiring unemployed registrants to renew once a week instead of only once a month, in order to keep their applications active. The second could be met to some extent by urging workers to give a telephone number at which messages can be left for them.

5. The logical independence of the placement and unemployment compensation functions needs to be clearly recognized. There is some tendency for their identity to be blurred by the fact that they originated together in the United States and that in most states they are closely related in day-to-day administration. The logic of the two programs, however, is quite distinct, and neither can be regarded as logically subordinate to the other.

Unemployment compensation draws the greater share of public attention because it involves taxation, cash payments, and direct adjudication of individual rights. Union and management officials naturally become preoccupied with tax levels, experience rating provisions, level and duration of benefit payments, eligibility of workers for benefits, and related issues. The function of directing available workers into vacant jobs is difficult to dramatize and easily neglected. During depression periods, in particular, the employment service tends to be regarded as an ancillary arm of the unemployment compensation system, with the twin functions of testing willingness to work and of getting benefit claimants off the fund as fast as possible by finding jobs for them.

This tendency should be resisted and the employment service should hew to its primary role, which does not depend at all on the existence of unemployment compensation systems. In selecting workers for placement, the service should be completely neutral as between registrants receiving compensation payments and other registrants. It should not give preference in referrals to compensation recipients in order to lighten the drain on the reserve fund. Nor should workers be referred to jobs at the behest of unemployment compensation officials merely to test their willingness to work. Referrals should be made only when there is reasonable likelihood of a satisfactory placement, and the

job without waiting to discover whether others in the office may be better qualified. The "active file" is supposed to provide a birds-eye view of all available workers, whether present in the office or not. Many registrants find jobs on their own, however, and fail to notify the service, so that many of the registrations on file at any time are useless. Moreover, it takes some time to send out post cards asking workers to report in to the office, and a vacancy may be filled before the registrant appears. The first difficulty might be met in part by requiring unemployed registrants to report in once a week, instead of only once a month, in order to keep their applications active. The second could be met to some extent by urging workers to give a telephone number at which messages can be left for them.

5. The logical independence of the placement and unemployment compensation functions needs to be clearly recognized. There is some tendency for their identity to be blurred by the fact that they originated together in the mid-thirties and that, in most states, they are closely related in day-to-day administration. The focus of the two programs, however, is quite distinct, and neither can be regarded as logically subordinate to the other.

Unemployment compensation draws the greater share of public attention because it involves taxation, cash payments, and direct adjudication of individual rights. Union and management officials naturally become preoccupied with tax levels, experience rating provisions, level and duration of benefit payments, eligibility of workers for benefit, and related issues. The function of matching available workers with vacant jobs is difficult to dramatize and easily ignored. During depression periods, in particular, the employment service tends to be regarded as an ancillary arm of the unemployment compensation system, with the twin functions of testing willingness to work and of getting benefit claimants off the fund as fast as possible by finding jobs for them.

This tendency should be resisted and the employment service should hew to its primary role, which does not depend at all on the existence of unemployment compensation systems. In selecting workers for placement, the service should be completely neutral as between registrants receiving compensation payments and other registrants. It should not give preference in referrals to compensation recipients in order to lighten the drain on the reserve fund. Nor should workers be referred to jobs at the behest of unemployment compensation officials merely to test their willingness to work. Referrals should be made only when there is reasonable likelihood of a satisfactory placement, and the

criteria should be no different for compensation claimants than for other workers.

6. The main point at which the two programs necessarily interlock is in the definition and application of the "suitable work" requirement. The meaning of "suitable work" is laid down by unemployment compensation officials, but the employment service bears the brunt of applying general definitions to specific situations. If a worker refuses referral to a job which seems to meet the accepted criteria of suitability, the employment service certifies this fact to the unemployment compensation department, which then decides whether the worker should be disqualified from benefits. In this process there is much room for difference of opinion and practice between employment service and unemployment compensation officials, arising partly from differences in the pressures impinging on them from unions and management and partly from differences in the kind of job they are doing.

The problem of the unemployment compensation officials is to determine a worker's *status,* to decide on his legal eligibility for benefit payments. They tend, therefore, to seek a definition of "suitable work" which can be applied to all workers under all circumstances. The purpose of employment service activities, however, is to attain the quickest and best adjustment of individual workers to available vacancies. From this standpoint, it would seem that the suitable work requirement should be adjusted to the circumstances of each case—whether the worker's displacement from his previous job is temporary or permanent, how long he has been unemployed, and what kinds of work will be available in the area within the visible future. If the displacement appears to be temporary, it is reasonable and efficient that the worker not be required to shift to another employment. If, on the other hand, the worker's job has permanently disappeared, he should be required to shift to the next best job available in the area and pressure to this effect should be increased the longer the period of unemployment. To say that, regardless of opportunities actually available and regardless of length of unemployment, no worker shall be required to take a job which is worse than his last job is an unrealistic policy calculated to delay necessary shifts within the labor force.

There should be written into unemployment compensation systems a "rule of reason" which would allow the suitable work requirement to be used as a lever for bringing about necessary labor market adjustments. While temporarily displaced workers should be given the full protection which they presently enjoy, permanently displaced workers

criteria should be no different for compensation claimants than for other workers.

4. The danger point at which the two programs necessarily interlock is in the definition and application of the "suitable work" requirement. The meaning of "suitable work" is laid down by unemployment compensation officials, but the employment service bears the brunt of applying general definitions to specific situations. If a worker refuses referral to a job which seems to meet the accepted criteria of suitability, the employment service reports this fact to the unemployment compensation authorities, which then decide whether the worker should be disqualified from benefits. In this process there is much room for difference of opinion and practice between employment service and unemployment compensation officials, arising partly from differences in the pressures impinging on them from unions and management and partly from differences in the kind of job they are doing.

The problem of the unemployment compensation officials is to determine a worker's status and to decide on his legal eligibility for benefit payments. They tend, therefore, to seek a definition of "suitable work" which can be applied to all workers under all circumstances. The purpose of employment service activities, however, is to attain the quickest and best adjustment of individual workers to available vacancies. From this standpoint, it would seem that the suitable work requirement should be adjusted to the circumstances of each case—whether the worker's displacement from his previous job is temporary or permanent, how long he has been unemployed, and what kinds of work will be available in the area within the visible future. If the displacement appears to be temporary, it is reasonable and efficient that the worker not be required to shift to another employment. If, on the other hand, the worker's job has permanently disappeared, he should be required to shift to the next best job available in the area, and pressure to this effect should be increased the longer the period of unemployment. To say that, regardless of opportunities actually available and regardless of length of unemployment, no worker shall be required to take a job which is worse than his last job is an unrealistic policy calculated to delay necessary shifts within the labor force.

There should be written into unemployment compensation systems a "rule of reason" which would allow the suitable work requirement to be used as a lever for promoting necessary labor market adjustments. While temporarily displaced workers should be given the full protection which they presently enjoy, permanently displaced workers

should he put under pressure to transfer to his previous alternative without "sitting out" the maximum benefit period. Unemployment compensation officials engaged in the application of sanctions should be required to accept the employment service's findings of fact on such matters as permanency of displacement, availability of alternative jobs, and transferability of skills.

It may be objected that this tightening up of present administrative practices will undermine employment standards by forcing unemployed workers into low-paid and unattractive jobs. There are two valid answers to this line of argument. First, it is not the function of the employment service to determine proper employment standards. It must necessarily take the existing structure of wages and working conditions as given. If the terms of employment in a particular plant are too low, they should be raised directly by trade union action or legal regulation rather than by trying to convert the employment service to a task for which it is not fitted. Second, workers permanently displaced by technical change or declining demand usually end up, on the average, with considerably poorer jobs than those they left. This is in the nature of the case, and it is unreasonable to expect the employment service to prevent it. Efforts to prevent it through the "suitable work" requirement will not mean that displaced workers will find better jobs in the end, but simply that they will take longer to reconcile themselves to taking the jobs which they must eventually take.

THE SCHOOL SYSTEM AND OCCUPATIONAL CHOICE

It was pointed out in Chapter V that the school system plays a strategic role in distributing young people among the various occupational levels. By the time of high school graduation, or at most within a few years after this time, a youngster is assigned rather definitely to professional or administrative work, to clerical or other white-collar employment, to a skilled craft, or to unskilled manual labor. There is abundant evidence that the way in which youngsters get sorted out at present leaves much to be desired. A full discussion of present defects and possible improvements would run far beyond the scope of this book and also beyond the writer's competence. The most that can be done here is to comment briefly on a few of the leading issues.

The problems come into clearest focus at the high school level. High school graduation, which until recently was restricted to a minority of the population, is rapidly coming to be customary for all young people. While some students still leave school prematurely for financial

should be put under pressure to transfer to the next best alternative without "sitting out" the maximum benefit period. Unemployment compensation officials engaged in adjudication of claims should be required to accept the employment service's findings of fact on such matters as permanency of displacement, availability of alternative jobs, and transferability of skills.

It may be objected that this tightening up of present administrative practices will undermine employment standards by forcing unemployed workers into low-paid and unattractive jobs. There are two valid answers to this line of argument. First, it is not the function of the employment service to determine proper employment standards. It must necessarily take the existing structure of wages and working conditions as given. If the terms of employment in a particular plant are too low, they should be raised directly by trade union action or legal regulation rather than by trying to convert the employment service to a task for which it is not fitted. Second, workers permanently displaced by technical change or declining demand usually end up, on the average, with considerably poorer jobs than those they left. This is in the nature of the case, and it is unreasonable to expect the employment service to prevent it. Efforts to prevent it through the "suitable work" requirement will not mean that displaced workers will find better jobs in the end, but simply that they will take longer to reconcile themselves to taking the jobs which they must eventually take.

THE SCHOOL SYSTEM AND OCCUPATIONAL CHOICES

It was pointed out in Chapter V that the school system plays a strategic role in distributing young people among the various occupational levels. By the time of high school graduation, or at most within a few years after this time, a youngster is assigned rather definitely to professional or administrative work, to clerical or other white-collar employment, to a skilled craft, or to low-skilled manual labor. There is abundant evidence that the way in which youngsters get sorted out at present leaves much to be desired. A full discussion of present defects and possible improvements would run far beyond the scope of this book, and also beyond the writer's competence. The most that can be done here is to comment briefly on a few of the leading issues.

The problems come into clearest focus at the high school level. High school graduation, which until recently was restricted to a minority of the population, is rapidly coming to be customary for all young people. While some students still leave school prematurely for financial

reasons, the percentage leaving on this account will decline steadily in future as income levels rise and greater security of income is provided through social insurance. The time is not far distant when all youngsters, except a small percentage with marked mental deficiencies, will complete high school.

As high school graduation becomes the general rule, the notion that a high school diploma entitles one to a superior occupational status will have to be abandoned. In the urban areas of the United States some 60 per cent of the job opportunities are in manual labor. It is obvious, therefore, that a large proportion of high school graduates will have to take manual jobs. Another 20 per cent of the opportunities are in clerical and sales jobs, many of which are not superior to manual labor either in skill or earnings.

This raises, first, a problem of curriculum. What sort of high school training is appropriate for youngsters of whom a large majority will spend their lives in low-skilled manual or white-collar occupations? The traditional academic curriculum geared to college entrance requirements does not entirely meet the need, nor is the answer to be found in multiplication of trade schools, commercial high schools, and the like. Apart from the undesirable implication that children enrolled in vocational schools are second-class citizens, vocational education as currently practiced involves serious waste of time and resources. There are few manual skills which cannot be learned on the job in three months or less, and few clerical skills which cannot be learned in six months. To spread out this training over several years of high school seems entirely unjustified. Moreover, the fixity of the schools' training facilities, combined with the shiftability of demand for specific skills, means that a large proportion of students receive training which bears no relation to their subsequent employment. The conclusion seems inescapable that vocational skills should normally be acquired on the job. Training on the job is realistic, rapid, and related to a concrete employment opportunity.

If one abandons the objective of inculcating vocational skills, what remains for the high school to do? There would appear to be at least three valid objectives: to develop personal interests which will make for fruitful use of leisure time in later life; to prepare the youngster for intelligent participation in public affairs at all levels, from the locality to the nation; and to prepare him also in a broad way for industrial citizenship. This last objective is quite different from vocational training in the usual sense. It is undesirable for high school

youths to spend time in practicing a specific semiskilled task. It is quite appropriate, however, for them to spend some time experimenting with a wide variety of manual operations in a general shop-type course in order to test their aptitudes and interests. It is desirable that they learn the rudiments of personnel practice, union policies, and union-management relations. It is desirable that they be given courses in vocational opportunities which will help them to make a reasonable choice of vocation.

My concern here is not to develop specific curricular suggestions, but simply to argue that there should be a standard or core curriculum for all high school youth.[1] We should not try to divide children at the end of the eighth grade into prospective manual workers, clerical workers, and professional and administrative workers, and consign these groups respectively to a trade school, a commercial high school, and a college preparatory school. All should go through a basic curriculum designed to meet the objectives noted above and, incidentally, to provide adult Americans with a solid base of common educational experience which can serve as a cohesive force in the community. This proposal would also meet some of the other problems noted in Chapter 4. There would no longer be any implication that high school graduation leads to a white-collar career and, consequently, less frustration when half the graduates find themselves entering manual labor. High school would become the common preparation for adult life at every occupational level. The problem of occupational choice would be left open until, say, the end of high school, a time at which the youngster is much better prepared to face this crucial choice than he is at the end of the eighth grade.

The school system could also do much more than is now being done to give students the data which they need to make sensible occupational choices. Present programs of vocational guidance need to be expanded and reoriented in certain respects. There seems at present to be (relatively) too much psychology and too little economics in vocational guidance: too much concentration on testing individual abilities and too little concern with actual employment opportunities. A test score which shows that an individual is excellently qualified for a dying occupation has little usefulness. In any event, what test scores usually show is a rather generalized aptitude or interest which

[1] The core curriculum might need to be supplemented in certain respects for the minority who propose to go on to college and who must meet college entrance requirements. This raises problems which are peripheral to the present study, however, and which we need not enter here.

youths to spend time in practicing a specific semiskilled task. It is quite appropriate, however, for them to spend time experimenting with a wide variety of manual operations in a general handicrafts course in order to test their capacities and interests. It is desirable that they learn the rudiments of personnel practice, union rules and policies, and union-management relations. It is desirable that they be given courses in occupational opportunities which will help them in making a reasonable choice of vocation.

My concern here is not to develop specific curricular suggestions, but simply to argue that there should be a standard or core curriculum for all high school youth.[7] We should not try to divide children at the end of the eighth grade into prospective manual workers, clerical workers, and professional and administrative workers, and consign these groups respectively to a trade school, a commercial high school, and a college preparatory school. All should go through a basic curriculum designed to meet the objectives noted above and, incidentally, to provide adult Americans with a solid base of common educational experience which can serve as a cohesive force in the community. This proposal would also meet some of the other problems noted in Chapter V. There would no longer be any implication that high school graduation leads to a white-collar career and, consequently, less frustration when half the graduates find themselves entering manual labor. High school would become the common preparation for adult life at every occupational level. The problem of occupational choice would be left open until near the end of high school, a time at which the youngster is much better prepared to face this crucial choice than he is at the end of the eighth grade.

The school system could also do much more than is now being done to give students the data which they need to make sensible occupational choices. Present programs of vocational guidance need to be expanded and reoriented in certain respects. There seems at present to be (relatively) too much psychology and too little economics in vocational guidance, too much concentration on testing individual abilities and too little concern with actual employment opportunities. A test score which shows that an individual is excellently qualified for a dying occupation has little usefulness. In any event, what test scores usually show is a rather generalized aptitude or interest which

[7] The core curriculum might need to be supplemented in certain respects for the minority who propose to go on to college and who must meet college entrance requirements. This raises problems which are peripheral to the present study, however, and into which we had better not enter here.

may be compatible with dozens of specific jobs. Choice among these jobs has to be based primarily on economic data.

It is worth noting that below the level of the skilled crafts youngsters going into manual labor are really choosing a *job* rather than an *occupation*. At this level there are no occupations, in the sense of a type of work which the youngster can expect to pursue throughout his life and which offers possibilities of substantial advancement. In many cases the youth chooses neither a job nor an occupation but an employer, and adapts himself to whatever job is vacant in the plant. Under conditions in which desirable jobs are filled increasingly through promotion within an enterprise, correct choice of an employer becomes particularly important.

During the last year or two of high school, students should be given a systematic basis for judging the relative attractiveness of different jobs and employers as well as their own capacities. They should be given full information on the occupational structure of the economy, prospective earnings in various occupations, the nature of the work and other nonwage characteristics, the amount and type of specialized training required, the trend of demand and the chances of securing employment, employers' hiring requirements and procedures, and the operation of the public employment service and other placement mechanisms. This information could probably best be provided through regular classroom courses supplemented by class visits to factories, stores, offices, and other places of employment, as well as "guest lectures" by people familiar with different major occupations. During the same period, each student should be given a battery of tests designed to discover occupational interests and aptitudes as well as capacity for further education. Finally, all this material should be drawn together in a series of counseling interviews with each student, which would continue until the student and his parents were satisfied that he had selected a feasible next step.[8]

Through this procedure young people leaving high school would divide themselves into four groups:

1. The largest group would comprise those going directly into

[8] The practical difficulties of such a program should not be overlooked. The number of people presently qualified to give occupational instruction and counseling at the high school level is extremely limited. Further, any effort at realistic instruction would undoubtedly subject the school system to the pressures to which the public employment service is already subjected. Employers whose work is relatively unattractive and underpaid, and who exist largely on the ignorance of successive generations of school graduates, would doubtless complain that their jobs were being "unfairly" presented in the schools and would demand more favorable treatment.

manual, sales, or clerical occupations requiring no preemployment training. The only problem here is one of placement, and the main issue is whether placement should be done by the high school or by the public employment service. It would probably be preferable to use the employment service because of its more extensive and continuous contacts with employers. The referral interviewers in the employment service, however, should be provided by the school authorities with a comprehensive dossier on each youngster, including both his academic record and the results of aptitude tests and counseling interviews.

2. Another group will choose to apprentice themselves to skilled trades. The main problem here is to ensure that the number of apprentices in each trade is kept in balance with prospective demand, including replacement of retiring workers and net expansion or contraction of the occupation. There is presently some tendency toward undertraining because many employers consider it cheaper to hire men who have been trained somewhere else than to institute their own apprenticeship programs. This is a problem which has to be worked out between employers, trade unions, government agencies responsible for fostering apprenticeship training, and agencies capable of forecasting labor demands. Present forecasts of occupational trends are usually on a national basis, and need to be extended to a regional basis in order to achieve maximum usefulness. Occupational forecasting on a regional basis can perhaps best be developed through state labor departments and state employment service systems, with some pioneering on methods by federal agencies and university research centers.

3. A considerable percentage of youngsters will select technical and subprofessional occupations for which some preemployment training is desirable—secretarial work, bookkeeping, elementary accounting, drafting, commercial photography, laboratory technicians, and the like. The appropriate training can probably best be provided by vocational colleges offering intensive specialized programs of study. These programs should above all be short and inexpensive, leaving further training and experience to be acquired on the job. The optimum period of preemployment training is probably not longer than six months for most occupations in this category.

4. Finally, a growing number of young people will choose to enter regular college courses which, in addition to their direct contribution to personal living, are a prerequisite to professional training and to executive positions. It seems clear in principle that selection of young people for college and postgraduate training should be based solely

manual, sales, or clerical occupations requiring no preemployment training. The only problem here is one of placement, and the main issue is whether placement should be done by the high school or by the public employment service. It would probably be preferable to use the employment service because of its comprehensive and continuous contacts with employers. The referral interviewers in the employment service, however, should be provided by the school authorities with a comprehensive dossier on each youngster, including both his academic record and the results of aptitude tests and counseling interviews.

2. Another group will choose to apprentice themselves to skilled trades. The main problem here is to ensure that the number of apprentices in each trade is kept in balance with prospective demand, including replacement of retiring workers and net expansion or contraction of the occupation. There is probably some tendency toward undertraining because many employers consider it cheaper to hire men who have been trained somewhere else than to institute their own apprenticeship programs. This is a problem which has to be worked out between employers, trade unions, government agencies responsible for fostering apprentice training, and agencies engaged in forecasting labor demands. Present forecasts of occupational trends are usually on a national basis, and need to be reduced to an area basis in order to achieve maximum usefulness. Occupational forecasting on an area basis can perhaps best be developed through state labor departments and state employment service systems, with some pioneering on methods by federal agencies and university research centers.

3. A considerable percentage of youngsters will select technical and subprofessional occupations for which some preemployment training is desirable—secretarial work, bookkeeping, elementary accounting, drafting, commercial photography, laboratory technicians, and the like. The appropriate training can probably best be provided by vocational colleges offering intensive, specialized programs of study. These programs should above all be short and inexpensive, leaving further training and experience to be acquired on the job. The optimum period of preemployment training is probably no longer than six months for most occupations in this category.

4. Finally, a growing number of young people will choose to enter regular college courses which, in addition to their direct contribution to personal living, are a prerequisite to professional training and to executive positions. It seems clear in principle that selection of young people for college and postgraduate training should be based solely

on ability, and that young people of adequate ability who cannot meet the costs of higher education should be assisted by scholarships or loan funds. This will probably require use of federal funds on a substantial scale, since adequate funds are not in sight either from private or state sources. This type of subsidy to higher education would appear to offer solid benefits, while involving minimum danger of undesirable government intervention in matters of university administration.

This proposal may seem inappropriate in a book devoted mainly to mobility *within* manual occupations, but I do not think it really is so. Free mobility out of manual labor is probably a good deal more important than free movement within the manual stratum. Equal access to educational opportunities and to the higher occupations, within limits set only by the abilities of the individual, is of the highest political and economic importance. On the political side, it helps to prevent the solidification of class lines so dangerous to a democratic society. On the economic side, it makes for maximum use of the natural abilities of the population. It also makes for more equal distribution of personal incomes, and achieves this result in a "liberal" way requiring no further intervention by government.

We have now considered the most important ways in which government can contribute to desirable movements of labor and an optimum distribution of individuals among jobs. A complete mobility policy would include a number of additional elements, but these must be omitted in a discussion which makes no pretense of being exhaustive.

In concluding the long journey of this book, I cannot forbear a final word on the overriding importance of a high aggregate demand for labor. The labor force is remarkably malleable, and the main thing needed to induce movements of labor is simply the existence of vacant jobs.

Adequate over-all demand is fundamental in two other respects. Without it, there is little point in worrying about optimum distribution of labor. What is the use of economizing labor if labor is chronically in excess supply? Again, without a high level of labor demand most proposals for improving labor mobility will be ineffective. It is all very well to advise high school students about the relative attractiveness of different occupations, set up an efficient employment service to fill vacant jobs, and pay the costs of moving and retraining workers from depressed areas. But if jobs are not available, what is the point of all this activity? Proper organization of the labor market achieves maximum results only under full employment conditions.

A P P E N D I X A

SUPPLEMENTARY TABLES

TABLE A-1

EMPLOYMENT SERVICE ACTIVE FILE AND UNEMPLOYMENT COMPENSATION RECIPIENTS, 1945–1949

(Data for Chart 1, Chapter I)

Year and Month	E.S. Active File	U.C. Recipients	Year and Month	E.S. Active File	U.C. Recipients
1945			*1948*		
Jan.	1,381	799	Jan.	4,443	3,500
Feb.	1,211	660	Feb.	4,546	2,876
March	961	504	March	4,264	3,112
April	905	512	April	4,429	2,868
May	1,264	682	May	3,951	2,581
June	2,496	1,470	June	4,325	3,312
July	2,580	2,242	July	5,832	4,949
Aug.	4,736	2,057	Aug.	5,354	4,176
Sept.	5,643	8,270	Sept.	4,195	3,782
Oct.	6,141	7,847	Oct.	3,645	2,582
Nov.	7,922	7,224	Nov.	3,717	2,815
Dec.	7,622	7,714	Dec.	5,375	3,588
1946			*1949*		
Jan.	7,944	8,578	Jan.	6,308	5,753
Feb.	8,962	8,556	Feb.	8,293	8,621
March	9,228	9,609	March	10,768	9,160
April	11,216	9,510	April	10,494	8,293
May	11,222	7,674	May	10,592	8,470
June	6,428	7,784	June	12,620	9,540
July	6,225	8,194	July	12,822	10,216
Aug.	7,302	7,643	Aug.	11,244	7,140
Sept.	6,071	5,581	Sept.	9,054	6,488
Oct.	4,342	3,428	Oct.	7,971	5,048
Nov.	4,061	2,364	Nov.	8,874	4,857
Dec.	3,732	2,743	Dec.	9,317	5,452
1947					
Jan.	5,134	3,264			
Feb.	4,237	2,897			
March	3,487	3,073			
April	4,010	3,209			
May	4,184	3,115			
June	4,888	3,434			
July	5,788	4,601			
Aug.	5,520	3,818			
Sept.	3,692	3,524			
Oct.	3,461	2,156			
Nov.	2,994	2,051			
Dec.	3,309	1,826			

TABLE A–2

EMPLOYMENT IN THIRTY-NINE MANUFACTURING COMPANIES, 1945–1949

(Data for Chart 2, Chapter I)

Year and Month	Employment	Year and Month	Employment
1945		*1948*	
Jan.	21,797	Jan.	19,655
Feb.	22,457	Feb.	20,039
March	23,649	March	20,074
April	23,422	April	19,450
May	23,275	May	19,624
June	22,477	June	19,476
July	21,519	July	19,659
Aug.	20,203	Aug.	19,534
Sept.	18,122	Sept.	19,658
Oct.	17,230	Oct.	19,506
Nov.	16,879	Nov.	19,815
Dec.	17,120	Dec.	19,843
1946		*1949*	
Jan.	17,846	Jan.	18,826
Feb.	17,981	Feb.	17,798
March	18,253	March	16,941
April	18,333	April	16,483
May	17,942	May	15,953
June	17,895	June	15,662
July	18,473	July	15,481
Aug.	18,626	Aug.	15,940
Sept.	18,881	Sept.	15,628
Oct.	19,133	Oct.	16,089
Nov.	19,098	Nov.	16,939
Dec.	19,611	Dec.	16,330
1947			
Jan.	19,438		
Feb.	19,671		
March	19,577		
April	19,594		
May	19,580		
June	19,586		
July	19,695		
Aug.	19,629		
Sept.	19,499		
Oct.	19,400		
Nov.	19,269		
Dec.	19,558		

TABLE A–3

Monthly Layoff Rate and Voluntary Quit Rate, Thirty-nine Manufacturing Companies, 1945–1949

(Data for Chart 3, Chapter I)

Year and Month	Layoffs (%)	Voluntary Quits (%)
1945		
Jan.	2.2	4.6
Feb.	1.5	4.3
March	0.9	5.1
April	1.0	5.0
May	1.8	5.2
June	3.3	4.4
July	3.0	5.3
Aug.	17.5	5.5
Sept.	7.0	7.0
Oct.	2.3	5.9
Nov.	0.7	4.9
Dec.	1.3	4.3
1946		
Jan.	2.1	5.7
Feb.	1.1	4.5
March	1.2	5.6
April	1.5	5.1
May	1.9	4.7
June	0.7	4.2
July	0.8	5.2
Aug.	0.2	6.6
Sept.	0.7	5.9
Oct.	0.2	7.1
Nov.	0.3	4.8
Dec.	1.1	3.6
1947		
Jan.	0.6	4.6
Feb.	1.6	4.2
March	1.0	4.0
April	1.1	4.3
May	0.6	4.8
June	0.5	3.2
July	1.0	4.0
Aug.	1.1	4.4
Sept.	2.0	4.0
Oct.	0.9	5.2
Nov.	0.6	3.5
Dec.	0.5	2.9
1948		
Jan.	0.7	3.7
Feb.	1.2	3.2
March	2.3	3.6
April	1.6	5.1
May	1.1	3.5
June	1.4	3.1
July	1.1	3.0
Aug.	1.3	3.4
Sept.	0.7	5.3
Oct.	0.8	3.6
Nov.	0.7	2.6
Dec.	2.0	2.3
1949		
Jan.	2.6	2.1
Feb.	6.2	1.7
March	5.9	2.0
April	4.0	1.5
May	2.5	1.6
June	3.0	1.3
July	2.5	1.4
Aug.	1.3	1.9
Sept.	1.0	1.6
Oct.	1.2	1.6
Nov.	1.3	1.2
Dec.	4.7	1.2

TABLE A-4

AVERAGE HOURLY AND WEEKLY EARNINGS, THIRTY-NINE MANUFACTURING COMPANIES, COMPARED WITH THE N.I.C.B. INDEX OF LIVING COSTS IN THE AREA (JANUARY, 1945 = 100)

(Data for Chart 4, Chapter I)

Year and Month	Average Hourly Earnings	Average Weekly Earnings	Cost of Living	Year and Month	Average Hourly Earnings	Average Weekly Earnings	Cost of Living
1945				*1948*			
Jan.	100	100	100	Jan.	121	107	128
Feb.	100	101	100	Feb.	121	107	127
March	103	101	99	March	119	106	126
April	103	102	99	April	122	107	128
May	105	104	100	May	122	111	129
June	101	98	100	June	122	108	129
July	102	97	100	July	123	108	130
Aug.	97	90	99	Aug.	124	106	130
Sept.	97	84	99	Sept.	125	110	131
Oct.	96	83	100	Oct.	126	113	129
Nov.	96	82	100	Nov.	125	108	128
Dec.	98	83	100	Dec.	126	108	127
1946				*1949*			
Jan.	100	90	100	Jan.	126	107	127
Feb.	101	90	—	Feb.	126	108	125
March	103	89	—	March	128	101	125
April	101	84	102	April	126	102	125
May	105	89	—	May	124	99	125
June	106	91	—	June	130	108	125
July	107	92	107	July	130	103	125
Aug.	108	92	—	Aug.	130	106	125
Sept.	110	97	—	Sept.	127	104	125
Oct.	111	101	112	Oct.	128	107	124
Nov.	112	100	—	Nov.	128	106	124
Dec.	111	98	—	Dec.	129	106	123
1947							
Jan.	112	98	114				
Feb.	114	98	—				
March	115	102	—				
April	115	100	—				
May	117	105	—				
June	117	107	123				
July	117	104	123				
Aug.	117	103	125				
Sept.	118	102	126				
Oct.	117	102	125				
Nov.	119	104	127				
Dec.	119	102	130				

TABLE A-5

RELATION OF TURNOVER RATE TO INTERINDUSTRY MOVEMENT
LIFETIME WORK HISTORIES
(Sample 1)

Average Length of Jobs Held (Years)	Total	Number of Changes of Industry (%)					
		0	1	2	3	4	5 or more
0.0–0.9	100	35	18	0	6	6	35
1.0–1.9	100	11	9	20	17	17	26
2.0–2.9	100	5	19	19	19	5	33
3.0–4.9	100	11	15	20	16	15	23
5.0–9.9	100	17	21	13	17	15	17
10.0–19.9	100	30	30	27	11	0	2
20.0 and over	100	79	17	4	0	0	0
Total	100	19	19	17	15	11	19

TABLE A-6

RELATION OF TURNOVER RATE TO INTEROCCUPATIONAL MOVEMENT,
LIFETIME WORK HISTORIES
(Sample 1)

Average Length of Jobs Held (Years)	Total	Number of Changes of Occupational Level (%)					
		0	1	2	3	4	5 or more
0.0–0.9	100	12	29	12	29	6	12
1.0–1.9	100	11	39	13	17	13	7
2.0–2.9	100	12	22	17	24	9	16
3.0–4.9	100	11	36	21	14	9	9
5.0–9.9	100	17	33	24	9	8	9
10.0–19.9	100	23	48	18	9	2	0
20.0 and over	100	54	34	8	4	0	0
Total	100	17	34	19	14	8	8

TABLE A–7

RELATION OF TURNOVER RATE TO GEOGRAPHICAL MOVEMENT, LIFETIME WORK HISTORIES

(Sample 1)

Average Length of Jobs Held (Years)	Total	Number of Changes of Locality (%)					
		0	1	2	3	4	5 or more
0.0–0.9	100	46	18	12	0	0	24
1.0–1.9	100	55	20	13	6	6	0
2.0–2.9	100	41	21	10	10	9	9
3.0–4.9	100	63	17	11	4	2	3
5.0–9.9	100	54	18	11	8	6	3
10.0–19.9	100	60	21	10	3	3	3
20.0 and over	100	80	8	8	0	0	4
Total	100	57	18	11	6	4	4

TABLE A–8

RELATION OF INTERINDUSTRY MOVEMENT TO INTEROCCUPATIONAL MOVEMENT, LIFETIME WORK HISTORIES

(Sample 1)

Number of Changes from One Industry to Another	Total	Number of Changes from One Occupational Level to Another (%)					
		0	1	2	3	4	5 or more
0	100	54	35	6	4	1	—
1	100	13	74	10	3	—	—
2	100	9	36	42	12	1	—
3	100	9	26	29	22	12	2
4	100	6	17	19	26	23	9
5 or more	100	2	13	12	23	13	37
Total	100	17	35	19	13	8	8

TABLE A-9

RELATION OF INTERINDUSTRY MOVEMENT TO INTEROCCUPATIONAL MOVEMENT, LIFETIME WORK HISTORIES

(Sample 2)

Number of Changes from One Industry to Another	Number of Changes from One Occupational Level to Another (%)						
	Total	0	1	2	3	4	5 or more
0	100	51	39	9	—	1	—
1	100	33	38	21	6	2	—
2	100	35	23	27	10	5	—
3	100	33	7	37	10	10	3
4	100	6	25	31	19	13	6
5 or more	100	8	8	33	33	18	—
Total	100	35	30	22	8	4	1

TABLE A-10a*

DIRECTION OF INTERINDUSTRY MOVEMENT, 1941

Industry from which Worker was Separated	Industry to which Worker Went (%)						
	Trade	Service	Trans-portation, etc.	Construction	Metal-working	Apparel	Other Manufacture
Wholesale and Retail Trade	—	18	4	0	41	5	16
Service Industries	9	—	2	3	52	3	15
Transportation, Communication, and Utilities	11	16	—	0	52	0	21
Construction	3	6	3	—	40	0	25
Metalworking	20	21	4	5	—	5	26
Apparel	7	20	0	0	41	—	19
Other Manufacture	10	15	2	2	56	0	—
Per cent of Area Employment, 1940	18	10	8	5	20	5	14

* The percentages in the rows of these tables do not total to 100, because not all industries in the area are included, and because some of the separated workers moved outside the area.

TABLE A–10b*

DIRECTION OF INTERINDUSTRY MOVEMENT, 1943

Industry from which Worker was Separated	Industry to which Worker Went (%)						
	Trade	Service	Trans-portation, etc.	Construction	Metal-working	Apparel	Other Manufacture
Wholesale and Retail Trade	—	13	5	2	38	3	16
Service Industries	16	—	3	2	46	3	17
Transportation, Communication, and Utilities	8	4	—	8	47	0	13
Construction	3	0	9	—	48	1	9
Metalworking	17	10	5	3	—	7	22
Apparel	6	7	1	0	48	—	28
Other Manufacture	12	9	5	3	47	7	—
Per cent of Area Employment, 1940	18	10	8	5	20	5	14

* The percentages in the rows of these tables do not total to 100, because not all industries in the area are included, and because some of the separated workers moved outside the area.

TABLE A–10c*

DIRECTION OF INTERINDUSTRY MOVEMENT, 1946

Industry from which Worker was Separated	Industry to which Worker Went (%)						
	Trade	Service	Trans-portation, etc.	Construction	Metal-working	Apparel	Other Manufacture
Wholesale and Retail Trade	—	15	3	1	19	3	20
Service Industries	13	—	5	2	17	6	14
Transportation, Communication, and Utilities	12	14	—	2	17	0	15
Construction	6	9	6	—	11	0	13
Metalworking	8	10	4	2	—	6	24
Apparel	7	9	2	0	28	—	18
Other Manufacture	12	8	6	4	27	6	—
Per cent of Area Employment, 1940	18	10	8	5	20	5	14

* The percentages in the rows of these tables do not total to 100, because not all industries in the area are included, and because some of the separated workers moved outside the area.

TABLE A–11a*

INTERCHANGE OF WORKERS BETWEEN SELECTED PAIRS OF INDUSTRIES, 1941

	Trade	Service	Trans-portation, etc.	Construction	Metal-working	Apparel	Other Manufacture
Trade	—	3.0	0.8	0.0	4.0	0.7	2.0
Service	—	—	0.5	0.9	9.0	1.1	3.0
Transportation, etc.	—	—	—	0.0	2.0	0.0	0.5
Construction	—	—	—	—	1.3	0.0	1.1
Metalworking	—	—	—	—	—	1.1	1.6
Apparel	—	—	—	—	—	—	0.5
Other Manufacture	—	—	—	—	—	—	—

* The figures in this Table, and those in Tables A-11b and A-11c below, show the number of people moving between each pair of industries, in both directions, reduced to a percentage of total employment in the two industries concerned.

TABLE A–11b

INTERCHANGE OF WORKERS BETWEEN SELECTED PAIRS OF INDUSTRIES, 1943

	Trade	Service	Trans-portation, etc.	Construction	Metal-working	Apparel	Other Manufacture
Trade	—	5.2	2.1	0.8	5.1	1.2	4.3
Service	—	—	1.1	0.6	4.3	1.2	4.8
Transportation, etc.	—	—	—	2.8	1.9	1.2	2.6
Construction	—	—	—	—	1.4	0.1	1.5
Metalworking	—	—	—	—	—	2.7	7.3
Apparel	—	—	—	—	—	—	4.0
Other Manufacture	—	—	—	—	—	—	—

TABLE A–11c

INTERCHANGE OF WORKERS BETWEEN SELECTED PAIRS OF INDUSTRIES, 1946

	Trade	Service	Trans-portation, etc.	Construction	Metal-working	Apparel	Other Manufacture
Trade	—	5.9	2.2	0.8	3.9	1.4	6.6
Service	—	—	4.0	1.5	4.4	2.9	5.2
Transportation, etc.	—	—	—	1.5	2.0	0.7	4.0
Construction	—	—	—	—	0.9	0.0	2.2
Metalworking	—	—	—	—	—	2.9	9.0
Apparel	—	—	—	—	—	—	3.5
Other Manufacture	—	—	—	—	—	—	—

TABLE A-12

ACTIVE FILE, PLACEMENTS, AND UNFILLED ORDERS AT THE LOCAL OFFICE OF THE STATE EMPLOYMENT SERVICE, 1944–1949

(Data for Chart 5, Chapter IV)

Year and Month	Active File (End of Month)	Placements During Month	Unfilled Orders (End of Month)	Year and Month	Active File (End of Month)	Placements During Month	Unfilled Orders (End of Month)
1944				*1947*			
Jan.	—	—	—	Jan.	5,134	1,510	1,052
Feb.	—	1,579	—	Feb.	4,237	1,214	1,034
March	974	1,736	—	March	3,487	1,492	1,402
April	895	1,419	—	April	4,010	1,544	1,379
May	1,057	1,669	3,501	May	4,184	1,451	1,239
June	1,069	1,917	3,406	June	4,888	1,393	886
July	973	1,677	2,832	July	5,788	1,427	766
Aug.	867	2,297	2,874	Aug.	5,520	1,192	1,114
Sept.	804	1,479	2,738	Sept.	3,692	1,578	1,238
Oct.	1,190	1,654	2,538	Oct.	3,461	1,765	1,372
Nov.	1,259	1,783	2,472	Nov.	2,994	1,467	1,269
Dec.	1,001	2,079	2,403	Dec.	3,309	1,305	869
1945				*1948*			
Jan.	1,381	2,705	2,506	Jan.	4,443	1,344	867
Feb.	1,211	2,530	3,095	Feb.	4,546	1,217	717
March	961	2,576	2,472	March	4,264	1,436	1,018
April	905	2,105	2,329	April	4,429	1,468	1,257
May	1,264	2,052	2,089	May	3,951	1,344	1,253
June	2,496	2,235	1,818	June	4,325	1,516	792
July	2,580	2,378	2,112	July	5,832	1,269	696
Aug.	4,736	1,750	2,455	Aug.	5,354	1,327	937
Sept.	5,643	1,070	2,863	Sept.	4,195	1,699	1,240
Oct.	6,141	1,401	2,335	Oct.	3,645	1,717	945
Nov.	7,922	1,387	1,972	Nov.	3,717	1,533	632
Dec.	7,622	1,121	1,931	Dec.	5,375	1,067	501
1946				*1949*			
Jan.	7,944	1,344	1,888	Jan.	6,308	1,009	407
Feb.	8,962	1,050	1,929	Feb.	8,293	916	459
March	9,228	1,282	1,680	March	10,768	1,184	530
April	11,216	1,155	1,884	April	10,494	1,053	559
May	11,222	1,235	1,909	May	10,592	1,059	454
June	6,428	1,208	1,875	June	12,620	1,527	420
July	6,225	1,446	1,651	July	12,822	1,063	540
Aug.	7,302	1,495	1,821	Aug.	11,244	1,717	488
Sept.	6,071	1,512	2,043	Sept.	9,054	2,446	515
Oct.	4,342	1,708	1,655	Oct.	7,971	2,241	425
Nov.	4,061	1,400	1,652	Nov.	8,874	1,281	339
Dec.	3,732	1,273	1,295	Dec.	9,317	815	355

TABLE A–13

FACTORS IN JOB SATISFACTION*

(%)

Factor	Left Last Job Because		Dissatisfied with Present Job Because		Satisfied with Present Job Because		Last 3 Jobs Rated "Good" or "Bad" Because (S2)		Int. in Transfer to Other Job in Plant Because (S2)		Would or Would Not Work in Other Specified Plants Because (S1)		What Makes a Job a "Good Job"? (S2)
	(S1)	(S2)	(S1)	(S2)	(S1)	(S2)	Good	Bad	Int.	Not Int.	Would Work	Would Not Work	
Wages	24	27	21	23	13	25	24	31	35	22	13	26	27
Physical Characteristics of the Job	23	22	17	15	10	12	18	36	16	15	12	26	21
Independence and Control	16	11	24	25	21	14	16	9	2	10	9	12	18
Job Interest	8	9	12	13	8	12	17	7	29	26	16	2	10
Fairness of Treatment	13	11	17	15	8	10	4	7	3	10	0	24	3
Relations with Fellow Workers	1	1	2	0	13	7	8	2	7	4	11	9	6
Steadiness of Work	0	0	0	0	9	10	3	3	2	4	0	0	3
Other	15	19	7	9	18	10	10	5	6	9	39	1	12
Total	100	100	100	100	100	100	100	100	100	100	100	100	100

* The symbols S1 and S2 refer to Samples 1 and 2 respectively.

TABLE A-14

PERCENTAGE INCREASE IN INCOME REQUIRED TO "LIVE COMFORTABLY," BY PRESENT FAMILY INCOME

(Sample 1)

Present Weekly Family Income (Dollars)	Size of Increase Required to "Live Comfortably" (%)							
	Total	No Increase	0–9%	10–19%	20–29%	30–39%	40–49%	50% and over
Less than 30	100	32	7	7	27	0	0	27
30–39	100	26	11	4	13	10	11	25
40–49	100	39	7	13	12	13	10	6
50–59	100	41	10	14	10	5	14	6
60–69	100	51	9	18	10	6	3	2
70–79	100	64	8	8	10	5	3	2
80 and over	100	79	7	0	0	7	0	7
Total	100	44	9	11	11	8	8	9

TABLE A-15

PROPORTION OF WORKERS REGARDING THEIR WAGE AS "FAIR" AND "UNFAIR," BY PRESENT WEEKLY EARNINGS

(Samples 1 and 2)

Present Weekly Earnings (Dollars)	Sample 1			Sample 2		
	Total (%)	Wage "Fair" (%)	Wage "Unfair" (%)	Total (%)	Wage "Fair" (%)	Wage "Unfair" (%)
Less than 30	100	67	33	100	50	50
30–39	100	62	38	100	40	60
40–49	100	61	39	100	67	33
50–59	100	72	28	100	75	25
60–69	100	73	27	100	91	9
70–79	100	83	17	100	80	20
80 and over	100	69	31	100	78	22
Total	100	70	30	100	75	25

TABLE A–16

RELATION OF PRESENT OCCUPATIONAL LEVEL OF RESPONDENT TO FATHER'S OCCUPATIONAL LEVEL AT TIME RESPONDENT BEGAN WORK

(Samples 1 and 2)

Occupational Level of Father (at Time Respondent Began Work)	Occupational Level of Respondent (Sample 1)				Occupational Level of Respondent (Sample 2)			
	Total	Sk.	Semisk.	Unsk.	Total	Sk.	Semisk.	Unsk.
Proprietor or Executive	100	43	40	17	100	35	59	6
Professional or Semi-professional	100	54	9	37	100	25	75	0
Clerical and Sales	100	38	31	31	100	45	44	11
Foreman	100	42	42	16	100	0	82	18
Skilled	100	50	32	18	100	33	62	5
Semiskilled	100	34	56	10	100	27	63	10
Unskilled	100	25	63	12	100	31	53	16
Service, Including Domestic Service	100	23	50	27	100	38	50	12
Farmer or Farm Laborer	100	38	31	31	100	22	56	22
Total	100	40	40	20	100	29	60	11

TABLE A–17

AGE DISTRIBUTION OF SAMPLES 1 AND 2, COMPARED WITH AREA LABOR FORCE, 1947

Age	Sample 1 (%)	Sample 2 (%)	Area Labor Force, 1947 (%)
14–24	6.3	17.5	19.1
25–44	46.1	65.9	45.6
45–64	40.9	15.4	30.5
65 and over	6.7	1.2	4.8
Total	100.0	100.0	100.0

TABLE A-18

OCCUPATIONAL DISTRIBUTION OF SAMPLES 1 AND 2, COMPARED WITH AREA LABOR FORCE, 1947

Occupational Level	Sample 1 (%)	Sample 2 (%)	Area Labor Force, 1947* (%)
Skilled	38	33	30
Semiskilled	41	57	49
Unskilled	21	10	21
Total	100.0	100.0	100.0

* This is a distribution of manual workers only. Service workers, exclusive of domestic servants, are included in the unskilled group. Data on the area labor force in Tables A-17 to A-19 are taken from Bureau of the Census, Series P-51, No. 4, "Labor Force Characteristics of the ——— Metropolitan District, April, 1947."

TABLE A-19

INDUSTRIAL DISTRIBUTION OF SAMPLE 1, COMPARED WITH AREA LABOR FORCE, 1940

Industry	Sample 1 (%)	Area Labor Force, 1940* (%)
Manufacturing	61	50
Construction	6	6
Transportation, Communication and Utilities	14	10
Wholesale and Retail Trade	7	22
Service Industries	12	12
Total	100.0	100.0

* This is a distribution of total employment in the five industry groups listed. These industries included in 1940 about 80% of the area labor force, and virtually all of the manual workers. The trade group includes a large white-collar segment, which accounts for it being underrepresented in our sample.

APPENDIX B Some Notes on Method

Discussion of methods has been held to a minimum in the body of this volume to avoid breaking the flow of the analysis. It is desirable now to say something more on this matter, both to aid the reader in evaluating the findings already presented, and to assist those who may wish to conduct similar studies in other areas.

This Appendix consists of three parts: (a) a description of the methods used in conducting the worker interviews, management interviews, union interviews, and area wage survey; (b) comments on types of work not done in this study but which might usefully be experimented with in future studies of other areas; (c) copies of the main questionnaires and interview schedules used in the study.

A. THE TECHNIQUES USED

In addition to the findings discussed in previous chapters, our study yielded as a byproduct many suggestions about what to do and what not to do in this kind of research. There are many things which we would have done differently had we known in advance all that we learned during three years of experimental investigation. It seems worth while to recount this experience, not just to document our findings, but also in order that later researchers may profit by our discoveries and our mistakes.

1. The Worker Interviews

Interviews with manual workers in the area absorbed more time and effort than any other phase of the study and yielded many of the most interesting conclusions. It will be useful to comment on three aspects of this work: the method of drawing the samples to be interviewed, the problems of conducting a successful interview, and the problems of coding and analyzing the results.

a. Sampling Methods

Two major groups of workers, referred to throughout this book as Samples 1 and 2, were interviewed during the study. Sample 1 was a cross section of all manual workers in the area. Both men and women were included, and workers in nonmanufacturing as well as manufacturing industries. Foremen and supervisors were excluded, as were clerical and other white-collar employees. The names of workers to be interviewed were drawn from the 1946 City Directory on a random basis, i.e., every *n*th name was selected throughout the book. The Directory listings indicate the individual's place of employment and usually the general nature of his work, so that manual occupations can be distinguished with reasonable precision. The 1946 Directory had certain limitations, however, with respect to coverage. Since listings for the Directory were taken in October, 1945, it did not include veterans who had not yet returned from war service or people who had left the city immediately after the end of the war because of postwar layoffs.

Sample 1 included 450 workers, or about 1 per cent of all manual workers in the area. The size of the group was determined by practical considerations of available time and funds, plus a calculation that a group of this size would yield adequate precision in primary tabulations. The characteristics of the workers in Sample 1 are compared with those of all workers in the area in Tables A-17 to A-19. It will be noted that the median age for Sample 1 is considerably above that for the area, due mainly to the exclusion of veterans already noted. For this and other reasons the sample also contains a bias in the direction of relatively immobile workers.

Since we were interested mainly in the nature of labor mobility, and particularly in voluntary movement from one job to another, we decided to draw a second sample made up exclusively of workers whose occupational listing in the 1947 Directory differed from their listing in the 1946 Directory or who were not listed in 1946 at all but were listed in 1947. These workers, in other words, had either returned from the service between October, 1945, and October, 1946 (the periods in which listings for the two directories were taken), or had gone to work for the first time, or had changed jobs during the period. Further, in order to provide a sharper focus in terms of industrial coverage, Sample 2 was limited to male workers currently employed in manufacturing industries.

The technique of selection was somewhat different from that for Sample 1. Every other page of the 1947 Directory was examined and male workers in manufacturing were checked. Where one of these workers was listed in a different job in 1946 or was not listed at all in 1946, his name was chosen. The names thus chosen, numbering about 2400, were then spotted on a block map of the city. The four hundred names desired for our sample were then selected, not by a sampling of individuals, but by a random sampling of blocks.

This block method of selection for Sample 2 was used because we had found during the work on Sample 1 that our interviewers spent an undue amount of time in simply trying to locate the interviewees. In many cases there was only one member of Sample 1 in a particular block. If that person was not at home on a particular evening the interviewer might have to travel some distance to the next person on the list, and often ended up by coming back without an interview. This mechanical difficulty was very much reduced, as we had expected, by the clustering of interviewees used in Sample 2. If one respondent was unavailable on a particular evening, it took little time for the interviewer to locate another person in the same block. We did not find that there was enough discussion of our interviews among respondents in the same neighborhood to interfere seriously with the reliability of the interviews.

The characteristics of the workers in Sample 2 are shown in Tables A-17 to A-19, and compared both with Sample 1 and with the area as a whole. It will be noted that the average age of Sample 2 is about ten years less than that of Sample 1, and that Sample 2 contains a considerably smaller proportion of skilled workers—28 per cent compared with 38 per cent in Sample 1. In view of these and other differences in the two groups, it was surprising to find how closely their responses agreed on most points. Numerous instances of such agreement have been noted in Chapters II–V above.

It should be noted that the number of interviews completed was in both samples considerably less than the number of names originally selected. There are two main reasons for this. First, there was a period of about eighteen months between the date at which the Directory listings were compiled and the date at which our interviewers called. This allowed time for a considerable number of people—7 per cent in Sample 1,

10 per cent in Sample 2—to leave the area, move to a new address in the area which could not be located, or die. Second, 5 per cent of those in Sample 1 and 3 per cent in Sample 2 either declined to be interviewed, could not be found at home after repeated visits, or were too inaccurate to give usable responses to the questions asked. The main effect of this shrinkage from the original samples is probably some under-representation of the most mobile elements in the labor force and of a group whose power of communication is impaired by low intelligence or other handicaps.

The deficiency in the samples would be serious if we were trying to reach quantitative conclusions about the behavior of the total labor force—for example, that a certain proportion of the labor force was unemployed in 1948, or that a certain percentage of workers in the city changed jobs during the year. Sampling errors are less serious for conclusions about workers' attitudes toward jobs and about typical practices of job hunting and general outlooks on the labor market. Somewhat greater precision could probably have been secured by using the block sampling technique of the Census Bureau, including all persons in the entire population in the selected blocks. For the kinds of questions we wanted to have answered, however, it is not certain that the gain in reliability would have been worth the increased cost of the more expensive procedure.

Samples 1 and 2 contained few unemployed workers because 1948 was a year of unusually high employment. During the first half of 1949, however, there was sufficient unemployment in the area so that it became feasible to explore a cross section of the unemployed. The best place at which to make contacts with this group was the local office of the State Employment Service. Sample 3, consisting of fifty unemployed manufacturing workers, was obtained by sitting in the Employment Service office for one week in April 1949 and interviewing workers after they had been interviewed by the regular placement staff of the service. Over half of the Service were most cooperative in passing workers on at the end of the regular interview, and the fact that our interview was conducted in the local office did not seem to prejudice the responses. Indeed, some workers told us things which, if reported back to Employment Service officials, might have led to cancellation or reduction of the worker's unemployment compensation benefits.

The chief limitation of this sample is that it included only workers using the Employment Service, which means mainly those currently in receipt of unemployment compensation benefits. It did not include many of the long-term unemployed who have exhausted their benefit rights or of workers not covered by the unemployment compensation system. This defect could not have been remedied, however, by supplementing the Employment Service sample by any other method relying mainly on the Service. The only way one could do a better job of sampling would be to take a cross section of the entire labor force during a period of substantial unemployment, in which case one would automatically obtain an adequate representation of unemployed workers.

4. Interviewing Technique

The interviews with members of Samples 1 and 2 were conducted in the workers' homes, and required usually between one and two hours to complete. We found that most workers can sustain a two-hour interview provided the interviewer establishes good rapport at the outset.

The technique used was that of a fixed-question, free-answer interview. The

13 per cent in Sample 2—to leave the area, move to a new address in the area which could not be located, or die. Second, 6 per cent of those in Sample 1 and 8 per cent in Sample 2 either declined to be interviewed, could not be found at home after repeated visits, or were too inarticulate to give usable responses to the questions asked. The main effects of this shrinkage from the original samples are probably some under representation of the most mobile elements in the labor force and of people whose power of communication is impaired by low intelligence or other handicaps.

This deficiency in the samples would be serious if we were trying to reach quantitative conclusions about the behavior of the total labor force—for example, that a certain proportion of the labor force was unemployed in 1947, or that a certain percentage of workers in the city changed jobs during the year. Sampling defects are less serious for conclusions about workers' attitudes toward past and present jobs, typical methods of job hunting, and general outlook on the labor market. Somewhat greater precision could probably have been secured by using the block sampling technique of the Census Bureau, including a precensus of the entire population in the selected blocks. For the kinds of questions we wanted to have answered, however, it is not certain that the gain in reliability would have been worth the added cost of the precensus procedure.

Samples 1 and 2 contained few unemployed workers because 1947 was a year of unusually high employment. During the first half of 1949, however, there was sufficient unemployment in the area so that it became feasible to explore a cross section of the unemployed. The best place at which to make contact with this group was clearly the local office of the State Employment Service. Sample 3, consisting of fifty unemployed manufacturing workers, was obtained by sitting in the Employment Service office for one week in April, 1949, and interviewing workers after they had been interviewed by the regular placement staff of the Service. The staff of the Service were most cooperative in passing workers on at the end of the regular placement interview, and the fact that our interview was conducted in the local office did not seem to prejudice the responses. Indeed, some workers told us things which, if reported back to Employment Service officials, might have led to cancellation or reduction of the worker's unemployment compensation benefits.

The chief limitation of this sample is that it included only workers using the Employment Service, which means mainly those in current receipt of unemployment compensation benefits. It did not include many of the long-term unemployed who have exhausted their benefit rights, or of workers not covered by the unemployment compensation system. This defect could not have been remedied, however, by sampling the Employment Service active file or by any other method relying mainly on the Service. The only way one could do a better job on this front would be to take a cross section of the entire labor force during a period of substantial unemployment, in which case one would automatically obtain an adequate representation of unemployed workers.

b. *Interviewing Technique*

The interviews with members of Samples 1 and 2 were conducted in the evening at the workers' homes, and required usually between one and two hours to complete. We found that most workers can sustain a two-hour interview provided the interviewer establishes good rapport at the outset.

The technique used was that of a fixed question, free-response interview. The

interviewers were provided with a list of key questions to be asked (see Schedules 1 and 2 below). Once the question had been raised, however, the worker was allowed to talk freely without any prompting by the interviewer. This was found to be more satisfactory than pinning the worker down to minute, specific answers as is sometimes done in attitude and public opinion surveys. It did mean that respondents spent a good deal of time talking about subjects which were irrelevant to the question asked; but embedded in the stream of irrelevancies would be solid pieces of pertinent material. This material, when screened out, seemed to give a more spontaneous indication of actual attitudes than would be secured from brief responses to detailed and highly restricted questions.

Interviewers were instructed to make no comments which might influence the respondent's answers. Certain devices were used, however, in order to encourage the respondent to talk as fully as possible on each subject: (a) An expectant pause by the interviewer after a question had been answered too briefly. This often made the respondent aware of the incompleteness of his answer and led him to say more. (b) Brief assenting comments, such as "That's very interesting," or "Oh, I see," frequently served to keep the conversation going. (c) In some cases the interviewer was able to draw out the respondent more fully by asking neutral questions such as, "That's very instructive, won't you tell me more about it?" or "Could you please explain that a little more?"

Note-taking during the interview was confined to a minimum in order not to restrain the free flow of discussion. Interviewers were required to prepare a full narrative report of the interview immediately after its completion, using the worker's own words as nearly as possible. These reports were later coded and transferred to punch cards for tabulation. In order to avoid bias in the reports, the questions themselves were not precoded nor did the interviewers know the coding system to be used in the final analysis.

The success of this whole procedure depends entirely on the quality of the interviewers, and securing a competent staff of interviewers proved to be the most difficult and important problem in the whole study. A good interviewer needs to understand the conceptual framework behind the questionnaire, he must be able to walk into a strange home and within five or ten minutes have the respondent talking freely to him, and he must be able to retain the details of a two-hour discussion sufficiently well that he can later sit down and reproduce it with a high degree of accuracy.

The last of these requirements is attained mainly through experience, and the first can be met by anyone of high intelligence after a brief training period. We found that the amount of previous training in the social sciences bore little relation to an interviewer's success. Students from the law school and other graduate schools of the University made as good interviewers as graduate students in economics or psychology. The rarest and most important qualification is the second—ability to establish good personal relations quickly and get the respondent talking freely. This quality seems to show no marked correlation with intelligence; some of our best students proved to be poor interviewers and had to be dropped. It seems rather to be a matter of personality and temperament, and a person without the right qualities of temperament cannot be turned into a satisfactory interviewer by any amount of training.

We found that women made as satisfactory interviewers as men, and that they had as good success with male respondents as with females. A considerable propor-

found the Negroes interviewed showed some discomfort [illegible] in response to our interviewers. This seemed to stem mainly from the fact that our interviewers were white, and suggests that in future studies it would be well to use Negro interviewers for interviews in Negro households. It is also important that workers with a poor command of the English language be interviewed by someone who speaks their tongue. If a third party sits in as interpreter, there are obvious possibilities of error and bias in the interview.

More generally, it is important that interviews be conducted with as little outside participation as possible by other members of the family. For example, if a man is interviewed with his wife present, he may be reluctant to disclose certain things about his job, such as his exact earnings. We also found a considerable tendency for wives to answer questions in place of the husband, or at least to prompt the answers, and [illegible] sometimes did this when husbands were being interviewed.

The best technique would doubtless be to interview the respondent in isolation and to record the complete interview mechanically, instead of relying on the interviewer's memory. It might be difficult to "sell" workers on a recording procedure, but the experiment would be worth making.

Other features of our interview procedure conformed to standard practice. Each schedule was pretested on workers not members of the sample, and revised in the light of this experience. Interviewers were also pretested, and those who did not reach reasonable proficiency by the second or third interview were dropped from the staff. After work on the sample itself had begun, the completed reports of each interview were carefully checked and any defects pointed out to the interviewer in question. In addition, a certain proportion of the interview reports, selected at random, were spot-checked by having a second interviewer visit the same individual. We did not, however, try to check workers' statements about their present jobs, their reasons for leaving previous jobs, and so on against the records of the companies concerned. We were interested mainly in determining what the worker thought about each matter rather than the objective facts of the situation.

Coding and Analysis

It has already been pointed out that the questions in the interview schedules were not precoded. We wished to avoid channeling the responses in predetermined directions, and believed that better results would be obtained if the categories to be used for analysis emerged directly from the data. The steps in the coding procedure were as follows:

1. After all interviews in a sample had been completed, we analyzed one quarter of them, selected at random, in order to determine the main kinds of response to each question. The responses which showed up most frequently became the categories to be used for coding of that question.

2. The most experienced and competent of our interviewers were selected to do the coding work. Four people worked on the coding of Sample 1. Only one was used for coding of Sample 2, clearly a preferable procedure in terms of uniformity of results.

3. The categories to be used were defined and explained in detail to each coder in order to make coding more uniform. After they began work the coded schedules were spot-checked in order to ensure that the coding system was being applied accurately and uniformly.

tion of the Negroes interviewed showed suspicion and resistance to our interviewers. This seemed to stem mainly from the fact that our interviewers were white, and suggests that in future studies it would be well to use Negro interviewers for interviews in Negro households. It is also important that workers with a poor command of the English language be interviewed by someone who speaks their tongue. If a third party sits in as interpreter there are obvious possibilities of error and bias in the interview.

More generally, it is important that interviews be conducted with as little participation as possible by other members of the family. For example, if a man is interviewed with his wife present, he may be reluctant to disclose certain things about his job, such as his exact earnings. We also found a considerable tendency for wives to answer questions in lieu of the husband, or at least to prompt his answers; and husbands sometimes did this when wives were being interviewed.

The best technique would doubtless be to interview the respondent in isolation and to record the complete interview mechanically instead of relying on the interviewer's memory. It might be difficult to "sell" workers on cooperating in this procedure, but the experiment would be worth making.

Other features of our interview procedures conformed to standard practice. Each schedule was pretested on workers not members of the sample, and revised in the light of this experience. Interviewers were also pretested, and those who did not show reasonable proficiency by the second or third interview were dropped from the staff. After work on the sample itself had begun the completed reports of each interview were carefully checked and any defects pointed out to the interviewer in question. In addition, a certain proportion of the interview reports, selected at random, were spot-checked by having a second interviewer visit the same individual. We did not, however, try to check workers' statements about their present jobs, their reasons for leaving previous jobs, and so on, against the records of the companies concerned. We were interested mainly in determining what the worker *thought* about a situation rather than the objective facts of the situation.

c. *Coding and Analysis*

It has already been pointed out that the questions in the interview schedules were not precoded. We wished to avoid channeling the responses in predetermined directions, and believed that better results would be obtained if the categories to be used for analysis emerged directly from the data. The steps in the coding procedure were as follows:

1. After all interviews in a sample had been completed, we analyzed one quarter of them, selected at random, in order to determine the main kinds of response to each question. The responses which showed up most frequently became the categories to be used for coding of that question.

2. The most experienced and competent of our interviewers were selected to do the coding work. Four people worked on the coding of Sample 1. Only one was used for coding of Sample 2—clearly a preferable procedure in terms of uniformity of results.

3. The categories to be used were defined and explained as clearly as possible to the people doing the coding. After they began work the coded schedules were spot-checked in order to ensure that the coding system was being applied accurately and uniformly.

4. The coded responses were then transferred to IBM punch cards for purposes of tabulation. For samples of this size machine tabulation proved much more economical than hand tabulation.

The most difficult coding problem arose on questions where respondents gave a variety of reasons for some attitude or action—for example, reasons for liking or disliking their present job. This presented two questions: first, *how many* of the reasons given should be coded and tabulated? Second, *which* reasons should be selected as most significant? Our general rule was to code no more than three elements in any response, mainly because few workers gave more than three reasons for any answer. Where a worker gave more reasons than this and it became necessary to select the three most significant items, this decision was made on the basis of the frequency with which a particular point was mentioned in the narrative report. Where the frequency was equal, the items mentioned first were selected for coding. This procedure doubtless involves some lack of accuracy, for the most significant element in a situation might emerge near the end of the discussion rather than at the beginning; but it seemed more reliable than any alternative procedure.

While this seemed to be the only feasible way of summarizing the great mass of our interview material, the reader should not take summary tabulations such as Table 14 in Chapter IV more seriously than they deserve. The material is essentially qualitative and any attempt to quantify it is suggestive rather than definitive. A real grasp of the attitudes and behavior involved comes only from going through the interview procedure oneself or, as second best, reading the full narrative reports of the interviews. This kind of knowledge, unfortunately, is not readily transmittable from one person to another; and much of the material presented in this book will be fully convincing only to people who have been through similar studies elsewhere.

2. Interviews with Management Officials

The first step on this phase of the study was to discuss our plans with the presidents of the local Chamber of Commerce and the local Manufacturers' Association. Out of these discussions emerged a four-man advisory committee of local business leaders with whom we consulted frequently over the course of the study. All our proposed questionnaires and procedures were fully discussed with this committee before being put into use. Members of the committee were most helpful in advising us on what kinds of material we would find in most companies, what kinds of question would be understood by management people, who to approach first in each company, and how to win their cooperation. Indeed, without this advice and without the general approval of the two leading business associations in the area we would have gotten very little information from management. It should be added that members of the advisory committee, while they were good enough to read and criticize drafts of our manuscript, never attempted to interfere in any way with objective analysis of the material.

Contact was established with some fifty manufacturing companies in the area. This included all companies with more than two hundred employees, and a small sample of those with less than two hundred employees. The companies studied employ about three quarters of all manufacturing workers in the area. The range of questions discussed in each company is shown in Schedules 4 and 5 below. We attempted to cover in as much detail as possible the wage system used by the company, the factors influencing specific changes in the plant wage level, the adjustment

of the firm in wage bargaining; the role of wage and labor conditions; the general personnel policies and hiring methods of the firm, its procedures for promotion and layoff, and the extent and channels of interplant movement of labor.

Most companies were visited five or six times during the course of the study, for interviews of one to two hours at a time. Interviews were normally with the president of the company, occasionally with the general manager or works manager. Because of the small scale and low mobility of most companies in the area, the chief executive of the company was readily available and is in close touch with day-to-day operations, so that it was not necessary to canvass numerous company executives in order to answer our questions. In some cases the president called in the personnel manager or plant superintendent while we were in conference, in order to amplify or check his own statements. Most companies in the area are so small that the personnel manager does only routine employment interviewing and has no policy-making function.

Before going out to interview a company official, we sent him an outline of the matters to be discussed that day, drawn from Schedules 4 and 5. This had the disadvantage of giving an executive opportunity to prepare a public relations statement on each point if he wished to do so. It had the great advantage, however, of setting the executive at his ease about the interview, of allowing opportunity for desirable advance preparation, and of focusing the discussion while avoiding the undesirable features of a formal questionnaire. On the whole, we found the technique very serviceable.

After completing an interview, we immediately dictated a summary of it, as close to verbatim form as possible, and mailed it back to the person interviewed for checking. This enabled us to correct inaccuracies, gather additional information on some points, and also served a useful purpose in demonstrating to management that we had grasped their reasoning and reported it accurately. All of the management interviewing was done by Dr. Shister, Mrs. [illegible], and myself. This is skilled work which cannot safely be delegated to an inexperienced person.

Our experience in talking with management people suggests two conclusions concerning research method. First, the best results are obtained from questions which relate to concrete events in the quite recent past. Management can say a good deal about the considerations behind a general wage increase made two months ago. They cannot, however, say anything very useful about an event which happened five years ago, nor can they give useful answers to abstract questions such as "What are the main factors which you take into account in deciding on general wage changes?" Confronted with a question of this type the executive retreats to symbols and rationalizations. Second, discussions with management people yield increasing returns over the course of time. In general, executives talked more freely and gave more meaningful answers on the third or fourth visit than on the first visit. Securing useful information depends largely on establishing a relation of personal confidence between interviewer and respondent, and this comes only slowly with the passage of time and with repeated personal contacts.

3. Interviews with Union Officials

We made contact with all of the unions represented in the manufacturing plants included in our study, and also with a number of unions in nonmanufacturing industries. The objective was to explore union objectives and strategy in wage negotiations

of the firm to wage increases, the role of wages in labor recruitment, the general recruitment tactics and hiring methods of the firm, its procedures for promotion and layoff, and the extent and channels of intraplant movement of labor.

Most companies were visited five or six times during the course of the study, for interviews of one to two hours at a time. Interviews were normally with the president of the company, occasionally with the general manager or works manager. Because of the small scale and local ownership of most companies in the area, the chief executive of the company was readily available and in intimate touch with day-to-day operations, so that it was not necessary to canvass numerous company executives in order to answer our questions. In some cases the president asked the personnel manager or plant superintendent to be present at our interviews in order to supplement his own statements. Most plants in the area are so small, however, that the personnel manager does only routine employment interviewing and has no policy-making functions.

Before going out to interview a company official, we sent him an agenda of the matters to be discussed that day, drawn from Schedules 4 and 5. This has the disadvantage of giving an executive opportunity to prepare a public relations statement on each point if he wishes to do so. It has the great advantage, however, of setting the executive at his ease about the interviewer's intentions, allowing opportunity for desirable advance reflection, and focussing the discussion while avoiding the undesirable features of a formal questionnaire. On the whole, we found the technique very serviceable.

After completing an interview, we immediately dictated a transcript of it in as close to verbatim form as possible and mailed this back to the person interviewed for checking. This enabled us to correct inaccuracies, elicited additional information on some points, and also served a useful purpose in demonstrating to management that we had grasped their reasoning and reported it accurately. All of the management interviewing was done by Dr. Shister, Mrs. Calsoyas, and myself. This is skilled work which cannot safely be delegated to an inexperienced person.

Our experience in talking with management people suggests two conclusions concerning research method. First, the best results are obtained from questions which relate to concrete events in the quite recent past. Management can say a good deal about the considerations behind a general wage increase made two months ago. They cannot, however, say anything very useful about an event which happened five years ago; nor can they give useful answers to abstract questions such as "What are the main factors which you take into account in deciding on general wage changes?" Confronted with a question of this type, the executive retreats to symbols and rationalizations. Second, discussions with management people yield increasing returns over the course of time. In general, executives talked more freely and gave us more significant answers on the third or fourth visit than on the first visit. Securing useful information depends largely on establishing a relation of personal confidence between interviewer and respondent, and this comes only slowly with the passage of time and with repeated personal contacts.

3. Interviews with Union Officials

We made contact with all of the unions represented in the manufacturing plants included in our study, and also with a number of unions in nonmanufacturing industries. The objective was to explore union objectives and strategy in wage negotiations,

and the circumstances surrounding specific wage settlements in the recent past. Discussions were held with the official in charge of negotiations on the union side—the local president, business agent, chairman of the negotiating committee, or international representative as the case might be.

Little need be said of this phase of the study, since the methods used were broadly similar to those used with management officials. An initial approach was made to the top AFL and CIO officials in the area, who facilitated our contact with individual locals. With this introduction, and with the usual promise that replies would be kept confidential, we found most local officials and international representatives willing to talk very frankly about their operations. As in the case of management people, we found that questions had to be presented very concretely and with reference to some recent situation in order to secure useful answers. As in the case of management, all interviews were written up immediately and sent back to the person interviewed for comment and correction.

4. Wage-Employment Survey of Manufacturing Plants

A statistical questionnaire on wages, employment, and labor turnover over the years 1940–48 was distributed to all the manufacturing companies cooperating in the study (see Schedule 6). Because of deficiencies of record-keeping in the smaller companies, and because of the difficulty of persuading some companies to do the amount of work required by the questionnaire, we received only twenty-six usable returns. The main results have been analyzed in Chapter VII.

This phase of the study presented more technical difficulties than any other. Some of the problems, well known to wage statisticians, should be noted here for the benefit of others who may wish to work on the wage structure of local areas:

a. Many firms do not keep good summary records of wages and employment, particularly for back years. Small firms are particularly deficient in this respect. An area wage survey is thus likely to end up as a survey of larger companies in the area and, since wage level and size of firm are strongly correlated, this means that one is getting only the upper portion of the wage range in the area.

b. There is no uniformity at all among employers in their interpretation of apparently simple terms. Not only must the terms used in the questionnaire be defined very carefully, but the investigator himself must visit each plant, explaining the meaning of the various terms, and make sure that the questionnaire has been completed in accordance with instructions. We spent a good deal of time in such visits, and without them the returns would have been entirely unusable.

c. It is desirable to obtain the basic aggregates required and then calculate ratios between them rather than leave these ratios to be calculated by the company. If derived figures are calculated by the company, there are almost certain to be differences in the methods used by different companies which impair the comparability of the results. Thus, one should obtain total employment, total accessions, and total separations during a period, from which turnover ratios can be calculated. Again, one should obtain total payroll, employment, and man-hours worked, and make one's own calculation of average hourly and weekly earnings. Ideally, straight-time hours should be separated from overtime hours, but few of the companies we studied were able to provide this information.

d. Proper comparison of the rates paid by different companies for what purports to be the same job is extremely difficult. Few occupations are found in enough com-

grades or subject to seniority [illegible] etc. If the job is [illegible] on a time basis in some plants and on an incentive basis in others, wage comparisons are meaningless. Actual job duties may vary widely, despite similarity of job titles and, while one can read detailed company specifications of job duties in each company, there is no quantitative method of adjusting the wage comparisons to take account of this factor. Because of these difficulties and others, we finally decided to abandon our attempt at occupational wage comparisons even within manufacturing.

6. We did compare the entrance rates for inexperienced workers in all area companies. While this sort of comparison is not open to all the objections just cited, it is still subject to some ambiguities. In some plants in the area, the starting rate is identical with the rate for the lowest job classification in the plant; in other plants it is a few cents below the lowest rated job. In most plants a new employee [illegible] at the starting rate for a fixed period, in others for [illegible], and in other plants he is quickly [illegible] promoted to a higher job. In spite of these defects, we felt that the comparison was more useful and meaningful than that for any specific job titles.

7. Employers' statements about general wage increases need to be analyzed as precisely as possible. If the increase was made on a percentage basis, it is necessary to calculate the cents-per-hour equivalent, and vice versa. One needs to make sure that the increase was actually applied uniformly to all job classifications. If changes were made in fringe payments as well, it is desirable to obtain the employer's estimate of the cents-per-hour equivalent of these changes so that one can calculate the total "package" involved.

We did not handle all of these problems as adequately as we would have liked, partly because some of them did not reveal themselves until we were well into our survey and it was too late to change course. We mention them here so that others may be forewarned and may make plans to cope with these difficulties before starting work.

SUGGESTIONS FOR FURTHER RESEARCH

My first suggestion would be that the techniques which have been found useful in this study might well be tried out in other areas, either as they stand or with necessary modification for local circumstances. In addition, however, I would hope that future studies might go beyond this one in a number of directions. This study opened up numerous areas which we were not able to explore adequately, but which are highly important for an understanding of labor market behavior.

1. Analysis of Workers' Psychological Characteristics

The worker interviews revealed numerous differences of behavior which could not be entirely explained by objective circumstances. Some workers had done much more voluntary shifting than others in the same age and skill classification. Some showed a high propensity to further [illegible], while others revealed very little. Some had worked a considerable distance up the occupational ladder, while others remained about where they had started. The interviews suggest that these behavior differences stem partly from differences of intelligence, physical vitality, personality [illegible], and other personal characteristics of the individual.

It would be interesting to make a study in which, in addition to the kind of information we obtained, the worker would be put through a series of psychological tests. The hypothesis would be that the test results would show a correlation with mobility

panies in an area to permit calculation of averages, dispersion, etc. If the job is paid on a time basis in some plants and an incentive basis in others, rate comparisons are meaningless. Actual job duties may differ widely despite similarity of job titles and, while one can and should obtain a specification of job duties from each company, there is no quantitative method of adjusting the wage comparisons to take account of this factor. Because of these difficulties and others, we finally decided to abandon any attempt at occupational wage comparisons even within manufacturing.

e. We did compare the entrance rates for inexperienced workers in different companies. While this sort of comparison is not open to all the objections just noted, it is still subject to some ambiguities. In some plants in the area, the starting rate is identical with the rate for the lowest job classification in the plant; in other cases, it is a few cents below the lowest rated job. In some plants a new employee stays at the starting rate for a few weeks, in others for several months, and in other plants indefinitely unless promoted to a higher job. In spite of these defects, we felt that the comparison was more clear-cut and useful than that for any specific job title.

f. Employers' statements about general wage increases need to be pinned down as precisely as possible. If the increase was made on a percentage basis it is necessary to calculate the cents-per-hour equivalent, and vice versa. One needs to make sure that the increase was actually applied uniformly to all job classifications. If changes were made in fringe payments as well, it is desirable to obtain the approximate cents-per-hour equivalent of these changes so that one can estimate the total "package" involved.

We did not handle all of these problems as adequately as we would have liked, partly because some of them did not reveal themselves until we were well into our survey and it was too late to change course. We mention them here so that others may be forewarned and may make plans to cope with these difficulties before setting to work.

B. SUGGESTIONS FOR FURTHER RESEARCH

My first suggestion would be that the techniques which have been found useful in this study might well be tried out in other areas, either as they stand or with necessary modification for local circumstances. In addition, however, I would hope that future studies might go beyond this one in a number of directions. This study opened up numerous vistas which we were not able adequately to explore, but which seem highly important for an understanding of labor market behavior.

1. Analysis of Workers' Psychological Characteristics

The worker interviews revealed numerous differences of behavior which could not be entirely explained by objective circumstances. Some workers had done much more voluntary shifting than others in the same age-and-skill classification. Some showed a high propensity to further movement, while others revealed very little. Some had worked a considerable distance up the occupational ladder, while others remained about where they had started. The interviews suggest that these behavior differences stem partly from differences of intelligence, physical vitality, personality structure, and other personal characteristics of the individual.

It would be interesting to make a study in which, in addition to the kind of information we obtained, the worker would be put through a series of psychological tests. The hypothesis would be that the test results would show a correlation with mobility

rates and other indicators of labor market behavior. This sort of work would call for use of trained clinical psychologists as interviewers and would require spending much more time with each worker than we did. There would also be a difficult problem of selecting appropriate tests and judging their validity. It seems likely, however, that this approach would yield significant results and would well repay the cost involved. Without it, there seems no possibility of giving a satisfactory explanation of the personal incidence of mobility.

2. The Labor Supply Situation of High-Wage and Low-Wage Companies

Our discussions with employers, officials of the public employment service, and others in the area left us with a strong impression that low-wage manufacturing plants have a considerably harder time in recruiting and retaining workers than do high-wage plants. We were not able in the time available, however, to secure much quantitative evidence in support of this impression. It would seem very useful to make a study in which, after identifying a few plants at the top of the area wage structure and a few at the bottom, the two groups of plants would be compared on such points as:

a. Number of applicants for work (relative to size of the plant labor force) and personal characteristics of these applicants.

b. Percentage of workers offered jobs with the company who refuse the offer.

c. Personal characteristics of the workers accepting jobs with the company.

d. Personal characteristics of the entire plant labor force, with especial attention to any possible indicators of labor efficiency.

e. Number and characteristics of workers quitting their jobs voluntarily, and purported reasons for quitting.

f. Percentage of job vacancies listed at the public employment service; number and characteristics of workers referred to the company by the public employment service.

g. Recruitment tactics other than use of the public employment service.

h. Hiring requirements of the company for various job classifications.

i. Average length of time between appearance of a vacancy in the plant and filling of the vacancy.

Careful comparison of even a half-dozen plants on these points might be very illuminating. The most significant results would probably be obtained on points b, c, d, f, and h. My hypotheses on these points would be that the low-wage companies have a higher percentage of their job offers refused, that the quality of those who accept is lower, that the quality of the entire plant labor force is consequently lower, that the low-wage companies list a higher percentage of their vacancies at the public employment service but receive relatively few and poor referrals, and that their hiring requirements are perforce lower than those of the high-wage companies.

3. Intensive Case Studies Within Individual Companies

In the course of trying to get a birds-eye view of the labor market as a whole we were not able to go very thoroughly into the operation of particular enterprises. Over the course of the study, however, we became convinced that it would be fruitful to dig intensively into individual companies on such matters as:

a. The determinants of management's wage decisions, particularly decisions concerning the general wage level of the plant. Our management interviews suggest that wage decisions are intimately related to pricing, sales estimates, financial manage-

ment, and other aspects of the business, and cannot be understood in isolation. Even if one is interested mainly in wages, therefore, it seems necessary to make a broad attack on the economics of the enterprise as a whole. One must understand management's general objectives and strategy in order to understand how wage levels fit into this strategy—sometimes, to be sure, as a minor element in the total picture.

b. The extent and determinants of intraplant movements of labor. As the walls around individual enterprises grow higher, intraplant movement becomes relatively more important. It would be interesting to sample the work force of an enterprise, examine the jobs held by these workers since joining the company, inquire into their interest in and expectation of future promotions within the plant, and explore the limits to intraplant promotion set by technology, management policies, and collective bargaining provisions. The one case study of this sort which we completed (see Chapter V) was very suggestive. Further work of this sort should help to define more clearly the way in which the average worker thinks of occupational progress, and also the objective limitations on such progress.

c. The effect of wage incentive systems on worker effort and output. Existing wage theory is largely the theory of hourly wage rates. A theory of incentive rates and earnings remains to be written. As a basis for such a theory, we need to know much more about workers' output reactions under incentive systems. This requires careful quantitative work on the dispersion of individual output rates within groups of workers on individual incentives, the behavior of these individual output rates over the course of time under substantially unchanged conditions, and the reaction of output rates to important changes—in general wage level of the plant, in hours of work, in work methods, in prospects for layoff or continued employment, or in the structure of the incentive system itself.

4. Additional Work on Nonmanufacturing Industries

This study was focussed entirely on manual labor and, within manual labor, largely on manufacturing establishments. It was noted in Chapter II, however, that there is much movement of manual workers between manufacturing and nonmanufacturing jobs. One suspects also that there is considerable movement from manual to white-collar occupations or, in any event, considerable competition between the two types of work for young people entering the labor market. This underlines the desirability of a more comprehensive study which would include interviews with white-collar as well as manual workers (perhaps even with the self-employed and with small proprietors), collection of wage information for a wide range of clerical as well as manual occupations, and examination of wage determination and hiring techniques in nonmanufacturing industries. Such an ambitious project would probably be feasible only in a relatively small city. If it could be done, however, it would yield valuable information on many matters with respect to which the present study must necessarily remain silent.

C. INTERVIEW SCHEDULES AND QUESTIONNAIRES

A brief comment on each of these schedules may be helpful to anyone interested in doing similar work elsewhere.

Schedule 1: This was used with our first worker sample, which was a cross section of all manual workers in the area. The weakest part of this schedule is Section B. Questions B.2.a., B.3.b., and B.3.d vielded suggestive results. Most of the other ques-

tions in Section B yielded relatively little, however, and were abandoned in Schedule 2. Schedule 1 was also somewhat longer than it should have been. Anyone who has not tried to record an employment history should be warned that this is a very time-consuming matter, since it is important to get an accurate accounting of all time since the person began work, including periods unemployed or out of the labor force.

Schedule 2: This was used with our second worker sample, consisting of male workers in manufacturing who had changed jobs within the previous year. It reflects our experience with Schedule 1 and is a briefer, tighter, generally more satisfactory questionnaire. Note that instead of obtaining a complete employment history we asked a series of questions about each job held since January 1, 1940. The interviewer was required to turn in one of these sheets for each job held by the worker since that time.

Schedule 3: This was used with a sample of unemployed workers, and proved generally satisfactory.

Schedule 4: This was used with some sixty manufacturing employers in the city.

Schedule 5: This was used with the same group of employers at a later date. It attempts to go more thoroughly into some of the questions raised in Schedule 4, Section D, and also to cover some additional issues which emerged as the study proceeded. Schedules 4 and 5 were pretested on a few cooperative employers and the questions which appear in them are, I think, the right questions to ask on these points. The difficulties which we encountered in securing answers, discussed briefly in Chapter VI and earlier in this Appendix, seem to be inherent in any investigation of managerial practices.

Schedule 6: This was used to secure wage and employment information from twenty-six of the larger manufacturing companies in the area. The apparent simplicity of this questionnaire conceals numerous technical difficulties (see the discussion in Section A of this Appendix, and also the instruction sheet attached to the questionnaire).

SCHEDULE 1

A. Occupational Choices

1. *Introduction*
   a. What kind of work are you doing now, where?
   b. How long have you been there?

2. *Choice of present job (if after August 1, 1945)*
   a. What did you do before, where?
   b. How did you happen to leave that job?
   c. How did you find out about your present job? Did anyone speak for you and if so, who?
   d. Did you have any other chances besides this one and if so, how did you happen to pick this job?
   e. How much did you know about the job before you took it?
   Kind of work ________ Wages ________ Conditions ________
   Steadiness ________ Chance of advancement ________
   f. Has it worked out as well as you expected?

3. Chances for advancement

a. Have you had any changes of work since you came to this company?
If so, have these changes been for the better?

b. Do you expect to go on to a better job with the company?
If "Yes," specify the job and why it is "better." If "No," give reasons.

4. Potential mobility within the area

a. Do you expect to stay with the company? Yes ________ No ________
If "Yes," what in particular makes you want to stick with the company?
If "No," what makes you feel this way? What are your plans for finding other work?

b. Supposing you were out of a job, how would you go about finding another?

c. Where would you try to get in first?

d. Are there any places where you wouldn't want to work? What makes you feel this way?

e. Do you know about any other plants that have jobs in your line of work?
If so, *what* do you know about them?

f. How do you find out about jobs and wages in other plants?

5. Geographical mobility

a. Do you know anything about jobs and wages in any city besides X?
If so, how did you hear about them?

b. Is there any place you would rather work than X?

c. Suppose you were offered a job somewhere else in the same state, a job just like the one you have now. How much more money would you have to get to make it worth while for you to move?

6. Occupational aspirations

a. If you had your choice, what kind of work would you most like to do?
Why?

b. Do you think there is any chance to get into that sort of work?

c. What would you like your children to do?

7. Choice of first job

a. When did you go to work and how did you happen to start work at that time?

b. What was your first regular job and how did you get it?

c. Did you consider taking any other jobs?
If "Yes," what were they and why did you pick this one?

d. How much did you know about the job before you took it?
Kind of work ________ Wages ________ Conditions ________
Steadiness ________ Chances of advancement ________

e. How did it work out? Did it lead to anything better?

f. When you were in school, what did you want to do? What did your parents want you to do?

B. Wages and Family Income

1. Response to wage incentives (to be used only for workers on incentives)

a. How are the rates set? Do you think they are set fairly?

b. How much do you make most weeks? ______ High ________ Low ________
Suppose you could be absolutely sure the rate wouldn't be cut. How much more could you turn out?

c. What is the most that anybody ever makes on your job?
What is the least that anybody makes?
Do you think there should be this much difference between men's earnings?

d. Would you rather work on a straight hourly rate?
If you could make what you're making now?
If you made less? How much less?

2. *Wage and income standards*

a. Do you think you are getting a fair wage for what you are doing?
What makes you feel that way? How much do you think you should get?

b. Are you doing any extra work besides your regular job? If so, give details.
How much of a raise on your regular job would you have to get to give up this extra work?

c. How much money does your family get besides what you earn? ________
Altogether, then, you have $________ a week to live on?
Are you able to save anything on this?
How much do you think a family your size *should* have to live comfortably and without worry? ________

d. Is your wife working?
If "No," when and why did she stop?
If "Yes," would she stop working if your pay was raised?
How much? ________

3. *Hypothetical choices*

a. How many hours a week do you work? ______
How many would you like to work? ______
(Specify whether overtime pay is included.)
If your pay was 10% higher, would you want to work more, same, or fewer hours?
If your pay was 10% lower, would you want to work more, same, or fewer hours?

b. Suppose wages are being raised in your plant. Here are two men, one getting $1.00 an hour, another $1.50 an hour. Should they both get 10 cents an hour, or should the low man get 10 cents and the high man 15 cents?

c. Suppose you were offered either of two jobs; one pays $1.00 an hour with no chance of getting ahead; the other starts at $.80 an hour but there is a fifty-fifty chance that within a year you could work up to a job paying $1.20 an hour. Which would you take?

d. Suppose you had a choice on your present job of getting a wage increase or getting a guarantee of steady work right through the year: which would you take?
(Point at which he would take the wage increase ______.)

e. Do you have a paid vacation? How long is it?______
(i. If he has one, would he give it up for a compensating wage increase?
ii. If he has no vacation, would he "buy" one week or two weeks by taking an equivalent reduction in wages?)

EMPLOYMENT HISTORY

(Start from the present and work back. Note periods of unemployment with dates as they occur in the job history. Note also periods out of the labor market with dates and reason.)

City	Company	Industry or Product	Job Description	Occup. Code	Started	Left

Which of these jobs did you like best? Why?

FACE-SHEET

1. Present job

Employer ______________ Industry or product ______________
Date hired ______________ Job ______________
Earnings at start Weekly $______ Hours______ Hourly $______
Earnings at present Weekly $______ Hours______ Hourly $______

2. Last previous job (if required)

Employer ______________ Industry or product ______________
Job ______________
Earnings at time of leaving Weekly $______ Hours______ Hourly $______

3. Personal and family data

Sex ______ Date of birth ______ Place of birth ______________
S, M, W, D.______________ White or colored ______________
Dependents ______________
Date of marriage ______ Wife's (or husband's) place of birth ______________
Father's place of birth ______________ Mother's place of birth ______________
Father's occupation (at time interviewee began work)______________
Present occupations of sisters and brothers: ______________
Education: grade school ______ high school ______ age at leaving ______
Date came to X ______ Years cont. residence ______ Own home?______
Union member? ______ Years union membership ______________
How far do you live from work? ______ How do you get to work?______
______________ How long does it take you to get from home to work? ______________
Have you any relatives working in the same plant? If so, indicate number and relationship. ______________
Have you other close friends in the plant? If so, specify. ______________
Do you think you would stay on the job if your friends (or relatives) left?______

Employment of other family members (earnings required only for children at home):

Wife __________ Occupation __________ Weekly earnings ________
Child __________ Occupation __________ Weekly earnings ________
Child __________ Occupation __________ Weekly earnings ________
Child __________ Occupation __________ Weekly earnings ________

SCHEDULE 2

1. *Introduction*
   a. What kind of work are you doing now, where?
   b. How long have you been there?
   c. Have you done the same kind of work ever since you came to the company? If not, specify changes.
2. *Employment history* (see attached sheets)
3. *Factors in job satisfaction*
   a. Do you expect to stay with the company?
   What makes you feel that way?
   If answer is "No," are you looking around for other work now?
   If so, how? If not, why not?
   b. Do you think you are getting a fair wage for what you are doing?
   What makes you feel that way?
   How much do you think you should get?
   c. Is there any other job in the company which you would rather have than your present job?
   If so, why? If not, why not?
   Do you think you could do this job?
   What do you think are your chances of getting it?
   d. What do you think are the main things a job should have to make it a good job?
   e. If you had your choice, what kind of work would you most like to do? Why?
4. *Choice of first job*
   a. When did you go to work?
   How did you happen to start work at that time?
   b. What was your first regular job?
   How did you get it?
   c. Did you look around for any other jobs?
   If "Yes," why did you pick this one?
   If "No," why not?
   d. How did it work out?
   Would you pick the same job if you had it to do over again? Why?
   e. When you were in school, what did you want to do? Why?
   What did your parents want you to do? Why?
5. *Questions for unemployed workers*
   a. Are you looking for a job now? If so, how? What kind of job? Why this particular kind?

b. Have you found any jobs that you did not take? If so, why did you not take them? How did you find them?

c. Have you found the State Employment Service helpful or not? Why?

Face Sheet

Present occupation__________ Present industry__________
Present weekly earnings__________ Hours__________ Hourly earnings__________
Date of birth__________ Place of birth__________ White or colored__________
S, M, W, D__________ No. of dependents__________
Father's employment (at time interviewee began work)
Occupation__________ Industry __________
Present employment of sisters and brothers
Occupation__________ Industry __________
Occupation__________ Industry __________
Occupation__________ Industry __________
Present employment of wife
Occupation__________ Industry __________
Present employment of employed children
Occupation__________ Industry __________
Occupation__________ Industry __________
Occupation__________ Industry __________
Education: grade school__________ high school__________ age at leaving__________
Vocational training: type__________ trade__________ years__________
Date came to X__________ Years cont. residence__________ Own home?__________
Union member?__________ Years union membership__________

Employment Record

(Separate sheet to be completed for each job held since Jan. 1, 1940.)

a. Dates__________ Co.__________ Location__________ Industry__________
Work assignments (list in chronological order work assignment held during employment with the company). Were the changes for the better? If so, why? If not, why?

b. How did you get the job? Did you shop around for other jobs? If not, why not? Did you go to the State Employment Service? Why? If not, why not?

c. Would you say it was a good job? Just fair? Poor? Why?

d. How did you happen to leave?

e. Note here any lapse of time between this job and the next, and how this time was spent.

SCHEDULE 3

1. Where did you work last?
   What kind of work were you doing?

2. How did you happen to leave?
   How long ago was that?

3. If answer to 2 is "laid off," would you like to go back to the same company if you had a chance?
   Do you think there is any chance of the company calling you back?

4. Have you done any looking around for a new job?
   If "No," why not? If "Yes," what have you done?
   Have you had any offers?

5. What kind of work would you most like to get?

6. If you couldn't get this, what other kinds of work would you be willing to take?

7. What is the lowest wage you would work for?

8. Would you take a job if it meant moving away from X? What about living in X and traveling to some other town to work?

PERSONAL DATA:

Years' service with last employer________________________
Earnings at time of leaving: hourly__________ weekly__________
Drawing unemployment compensation? How long__________ Rate_____
Sex__________ Age__________ Dependents__________

SCHEDULE 4

STUDY OF WAGE AND EMPLOYMENT PRACTICES

Note: This is not a questionnaire. It is an agenda for the discussion which you will have with our staff representative. It is sent you in the belief that advance reflection on these points will shorten the discussion and conserve your time. The information you provide on these subjects will be treated as strictly anonymous and confidential.

A. KIND OF WAGE SYSTEM USED

1. *Organization for handling wages*
   Responsibility for setting individual job rates and piece prices
   Responsibility for decisions on general wage changes
   Responsibility for negotiating with the union (if a union exists)

2. *Wage structure of the plant*
   Use made of job rating
   Kind of incentive system used (if any)
   The problem of "loose" incentive rates
   The problem of keeping earnings of incentive workers in line with those of hourly rated workers
   Are general wage changes made on a cents-per-hour or a percentage basis?
   How are they applied to incentive jobs?

B. FACTORS AFFECTING DECISIONS TO CHANGE WAGES

1. *Wage changes made since beginning of 1946*
   When were general changes made, and what were the circumstances?

2. *Factors influencing wage decisions*
   Importance attached to wage changes by other X companies
   Importance of wage changes by competitors outside X

4. Have you had any [illegible] for a new job?
If "no," why not? If "yes," what have you done?
Have you had any offers?

5. What kind of work would you most like to do?

6. If you couldn't get this, what other kinds of work would you be willing to take?

7. What is the lowest wage you would work for?

8. Would you take a job if it meant moving away from X? What about living in X and traveling to some other town to work?

Personal Data

Year of leaving the last employer
Earnings at time of leaving [illegible] ______ week
Drawing unemployment compensation? How long? ______ Rate ______
Sex ______ Age ______ Residence ______

SCHEDULE 4

Survey of Wage and Employment Practices

Note: This is not a questionnaire. It is an agenda for the discussion which you will have with our field representative. It is our belief that advance reflection on these points will shorten the discussion and conserve your time. The information you provide on these subjects will be treated as strictly anonymous and confidential.

A. Kind of Wage System Used

1. Organization for handling wages
Responsibility for setting individual job rates and piece prices
Responsibility for decisions on general wage changes
Responsibility for negotiating with the union (if a union exists)

2. Wage structure of the plant
Use made of job rating
Kind of incentive system used (if any)
The problem of "loose" incentive rates
The problem of keeping earnings of incentive workers in line with those of hourly rated workers
Are general wage changes made on a cents-per-hour or a percentage basis?
How are they applied to incentive jobs?

B. Factors Affecting Decisions on Changes in Wages

1. Wage changes since [illegible]
When were general changes made and what were the circumstances?

2. Factors influencing wage changes
Importance of desire to match changes by other X companies
Importance of wage changes by competitors outside X

Importance attached to the labor supply situation—turnover, rumors of unfilled jobs, etc.?

Importance of the financial position of the company, method of estimating how much of a wage level the company can stand?

Which of these factors is most important at present?

Which was most important before the war?

7. *Effects of collective bargaining on wage increases?*

Has collective bargaining

a. Pushed wages in the plant up higher than they should be?

b. Changed the way in which general wage increases are made?

c. Changed your method of setting job rates?

d. Affected your wage incentive system?

C. Effects of Wage Changes on the Business

(In order to get down to cases we would like to discuss the effects you noticed after your last wage increase. We do not want detailed facts or figures about your business, but would be interested in your general impression and judgment on the following points.)

1. *Effect upon labor supply*

Did the wage increase make it easier to get additional workers or to hold the workers you already had?

2. *Effect on worker effort*

Did workers, particularly incentive workers, increase or slacken their output after the wage increase?

3. *Effect on production schedule*

Did the wage increase cause you to reduce your scheduled production by cutting overtime or dropping product lines which had become unprofitable?

4. *Effect on use of labor*

Did the wage increase cause you to make a special effort to reduce costs by raising the efficiency of direct labor, reducing the use of indirect labor, eliminating certain operations, or making other changes in methods?

5. *Effect on use of machinery*

Did you, as a result of the wage increase, put in any new labor-saving machinery which you would not have put in otherwise?

6. *Effect on pricing of products*

Did the wage increase cause you to raise prices or reduce discounts on products? If so, was the price increase sufficient to cover the increase in labor costs?

D. Recruitment, Training and Promotion

1. *Recruitment and hiring methods*

Relative importance of the various applicant sources with you [illegible]? Most effective methods of recruitment [illegible] U.S.E.S.? Methods for screening applicants, hiring them and assigning them to jobs. Extent to which workers refuse jobs on [illegible] and reasons for this.

Importance attached to the labor supply situation—turnover, number of unfilled jobs, etc.
Importance of the financial position of the company; method of estimating how high a wage level the company can stand
Which of these factors is most important at present?
Which was most important before the war?

3. *Effects of collective bargaining (where it exists)*
Has collective bargaining
a. Pushed wages in the plant up higher than they should be?
b. Changed the way in which general wage increases are made?
c. Changed your method of setting job rates?
d. Affected your wage incentive system?

C. Effects of Wage Changes on the Business

(In order to get down to cases, we would like to discuss the effects you noticed after your last wage increase. We do not want detailed facts or figures about your business, but would be interested in your general impression and judgment on the following points.)

1. *Effect on labor supply*
Did the wage increase make it easier to get additional workers or to hold the workers you already had?

2. *Effect on worker effort*
Did workers, particularly incentive workers, increase or slacken off on their output after the wage increase?

3. *Effect on production volume*
Did the wage increase cause you to reduce your scheduled production by reducing overtime or dropping product lines which had become unprofitable?

4. *Effect on use of labor*
Did the wage increase cause you to make a special effort to reduce costs by raising the efficiency of direct labor, reducing the use of indirect labor, eliminating certain operations, or making other changes in methods?

5. *Effect on use of machinery*
Did you, as a result of the wage increase, put in any new labor-saving machinery which you wouldn't have put in otherwise?

6. *Effect on pricing of products*
Did the wage increase cause you to adjust prices on some or all of your products? If so, was the price increase sufficient to cover the increase in labor costs?

D. Problems of Hiring and Promotion

1. *Recruitment and hiring methods*
Reasons why workers apply for work with you instead of somewhere else
Most effective methods of recruitment; effectiveness of S. E. S.
Methods for screening applicants, hiring them, and assigning them to jobs
Extent to which workers refuse jobs offered them, and reasons for this

2. *Sources of labor*

From what kinds of work do most of your applicants come? When you lose people, where do they most frequently go?

Have you found that workers from certain other plants or industries are particularly well adapted (or poorly adapted) for work with you?

What do you do about men who apply for work with you while they are still working in another plant?

3. *Promotion practices*

Extent to which you try to fill vacancies on production jobs from within the plant, and methods used for this. Main lines of promotion in the plant

Extent to which vacancies are actually filled from inside the plant

Proportion of long-service workers who have moved up appreciably during their service with the company, and reasons for this

SCHEDULE 5

Study of Hiring, Promotion, and Layoff Practices

Note: This is a discussion agenda, not a questionnaire. It is sent you in the belief that advance reflection on these points will shorten the discussion and conserve your time. The information you provide on these subjects will be treated as strictly anonymous and confidential.

A. Hiring

1. What kinds of jobs do you fill mainly by hiring from the outside? What kinds by transfers of present employees?

2. How many applications for work have you on file at present? Are you able to fill many of your vacancies from the file?

3. How many unfilled vacancies have you at present? How many of these are listed at the State Employment Service?

4. What percentage of your new hires are referred to you by the Employment Service?

5. Does the employment manager or the foreman have main responsibility for selection and placement?

6. What is the practice concerning starting rates and probationary period?

7. Do you have a good deal of turnover among the newer employees? If so, what do you think are the main reasons?

B. Transfer and Promotion

1. What procedure do you use for filling vacancies:
   a. by transfers within a department?
   b. by transfers between departments?
   Are workers selected for promotion to higher jobs on the basis of general proficiency, length of service, or specialized skills?

2. Do you find that most workers are actively interested in promotion to higher jobs and willing to prepare themselves for it? What steps have you taken to stimulate interest in promotion?

3. If there is a union in the plant, has the union had any effect on your procedure for filling vacancies from inside the plant?

4. Are there any definite promotion "ladders" in the plant (e.g., second shift to first shift, day work to incentive work, helper to machine operator to setup man, lower labor grades to higher labor grades)?

5. The wage differentials between various grades of work have been considerably reduced in recent years. Have you found that this makes it harder to induce workers to prepare themselves for, or accept promotion to, the more skilled jobs?

6. Where a worker's job is eliminated by the discontinuance of a particular operation, what provision (if any) is made for placing him somewhere else in the plant?

7. Have you had difficulty recently in filling foremanships, and what are you doing about this problem?

C. Reductions in Work Force

1. Have you made any temporary or permanent reductions in work force during the past year or so? If so, were layoffs made on the basis of seniority, efficiency, or some other basis?

2. If you were reducing your production schedules in the future, would this be taken care of by dropping extra shifts, reducing hours, laying off workers from the first shift, or some combination of these?

3. If there is a union in the plant, what layoff procedure (if any) is specified in the union contract?

4. When workers are laid off for a temporary period, do most of them wait around to be recalled to your plant, or do they seek work in other plants? Are workers with high seniority more likely to wait around than those with low seniority?

SCHEDULE 6

(This schedule requested information for each year from 1940 through 1948. In order to conserve space, however, only one year is shown here.)

A. NMTA Labor Grade Rates

		1940 Rate Range Minimum	1940 Rate Range Maximum
Male Grade	11		
	10		
	9		
	8		
	7		
	6		
	5		
	4		
	3		
	2		
	1		
Female	111		
	110		
	109		
	108		
	107		

B. Starting Rates

	1940
Male	
Female	

C. Average Hourly Earnings (exclusive of office help)

Including overtime
Excluding overtime
Scheduled work week (hours)

D. General Wage Changes

	1940
Date	
Amount	
How applied	

E. Separations

	1940
Total number of people separated during year	
Voluntary quits	
Other	

5. Number of employees (exclusive of office help, average for year) 1940

Male
Female

1940

6. Hourly Rates and Earnings	Average Earnings	Rate Range Minimum	Maximum
Highest rated job in plant			
Lowest rated job in plant (specify jobs)			

All information obtained on this form will be summarized so as to obscure the identity of the contributing firms. Your cooperation in obtaining this information will be greatly appreciated.

Section 4—Labor Grade Rates

Section 4 on the preceding page is to be used in supplying information for the years during which you have used the National Metal Trades Association job grade system. Rate ranges and earnings should be those in effect as of July 1 each year. Figures given under "minimum" and "maximum" should be the established ranges for grades rather than lowest or highest rates actually paid.

Section 5—Starting Rates

If inexperienced workers are hired at a special rate below the minimum of the lowest labor grade and remain at this rate for a certain period, please indicate this starting rate here.

Section 6—Average Hourly Earnings

These figures should cover the last complete payroll period before July 1 of each year. The scheduled work week should be the normal work week of your plant.

Section 7—General Wage Changes

This refers to general increases (or lowered) increases. The date given should be the effective date of the increase. The amount should be the flat hourly amount in cents per hour (where given on that basis) or the equivalent in cents per hour (where granted on a percentage basis). It should be indicated also whether the increase was actually applied on an absolute (cents per hour) or percentage basis.

Sections 8 and 9—Separations and Employment

The separation figure should comprise (1) the total number of people who quit during the year, and (2) the total number who were otherwise separated during the year.

The figure for the number of employees should be the average for each year; the average for 1949 will comprise only the period from January 1, 1949, to the present.

F. Number of Employees (exclusive of office help; average for year)		1940	
Male			
Female			

		1940	
	Average	Rate Range	
G. Hourly Rates and Earnings	Earnings	Minimum	Maximum
Highest rated job in plant			
Lowest rated job in plant (specify jobs)			

All information obtained on this form will be summarized so as to obscure the identity of the contributing firms. Your cooperation in obtaining this information will be greatly appreciated.

Section A—Labor Grade Rates

Section A on the preceding page is to be used in recording information for the years during which you have used the National Metal Trades Association job grade system. Rate ranges and earnings should be those in effect as of July 1 each year. Figures given under "minimum" and "maximum" should be the established ranges for grades rather than lowest or highest rates actually paid.

Section B—Starting Rates

If inexperienced workers are hired at a special rate below the minimum of the lowest labor grade and remain at this rate for a certain period, please indicate this starting rate here.

Section C—Average Hourly Earnings

These figures should cover the last complete payroll period before July 1 of each year. The scheduled work week should be the normal work week of the plant.

Section D—General Wage Changes

This refers to general (across-the-board) increases. The date given should be the effective date of the increase. The amount should be the flat hourly amount in cents per hour (where given on that basis) or the equivalent in cents per hour where granted on a percentage basis. It should be indicated also whether the increase was actually applied on an absolute (cents-per-hour) or percentage basis.

Sections E and F— Separations and Employment

The separation figure should comprise (1) the *total* number of people who quit during the year, and (2) the *total* number who were otherwise separated during the year.

The figure for the number of employees should be the *average* for each year; the average for 1948 will comprise only the period from January 1, 1948, to the present.

Section G—Hourly Rates and Earnings

Rate ranges and earnings should be those in effect as of July 1 each year. Figures given under "minimum" and "maximum" should be the established ranges for grades rather than lowest or highest rates actually paid. Where average hourly earnings of workers in each grade have been compiled and are available, please record these figures in the column headed "Average Earnings." Please indicate also whether the figure includes or excludes overtime; straight-time hourly earnings are preferable if available.

INDEX

INDEX